Israel and the Palestinian refugee issue

Examining the development of Israel's policy toward the Palestinian refugees, this book spans the period following the first Arab-Israeli War (in 1947–1949) until the mid 1950s, when the basic principles of Israel's policy were finalized.

Israel and the Palestinian refugee issue outlines and analyzes the various aspects that, together, created the mosaic of the "refugee problem" with which Israel has since had to contend. These aspects include issues of repatriation, resettlement, compensation, blocked bank accounts, internal refugees, and family reunification.

Drawing on extensive archival research, this book uses documents from Israeli government meetings, from the Foreign Affairs and Defense Committee, and from the office of the prime minister's advisor on Arab affairs to address the many diverse aspects of this topic, and will be essential reading for academics and researchers with an interest in Israel, the Middle East, and Political Science more broadly.

Dr. Jacob Tovy is specializing in the political history of the Jewish community in Palestine during the British Mandate period and the State of Israel during the first decade following its establishment. To date he has published three books in Hebrew; this is his first book in English.

Israeli History, Politics and Society

Series Editor: Efraim Karsh, Kings College London

This series provides a multidisciplinary examination of all aspects of Israeli history, politics and society, and serves as a means of communication between the various communities interested in Israel: academics; policy-makers; practitioners; journalists and the informed public.

1. **Peace in the Middle East: The Challenge for Israel**
   Edited by Efraim Karsh

2. **The Shaping of Israeli Identity: Myth, Memory and Trauma**
   Edited by Robert Wistrich and David Ohana

3. **Between War and Peace: Dilemmas of Israeli Security**
   Edited by Efraim Karsh

4. **US-Israeli Relations at the Crossroads**
   Edited by Gabriel Sheffer

5. **Revisiting the Yom Kippur War**
   Edited by P R Kumaraswamy

6. **Israel: The Dynamics of Change and Continuity**
   Edited by David Levi-Faur, Gabriel Sheffer and David Vogel

7. **In Search of Identity: Jewish Aspects in Israeli Culture**
   Edited by Dan Urian and Efraim Karsh

8. **Israel at the Polls, 1996**
   Edited by Daniel J Elazar and Shmuel Sandler

9. **From Rabin to Netanyahu: Israel's Troubled Agenda**
   Edited by Efraim Karsh

10. **Fabricating Israeli History: The "New Historians", second revised edition**
    Efraim Karsh

11. **Divided against Zion: Anti-Zionist Opposition in Britain to a Jewish State in Palestine, 1945–1948**
    Rory Miller

12. **Peacemaking in a Divided Society: Israel after Rabin**
    Edited by Sasson Sofer

13. **A Twenty-Year Retrospective of Egyptian-Israeli Relations: Peace in Spite of Everything**
    Ephraim Dowek

14. **Global Politics: Essays in Honor of David Vital**
    Edited by Abraham Ben-Zvi and Aharon Klieman

15. **Parties, Elections and Cleavages: Israel in Comparative and Theoretical Perspective**
    Edited by Reuven Y Hazan and Moshe Maor

16. **Israel and the Polls 1999**
    Edited by Daniel J Elazar
    and M Ben Mollov

17. **Public Policy in Israel**
    Edited by David Nachmias
    and Gila Menahem

18. **Developments in Israeli Public Administration**
    Edited by Moshe Maor

19. **Israeli Diplomacy and the Quest for Peace**
    Mordechai Gazit

20. **Israeli- Romanian Relations at the End of Ceauceşcu's Era,**
    Yosef Govrin

21. **John F Kennedy and the Politics of Arms Sales to Israel**
    Abraham Ben-Zvi

22. **Green Crescent over Nazareth: The Displacement of Christians by Muslims in the Holy Land**
    Raphael Israeli

23. **Jerusalem Divided: The Armistice Region, 1947–1967**
    Raphael Israeli

24. **Decision on Palestine Deferred: America, Britain and Wartime Diplomacy, 1939–1945**
    Monty Noam Penkower

25. **A Dissenting Democracy: The Case of "Peace Now", An Israeli Peace Movement**
    Magnus Norell

26. **British, Israel and Anglo-Jewry 1947–1957**
    Natan Aridan

27. **Israeli Identity: In Search of a Successor to the Pioneer, Tsabar and Settler**
    Lilly Weissbrod

28. **The Israeli Palestinians: An Arab Minority in the Jewish State**
    Edited by Alexander Bligh

29. **Israel, the Hashemites and the Palestinians: The Fateful Triangle**
    Edited by Efraim Karsh
    and P R Kumaraswamy

30. **Last Days in Israel**
    Abraham Diskin

31. **War in Palestine, 1948: Strategy and Diplomacy**
    David Tal

32. **Rethinking the Middle East**
    Efraim Karsh

33. **Ben-Gurion against the Knesset**
    Giora Goldberg

34. **Trapped Fools: Thirty Years of Israeli Policy in the Territories**
    Schlomo Gazit

35. **Israel's Quest for Recognition and Acceptance in Asia: Garrison State Diplomacy**
    Jacob Abadi

36. **H V Evatt and the Establishment of Israel: The Undercover Zionist**
    Daniel Mandel

37. **Navigating Perilous Waters : An Israeli Strategy for Peace and Security**
    Ephraim Sneh

38. **Lyndon B Johnson and the Politics of Arms Sales to Israel: In the Shadow of the Hawk**
Abraham Ben-Zvi

39. **Israel at the Polls 2003**
Edited by Shmeul Sandler, Ben M. Mollov & Jonathan Rynhold

40. **Between Capital and Land: The Jewish National Fund's Finances and Land-Purchase Priorities in Palestine, 1939–1945**
Eric Engel Tuten

41. **Israeli Democracy at Crossroads**
Raphael Cohen-Almagor

42. **Israeli Institutions at Crossroads**
Raphael Cohen-Almagor

43. **The Israeli-Palestine Peace Process Negotiations, 1999–2001: Within Reach**
Gilead Sher

44. **Ben-Gurion's Political Struggles, 1963-67: A Lion in Winter**
Zaki Shalom

45. **Ben-Gurion, Zionism and American Jewry: 1948–1963**
Ariel Feldestein

46. **The Origins of the American-Israeli Alliance: The Jordanian Factor**
Abraham Ben-Zvi

47. **The Harp and the Shield of David: Ireland, Zionism and the State of Israel**
Shulamit Eliash

48. **Israel's National Security: Issues and Challenges since the Yom Kippur War**
Efraim Inbar

49. **The Rise of Israel: A History of a Revolutionary State**
Jonathan Adelman

50. **Israel and the Family of Nations: The Jewish Nation-State and Human Rights**
Alexander Yakobson and Amnon Rubinstein

51. **Secularism and Religion in Jewish-Israeli Politics: Traditionists and Modernity**
Yaacov Yadgar

52. **Israel's National Security Law: Political Dynamics and Historical Development**
Amichai Cohen and Stuart A. Cohen

53. **Politics of Memory: The Israeli Underground's Struggle for Inclusion in the National Pantheon and Military Commemoralization**
Udi Lebel

54. **Social Mobilization in the Arab/ Israeli War of 1948: On the Israeli Home Front**
Moshe Naor

55. **Britain's Moment in Palestine: Retrospect and Perspectives, 1917–1948**
Michael J. Cohen

56. **Israel and the Palestinian Refugee Issue: The Formulation of a Policy, 1948–1956**
Jacob Tovy

Israel: The First Hundred Years (Mini Series)
edited by Efraim Karsh

1. Israel's Transition from Community to State
2. From War to Peace?
3. Politics and Society since 1948
4. Israel in the International Arena
5. Israel in the next Century

Israel and the Palestinian refugee issue

The formulation of a policy, 1948–1956

Jacob Tovy

LONDON AND NEW YORK

First published 2014
by Routledge
2 Park Square, Milton Park, Abingdon, Oxon OX14 4RN

and by Routledge
711 Third Avenue, New York, NY 10017

Routledge is an imprint of the Taylor & Francis Group, an informa business

© 2014 Jacob Tovy

The right of Jacob Tovy to be identified as author of this work has been asserted by him in accordance with sections 77 and 78 of the Copyright, Designs and Patents Act 1988.

All rights reserved. No part of this book may be reprinted or reproduced or utilised in any form or by any electronic, mechanical, or other means, now known or hereafter invented, including photocopying and recording, or in any information storage or retrieval system, without permission in writing from the publishers.

Trademark notice: Product or corporate names may be trademarks or registered trademarks, and are used only for identification and explanation without intent to infringe.

British Library Cataloguing in Publication Data
A catalogue record for this book is available from the British Library

Library of Congress Cataloging in Publication Data
A catalog record for this title has been requested

ISBN: 978-0-415-65999-4 (hbk)
ISBN: 978-1-315-81648-7 (ebk)

Typeset in Times New Roman
by Taylor and Francis Books

Printed and bound in the United States of America by Publishers Graphics,
LLC on sustainably sourced paper.

This book is dedicated to my parents, David and Malka Tovy, inspiring in their knowledge and love of the written word

Contents

Preface		xiii
Acknowledgements		xvii

Introduction: the evolution of the Palestinian refugee problem during the 1948 Arab-Israeli War		1
1	Israel's policy towards the emerging refugee problem, spring–winter 1948	13
2	The Lausanne Conference and the refugee problem	36
3	Shifting the emphasis for solving the refugee problem: from a political approach to an economic one	72
4	The refugee problem and Abdullah's Jordan	87
5	An exchange transaction: paying compensation in exchange for the resettlement of the refugees	107
6	Israel and the compensation issue prior to the Paris Conference and during its proceedings	136
7	Two political matters linked to the compensation issue	160
8	The resettlement question following the 6th United Nations General Assembly	170
9	Toughening Israel's position: compensation policy since the winter of 1952	200
10	The Alpha Plan	219

xii *Contents*

11 Three secondary aspects of the refugee problem where progress
    has been achieved   242

Conclusion   272

    Bibliography   282
    Index   297

Preface

In the fall of 1999, a new stage in the Israeli-Palestinian political process began. After six years of focusing on interim agreements, the two parties embarked on negotiation of a permanent status agreement that was supposed to resolve the core problems that divided the two sides: the country's borders and the status of Jerusalem (a legacy of the 1967 war) and the refugee problem (the result of the 1948 war). At first glance, this seemed to be a mission impossible since the gulf between their positions was very deep. The Palestinians demanded that an independent Palestinian state be established in all of the West Bank and Gaza, a polity whose capital would be East Jerusalem. They also demanded that Israel recognize its moral, legal, and political responsibility for creation of the refugee problem and accept the principle of repatriation. Their spokespersons hinted that, in practical terms, Israel would have to absorb several hundred thousand refugees, particularly those situated in Lebanon. In addition to this, Israel, it was claimed, must compensate the refugees for their abandoned assets and the lost income they could have accrued from them, as well as compensation for decades of hardship they suffered as refugees. Israel, by contrast, refused to commit *publicly* to the idea of a Palestinian state and expressed its readiness to hand over to the Palestinians only approximately two-thirds of the West Bank and Gaza, although under no condition would it hand over any part of the Jerusalem metropolitan area. Israel refused to take responsibility for the creation of the refugee problem or accept the principle of repatriation; it did, however, agree to transfer monetary compensation to an international body that would engage in rehabilitation of the refugees (in this context, Israel sought to raise the issue of abandoned Jewish property in Arab countries) and expressed willingness to absorb a very limited number of Palestinian refugees, but only on humanitarian grounds or for the purpose of family reunification. Officially, Israel refrained from enumerating how many refugees would be allow to return, but according to unofficial utterances by Israeli representatives Israel was talking about 20,000 to 40,000 refugees who would be permitted to return over a generation. The Palestinians viewed this as a mockery, since they held that there were 4 million refugees and their offspring throughout the Middle East and elsewhere.

xiv *Preface*

In late January 2001, after a number of rounds of talks, attempts by Israel and the Palestinians to reach a permanent accord came to naught. During the entire period of negotiations, Israel's leaders conceded and retreated from their principles on most of the issues on the agenda. They agreed to the establishment of a Palestinian state on 95 percent of the West Bank and Gaza whose capital would be East Jerusalem, and even agreed to limited Palestinian control of the Old City. On the refugee issue, however, Israel was unwilling to compromise at all. Israeli negotiators explained to their Palestinian interlocutors that if Israel would take upon itself responsibility for creation of the Palestinian tragedy, Israel would be marked as a "nation born in sin" and the Jewish state's moral legitimacy would be put in question. The Israelis further argued that if Israel would accept the principle of repatriation, millions of refugees could try to seek redress to their "Right of Return" in international courts, and should they succeed in realizing "their rights" through such channels, Israel as a Jewish-Zionist state would cease to exist.

Hence, Israel's leaders believed that should they respond positively to Palestinian demands on the refugee question, in contrast to territorial questions including Jerusalem, it would shake both the moral foundations and physical underpinnings of the Jewish state as it exists, and lead to its collapse.[1] The majority of the Jewish public in Israel supported their leaders' position, an attitude reflected in public opinion polls at the time.[2] The Palestinian picture was the inverse of the Israeli one – sanctifying the right of all refugees to return to their former places of residence before the war.[3]

Deliberations on the Palestinian refugee problem during permanent status talks were the most prolonged and most substantive on this matter held to that point by official Israeli and Arab parties of any kind since the creation of the problem in the closing years of the 1940s. The roots of Israel's position on this issue, as expressed in the course of the years 1999 to 2001, can be found in the 1948 war and the first years of statehood when Israeli policy crystallized on its variant aspects: repatriation, resettlement, compensation for abandoned Arab property, blocked bank accounts, family reunification, and the internal refugees ("present absentees").[4]

The research at hand is designed to share with the reader how Israeli policy on the refugee question took form, with all its components and twists and turns, as policy took shape in the years 1948 to 1956. When existing research literature deals with Israeli refugee policy it does so fragmentarily from a thematic and chronological standpoint, only citing limited or isolated instances; moreover, most of the research raises the issue of the refugees in its Israeli context, doing so merely as a side issue to a much broader discussion of other topics. Only a handful of studies focus on Israeli policy towards the refugee problem, and those, as noted above, address merely some of the issues or deal only with very limited time slots.

The work at hand, by contrast, examines all the historical junctures when the Palestinian refugee problem was raised on the State of Israel's diplomatic

Preface xv

and security agenda, during which Israeli policy on this issue took form. The volume also presents other junctures that to date have not been mentioned in the research literature at all or have been given marginal attention. Both have been combined in the research, enabling me to draw a clear and coherent composite picture of the emergence of refugee policy as it developed in Israel.

Notes

1 The talks between Israel and the Palestinians regarding a permanent arrangement, and in particular those that took place at Camp David (in July of 2000) and at Taba (in January of 2001), generated numerous news reports, substantial amounts of press and internet website commentary, published interviews with participants, memoirs (most of which were written by Israelis and Americans), and research publications (based primarily on non-classified material). The following is a list of the sources that were relied upon here: Yossi Beilin, *Manual for a Wounded Dove*, Tel Aviv: Yedioth Ahronoth, 2001 (Hebrew); Shlomo Ben Ami, *Scars of War, Wounds of Peace: The Israeli-Arab Tragedy*, Oxford: Oxford University Press, 2007, pp. 240–84; Yossef Bodansky, *The High Cost of Peace: How Washington's Middle East Policy Left America Vulnerable to Terrorism*, Roseville, CA: Prima Publishing, 2002, pp. 309, 408; Bill Clinton, *My Life*, New York: Alfred A. Knopf, 2004, pp. 911–6; Chris Doyle, *Camp David II – A Synopsis: What Was Discussed at the Camp David Summit, July 2000*, London: Council for the Advancement of Arab-British Understanding, 2000; Akram Hanieh, "The Camp David Papers", *Journal of Palestine Studies* 30(2), 2001, pp. 75–97; Martin Indyk, *Innocent Abroad: An Intimate Account of American Peace Diplomacy in the Middle East*, New York: Simon and Schuster, 2009, pp. 288–376; Bruce Maddy-Weitzman and Shimon Shamir (eds), *The Camp David Summit: What Went Wrong?*, Brighton and Portland: Sussex Academic Press, 2005; Itamar Rabinovich, *The Lingering Conflict: Israel, the Arabs and the Middle East 1948–2011*, Washington, DC: Brookings Institution Press, 2011, pp. 87–127; Dennis Ross, *The Missing Peace: The Inside Story of the Fight for Middle East Peace*, New York: Farrar, Straus and Giroux, 2004, pp. 591–758; Gilead Sher, *The Israeli-Palestinian Peace Negotiations, 1999–2001: Within Reach*, London: Routledge, 2006; Jacob Tovy, "Negotiating the Palestinian Refugees", *Middle East Quarterly* 10(2), 2003, pp. 44–50; Tim Youngs, *The Middle East Crisis: Camp David, the "Al-Aqsa Intifada" and the Prospects for the Peace Process*, London: UK House of Commons Library, 2001; Robert Malley and Hussein Agha, "Camp David: The Tragedy of Errors", *New York Review of Books*, 9 August 2001; PLO Negotiations Affairs Department – Negotiations Process, see www. nad-plo.org; Le Monde Diplomatique, "The Middle East: How the Peace was Lost", available at http://mondediplo.com/2001/09/01middleeastleader? var_recherche-camp + david.; articles in the American Press on the Camp David talks: *USA Today*, 21, 28 July 2000; *The Washington Post*, 26, 29, 30 July 2000 and 16 August 2000; *The New York Times*, 2 August 2000; on President Clinton's proposals and the responses of the two parties: *USA Today*, 27 December 2000; *The Washington Post*, 22, 23, 27 December 2000 and 4, 6, 7 January 2001; *The New York Times*, 26, 28 December 2000; on the Taba Conference: *The Washington Post*, 29 January 2001.

2 http://spirit.tau.ac.il/socant/peace/peaceindex/2000/data/july2000d.doc.

3 http://www.jmcc.org/publicpoll/results/1999/no.34.htm; http://www.jmcc.org/publicpoll/results/2000/no.37.htm; for additional surveys of Palestinian public

xvi *Preface*

opinion regarding the refugee problem, see Isabelle Daneels, *Palestinian Refugees and the Peace Process: An Analysis of Public Opinion Surveys in the West Bank and the Gaza Strip*, Jerusalem: Jerusalem Media and Communication Centre, 2001.

4 The subject of the refugees was discussed at length at the Lausanne Conference held in the summer and spring of 1949, but, as this study will show, Israel had not yet formulated a completely coherent position on the issue at that time.

Acknowledgements

The first edition of this book was published in Hebrew in late 2008 by the publishing house of the Ben-Gurion Research Institute for the Study of Israel and Zionism at Ben-Gurion University of the Negev, and was based on a PhD thesis written in the University of Haifa. I am deeply grateful to my doctoral supervisors, Professor Yoav Gelber and Professor Nathan Yanai, for their tireless support and astute advice. I would also like to thank the Herzl Institute for Research and Studies on Zionism at the University of Haifa for its generous financial assistance. I wish to express my gratitude to Daniella Ashkenazy, who translated this book from the Hebrew edition, for her excellent skills as a wordsmith. Finally, I owe special thanks to Professor Efraim Karsh, with whom I made the first connection in the autumn of 2009 regarding the possibility of publishing my research in English. His firm support paved the way for this English edition.

Introduction

The evolution of the Palestinian refugee problem during the 1948 Arab-Israeli War

On 29 November 1947, the United Nations General Assembly passed Resolution 181 terminating the British Mandate in Palestine (*Eretz Yisrael* in the Jewish terminology) and partitioning the country into two states: one Jewish, one Arab.

Upon hearing the results of the vote on the radio, masses of Jews filled the streets of their cities and towns to dance and celebrate. The heads of the Jewish community in Mandate Palestine rushed to publicly declare their readiness to accept the international community's decision. By contrast, the Palestinians, who believed an Arab polity should be established in all of Mandate Palestine, responded with fury and the following day embarked on acts of violence to block the resolution's implementation. A bus with Jewish passengers was attacked near Lod airport, killing five passengers. The Arab Higher Committee (the organization of Palestinian Arab political leadership) called a general strike, and following this the Jewish commercial district adjacent to Jaffa Gate in Jerusalem was ransacked and set aflame. Anti-Jewish riots also took place in Beirut, Damascus, Cairo, and Baghdad. From his residence in Beirut, the political-religious leader of Palestinian-Arabs Haj Amin al-Husseini declared that the Arabs viewed Resolution 181 as null and void, and therefore the Palestinian people had no intention of honoring it. Similar declarations were heard among member states of the Arab League.[1]

Thus, the foundations were laid for a bloody confrontation that lasted until the beginning of 1949 between the Jewish community in Mandate Palestine (and afterwards the State of Israel) and the Palestinian people (and neighboring Arab countries). In this violent campaign one of its core ramifications was the Palestinian refugee problem.

The official Israeli narrative regarding the refugee issue took shape in the second half of 1948 and crystallized into a coherent treatise the following year. According to this narrative, had Arab leaders not decided to oppose by force the establishment of a Jewish state in blatant violation of the UN decision – first by activating local Palestinian forces and the Arab Liberation Army,[2] afterwards through direct military intervention – the flight of refugees would not have taken place. According to the Israeli version, this flight was accelerated at various stages of the war as a result of several actions taken by

2   Introduction

the Arabs: the call of Arab leaders to the Palestinian population to temporarily abandon their homes until the battle could be won; dissemination of false scare propaganda by Arab media and Arab leaders regarding the behavior of Jewish soldiers towards the Palestinian population; the flight of Palestinian society's social, economic, religious, and political leadership immediately after the outbreak of hostilities; and the abusive behavior of members of the Arab Liberation Army and other Arab volunteers towards the local Palestinian population. According to this narrative, Israel held no responsibility whatsoever for the creation of the refugee problem.[3]

Up until the beginning of the 1980s, this view, held by the Israeli establishment, was reflected in the overwhelming majority of local literature, academic and non-academic, devoted to events during the 1948 Arab-Israeli war.[4]

Research into the Palestinian refugee problem and its roots was shaken towards the mid 1980s when archival material concerning events during the 1948 war was declassified and exposed to public scrutiny in Israel, Britain, and the United States. New Israeli research, based among other things on ample documentation found in the various archives, demonstrated that Israel was also responsible for the creation of this problem, first and foremost due to expulsions carried out by its forces. Contrary to earlier Israeli works, these studies, in essence, adopted a critical and revisionist perspective, clear and well defended as befits academic research. Their findings challenged the dominant official narrative regarding the roots of the Palestinian refugee problem.[5] Examination of new research revealed that while all agree that Israel was responsible to one degree or another for the creation of the refugee problem, opinions are divided as to the scope of this responsibility. That is to say, there are those who argue that Israeli culpability for the problem is equal to that of the Palestinians, while others place most of the blame on Israel.[6]

Revisionist interpretations of the refugee issue were harshly criticized by various Israeli scholars. Although most objectors don't totally reject the revisionist thesis that points out cases where Palestinians were expelled by force, for the critics, if Israel bears some degree of responsibility, it is significantly smaller than Arab-Palestinian culpability. Expulsion of non-combatants, the most deliberate and brutal manifestation of Israeli responsibility, was in their estimation much more limited than what most of the new research claimed. Opponents to the revisionist perspective also lashed out to criticize the quality of their rivals' work. They held that the documentation upon which the new research was founded was often used in a biased and distorted manner to make the archival material compatible with the authors' basic assumptions.[7]

When we set forth to present the core factors that brought about the creation of the Palestinian refugee problem during the 1948 Arab-Israeli war, based on analysis of various studies, the following picture emerged:

The first wave: December 1947 to March 1948

During the first four months of the conflict, most of the action was terrorist attacks against Jewish civilian targets perpetrated by irregular Arab forces – locals and volunteer combatants from Arab countries. These operations included throwing bombs into Jewish crowds in mixed cities; shooting at isolated Jewish settlements; and harassment of Jewish transportation on major traffic arteries. The Haganah (the military arm of the organized Jewish community of Mandate Palestine) generally refrained from initiating operations of its own, and its actions were limited to responding to and repelling Arab attacks. As much as one can determine, at this stage Palestinian Arabs had the upper hand, and indeed the number of Jewish casualties grew from day to day.[8]

Arab achievements on the battlefield did not, however, prevent the flight of some 50,000 to 75,000 Palestinian Arabs from their homes during this period; the escapees constituted from 4 to 6 percent of the sum total of 1.3 million Arabs residing west of the Jordan River in late 1947. A relatively large proportion of those taking flight were upper-middle-class families and wealthy prominent Palestinian families from Jaffa, Jerusalem, Haifa, and a number of villages in the Sharon region.[9] Besides such social and economic elites, there were also Palestinian villagers who, over the years, had migrated to Arab and mixed cities and after the outbreak of hostilities rushed to return to their villages. Many thousands of the escapees were citizens of neighboring countries: Lebanese, Syrians, and Egyptians who recently arrived in Mandate Palestine and also decided with the outbreak of the confrontation to go back to their countries of origin.[10] In the first wave of flight, the Palestinians fled primarily to the heavily Arab-populated section in the interior of the country, particularly to Nazareth and Nablus, as well as to neighboring Arab countries. While most of the escapees expected a swift Arab victory, they decided to avoid the dangers and discomforts of wartime by leaving their homes until the fighting was over.[11]

The second wave: April to 15 May 1948

In light of the stark military realities facing the Jewish community in Mandate Palestine as well as geopolitical considerations, on 19 March 1948 the United States recommended to the Security Council that a temporary trusteeship under UN auspices be established in the country. Faced with the double jeopardy to the future of a Jewish state – in the diplomatic as well as the military theater – the heads of the Jewish community and the Haganah commanders decided to change strategy in the confrontation with the Arabs: to abandon a defensive footing and go on the offensive. This took the form of what became known as Plan D, a plan of action prepared by the Haganah in early March 1948 to win the battle against the irregular Arab forces in Mandate Palestine. The plan of action was designed to achieve two objectives: first of all the defeat of the enemy at the door would enable the Jewish forces to take and control Palestinian concentrations situated in areas allotted to the Jewish state

4   *Introduction*

under the Partition Plan and to establish territorial contiguity between major Jewish areas. Fulfillment of this objective would assist the Haganah in the coming days to meet the challenge of a pending invasion by neighboring Arab armies. Second, if a Jewish victory in the field was decisive, this would demonstrate to the international community, and first and foremost the United States, that the Jewish community was able to ensure its own independence and was therefore worthy of the United Nations' support for a Jewish state.[12]

Two months after the launch of Plan D, a completely new reality emerged: the local Palestinian forces were defeated and with them the Arab Liberation Army. Consequently, almost all the territory allotted to the Jewish state was occupied by Jewish forces and the Arab population of these areas left, most from mixed urban centers (Tiberias, Haifa, Jaffa, Safed, and Acre). At the same time, the departure of Arabs from their villages in the Sharon region was completed, and a number of villages along the main road linking Tel-Aviv to Jerusalem were abandoned by their inhabitants. All told, in the second wave, some 200,000 to 300,000 Palestinian Arabs left for neighboring countries – Lebanon, Syria, Egypt, and Trans-Jordan – as well as for heavily populated Arab areas within Mandate Palestine, in particular Nablus and Hebron.[13] It should be noted that, at this stage, Jewish leaders attempted to prevent the flight of Arabs, in Haifa for example.[14]

The departure of Palestinian Arabs in the months of April and May 1948 was the result of several factors, direct and indirect:

1   The general deterioration that followed the outbreak of hostilities in December 1947 accelerated greatly during this period due to escalation in the level of fighting between the two sides, following the Haganah's adoption of an offensive footing and a sharp rise in armed operation of irregular Arab forces. This was paralleled by the sudden vacuum created by the waning of a British Mandatory presence as 14 May and the close of the Mandate approached. This deterioration led to general chaos: law and order was not enforced; difficulties in transportation and supply of essential goods and services increased, and economic activities came to a near standstill. It was primarily the Palestinian population that suffered from growing chaos; unlike the Jewish community, which during three decades of British Mandatory administration had built a network of economic and social institutions in preparation for statehood, the Arab community had no alternative systems to rely on once British civil services and other functions ceased to operate. The collapse of Palestinian society under such conditions undermined the ability of Palestinians to withstand the exigencies of war and amplified the stream of refugees.[15]

2   The thousands of wealthy families who left the country in the first wave of flight were joined in the second wave by much of the political leadership of Palestinian society, as well as members of the free professions and other educated classes: village heads, senior civil servants in the former Mandate

government, political functionaries, judges, teachers, physicians, lawyers, businesspeople, and even clergy. The flight of these key sectors of society who were models for the Palestinian masses affected simple rank-and-file Palestinians, who found themselves leaderless in a state of crisis.[16]

3 In some areas, Arab residents were ordered by the Arab Higher Committee or local Arab commanders to leave their homes, primarily for strategic reasons. Having said that, one cannot conclude that this factor carried substantial weight among all the factors that led Palestinians to abandon their homes.[17]

4 Sweeping defeats among Arab forces in many cities and villages in the spring of 1948 led many Palestinians to conclude that the mélange of Arab militias operating in the war zone was incapable of providing them with protection against the Jews, and it would be wise to seek shelter elsewhere.[18]

5 Relations between the groups of volunteers who arrived from Arab countries and the local Palestinian population left much to be desired. The volunteers' behavior towards the civilian population was harsh and oppressive, generating among the Palestinians fear of those who were supposed to be their saviors. Such a flawed relationship only further undermined the endurance of Palestinians.[19]

6 As Jewish military pressure increased in April, the Palestinians became apprehensive that now that the Jews had the upper hand, they would take terrible revenge on the Palestinians for numerous atrocities the latter had committed over the years against Jews in the course of the conflict. The massacre that Jewish forces committed at the Palestinian village of Dir Yassin on 9 April 1948,[20] and the widespread publicity the carnage was given by the Arab media and by the local Arab leadership, further entrenched trepidations and magnified fears. Arab media and Arab leaders had already spread horror stories (most of them fabrications) regarding the bestial behavior of Jewish soldiers towards Palestinian non-combatants, thus unwittingly adding to Palestinian anxieties, and indirectly adding momentum to the flight.[21]

7 The psychological warfare conducted by Jewish forces against Arab forces, and sometimes against the civilian population, to bring about their swift surrender further aggravated the low spirits and despair that enveloped Palestinian Arabs and spurred on their exit.[22]

The third wave: 15 May 1948 to February 1949

Most of the factors that led to the Palestinian exodus in the second stage of fighting continued into the third stage, parallel to an additional factor that arose from a new stance adopted by the Jews towards the Arabs in the country.[23]

On 14 May 1948, the head of the Jewish community in Mandate Palestine, David Ben-Gurion, declared the establishment of the State of Israel at a

6   Introduction

meeting of the People's Council. The next day, the armies of five Arab states invaded the newborn state. The Jewish community, which found itself in an all-out war against five regular Arab armies, changed its policies towards the Palestinian population from top to bottom. At this stage of the fighting, Palestinians were expelled from their homes. At the beginning of June, the newly established Israeli army (the IDF) expelled the inhabitants of the village Nabi Rubin (southwest of Rishon Le-Zion), sending them southward onto the sand dunes leading to the Arab village Yibna. In the second week of July, Israeli soldiers pressed the inhabitants of the village Yahudiya (east of Tel-Aviv) and other nearby Arab villages to leave. Two days later, on 12 July, the cities of Ramle and Lod were occupied. A small number of their inhabitants fled at the beginning of the battles, while most were expelled later. This pattern of occupation and expulsion repeated itself to one degree or another in various places of the country up until the beginning of 1949.[24]

Such expulsions were primarily the product of the harsh realities the Jewish community faced, with five invading armies. The inability of the United Nations to prevent the Arab attack on the tiny Jewish community (only 650,000 souls) left the Jews standing alone against the Arab world. In order to prevail and ensure the security of the Jewish state in the future, Israeli commanders adopted a strategy that encouraged the expulsion of a portion of the Palestinian population, and government echelons, while aware of this, chose to remain silent. This strategy enabled the IDF to dispatch Israeli forces to engage invading Arab armies, eliminating the need to police Palestinian villages to the rear that had surrendered. The expulsion also had long-term ramifications since it paved the way to shape and consolidate a stable polity with a Jewish majority, without a large hostile Arab minority within.[25]

In the third wave, some 300,000 Palestinian Arabs fled or were expelled to areas of the country occupied by invading Trans-Jordanian forces (i.e. the West Bank, as it would be renamed), as well as to the Gaza Strip and Lebanon. Most of the escapees were inhabitants of Lod, Ramle, Beersheva and Majdal (Ashkelon), and villages in the Upper and Lower Galilee, and Bedouin from the northern Negev.[26]

Israeli and western scholars who examined the refugee issue believe that the heads of the Jewish community in Mandate Palestine (and later Israeli leadership) had no official and premeditated policy to expel Arabs from the Jewish state's territory.[27] Support of this conclusion can be found in archival documentation, which substantiates that those at the helm of the Jewish state were taken aback by the exodus of the Palestinians and expressed their astonishment in closed meetings, internal correspondence, and talks with foreign colleagues. There would have been no sense of surprise had this transfer of population been planned.[28] At the same time, the longer the exodus continued – creating a totally new demographic reality in areas slated to be a Jewish state – Jewish leaders' surprise and consternation was replaced by a sense of relief and satisfaction in light of the demographic-strategic transformation the departure forged that was, in essence, favorable for the Jews.[29] Therefore, those leaders

Introduction 7

did very little to curb independent initiatives by commanders in the field to expel Palestinians.[30]

It is hard to calculate the exact number of Palestinians who became refugees in the wake of the 1948 Arab-Israeli war. This is stymied by a number of factors:

1 It was impossible to know the exact size of the Palestinian population that lived prior to the war in areas that became the State of Israel. There were three reasons for this: the number of Arabs from neighboring countries residing illegally in Mandate Palestine prior to the outburst of hostilities was unknown; some 100,000 Bedouin had been in constant motion, wandering back and forth across the borders between Sinai, Trans-Jordan, and Mandate Palestine; the collapse of civil services during the 15 months of intermittent fighting thwarted any possibility of calculating the natural growth rate of the Palestinian population during this period.
2 Fallacious reports pushed the number of Palestinian refugees upward: first of all, inflating the number of persons in one's family was common among the Palestinian population, with family heads reporting non-existent births and refraining from reporting actual deaths. Such maneuvers were designed to artificially increase the assistance one's family could receive from relief agencies. Second, there were civilians in the countries to which refugees fled who also declared that they were refugees in order to receive material assistance from relief agencies.
3 In some places where refugees concentrated, particularly in Trans-Jordan, the authorities, for political reasons, exhibited a lack of will to cooperate with UNRWA personnel (the special United Nations agency mandated to care for Palestinian refugees)[31] in conducting a census to determine the exact number of refugees.[32]

In its May 1950 interim report to the secretary-general of the United Nations, UNRWA reported that apparently it would not be able to provide – today or in the future – a precise declaration of the number of genuine refugees as a result of the war in Palestine. In UNRWA's estimation, it was near impossible to define the word "refugee" as required by its work, without leaving certain groups of people beyond this definition who in fact merited such status, or conversely, including groups that apparently should not have received relief assistance.[33] Nevertheless, the agency knew that in order to function it must define who is a refugee. After a number of deliberations, UNRWA stipulated that "a refugee is a person in need, who as a result of the war in Palestine lost his home and livelihood."[34] Within a short time, however, it became clear to the UN agency that its definition of refugee was too general and did not clarify how to relate to certain groups such as the Bedouin population for whom the concepts of "home" and "place of work" were too specific and irrelevant, or villagers who lost their lands (that is, their livelihoods) but not their homes, and therefore were ineligible for refugee status. The definition also enabled subjects of Arab states who had spent a short time in

8 Introduction

Mandate Palestine prior to the war and had gone home when Palestine became a war zone to claim refugee status. Moreover, it was even possible to register as UNRWA refugees citizens of neighboring states who lived along the border of Mandate Palestine and fled due to the fighting. In the years 1953 to 1954 UNRWA set new criteria that sought to provide a suitable answer for all the special cases: the new definition stipulated that only persons who had lived in Mandate Palestine for a period of two years or more before the outbreak of hostilities in 1948 and as a result of the fighting lost their homes (and/or) their source of livelihood were entitled to refugee status.[35] In the end, however, even the new definition was unable to create an orderly and reliable list of UNRWA refugees since adding or removing a person from the list was in the hands of UNRWA's Palestinian machinery or rested on the testimonies and confirmations of *mukhtars* (village heads) that did not necessarily reflect the truth.[36] Evidence that the problem continued to exist is reflected in a UNRWA communiqué in the summer of 1954 that cited there were some 120,000 invalid names on refugee rolls: people whose names appeared more than once, or people who pretended to be refugees.[37]

On 30 June 1950 (a year and a half after the end of the war), according to UNRWA's records there were 914,221 registered Arab refugees. Another 45,800 refugees remained in Israeli territory, two-thirds of them Arabs and a third Jews – thus, the sum total of war refugees tallied at the time stood at 960,021 souls.[38] Another UN body – the Economic Survey Mission for the Middle East[39] – stated in November 1949 after a two-month investigation that there were 726,000 Arab refugees.[40]

The US State Department put the number of refugees somewhere between the two figures.[41] The British estimated in 1949 that the number of refugees was in the vicinity of 800,000. The two rival sides tended to exaggerate their estimates. Since 1949, official Arab spokespersons have held that the correct number ranged from 900,000 to a million Palestinians,[42] while Israeli representatives have put their number at half a million.[43] The goal of the Israelis was to reduce the scope of the problem in order to push the refugee issue and its negative political ramifications off the international agenda.[44] The Arabs in contrast

Table 1 Breakdown of Palestinian refugee populations in neighboring Arab countries, according to UNRWA data for the years 1950 to 1956 UNRWA, A/3686, p. 12.

	June 1950	June 1951	June 1952	June 1953	June 1954	June 1955	June 1956
The Gaza Strip	198,227	199,789	204,356	208,560	212,600	214,601	216,971
The Kingdom of Jordan	506,200	465,741	469,576	475,620	486,631	499,606	512,706
Lebanon	127,600	106,896	104,901	102,095	101,636	103,600	102,625
Syria	82,194	82,861	84,224	85,473	86,191	88,179	89,977
Total	914,221	855,287	863,057	871,748	887,058	905,986	922,279

Introduction 9

sought to set the estimate as high as possible, both to increase the scope of international humanitarian aid received, and to intensify the scale of human tragedy (and between the lines, to magnify Israel's sense of guilt). Differences of opinion over the exact number of refugees can also be found among scholars who studied the issue.[45] I accept the position of Benny Morris, who in the absence of clear and precise data, preferred to set a number with wide margins – between 600,000 and 760,000 Palestinian refugees.[46]

Notes

1 Baruch Kimmerling and Joel S. Migdal, *Palestinians: The Making of a People*, New York: The Free Press, 1993, pp. 140–41; Meron Medzini (ed.), *Israel's Foreign Relations: Selected Documents, 1947–1974*, Jerusalem: Ministry for Foreign Affairs, 1976, pp. 110–11; Mark Tessler, *A History of the Israeli-Palestinian Conflict*, Bloomington, IN: Indiana University Press, 2009, p. 261.

2 By March 1948 some 5,000 Arab volunteers reached Palestine to fight against the Jews. Most of them were from the urban slums of Iraq, Syria and Lebanon. They were organised as the Arab Liberation Army.

3 ISA, MFA 364/3, The Problem of the Palestinian Refugees from Eretz Yisrael – Memorandum by A. Goren, 27 September 1948; ISA, MFA 2445/3, Memorandum on an Arrangement for Arab Refugees; ISA, MFA 9/949/8, Information Division, Official Publications, Vol. 2, 1948–1964: Israel and the Arab Refugees: A Survey of the Problem and Its Solutions. Throughout the period under discussion, Israel followed this official position regarding the creation of the refugee problem. See, for example: ISA, MFA 339/7, David Uriel, The Arab States and the Refugee Problem – Memorandum, 7 October 1951; ISA, MFA 9/953/4, Information Division, Official Publications, Vol. 2; 1948–1964: The Arab Refugees; ISA, MFA 9/958/2, Information Division, The Arab Refugees' Problem: Need for Candor; ISA, MFA 9/961/5, Information Division, The Arab Refugees: Arab Statements and the Facts.

4 See, for example: Chief Education Officer (Information Branch), *The War of Independence*, Jerusalem: Israel Information Center, 1980, p. 20 (Hebrew); Natanel Lorech, *The History of the War of Independence*, Tel Aviv: Massada, 1958, pp. 540–41 (Hebrew); Yehuda Slutsky, *History of the Hagana (Vol. 3: From Resistance to War)*, Tel Aviv: Am Oved, 1972, pp. 1362–4, 1547–8 (Hebrew); Ephraim Talmy, *Who's and Who's: The Lexicon of the War of Independence*, Tel Aviv: Davar, 1965, pp. 82, 229 (Hebrew).

5 For an in-depth examination of the Israeli discourse on the sources of the Palestinian refugee problem, see: Rafi Nets-Zehngut, "Origins of the Palestinian Refugee Problem: Changes in the Historical Memory of Israelis/Jews, 1949–2004", *Journal of Peace Research* 48(2), 2011, pp. 235–49.

6 See, in this context, the following essays: Simha Flapan, *The Birth of Israel – Myths and Realities*, London: Croom Helm, 1987, pp. 85–90; Benny Morris, *The Birth of the Palestinian Refugee Problem, 1947–1949*, Tel Aviv: Am Oved, 1991, pp. 382–94 (Hebrew); Yoram Nimrod, *War or Peace? Formation of Patterns in Israel-Arab Relations, 1947–1950*, Givat Haviva: The Institute for Peace Research, 2000, p. 212 (Hebrew); Ilan Pappe, *The Making of the Arab-Israeli Conflict 1947–1951*, New York: St Martin's Press, 1992, p. 88; Tom Segev, *1949: The First Israelis*, New York: The Free Press, 1986, p. 26.

7 See, in this context, the following essays: Efraim Karsh, "Falsification out of Awareness? Falsification out of Blindness? – Benny Morris on the 'Transfer' Issue," *Alpayim* 13, 1996, pp. 212–32 (Hebrew); and *Fabricating Israeli History: The "New Historians,"* London: Frank Cass, 1997; Elhannan Orren, "From the Transfer

10 *Introduction*

Proposal of 1937–1938 to the 'Transfer De Facto' of 1947–1948," *Iyunim Bitku-mat Israel* 7, 1997, 75–85 (Hebrew); Shabtai Teveth, "The Palestinian Refugee Problem and Its Origins (Review Article)," *Middle Eastern Studies* 26(2), 1990, pp. 214–50; and, "Integrity and Rewriting Documents," *Alpayim* 13, 1996, pp. 233–56 (Hebrew).

8 Kimmerling and Migdal, *Palestinians*, pp. 140–5; Yaacov Shimoni and Evyatar Levine, *Political Dictionary of the Middle East in the Twentieth Century*, London: Weidenfeld and Nicolson, 1972, p. 36; Tessler, *A History of the Israeli-Palestinian Conflict*, p. 263; According to Yoav Gelber, by May of 1948, more than 2,000 people had been killed in the hostilities: 895 Jews, 991 Arabs, 123 British soldiers and policemen, and 38 unidentified persons: Yoav Gelber, *Palestine 1948: War, Escape and the Emergence of the Palestinian Refugee Problem*, Brighton: Sussex Academic Press, 2001, p. 85.

9 See, for example, the city of Jaffa. According to the Haganah Intelligence Service, "60 percent of Jaffa's rich Christians" departed from the city, as well as many middle-class Muslims and the majority of the residents of the well-off northern section of Jabaliyya, all in the first month of the confrontation. According to one report, 15,000 Arab residents had left Jaffa by the middle of January 1948. Itamar Radai, "Jaffa, 1948: The Fall of a City," *The Journal of Israeli History* 30(1), 2011, p. 30.

10 During a cabinet discussion of Israel's position regarding political settlements with the Arab countries, the minister of police, Behor Shitreet, told his colleagues that the point to be emphasized concerning the refugee issue was that "tens of thousands [of] non-Palestinian Arabs had been living in Haifa and Jaffa; they were Lebanese, Syrian, and Hauranese. Their return should certainly not be discussed, because they have no connection to the country. They came here and entered into commerce. Almost the entire Arab street, and the entire market, were populated by Syrian Damascenes." ISA, Government Meeting, 14 March 1949, p. 6. At a cabinet meeting held one month later, Minister Shitreet repeated this assertion: "regarding the refugees there were many Syrians, Lebanese and Egyptians here in Eretz Yisrael and their return should certainly not be considered." ISA, Government Meeting, 11 April 1949, p. 8; see also: Gelber, *Palestine 1948*, pp. 76, 116.

11 Moshe Efrat, "The Palestinian Refugees: Social and Economic Survey 1949–1974," MA thesis, Tel Aviv University, 1976, pp. 1–2 (Hebrew); Rony E. Gabbay, *A Political Study of the Arab-Jewish Conflict–The Arab Refugee Problem (A Case Study)*, Geneva: Librairie E. Droz, 1959, pp. 65–8; Gelber, *Palestine 1948*, pp. 74, 76, 82; Mordechai Lahav, *50 Years of the Palestinian Refugees, 1948–1999*, Haifa: self-published, 2000, pp. 23, 124, 392 (Hebrew); Morris, *The Birth*, pp. 50–2, 86–90; Pappe, *The Making*, pp. 87–8; According to Charles Douglas-Home, "Arabs have a habit of fleeing from situations of uncertainty, turbulence or foreboding, and of returning when peace is restored or when word reaches them that their fears were unfounded. It has happened over and over again in the Arab world." Charles Douglas-Home, *The Arabs and Israel: A Background Book*, London: The Bodley Head Ltd., 1968, p. 38.

12 David Tal, *War in Palestine, 1948: Strategy and Diplomacy*, London: Routledge, 2004, pp. 86–8.

13 Efrat, "The Palestinian Refugees: Social and Economic Survey," p. 3; Gabbay, *A Political Study*, p. 86; Morris, *The Birth*, pp. 91–183, 401; Terence Prittie and Bernard Dineen, *The Double Exodus–A Study of Arab and Jewish Refugees in the Middle East*, London: The Goodhart Press, 1970, p. 5.

14 Gelber, *Palestine 1948*, pp. 107–8; Tamir Goren, *The Fall of Arab Haifa in 1948*, Sede Boqer: The Ben-Gurion Research Institute, 2006, pp. 228–32 (Hebrew); Don Peretz, *The Palestine Arab Refugee Problem*, New York: Rand Corporation, 1969, p. 9; Joseph B. Schechtman, *The Arab Refugee Problem*, New York: Philosophical Library, 1952, pp. 7–9.

Introduction 11

15 Gabbay, *A Political Study*, pp. 85–6; Gelber, *Palestine 1948*, pp. 98, 116; Lahav, *50 Years*, p. 394; Morris, *The Birth*, pp. 96–7, 180; Peretz, *The Palestine Arab Refugee Problem*, p. 10; Avraham Sela, "The Palestinian Arabs in the 1948 War," in Moshe Maoz and Benjamin Z. Kedar (eds), *The Palestinian National Movement: From Confrontation to Reconciliation?*, Tel Aviv: Ministry of Defence, 1996, p. 170 (Hebrew).

16 Gabbay, *A Political Study*, pp. 86–7; Morris, *The Birth*, pp. 180, 182; Pappe, *The Making*, p. 99; Peretz, *The Palestine Arab Refugee Problem*, p. 10.

17 Efrat, "The Palestinian Refugees: Social and Economic Survey," p. 2; Gabbay, *A Political Study*, p. 94; Morris, *The Birth*, p. 387; Nimrod, *War or Peace?*, p. 202; Sela, "The Palestinian Arabs," p. 168.

18 Aharon Cohen, *Israel and the Arab World*, New York: Funk and Wagnalls, 1970, p. 432; Gabbay, *A Political Study*, p. 95; Gelber, *Palestine 1948*, p. 108; Lahav, *50 Years*, p. 394; Pappe, *The Making*, p. 94.

19 Cohen, *Israel and the Arab World*, p. 459; Gabbay, *A Political Study*, p. 92; Morris, *The Birth*, pp. 33–4; on page 142, Morris noted that "the acts of murder, looting and rape committed by undisciplined members of the Arab irregular forces" contributed to the atmosphere of general despair that gripped the Arab residents of Jaffa and reinforced their tendency to leave; Nimrod, *War or Peace?*, p. 201.

20 For an in-depth examination of the subject of Dir Yassin, see Benny Morris, "The Historiography of Deir Yassin," *The Journal of Israeli History* 24(1), 2005, pp. 79–108.

21 Cohen, *Israel and the Arab World*, pp. 459–60; Douglas-Home wrote about that: "There were atrocities and rumours of atrocities on both sides to speed them on. Both sides indulged in atrocity propaganda, just as both sides indulged in atrocities. Perhaps the main difference between their propaganda, however [...] was that the Arab population to whom their propaganda was direct was a less critical, more gullible, and more simple audience than the Jews. They were taught to hate the Jews, but their belief that the Jews possessed the very characteristics which they were taught to hate only helped to increase their terror, and persuaded them to flee before what they had every reason to believe must be a great wrath to come." Douglas-Home, *The Arabs and Israel*, p. 39; Gabbay, *A Political Study*, pp. 87–91; Lahav, *50 Years*, p. 394; Morris, *The Birth*, pp. 181–2.

22 Gabbay, *A Political Study*, pp. 83–4; Morris, *The Birth*, pp. 171–3.

23 Gabbay, *A Political Study*, p. 108; Lahav, *50 Years*, p. 395; Benny Morris wrote the following concerning this issue: "The 'Haganah' attacks came during the months of April and May [...] The cumulative effect of the Fears, defeats, the departure of the wealthy families, and the acts of theft and looting in both towns and villages now began to overcome the natural aversion to the abandonment of homes and property and to exile [...] The Arabs' ability to endure was weakened and a general blind panic spread." Morris, *The Birth*, p. 384.

24 Gabbay, *A Political Study*, pp. 108–9; Gelber, *Palestine 1948*, pp. 150–1, 161–2, 208, 224–5; Morris, *The Birth*, pp. 94, 390; Sela, "The Palestinian Arabs," pp. 171–2.

25 Gabbay, *A Political Study*, pp. 109–10; Morris, *The Birth*, pp. 386–7.

26 Gabbay, *A Political Study*, pp. 108–12; Morris, *The Birth*, pp. 265–315.

27 Flapan, *The Birth*, pp. 87, 90; Gabbay, *A Political Study*, pp. 97, 109–10; Morris, *The Birth*, pp. 291, 382, 390–91; Prittie and Dineen, *The Double Exodus*, p. 7. Palestinian researchers have claimed that the Zionist leadership began to contemplate the idea of transfer years before the 1948 war; as proof, they point to the fact that the subject was discussed by Zionist leaders during the second half of 1937 and the beginning of 1938, after the publication of the Peel Commission Report, which proposed the transfer of Arabs out of the territory of the Jewish state. Alec D. Epstein and Michael Uritsky, "What Happened and What Did Not Happen: The Yishuv, the End of the Mandate, and the Emergence of the

12 Introduction

Refugee Problem," *Gesher* 149, 2004, pp. 58–63 (Hebrew). The Zionist leaders did hold talks on the subject, but the historical fact is that the idea was never approved.

28 PDD, Document 483, Meeting: M. Shertok, E. Epstein – G. Marshall, R. Lovett, D. Rusk, Washington, 8 May 1948; ISA, Provisional Government Meeting, 8 June 1948, p. 22; DEPI, Vol. 1, Document 189, M. Shertok to N. Goldmann, 15 June 1948. James McDonald, the first American ambassador to Israel, wrote in his memoir that the Israeli leadership "had been quite unprepared for the Arab exodus; no responsible Zionist leader had anticipated such a 'miraculous' clearing of the land." James G. McDonald, *My Mission in Israel, 1948–1951*, New York: Simon and Schuster, 1951, p. 176.

29 Michael Bar-Zohar, *Ben-Gurion: A Political Biography*, Tel Aviv: Am Oved, 1977, pp. 703, 775 (Hebrew); Israeli President Chaim Weizmann told Ambassador McDonald that the Arab exodus provided a "miraculous simplification of Israel's tasks." McDonald, *My Mission*, p. 176.

30 An internal Ha-Shomer Ha-Tzair document, drafted by Aharon Cohen in October of 1948, contained the following statement: "The Arabs' flight was not part of a Zionist program that had been planned in advance, but once it began, it was encouraged by important Jewish elements, for military and political reasons." Cited in Ronit Barzily and Mustafa Kabha, *Refugees in their Homeland: Internal Refugees in the State of Israel, 1948– 1996*, Givat Haviva: The Institute for Peace Research, 1996, p. 6 (Hebrew); Gabbay, *A Political Study*, p. 110.

31 On the circumstances of its establishment and the area in which it operated, see Chapter 1.

32 Gabbay, *A Political Study*, pp. 169–74; Deborah Kaplan, *The Arab Refugees: An Abnormal Problem*, Jerusalem: Rubin Mass, 1959, pp. 122, 127–8; Morris, *The Birth*, pp. 397–9; Walter Pinner, *How Many Arab Refugees ? A Critical Study of UNRWA's Statistics and Reports*, London: Macgibbon and Kee, 1959.

33 UNRWA, A/1451/Rev. 1, p. 3.

34 Gabbay, *A Political Study*, p. 170.

35 UNRWA, A/2717, p. 2.

36 Efrat, "The Palestinian Refugees: Social and Economic Survey", p. 9.

37 Benjamin N. Schiff, *Refugees unto the Third Generation: U.N. Aid to Palestinians*, Syracuse, NY: Syracuse University Press, 1995, pp. 23–4.

38 UNRWA, A/3686, p. 12.

39 On the circumstances of its establishment and the area in which it operated, see Chapter 3.

40 UNESM, A/1106, p. 22.

41 See the data presented in Chapter 2, under the heading 'The parties' position towards the refugee problem on the eve of the Lausanne Conference.'

42 ISA, MFA 2566/13A, The Palestinian Refugee Problem (Review 4), 20 April 1949; Morris, *The Birth*, p. 397.

43 ISA, MFA 2015/7, The Arab Refugee Problem, 26 November 1950.

44 Haya Bambaji-Sasportas, "Whose Voice Is heard/Whose Voice Is Silenced: The Construction of 'The Palestinian Refugee Problem' Discourse in the Israeli Establishment, 1948–1952," MA thesis, Ben-Gurion University, 2000, pp. 38–9 (Hebrew).

45 See the data presented by the following researchers: Bambaji-Sasportas, "Whose Voice Is heard," p. 38, n. 2; Efrat, "The Palestinian Refugees: Social and Economic Survey," pp. 16–18; and "The Palestinian Refugees: The Socio-Economic Integration in their Host Countries," *Orient* 42(1), 2001, p. 47; Gabbay, *A Political Study*, p. 177; Pinner, *How Many Arab Refugees?*, pp. 24–8; Shimoni and Levine, *Political Dictionary*, p. 325.

46 Morris, *The Birth*, p. 399.

1 Israel's policy towards the emerging refugee problem, spring–winter 1948

Rejection of the principle of repatriation[1]

The heads of the Jewish community in Mandate Palestine only began to seriously address the flight of the Palestinians at the end of April 1948 when a trickle turned into a rising surge, particularly from the mixed cities of Haifa and Jaffa.[2] The core issue that concerned Jewish leadership in this context was the question of repatriation. From statements uttered in this regard, it is evident that the heads of the Jewish community had deep reservations concerning the possibility that the refugees would return to their homes. Thus Moshe Sharett, head of the Jewish Agency's Political Department (the organization of Jewish political leadership in Mandate Palestine), wrote in a 25 April telegram from New York to officials in his home office in Tel Aviv: "Suggest [we] consider issuing warning [to] Arabs now evacuating – cannot be assured of return."[3] Two weeks later, Sharett told US Secretary of State George Marshall that the Arab states bear now the burden of "feeding, clothing and sheltering masses of refugees." He demonstratively refrained from suggesting the return of those taking flight.[4] The Chair of the Jewish Agency David Ben-Gurion stated after the fall of Haifa to Haganah forces that while one should treat any Arab who remained in Haifa with "civil and human equalitarianism, it is not our job to take care of the return of the Arabs."[5] Similar sentiments concerning Palestinian Arab refugees from Haifa were expressed by Golda Meir, a member of the Jewish Agency Executive. In a speech delivered on 11 May at a meeting of Mapai's Centre (a left-wing socialist party that headed the Zionist establishment), she clarified to all those present: "I say I am not willing to make extraordinary arrangements to bring back Arabs."[6] This position was further entrenched in the course of political-defense consultations that took place on 1 June in Tel Aviv, two weeks after declaration of independence. Participating were newly appointed ministers and senior officials in the State of Israel. The participants agreed that the refugees should not be helped to return and directives should be issued in this regard to army commanders.[7] Parallel to this, the heads of the IDF themselves warned the political echelons regarding the grave ramifications return of the Palestinian Arab refugees would have in terms of the ability of the army to deal with the invading armies of neighboring Arab states.[8]

14 *Israel's policy towards the emerging refugee problem*

The Israeli leadership's position towards the refugee problem was not the fruit of a comprehensive and in-depth debate of the issue. The dramatic developments on the military and political fronts since March did not leave room for such a luxury.[9] Only when the first ceasefire came into force on 11 June was it possible to sit and weigh seriously formulation of an official policy on this issue – at the heart of the matter, the question of repatriation. Realities demanded such a clarification in light of the escalation of the problem: at this point in time, there were already 300,000 refugees, and consequently world attention was focused on the crisis. Public opinion in the west was mobilized and European and American relief funds were established to ease the distress of the refugees. The envoy appointed by the United Nations to deal with the Middle East conflict, Swedish Count Folke Bernadotte, clarified prior to his arrival in Israel on 17 June that he intended to focus his efforts on finding a solution to the problem of the Palestinian refugees.[10]

On 16 June, the eve of his arrival, the Israeli cabinet convened and deliberated at length the refugee issue and especially the question of repatriation. The first speaker, Foreign Minister Sharett, delineated in a sharp and resolute speech the outlines of the anticipated solution:[11]

> I believe that we need to be prepared to pay for land. It's not a matter of us buying it one person at a time. But this needs to be a question of government-[level] negotiations, that we will pay for assets and land and this will serve for their settlement in other countries. But they are not returning. And this is our policy: That they're not returning […] They need to get used to the idea that this matter is a lost cause and this change is a change that won't reverse.

Sharett's rationale rejecting repatriation touched on every possible aspect of life in the young state:

> In my eyes, this is the most surprising thing: The emptying out of the Arab community […] There will be a need to explain the tremendous importance of this transformation that took place from a settlement perspective, from a security perspective, from the perspective of the robustness of the state's structure and solution to vital social and very grave political problems that have cast their shadow on the entire future of the state.

Immediately after Sharett, Prime Minister and Minister of Defense David Ben-Gurion took the floor. His solution to the refugee problem was similar to the foreign minister's, although his rationale was based primarily on security and military considerations.

> We didn't make war. They made the war. Jaffa made war against us. Haifa made war against us. Beit Shaan carried out a war against us. And I don't want that they will make war against us again. Because that

wouldn't be righteousness, rather [it would be] a folly. That's to be a foolish pious man. Must we bring the enemy back so that again it can make war against us in Beit Shaan? No! You made war – You lost. I have no obligation to maintain Beit Shaan. They lost and they fled [...] I will be in favor of this that they won't return even after the war.

The prime minister's and foreign minister's resolute stand against repatriation of the refugees won broad support in the cabinet. An exception was the minister of agriculture, Aharon Zisling from Mapam (a left-wing socialist party). Zisling expressed strident opposition to the proposed line. Hundreds of thousands of refugees, "they and their young offspring, will carry with them ambitions for revenge, payment and repatriation", he warned, and there will be those who will stir up the Arab masses for war with Israel. Thus we cede with our own hands, added Zisling with pathos, "the hope of an alliance and peace with [Palestinian] forces that could be our allies in the Middle East." He concluded:

This orientation of prohibiting the Arabs' return, that is to say, that we won't approach this matter neither through settlement afterwards, nor through dialogue, nor through transfer from one part of the country to another, nor through constructive action that will generate trust [...] rather coming with a disallowance, by shutting [the door] and preventing return after the war – this must surely be a stumbling block for us.[12]

The sentiments expressed by Minister Zisling reflected the outlook that was current within Mapam vis-à-vis the refugee issue. Thus, a month earlier, Meir Ya'ari, one of Mapam's senior leaders and the movement's most prominent ideologue, said in a speech before a mass meeting:

Alas, a great fear has descended upon the Arab masses [...] Hundreds of thousands have fled [...] yet are we interested that a refugee problem will be created with a belt of hostility around us? We will not be able to maintain our independence if we will be encircled with eternal animosity around us.[13]

In keeping with this outlook, on 15 June, Mapam's political committee passed a decision that implied that repatriation should be allowed at the end of the war.[14]

In theory, the decision was supposed to be the product of a compromise between the party's two factions – Ha-Shomer Ha-Tzair and the Ahduth Ha-Avodah–Po'alei Zion Movement – however, in practice, the decision was closer to the line adopted by Ha-Shomer Ha-Tzair. Members of Ahduth Ha-Avodah, who held an "activist" approach to foreign relations and security issues, tended to reject repatriation,[15] while members of Ha-Shomer Ha-Tzair, who championed Jewish-Arab fraternity, believed all those refugees who desired to return to their homes at the end of hostilities should be allowed to do so.[16] Mapam's party newspaper *Al Ha-Mishmar*, where Ha-Shomer Ha-Tzair members held a dominant position, reflect this stance in a 22 July editorial:

16 Israel's policy towards the emerging refugee problem

The government of Israel must announce to the Arab refugees in a clear manner: Their property, their fields and their rights are safeguarded for them, and at the end of the war all (those) who want to return – the gates are open before him.[17]

In the following months, Ha-Shomer Ha-Tzair members set the tone on the question of repatriation, and Mapam's official position reflected their worldview.[18]

The ruling Mapai party's outlook differed, and its leaders Ben-Gurion and Sharett clarified this in the cabinet meeting. According to the Intelligence Service (which was responsible for censorship of newspapers and mail), public opinion in Israel favored this stance,[19] but nevertheless Mapai could not ignore Mapam's conciliatory position. Mapam, after all, was Mapai's primary coalition partner in the government, and no less important, Mapam was Mapai's natural ally due to their shared socialist ideological values. Moreover, Mapam was held in esteem by the Israeli public, and only Mapai held more prestige in the eyes of the public. This was reflected in the outcome of the country's first parliamentary elections: Mapam garnered more seats in the Knesset than any of the other parties in parliament, except for Mapai.[20] The prestige and power of the Mapam movement rested on the fact that Mapam's cadres occupied a prominent place in the upper echelons of the military and security establishment of the young state. They also held a weighty position among senior civil servants, and many kibbutz settlements were associated with Mapam, both socially and politically. It is therefore not surprising that at the 16 June cabinet meeting described above, Ben-Gurion closed the meeting without taking a vote on the issue of repatriation. It is possible that had Ben-Gurion passed an official decision harshly rejecting on the spot the principle of repatriation, Mapam would have been forced to leave the coalition government, dealing a heavy blow to national unity in time of war.

The desire to prevent a coalition crisis forced Ben-Gurion and Sharett to adopt a more flexible and less strident position than the one they expressed during cabinet deliberations, that is, a position that did not totally reject repatriation.[21] A cue to the position taking shape can be seen in a 20 June interview that the Director of the Middle East Division in the Ministry of Foreign Affairs Eliahu Sasson gave to the *New York Herald Tribune*. Sasson declared that selective repatriation of refugees could be possible if this would be part of a peace treaty with the Arab states.[22] It is unclear whether these sentiments were made of Sasson's own volition or on orders from the foreign minister; either way, for a number of weeks they remained the only political statement on record regarding Israel's position on the refugee question, and Israeli representatives abroad relied on this utterance when they were requested to clarify their government's position. Official confirmation of Sasson's statement came on 22 July in a telegram sent by Foreign Minister Sharett to the Israeli delegation at the United Nations:

2. No question [it is out of the question] allowing Arabs return while state of war continuing, as would mean introduction fifth column, provision

bases for enemies from outside and dislocation law order inside. Exceptions only in favour special deserving cases compassionate grounds [humanitarian grounds], subject security screening [...] 4. Question Arab return can be decided only as part peace settlement with Arab States and in context its terms, when question confiscation property Jews neighboring countries and their future will also be raised.[23]

Thus, the Israeli leadership agreed that in the framework of comprehensive peace talks with its neighbors, Israel would agree to discuss the repatriation issue and perhaps even allow some number of refugees to return to their homes, once an agreement was achieved. On the other hand, Mapam's demand to permit immediate repatriation after termination of hostilities was not accepted, and in any case the possibility of refugees returning during the war was out of the question. Already on 18 June Foreign Minister Sharett told the UN Envoy Bernadotte that "the question [of repatriation] could not be discussed while war was on."[24] On 28 July, after lengthy discussion, the Israeli government passed its first official decision vis-à-vis the Palestinian refugee problem, stating that "as long as the war continues, there is no agreement to repatriate the refugees."[25]

In a 24 July conversation that the director of the British Commonwealth Division in the Ministry of Foreign Affairs, Michael Comay, conducted with the deputy head of the American Delegation to the United Nations, Philip Jessup, Israel's position was relayed to the Americans, according to which a linkage exists between the repatriation issue and a peace agreement.[26] Two days later, UN Envoy Bernadotte was also updated in a meeting with Sharett as to the Israeli position.[27]

In the meantime, the refugee question became a burning issue in the Arab world. On 5 July, the secretary of the Arab League, Abd al-Rahman Azzam, turned to the secretary-general of the United Nations, Trygve Lie, requesting assistance be provided to the refugees. In this request, the first of its kind from the Arab states, emphasis was placed on the tremendous suffering masses of Palestinian refugees faced.[28] In a 24 July meeting between Bernadotte and Azzam in Beirut, Azzam reiterated the request, pointing to "the wretched living conditions which Arab refugees are subject to," some 300,000 to 400,000 souls, he claimed.[29]

The Arab request resonated well. The International Red Cross rapidly mobilized its assistive machinery to deal with the humanitarian crisis,[30] and Bernadotte called upon Israel to allow the immediate repatriation of a limited number of refugees among those requesting to do so.[31]

Israel, however, was not impressed by the international uproar. In a 1 August reply to the UN envoy, Sharett reiterated Israel's position that rejected repatriation of refugees as long as the war continued and coupled discussion of solutions with a peace agreement. Yet even should this precondition be met and a peace agreement achieved, Israel offered no guarantee that it would permit unlimited repatriation within its borders. The opposite seemed far more likely. Bernadotte had been told:

18 *Israel's policy towards the emerging refugee problem*

> The long-term interests of the Jewish and Arab populations; the stability of the State of Israel and the durability of the basis of peace between it and its neighbours [...] will all be relevant to the question of whether, to what extent and under what conditions [the refugees would return].[32]

In his remarks, the foreign minister alluded to an alternative solution to the repatriation principle: resettlement of the refugees in the Arab countries. This alternative, which was raised by Israel with Bernadotte and afterwards also with the United States, was designed to balance the scales in the face of growing demands from both quarters for repatriation of a large number of refugees.

In a conversation Sharett had with Bernadotte on 10 August, the foreign minister allowed himself to state things more clearly and in detail vis-à-vis the resettlement issue:

> I indicated the vast potentialities of absorption in Syria and Iraq, instancing Jamil Mardam's[33] statement to me that the District of Damascus alone could take in one million more people [...] as well as the continuous clamour of Iraq for more population. The resettlement of 300,000 people in these countries was not merely practicable, but in the measure in which it would be accompanied by an investment of new capital obtained from the realization of [abandoned Arab] assets in Palestine, it would be a distinct boon to the countries and Governments concerned.

The foreign minister went on to explain why it was advisable not to implement the principle of repatriation:

> The State of Israel would much more quickly achieve its full internal stability, and its peaceful relations with the Arab world would be put on a much firmer footing. However pampered the Arab minority in the State of Israel might be, they would always complain of unfair treatment, and their complaints would always act as an irritant in the relations between Israel and her neighbours and serve as a perpetual excuse for the latter to try and interfere in the affairs of the former. In the long run it was in the interests of all concerned that the Arab minority in the State of Israel be a small and not a large one.[34]

Documentation evidences to what extent serious and in-depth investigation of resettlement occupied policymakers in Israel since August. Bernadotte's pressure on the repatriation issue; the pending arrival in the country of James McDonald, the United States' first diplomatic representative in Tel Aviv; and the need to settle the fate of abandoned Arab land all fueled such intensive activity. A memorandum prepared in the Ministry of Foreign Affairs at the beginning of August entitled "Proposals for Immediate Actions Tied to Preventing Return of the Arab Refugees to Israel before Setting Permanent Policy towards This

Israel's policy towards the emerging refugee problem 19

Problem" raised several paths of action: first, detail the present location of the refugees; second, survey abandoned property; third, estimate the value of these assets from several perspectives; fourth, formulate proposals for a plan to resettle the refugees in various regions of the Arab world.[35]

On 18 August, Ben-Gurion ordered a large meeting to examine the Israeli position vis-à-vis the refugee issue. The gathering included, in addition to the prime minister, the following participants: Foreign Minister Sharett; Minister of Minorities Behor Shitreet; Minister of Finance Eliezer Kaplan; Director-General of the Ministry of Finance David Horowitz; director of the Political Division and advisor on Special Affairs in the Ministry of Foreign Affairs Reuven Shiloah; Deputy Director of the Middle East Division in the Ministry of Foreign Affairs Yaacov Shimoni; a clerk in the Middle East Division, Ezra Danin; director of the Jewish National Fund's Land and Forest Department Yosef Weitz; advisor to the government of Israel on land issues and cartography specialist Zalman Liff; and others. The next day, when Shimoni came to summarize the meeting, he wrote that "the opinions of the participants was uniform, and the desire to do everything possible in order to prevent the return of the refugees was shared by all."[36] Ben-Gurion's inscription [in his diary] on the consultations reveals that during the meeting the prime minister's attention was focused primarily on the idea of resettlement.[37]

In the wake of the meeting, on 29 August Ben-Gurion appointed a committee of three – Yosef Weitz, Zalman Liff, and Ezra Danin – "the Retroactive Transfer Committee," as Weitz later dubbed it. In his memoirs Weitz cited that according to the letter of appointment the committee was mandated to "submit to him [the prime minister] a proposal on the feasibility of settling the Arabs of Eretz Yisrael in the Arab countries."[38] On 26 October, the commission reported to Ben-Gurion on its principle findings. The commission rejected unequivocally the notion of repatriation on the following grounds: the departure of the Arabs was the most realistic solution to the problem of Mandate Palestine, a solution already noted in the past by many people in the world; agreement with the principle of repatriation would be a political mistake on Israel's part; return of the refugees would place a heavy economic burden on the state, as they would return empty-handed to a ravaged economy; and the animosity that the refugees harbored towards the Jewish community for their suffering, augmented by incitement against Israel carried out by Arab countries, would transform them into a kind of "fifth column" for the State of Israel. The commission concluded that the solution to the refugee problem resided in realization of the idea of resettlement. Palestinian refugees, the commission held, must remain in the Arab states "in order to settle in them permanently and build their households anew from the foundations." In its judgment, "this is also the desired and the most rational solution to this problem from an Arab perspective." The commission believed that three Arab countries were most suitable to absorb the refugees – Iraq, Syria, and Trans-Jordan – since their populations were sparse and in need of much manpower to develop the huge tracts of land within their borders. In addition, these countries could absorb

20   *Israel's policy towards the emerging refugee problem*

the refugees well, in light of the affinity that exists between the Palestinians and the local populations from a religious, linguistic, cultural, and national standpoint.[39]

The commission's reasoning faithfully reflected the outlook that also began to take shape among the Israeli public at large regarding a just solution to the problem of the Palestinian refugees. This perception of the problem and its solution took final shape in the coming months and became the official line of Israeli public diplomacy regarding resolution of the refugee problem.[40]

On 20 August McDonald met with Ben-Gurion and clarified to the Israeli prime minister that the United States was considering steps on the refugee question that would be distasteful to Israel. The United States, McDonald continued, might even go so far as to impose sanctions to force Israel to accept the American position on this subject. The prime minister replied that as long as Arab armies were on Israeli territory the repatriation of Palestinian refugees would be disastrous. "We cannot return an enemy to the country," he asserted adamantly, "even if sanctions would be placed on us."[41] Two weeks later, McDonald met with Sharett and presented the foreign minister with several American proposals to solve the Arab-Israeli conflict. On the refugee issue, it was proposed that the State of Israel "consider some constructive measures for the alleviation of Arab refugee distress."[42] Israel's response came swiftly, and on 8 September, in the course of a meeting between Ben-Gurion and Sharett with McDonald, the American diplomat was told that a comprehensive solution to the refugee problem would be achieved only in the framework of a peace agreement, and even then most of the refugees would have to resettle in Arab lands. For the time being, Israel would agree to absorb a very small number of refugees, solely on humanitarian grounds.[43]

Sharett allowed himself to be far more frank in a letter to Chaim Weizmann, president of the Provisional Council of State:

> With regard to the refugees, we are determined to be adamant while the war lasts [...] As for the future, we are equally determined – without, for the time being, formally closing the door to any eventuality – to explore all possibilities of getting rid, once and for all, of the huge Arab minority which originally threatened us.[44]

In preparation for the deliberation of the Palestine question in the 3rd United Nations General Assembly, the Israeli government discussed in its 12 September cabinet meeting what position the Israeli diplomatic delegation to the United Nations should take on the political issues that would be raised, such as the refugee problem, the borders of the Jewish state, and the fate of Jerusalem. Foreign Minister Sharett presented to his colleagues in the cabinet his ministry's recommendations on each of the topics. In regard to the refugee problem, the Israeli delegation should declare formally that "the question remains open, in anticipation of peace," while at the same time informal discussions would be conducted with other delegations to garner supporters for resettlement.

Most of the ministers in the cabinet supported the Ministry of Foreign Affairs' recommendation. The only exception was, again, Mapam's ministers, who were joined this time by Moshe Shapira from the United Religious Front (the Minister of Health who also held the Immigration portfolio). Mapam Minister Zisling reiterated his party's stand. Israel, he said, must tell the world that "we are willing to discuss immediately arrangement of the return of the Arab refugees, if neighboring governments will withdraw their armies from the country's [international] borders."

Zisling's party colleague, Minister of Construction and Housing Mordechai Bentov (who also held the Labor portfolio), requested to explain the logic behind this approach:

> If we would say we are prepared to repatriate them the minute the invading armies will leave the country, we would be sticking a wedge between the Arab states and the refugees. The refugees will claim that the main stumbling block to their return are the Arab armies sitting in the country, because the minute these armies leave – we will be prepared to return them to their [previous] places [of residence]. This posture will be a wedge that will be hard for the Arab [states] to remove and to settle the problem.

Hearing these arguments, Ben-Gurion burst in and slung at Bartov: "If such a thing will be done without a permanent peace agreement – the invaders will return again to the country." Minister Shapira replied that while the Arabs wouldn't accept the conditional that they remove their armies from the country, nevertheless "we must appear before the world and say we are willing to repatriate a significant number of refugees." In response to the Mapam minister and Minister Shapira's suggestion, Foreign Minister Sharett reiterated the core position that guided him and the prime minister regarding repatriation ever since the government's 16 June cabinet meeting:

> As for the refugees, from a tactical standpoint I am prepared [to] move closer to your point of view, and I was impressed with the wedge argument […] but […] I can't say that we will repatriate the refugees when I'm against returning [them]. And if I say that the question will be solved when the invaders leave the country – I stir up hope. It may be that the armies will leave the country, and then I will have to say publicly that I don't want the refugees back.

At the end of deliberations, the majority of the ministers voted seven in favor and three against the recommendation that repatriation would not be discussed except when peace agreements would be discussed.[45]

The government's decision made Israel's declared position since July official policy. Ben-Gurion and Sharett didn't intend to surrender to Mapam's ongoing pressure to present a more conciliatory position ("permit repatriation with termination of hostilities") but at the same time they refrained, again, from

22 Israel's policy towards the emerging refugee problem

officially adopting a rigid position that would totally reject repatriation within the framework of the cabinet. Mapam was liable to stir up coalition problems; no less important, such a move would have angered Washington, which was pushing to solve the refugee problem through repatriation of many Palestinians back to their homes, now in Israel. While still at war, Israel could not allow itself to open a diplomatic front with the strongest power in the world.

And at the same time, despite the cabinet's decision, Ben-Gurion and Sharett remained faithful to their fundamental position, which viewed the return of masses of Palestinian refugees, even in peacetime, as a concrete peril to the Jewish state; and therefore they urged Israeli diplomats at the United Nations to work behind the scenes to promote the idea of resettlement. Put more candidly, they should work vigorously to derail repatriation as a solution.

In a telegram to Eliahu Sasson (who was in Paris at the time), Yaacov Shimoni reported that in its formal appearances, the Israeli delegation to the United Nations would need to present the policy position passed by the government. In its informal appearances and private talks, however, it should declare that the government of Israel was prepared to discuss the repatriation of refugees only "in the event and on condition that the Arab states would seriously set about resettling [most of] the refugees outside of Israel." This directive, Shimoni revealed, "was not from the government – because deliberation of such a directive in the cabinet would have stirred up controversy [between] the parties which they wanted to prevent, rather, [the directive] was the Foreign Minister's alone."[46]

The diplomatic battle to repatriate the refugees reached its peak on 20 September with publication of Bernadotte's report on his efforts to mediate the Middle East conflict.[47] The report was completed on 16 September, the day before a Jewish terrorist squad assassinated the UN envoy in Jerusalem. In the report, Bernadotte supported repatriation of Arab refugees to their homes "at the earliest practical date" although he was cognizant of the radical changes that had taken place and were still taking place on the ground – the influx of masses of Jewish immigrants to Israel who occupied abandoned Arab houses, a process that was liable to prevent the return of masses of Arab refugees. Bernadotte noted: "The vast majority of the [Arab] refugees may no longer have homes to return to and their re-establishment in the State of Israel presents an economic and social problem of special complexity." Bernadotte also recommended that Israel pay "suitable compensation" for abandoned property of refugees who had fled and did not plan to return. Also, he supported establishment of a new body, "Conciliation Commission for Palestine," whose task would be to promote peace in the region under UN auspices, including promoting a solution to the Arab refugee problem.[48]

The UN envoy's recommendation to implement the principle of repatriation did not prompt Israel to reconsider its approach to this issue. In its reply to the report, Israel had to walk a fine line in light of the awkward and sensitive position in which it found itself: on one hand, the Swedish diplomat had been assassinated by Israelis; on the other hand, Bernadotte's recommendations, beyond the repatriation issue, such as internationalization of Jerusalem and transferring the Negev (the southern part of Israel) to the Arabs were an abomination in Israeli eyes. The delicate situation demanded an extremely carefully phrased reply that would express regret about the assassination without leaving any doubt as to Israel's position so that at no time in the future could the answer be interpreted as Israeli willingness to concede on these cardinal issues. Thus in the Israeli response to the Bernadotte report, submitted on 23 September, Israel ignored the UN envoy's call to recognize the refugees' right to return.[49]

In consultations in early October that the foreign minister conducted with the Israeli delegation at the UN, Sharett clarified:

> On the refugee question our position is that strong propaganda should be carried out in discussions with the delegations for the settlement of the refugees in the Arab states, stressing the broad possibilities. It should be explained that over time, this will be to the benefit of these countries, to the benefit of the settlers and their offspring and to the benefit of the [Middle] East as a whole, by reducing as much as possible the area [points] of friction.

The minister did not reject repatriation of a limited number of refugees to Israel, but he reiterated and declared that "if to repatriate, then only under conditions of peace."[50] In an additional discussion several days later, the legal advisor to the Israeli delegation, Yaacov Robinson, said that the international community must be convinced that "a dynamic solution" must be found to the refugee problem that will bring about their settlement in new places.[51] In this spirit, Sharett clarified to his French colleague, Robert Schuman, that "the most radical solution" to the Palestinian refugee problem will be their resettlement in neighboring countries.[52] Towards mid November, the foreign minister went to Paris to launch a diplomatic offensive against Bernadotte's recommendations. In a 15 November speech before the Ad Hoc Political Committee of the United Nations, Sharett again stated that the key to a solution of the refugee problem rested on the principle of resettlement.[53]

Israel was not the only one rejecting the Swedish mediator's report. The Arab bloc rejected it on the spot. This rejection was related to the refusal of the Arabs to recognize the very existence of a Jewish state, clearly reflected in the wording of the report. In addition, Bernadotte gave serious territorial dividends to Trans-Jordan's monarch, King Abdullah, a thorn in the side of the other Arab rulers. Consequently, in a meeting of the Political Committee of the Arab League in Cairo, the Arabs rejected the mediator's report, floating a plan to establish an un-partitioned [Arab] polity in Palestine that would guarantee protection of its Jewish minority.[54]

While Israel was concentrating on the political aspects of the refugee problem, the international community sought to deal with the humanitarian dimension. On 20 October, the Political Committee of the UN General Assembly held its

24   *Israel's policy towards the emerging refugee problem*

first discussion of the Arab refugee question. Acting UN Mediator on Palestine Ralph Bunche presented an account of the refugees' situation and emphasized that immediate assistance to ease their distress was needed. Discussion ran for several sessions during the last days of October and the beginning of November, and closed with a General Assembly resolution decision on 19 November 1948 to establish UNRPR – the United Nations Relief for Palestine Refugees. The objective of the new body was to provide for the basic survival requirements of Arab refugees and coordinate the operations of relevant relief bodies. The body was mandated to operate for a period of nine months, from 1 December 1948 to 31 August 1949,[55] since it was assumed that by then the Palestinian refugee problem would be terminated.[56]

Three weeks later, on 11 December 1948, the General Assembly passed Resolution 194(3). Thirty-five member states voted in favor, including the United States and Great Britain, fifteen voted against, and eight abstained. Passage of Resolution 194(3) was based on a number of the Bernadotte report's recommendations, primarily those related to the refugee issue. The Resolution's 15 clauses dealt with various matters raised on the international agenda in the wake of the war in Mandate Palestine.

Clause 2 mandated the establishment of a Conciliation Commission consisting of three member states of the United Nations to mediate the Arab-Israeli conflict and bring about conciliation. Clause 5 called on the governments concerned to seek agreement, by negotiation – direct or indirect (through the Conciliation Commission), with the objective of reaching a final settlement of all questions outstanding between them. Clause 11 dealt with the refugee problem. In the first part it states that the General Assembly:

> resolves that the refugees wishing to return to their homes and live at peace with their neighbours should be permitted to do so at the earliest practicable date, and that compensation should be paid for the property of those choosing not to return and for loss of or damage to property which, under principles of international law or in equity, should be made good by the Governments or authorities responsible.

The second half of the clause stated as follows: "instructs the Conciliation Commission to facilitate the repatriation, resettlement and economic and social rehabilitation of the refugees and the payment of compensation."[57]

In the history of the Arab-Israeli conflict, realization of Clause 11 of Resolution 194(3) became a core propaganda tool in the hands of the Arabs every time they wished to gore Israel and undermine its standing in world public opinion. The Arabs argued that this clause granted the immediate and inalienable "Right of Return" to all Palestinian refugees who wish to do so, and that Israel's ongoing opposition to full implementation of this principle made Israel a rogue state that brazenly flaunts the legal decisions of the international community. Yet this political application of Resolution 194(3) by the Arabs was totally contrary to their own voting record on 11 December

Israel's policy towards the emerging refugee problem   25

1948: all the Arab states in the United Nations – Egypt, Syria, Lebanon, Iraq, Saudi Arabia, and Yemen[58] – chose to vote *against* the resolution. According to Arab historian Fred Khouri, the Arab vote against Resolution 194(3) was a continuum to their opposition to the Partition Plan of November 1947, since Resolution 194(3) embodied recognition of a sort of the existence of a Jewish state and, in any case, acceptance of the loss forever of most of Palestine.[59]

Khouri's assessment is supported by Bernadotte's report of 16 September in which the UN envoy stated that the Arab states "would reject any recommendation [that the international community will submit to them] for acceptance of the Jewish state or its recognition."[60]

Yet several weeks after passage of the resolution, the Arabs decided to change their position. Already at the beginning of 1949 several Arab leaders realized that in light of their own military weakness, the Arabs could only benefit by embracing Resolution 194(3). It became clear to them that on their own (that is, on the field of battle) they could not gain any of the significant territorial or demographic concessions they sought to squeeze out of Israel, concessions they felt were promised to the Arabs by UN Resolution 194(3).[61]

Arab reliance on Clause 11 to justify "the right" of the refugees to return immediately and unconditionally to their homes was totally baseless. While the General Assembly called upon Israel to allow repatriation of refugees, it linked such a move to several preconditions. First of all, it was stipulated that Arab refugee returnees must be wiling to live in peace with their Jewish neighbors. This conditional seemed impossible to measure, since there was no way to validate the peaceful intentions of each and every refugee interested in repatriation. A simple declaration could hardly suffice. Infiltration by criminal and terrorist elements among the Palestinian refugees in the 1950s, parallel to incitement against Zionism frequently voiced by Palestinian leaders, gradually crystallized opinions among Israelis that the refugees' intentions were far from peaceful. Even if one could find a Palestinian refugee who was honestly interested in returning to his home to live at peace with his Jewish neighbors, he couldn't do so on the spot. After all, the General Assembly had clarified that repatriation could take place only "at the earliest practical date." In other words, the UN intended to say that repatriation of the refugees ("peace-lovers") inside Israel's borders could be implemented only when a change in conditions made this possible. The United Nations refrained, however, from stating exactly what conditions needed to be realized in order to reach the point where repatriation was executable. The resolution also did not stipulate who among the sides – Israel, the Arabs, or the international community – would have the authority to determine whether "the earliest practical date" had arrived. Yet if one takes into account the fact that Israel is the only sovereign in the areas from which the refugees departed and to which they are supposed to return, it is clear that practically the decision about when the refugees could return to their homes was in its hands. In practice, Israel could determine that it would be possible to permit mass repatriation only when

26 *Israel's policy towards the emerging refugee problem*

there would be a comprehensive and lasting peace between the Jewish state and its rival Arab neighbors. Until then, as long as a state of hostilities – whether a cold war or a shooting war – existed between the two sides, conditions that could allow a return did not exist, be they security, political, or fiscal. In other words, the "practical date" had not arrived.

Israel, of course, quickly seized the provisos that appear in Resolution 194 (3) to demonstrate that the refugees were not given free rein to return to their homes. Thus, Foreign Minister Sharett, speaking to the Knesset on 15 June 1949 in deliberations on Israel's foreign policy, said:

> And again they buffet us with the 11 December resolution. But even that resolution which seemingly requires the return of the refugees who want to [return], qualifies on the spot this obligation with two provisos. First of all, only peace-seekers are entitled to return. Who will examine the sincerity of the desire for peace among returning masses, and who will guarantee the stability of this desire? Secondly, [the refugees] should be returned "at the earliest practical date." Who decided that this possible date has already arrived?[62]

Israel clung to this interpretation of Resolution 194(3) throughout the period studied in the research, and in fact continues to do so ever since.[63]

In closing, it is important to keep in mind that Clause 11, which addressed the Palestinian refugee problem, was only one component of Resolution 194 (3), which envisioned a final settlement of *all* disputes between the parties. The Arabs continued to demand implementation of this clause only (and exclusively in keeping with their own interpretations), separate from all the other issues.

Blocking the feasibility of repatriation

In addition to Israel's political stand, what put an end to repatriation *in practice* were the physical, demographic and legal realities that took form parallel to and following the departure of the refugees. Such facts on the ground thwarted any possibility that the Palestinian refugees would ever return to their homes and their previous lives.

At the outset, this was the product of purely military exigencies. Buildings in Palestinian villages and Arab neighborhoods in mixed cities and sometimes entire settlements were erased in the storm of battle. The Haganah, and its successors the IDF, sometimes razed Arab settlements after they were occupied by Israeli forces, in order to prevent them from providing cover for enemy forces.[64] But from the second half of 1948, as the view that the departure of the Arabs was a fait accompli took root, demolition of the Arab sector and control over what remained became a vehicle to perpetuate the Israeli leadership's position that categorically rejected implementation of the principle of repatriation.[65]

A fateful demographic development during the war and the two years that followed – the immigration of hundreds of thousands of Jews to Israel – further diminished the possibility that the Palestinians would be able to return and provided additional justification for Israel's policies towards the real estate assets of the Arab refugees.[66]

In the second half of 1948, 102,000 Jewish immigrants arrived in Israel. In the following year, some 240,000 more arrived; and in the years 1950–1951 another 350,000 Jews flooded the country. All told, Israel absorbed during its first three and a half years of statehood close to 700,000 Jewish immigrants, doubling the pre-state Jewish population.[67] Half of the immigrants came from Arab countries. In most cases, local Arab regimes limited the property Jews could take with them, forcing many to abandon their assets and arrive in Israel destitute.[68] The realities of finding shelter for such masses, all the more so in the midst of a fierce and destructive war, led to the rapid repopulation of abandoned Arab homes by homeless Jewish immigrants. Israel considered itself entitled to do so under prevailing circumstances. In its view, such abandoned properties were the assets of a people who had consciously and willingly declared a genocidal war on the Jews of Mandate Palestine in clear contravention of the UN Partition resolution. This war had imposed huge outlays on the fledgling Jewish state; parallel to this there was the economic burden of absorbing masses of immigrants. Both pressures made it imperative to exploit the assets of enemy Palestinians.[69]

The scope of abandoned Palestinian property is subject to controversy, just as the number of refugees is. According to Mandate records there were 434 Palestinian villages and 12 mixed cities in 1946. At the close of the 1948 Arab-Israeli war, there were 88 Arab villages and 7 mixed cities.[70] From the statistics of Israel's state custodian for absentees' property, a state official appointed to administer the abandoned property of Palestinians, the custodian was given custody of 4 million dunam of land that belonged to Arabs prior to the war: 2.5 million dunam of cultivated land and 1.5 million dunam of uncultivated land.[71] According to official Israeli data, the urban property abandoned by Arabs included 46,000 dunam of land, of which 3,300 dunam were built-up sectors that contained approximately 9,000 residences, 9,700 shops, and 1,200 offices. The estimated value of urban land at the time was 13 million pounds sterling, and the estimated value of buildings 12 million pounds sterling. In the villages, beyond millions of abandoned dunam, there were also thousands of buildings. Most served as residences, a smaller number as public buildings. Beyond these assets, infrastructure of various kinds also remained in Arab villages: wells, water pumps and pipes for irrigation and drinking water, power lines, and sewage and drainage systems.[72]

The estimates of the "Refugees Office" – a technical body established by the Conciliation Commission to examine the compensation issue – were totally different from the state custodian for absentees' property's assessment.[73] At the close of August 1951, based on a three-month survey, the Refugees Office claimed that Arab abandoned lands stood at 16,324,000 dunam: that is, nearly 80 percent of the surface area of the State of Israel within the 1949 armistice lines. Within this area, the extent of abandoned cultivated lands was approximately 4.5 million dunam.[74] The Refugees Office estimated that the monetary value of abandoned lands was 100,383,784 pounds sterling, according to the following division: 69,525,144 pounds sterling for rural lands; 21,608,640 for urban lands; and 9,250,000 for land in the Jerusalem area.[75]

It was impossible to accurately calculate the value of abandoned Arab movable property since it was difficult to appraise the value of certain articles of property, and all the more difficult to know what the refugees had taken with them and what they had left behind. Averaging out three methods of calculating assets, the Refugees Office approximated that the sum value of abandoned moveable property was 20 million pounds sterling.[76] The Israeli custodian, by contrast, estimated the value of Arab movables under his administration at the outset of 1951 at only 4 million pounds sterling.[77] According to Refugees Office data, the sum value at the outset of the 1950s of all Arab abandoned assets, movables and immovables, was nearly 120 million pounds sterling. This appraisal became the official assessment of the Conciliation Commission. Besides immovable and moveable property, more than 3 million pounds sterling in blocked bank accounts, unknown sums of cash and valuables (in homes and in safety deposit boxes), as well as commercial stock were left by the refugees.[78]

An in-depth analysis derived 50 years after the 1948 war by economics historian Frank Lewis arrived at higher figures. The value of rural land at 1950s market values stood at 169 million pounds sterling.[79]

In contrast with these estimates, the Arab League assessed the value of all abandoned Arab property in Israel at a flat 2 billion pounds sterling: 1.1 billion in land; 660 million in agricultural land; 200 million in real estate; and more than 7 million pounds sterling in blocked bank accounts.[80] Other Arab parties also provided their own high assessments of the value of abandoned Palestinian property.[81]

Already in the midst of the war, the Israeli leadership was forced to establish machinery to oversee abandoned Palestinian property so it would not be damaged or plundered; thus, in late March 1948 the Haganah High Command established a commission designed to deal with Arab assets. A short time later, the commission was transferred to a special division set up by the High Command to deal with all Arab affairs.[82] The commission dealt primarily with Arab properties in the rural sector that in late March–early April 1948 were the first to fall into Jewish hands. Parallel to this, with the occupation of Arab sections of mixed cities, local commissions were formed to deal with urban Arab assets.

On 24 June, the Provisional Council of State approved the Abandoned Areas Ordinance, 5708–1948, which stated that handling of abandoned Arab property was within the authority of the government, and the prime minister, or ministers authorized by him, could issue ordinances in this regard. The minister of finance was assigned executor of the ordinance, and a state custodian for the

Arab abandoned property was appointed. At the beginning of July, a ministerial committee for abandoned property was established. Members of the committee were Prime Minister and Minister of Defense David Ben-Gurion; Foreign Minister Moshe Sharett; Minister of Finance Eliezer Kaplan; Minister of Agriculture Aharon Zisling; Minister of Minorities Behor Shitreet; and Minister of Justice Pinhas Rosen. On 26 July the committee decided that the Ministry of Agriculture would handle abandoned agricultural property. Hence, the state custodian for the abandoned property, who was chief supervisor of Palestinian abandoned property and who operated under the auspices of the Ministry of Finance, dealt primarily with abandoned property in the cities, while the Ministry of Agriculture dealt with abandoned property in villages.[83]

On 12 December 1948 the Emergency Regulations Relating to Absentees' Property, 5709-1948 were published. The legal force of the regulations was extended from time to time until 31 March 1950, when the Absentees' Property Law, 5710-1950 came into force. These regulations defined the legal standing of the abandoned property and contained substantive limitations in their regard. They were worded in a format similar to the 1939 Mandatory Regulations of Commerce with the Enemy, based on the following principles:

1 to prevent the enemy – whether they are absent from the country or whether they are under arrest or under supervision – from using their assets or enjoying them for the duration of the war;
2 to enable the state to use these assets temporarily;
3 to protect them on behalf of their owners in order to return them when the state of emergency would be lifted or to use them to dispose of counter claims or war damage.

Hence, the state custodian was solely a temporary office, and the official's primary duty was to protect the assets for an interim period. The custodian was not entitled to decide the fate of the assets placed temporarily in his care; was prohibited from discharging them from his authority, except to the property owner; and was prohibited from transferring them to another or leasing them out for more than five years. That is to say, the 12 December regulations strictly restricted the authority of the government to fully or permanently utilize in an effective manner the assets of absentees for Jewish settlement purposes or absorption of Jewish immigrants. These problems demanded an immediate solution, and in order to secure the fiscal investment already made in these assets and those that would be made in the future, it was necessary to convert their status from temporary possession of absentees' property to that of permanent possession.[84]

In March 1949, Advisor to the Prime Minister on Land Issues Liff suggested a legal arrangement that would enable permanent transfer of absentees' properties to entities engaged in reconstruction of war damage, Jewish settlement activity, and Jewish immigrant absorption.[85] The legislation that Liff recommended

30 *Israel's policy towards the emerging refugee problem*

was based on legal precedents in other countries that had refugee problems of their own.

After numerous deliberations, on 14 March 1950 the Knesset passed the Absentees' Property Law, 5710-1950. According to the law, the state custodian for absentees' property was transformed from a *trustee* of abandoned assets to the *owner* of abandoned assets, albeit with certain restrictions. According to the law "all rights that the absentee held to the property pass to the Custodian at the time of transfer of the property."[86] The concept "absentee" was defined in the Absentees' Property Law as follows:

> A person who, at any time during the period between the 16th Kislev, 5708 (29th November, 1947) and the day on which a declaration is published, under section 9(d) of the Law and Administration Ordinance, 5708–1948, that the state of emergency declared by the Provisional Council of the State on the 10th Iyar, 5708 (19th May, 1948) has ceased to exist, was a legal owner of any property situated in the area of Israel or enjoyed or held it, whether by himself or through another, and who, at any time during the said period: (1) was a national or citizen of the Lebanon, Egypt, Syria, Saudi-Arabia, Trans-Jordan, Iraq, or the Yemen, or (2) was in one of these countries or in any part of Palestine outside the area of Israel, or (3) was a Palestinian citizen and left his ordinary place of residence in Palestine (a) for a place outside Palestine before the 27th Av, 5708 (1st September, 1948); or (b) for a place in Palestine held at the time by forces which sought to prevent the establishment of the State of Israel or which fought against it after its establishment.[87]

The return to Israel of a person who had previously been an absentee and now resided legally in Israel did not exempt such a person's property from being designated "absentee property" from a legal standpoint. Over time, an administrative norm developed to label such residents "present absentees," although this concept is not a technical legal term. Nevertheless, the custodian was entitled to use his judgment (while at the same time, taking into account the recommendations of a special committee appointed by the government under the law) and could allow a person situated at the time legally in Israel and defined as a "present absentee" to no longer be considered an "absentee" and return his property.[88]

According to one scholar of the period, the Absentees' Property Law was the first step in the legal campaign designed to bridge the gap between the "de-Arabization" of Arab abandoned assets and the "Israelification" of that property. That is to say, the Absentees' Property Law marked the beginning of the process of institutionalized transfer of Palestinian-Arab refugees' property to Jewish-Israeli hands.[89] Institutions and organizations engaged in development of the State of Israel were thus able to operate without apprehension in regard to the ultimate fate of their investments, should political changes of demographic and spatial significance arise.[90]

Israel's policy towards the emerging refugee problem 31

The custodian's title to Arab absentees' property was limited in order to ensure that such properties would be used exclusively for the national objectives for which they were earmarked; thus, for example, it was stipulated that the custodian was not permitted to sell absentees' properties except to a special body called "The Authority for the Development of the Country." Moreover, it was stipulated that the custodian was entitled to lease transferred real estate for a period of up to six years, but only to the Development Authority or to any lessee whose lease contract stipulated that the tenant undertook to cultivate or develop the property to the custodian's satisfaction.[91]

The Authority for the Development of the Country (or, in short, the Development Authority) was established by legislation entitled the Development Authority Law (Transfer of Properties) 5710–1950. It was clear to the law's architects that the state custodian for absentees' property was not a suitable authority to develop abandoned Arab assets, and it was designed primarily to locate, centralize, and protect such assets.

The primary drive behind establishment of the new authority was thus to construct a supreme governmental institution that could take absentees' properties from the hands of the custodian and utilize them to develop the country. The Development Authority's missions were numerous and varied. They included among other things: development of infrastructure, absorption of mass Jewish immigration, and reconstruction of the ravages of war. To fulfill its roles, the Development Authority was authorized to buy, rent, lease, alter, improve, or develop abandoned Arab assets. After it received abandoned property, the Development Authority could sell or rent it solely to the state, to institutions that the state approved, or to the Jewish National Fund,[92] which was designated first in line to purchase abandoned lands.[93] An entity to which the Development Authority sold or rented abandoned Arab property had no right to transfer the property to a third party without the approval of the authority. The objective was, of course, to prevent a situation where abandoned Arab property would fall out of Jewish hands and return to Palestinian Arab ownership.

Notes

1 The term "repatriation" refers to the return of Palestinian refugees to locations within the borders of the State of Israel. The term "resettlement" refers to the settlement of Palestinian refugees in Arab countries.
2 PDD, Editorial Note (p. 666); and see the references to the cables indicated there.
3 PDD, Document 410, M. Shertok to R. Zaslani, 25 April 1948.
4 PDD, Document 483, Meeting: M. Shertok, E. Epstein – G. Marshall, R. Lovett, D. Rusk (Washington, 8 May 1948).
5 David Ben-Gurion, *War Diary*, Tel Aviv: Ministry of Defence, 1982, p. 382 (Hebrew).
6 ILPA, 48/23, Central Committee Meeting, 11 May 1948, p. 13.
7 Ben-Gurion, *War Diary*, p. 477.
8 Yoav Gelber, *Jewish-Transjordanian Relations, 1921–1948*, London: Frank Cass, 1997, p. 277; Benny Morris, *The Birth of the Palestinian Refugee Problem, 1947–1949*, Tel Aviv: Am Oved, 1991, p. 193 (Hebrew).

32 *Israel's policy towards the emerging refugee problem*

9 Shelly Fried noted in his doctoral dissertation that at the cabinet meetings held until the middle of June 1948, "the refugees were [mentioned as] an aside to whatever had occurred, without any substantive discussion; they were noted in the context of a disordered report and discussion, usually during a review of the 'military situation' or 'the situation at the front'." Shelly Fried, "'They Are Not Coming Back' – The Crystallization of Israeli Foreign Policy toward Possible Solutions of the Palestinian Refugee Problem, 1947–1956: From the UN Partition Resolution to the Suez Campaign," PhD thesis, Tel Aviv University, 2003, p. 14 (Hebrew).

10 Morris, *The Birth*, p. 194; until a political solution could be found, Bernadotte was engaged in a vigorous effort to raise funds, food, and equipment, in an attempt to provide for the immediate needs of the numerous refugees. As part of that effort, he sent emotional appeals to various organizations and countries throughout the world. Elad Ben-Dror, *The Mediator: Ralph Bunche and the Arab-Israeli Conflict, 1947–1949*, Sede Boqer: The Ben-Gurion Research Institute, 2012, p. 126 (Hebrew).

11 Two days before he stated his position regarding the Palestinian refugee problem at the cabinet meeting held on 16 June, Foreign Minister Sharett expressed the same view during a deliberation at a Mapai Central Committee meeting and in a letter sent to Nahum Goldmann, president of the World Jewish Congress. Ariel Leibovich, "The Palestinian Refugee Issue in Israeli Foreign Policy 1948–1967," PhD thesis, University of Haifa, 2012, p. 90 (Hebrew); Gabriel Sheffer, *Moshe Sharett: Biography of a Political Moderate*, Oxford: Clarendon Press, 1996, p. 354.

12 ISA, Provisional Government Meeting, 16 June 1948, pp. 19–47.

13 Shulamit Carmy and Henri Rosenfeld, "The Time When the Majority of the Israeli 'Cabinet' Decided 'Not to Block the Possibility of Return of the Palestinian Refugees', and How and Why this Policy Was Defeated?" *Medina Vechevra* 2 (3), 2001, pp. 384–5 (Hebrew).

14 HHA, Aharon Cohen Papers 10.95.11 (1), "Our Policy towards the Arabs during the War" (Decisions of the Mapam Political Committee, 15 June 1948), Secretariat of Mapam Center, 23 June 1948.

15 Shaul Paz, "Between Ideology and Pragmatism: Mapam's Perceptions and Positions with Regard to Israel's Foreign and Defence Policy in the Years 1948–1954," PhD thesis, The Hebrew University, 1993, pp. 92–4 (Hebrew).

16 Paz, "Mapam's Perceptions," pp. 94–6; regarding the positions on the refugee problem of the two parties comprising Mapam, see Morris, *The Birth*, pp. 437–56.

17 *Al Ha-Mishmar*, 22 July 1948.

18 Paz, "Mapam's Perceptions," pp. 99–108.

19 IDFA, 2384/50/8, Intelligence Report No. 1, From IS [Intelligence Service] Headquarters, dated 30 August 1948.

20 In the elections held on 25 January 1949, Mapai won 46 Knesset seats and Mapam won 19.

21 At the 24 July 1948 meeting of the Mapai Central Committee, Sharett made very clear that "Our intention must be to prevent, as much as is possible, the Arab's return." However, he also emphasized that this resolute position should be expressed only "when necessary and against the background of the circumstances prevailing at that time." As of the current time, he noted, "we do not need to state it [explicitly]." See Yemima Rosenthal (ed.), *Moshe Sharett – The Second Prime Minister: Selected Documents (1894–1965)* Jerusalem: Israel State Archives, 2007, pp. 361–3 (Hebrew).

22 DEPI, Vol. 1, Document 345, M. Comay to M. Shertok, 19 July 1948, Note 2.

23 DEPI, Vol. 1, Document 357, M. Shertok to M. Comay, 22 July 1948. Sharett reiterated this stance two days later during a deliberation at a Mapai Central Committee meeting. See: Sharett, Yaakov ans Rina Sharett (eds), Speaking Out: Israel's Foreign Minister's Speeches, May–December 1948, Tel Aviv: Moshe Sharett Heritage Society, 2013; p. 308 (Hebrew).

Israel's policy towards the emerging refugee problem   33

24 DEPI, Vol. 1, Document 205, Meetings: M. Shertok – Count Bernadotte and Assistants (Tel Aviv, 17 and 18 June 1948).
25 ISA, Provisional Government Meeting, 28 July 1948, pp. 11–26.
26 DEPI, Vol. 1, Document 375, M. Comay to P. Jessup, 24 July 1948.
27 DEPI, Vol. 1, Document 380, Meeting: M. Shertok – Count Bernadotte and Assistants, 26 July 1948.
28 ISA, MFA 1989/4, 5 July 1948; ISA, MFA 1989/4, Document on the UN's Initial Treatment of the Arab Refugees, 2 July 1954; Moshe Efrat, "The Palestinian Refugees: Social and Economic Survey 1949–1974," MA thesis, Tel Aviv University, 1976, p. 3 (Hebrew).
29 Folke Bernadotte, *To Jerusalem*, trans. Joan Bulman, London: Hodder and Stoughton, 1951, p. 185.
30 Dominique D. Junod, *The Imperiled Red Cross and the Palestine–Eretz-Yisrael Conflict 1945–1952*, London: Kegan Paul International, 1996, p. 254; for a review of the Red Cross' activity among the Palestinian refugees from this period until the beginning of 1950, see Channing B. Richardson, "The United Nations and Arab Refugee Relief, 1948–1950: A Case Study in International Organization and Administration," PhD thesis, University Microfilms, 1951, pp. 103–79.
31 DEPI, Vol. 1, Document 390, J. Reedman to M. Shertok, 28 July 1948.
32 DEPI, Vol. 1, Document 406, M. Shertok to Count Bernadotte, 1 August 1948.
33 The Syrian prime minister at the time. During the 1930s, Mardam had met with Zionist leaders and representatives, including Sharett.
34 DEPI, Vol. 1, Document 441, Meeting: M. Shertok – Count Bernadotte (Jerusalem, 10 August 1948).
35 ISA, MFA 2566/13, Proposals for Immediate Measures Related to the Prevention of the Return of Arab Refugees to Israel before a Final Policy Relating to the Problem Is Established, 5 August 1948.
36 ISA, MFA 2570/11, Shimoni to Sasson, 19 August 1948.
37 Ben-Gurion, *War Diary*, pp. 652–4.
38 Joseph Weitz, *My Diary and Letters to the Children*, vol. 3, Ramat Gan: Massada, 1965, p. 336 (Hebrew).
39 ISA, MFA 2445/3, Memorandum on an Arrangement for Arab Refugees, undated.
40 According to Haya Bambaji-Sasportas, "[T]his report was the first text that formulated the Israeli narrative of the 'refugee problem' – its creation and its resolution." Haya Bambaji-Sasportas, "Whose Voice Is heard/Whose Voice Is Silenced: The Construction of 'The Palestinian Refugees Problem' Discourse in the Israeli Establishment, 1948–1952," MA thesis, Ben-Gurion University, 2000, p. 55 (Hebrew).
41 Ben-Gurion, *War Diary*, p. 657.
42 DEPI, Vol. 1, Document 493, Statement Delivered by James McDonald at a Meeting with M. Shertok (Tel Aviv, 6 September 1948).
43 FRUS, 1948, V, p. 1385, The Special Representative of the United States in Israel (McDonald) to the Secretary of State, 9 September 1948.
44 DEPI, Vol. 1, Document 352, M. Shertok to C. Weizmann, 22 August 1948.
45 ISA, Provisional Government Meeting, 12 September 1948, pp. 1–24.
46 DEPI, Vol. 1, Document 515, Y. Shimoni to E. Sasson, 16 September 1948.
47 On Bernadotte's mission in Palestine, see Amitzur Ilan, *Bernadotte in Palestine 1948: A Study in Contemporary Humanitarian Knight-Errantry*, Basingstoke: Macmillan, 1989, pp. 49–193.
48 Morris, *The Birth*, p. 208; for a comprehensive analysis of the report, see Sune Persson, *Meditation and Assassination: Count Bernadotte's Mission in Palestine, 1948*, London: Ithaca Press, 1979, pp. 187–205.
49 Fried, "They Are Not Coming Back," p. 69; Morris, *The Birth*, pp. 208–9.

34 Israel's policy towards the emerging refugee problem

50 DEPI, Vol. 2, Document 4, Meeting of the Israeli Delegation to the United Nations General Assembly (Paris, 3 October 1948).

51 DEPI, Vol. 2, Document 21, Meeting of the Israeli Delegation to the United Nations General Assembly (Paris, 11 October 1948).

52 DEPI, Vol. 2, Document 45, Meeting of the Israeli Delegation to the United Nations General Assembly (Paris, 21 October 1948).

53 Fried, "They Are Not Coming Back," p. 72; Sheffer, *Moshe Sharett*, p. 412.

54 Ruth Ninburg-Levy, "The Arab Position at Lausanne Conference, 1949," MA thesis, University of Haifa, 1987, pp. 35–6 (Hebrew).

55 DEPI, Vol. 2, Document 45, Meeting of the Israeli Delegation to the United Nations General Assembly (Paris, 21 October 1948), Note 11; Rony E. Gabbay, *A Political Study of the Arab-Jewish Conflict – The Arab Refugee Problem (A Case Study)*, Geneve: Librairie E. Droz, 1959, pp. 121–2; George J. Tomeh (ed.), *United Nations Resolutions on Palestine and the Arab-Israeli Conflict, 1947–1974*, vol. 1, Washington, DC: Institute for Palestine Studies, 1975, pp. 17–18. On UNRPR's activity, see Dennis C. Howley, *The United Nations and the Palestinians*, Hicksville, NY: Exposition Press, 1975, pp. 11–17.

56 According to Howard Kennedy, the first director of the UNRWA, the UNRPR was established on the assumption that the refugee problem would be resolved within a few months. Abid Husni Gama, *The United Nations and the Palestinian Refugees: An Analysis of the United Nations Relief and Works Agency for the Palestine Refugees in the Near East, 1 May 1950–30 June 1971*, Ann Arbor, MI: University Microfilms International, 1972, p. 119.

57 Tomeh, *United Nations Resolutions*, pp. 15–16.

58 At this time, neither Trans-Jordan nor Israel had yet become members of the United Nations.

59 Fred J. Khouri, "United Nations Peace Efforts," in Malcolm H. Ker (ed.), *The Elusive Peace in the Middle East*, Albany, NY: State University of New York Press, 1975, pp. 31–2.

60 Persson, *Meditation and Assassination*, p. 187; George Marshall, the United States secretary of state, argued in this connection that the "British object strongly to leaving settlement of Palestine question to negotiation between parties. Their view is that Arabs cannot negotiate [with Israel] because negotiation involves recognition of partition (and existence of Jewish State) which they cannot do. Arabs, according to British, will never agree directly or indirectly as result of negotiations to partition." FRUS, 1948, V, p. 1606, The Secretary of State to the Acting Secretary of State, 17 November 1948.

61 Khouri, "United Nations," p. 32.

62 *Knesset Minutes*, vol. 1, 15 June 1949, p. 721.

63 Abba Eban, *Voice of Israel*, New York: Horizon Press, 1957, pp. 220–1.

64 Morris, *The Birth*, pp. 214–19.

65 Morris, *The Birth*, p. 220.

66 According to sociologists Shulamit Carmy and Henri Rosenfeld, the mass immigration of Jewish refugees provided the strongest support for the no-return policy. Carmy and Rosenfeld, "The Time," p. 393.

67 Moshe Sicron, *Immigration to Israel, 1948–1953*, Jerusalem: The Falk Institute for Economic Research in Israel and the Central Bureau of Statistics, 1957, p. 45.

68 A notable case was that of the Jews from Iraq. See Moshe Gat, *The Jewish Exodus from Iraq, 1948–1951*, London: Frank Cass, 1997, pp. 144–9; ISA, MFA 2014/11, Jewish Refugees from the Arab Countries, 31 August 1956.

69 During the first year of Israel's existence, more than half of the Jewish immigrants moved into abandoned Arab houses or onto abandoned Arab land. See Morris, *The Birth*, p. 263. In 1954, approximately one third of the Jewish immigrants who had arrived in Israel since the establishment of the state (about 250,000 people)

Israel's policy towards the emerging refugee problem 35

were living in urban areas that had been abandoned by Arabs. See Don Peretz, *Israel and the Palestine Arabs*, Washington, DC: The Middle East Institute, 1958, p. 143; for more on this subject, see Yossi Goldstein, "The Great Aliyah and the Palestinian Villages: The Settlement Dynamics, 1948–1951," *Social Issues in Israel* 12, 2011, pp. 32–62 (Hebrew); Ruth Kark, "Planning, Housing, and Land Policy 1948–1952: The Formation of Concepts and Governmental Frameworks," in Ilan S. Troen and Noah Lucas (eds), *Israel First Decade of Independence*, Albany, NY: State University of New York Press, 1995, pp. 461–95.

70 Charles S. Kamen, "After the Catastrophe I: The Arabs in Israel, 1948–1951," *Middle Eastern Studies* 23(4), 1987, pp. 456–7.

71 ISA, MFA 2474/11, Summary of Remarks Delivered by M. Shtener, the Custodian for Absentee Property, to the Commercial and Industrial Club on 16 January 1953.

72 Arnon Golan, *Wartime Spatial Changes: Former Arab Territories within the State of Israel, 1948–1950*, Sede Boqer: The Ben-Gurion Research Institute, 2001, p. 12 (Hebrew).

73 On the differences between Israel's and the UN's estimations of the size of abandoned Arab lands, see Haim Sandberg, *The Lands of Israel: Zionism and Post-Zionism*, Jerusalem: self-published, 2007, pp. 66–9 (Hebrew).

74 UNPCC, A/1985, p. 11.

75 UNPCC, A/1985, p. 13.

76 UNPCC, A/1985, pp. 14–15; Peretz, *Israel and the Palestine Arabs*, p. 147.

77 Gabbay, *A Political Study*, p. 348.

78 ISA, MFA 2451/19, The Blocked Deposits, 22 October 1952.

79 Frank D. Lewis, "Agricultural Property and the 1948 Palestinian Refugees: Assessing the Loss," *Explorations in Economic History* 33(2), 1996, pp. 169–94.

80 ISA, MFA 1989/10, Subject: "The League Has Submitted to the United Nations Its Conclusions Concerning the Size of the Refugee Property," 22 March 1957; David P. Forsythe, *United Nations Peacemaking – The Conciliation Commission for Palestine*, Baltimore, MD: The Johns Hopkins University Press, 1972, p. 115; Peretz, *Israel and the Palestine Arabs*, p. 143.

81 Michael R. Fischbach, *Records of Dispossession: Palestinian Refugee Property and the Arab-Israeli Conflict*, New York: Columbia University Press, 2003, pp. 215–17.

82 Golan, *Wartime Spatial Changes*, p. 13.

83 Peretz, *Israel and the Palestine Arabs*, p. 149.

84 Aharon Liskovsky, "'Resident Absentees' in Israel," *The New East* 10(3), 1960, p. 187 (Hebrew).

85 Golan, *Wartime Spatial Changes*, p. 16.

86 Liskovsky, "'Resident Absentees'," p. 187.

87 Liskovsky, "'Resident Absentees'," p. 186.

88 Liskovsky, "'Resident Absentees'," pp. 186, 188.

89 Baruch Kimmerling, *Zionism and Territory: The Socio-Territorial Dimensions of Zionist Politics*, Berkeley, CA: University of California Press, 1983, p. 135.

90 See, in this context, Alexander Kedar, "Israeli Law and the Redemption of Arab Land, 1948–1969," SJD thesis, Harvard University, 1996.

91 Golan, *Wartime Spatial Changes*, p. 18; Liskovsky, "'Resident Absentees'," p. 187.

92 A Zionist institution established at the beginning of the twentieth century for the purpose of purchasing land in Mandate Palestine for Jewish settlement.

93 Golan, *Wartime Spatial Changes*, p. 17; Michal Oren-Nordheim, "The Crystallization of Settlement Land Policy in the State of Israel from Its Establishment and during the First Years of the Israel Lands Administration (1948–1965)," PhD thesis, The Hebrew University, 1999, pp. 147–67 (Hebrew); Peretz, *Israel and the Palestine Arabs*, pp. 179–81.

2 The Lausanne Conference and the refugee problem

The parties' position towards the refugee problem on the eve of the Lausanne Conference

The armistice agreements signed in the first quarter of 1949 by Israel and three of its Arab neighbors (Egypt, Lebanon, and Trans-Jordan) brought relative calm to the region that had been in a state of war since December 1947. The new situation made it possible to set in motion a political initiative to advance resolution of the core problems (borders, refugees, and Jerusalem) that separated the rival camps.

The Conciliation Commission was mandated to mediate between Israel and its neighbors. In General Assembly Resolution 194(3) it was stated that the commission had "to undertake, upon the request of the Security Council, any of the functions now assigned to the United Nations Mediator on Palestine or to the United Nations Truce Commission." This meant that the commission was "to take steps to assist the Governments and authorities concerned to achieve a final settlement of all questions outstanding between them." The General Assembly directed the commission to establish secondary bodies and engage technical experts (to whatever extent it deemed necessary) to effectively carry out its mission. The commission was also asked to submit a periodic progress report to the UN secretary-general, and he would passed it on to the security council and UN member states. The leaderships of Israel and the Arab states were called upon to cooperate fully and absolutely with the commission.[1]

The three countries appointed to serve as members of the commission were the United States, France, and Turkey. The United States was chosen due to its position as the strongest global power; as such it possessed the ability to impose a settlement on the rival parties. France joined due to its close ties with the Arab world, and Turkey was the only Muslim country that had recognized Israel de facto and therefore was expected to serve as a bridge between the Arab-Muslim camp and Israel.[2]

On 24 January 1949 the Conciliation Commission set up its headquarters at "the Government House" in the neutral zone of Jerusalem and shortly afterward began to hold consultations with representatives of the sides. In its discussions in Israel it became clear to the commission that the transitory and unofficial call heard from the direction of Tel-Aviv in the second half of 1948 to resolve the refugee problem by resettling the majority of the refugees in Arab countries[3] had now become a transparent and official demand.[4] There were two reason that those at the helm, Ben-Gurion and Sharett, considered it good and proper to take this position: first of all, the potential that a political conflict would develop with the United States on the repatriation issue seemed less perilous now after the war; and second, in early March 1949 a new government had been formed without Mapam, and there was no longer the need to take into account its conciliatory point of view on the refugee question.

On 1 February, Military Governor of Jerusalem Dov Yosef (who in March would be appointed to a cabinet post) met with the French member of the Conciliation Commission, Claude de Boisanger. Yosef said that Israel understood that the concern for the refugees was fundamentally humanitarian in nature, but "what happened, happened and the past can't be restored." The situation had changed since the refugees left the country, he stated. De Boisanger said that he well understood that the solution to the refugee problem was for them to reside in neighboring Arab countries. Yosef responded that on the basis of such a solution, the commission would encounter "good will on the part of our government to deal with the problem."[5] Approximately a week later, Foreign Minister Sharett met with the Conciliation Commission. Sharett said that although Israel did not reject repatriation of a set number of refugees after peace came, this would not solve the problem. The real solution was to be found in resettlement in other places. To justify his position, Sharett relied on the reasons already raised in the report of the Retroactive Transfer Committee. The return of the refugees, stated the foreign minister, would require a supreme financial effort by the state, would undercut its political stability, and would create grave security problems. All these wouldn't happen if the refugees were resettled in Trans-Jordan, Syria, and Iraq.[6]

The Conciliation Commission set out from Tel-Aviv for a several-day tour of neighboring Arab capitals. Arab rulers whom they met with claimed that the repatriation issue was at the top of their preferences.[7] They demanded that Israel allow every refugee who was interested to return to their former home to do so.[8] The Trans-Jordanians, in contrast with the general Arab position, announced their willingness to absorb the refugees that had arrived into their country. They suggested that Israel would deposit payment of compensation for the Palestinians' abandoned assets into a central fund that would deal with resettlement of the refugees.[9]

When they returned to Israel on 24 February, the commission members reported to Sharett that the refugee problem was a key cause of political incitement in the Arab countries. Sentiments in the Arab street, the foreign minister was told, were inflamed by the wretched state of masses of refugees and this state of affairs worried Arab rulers.[10] The commission mused out loud – couldn't Israel make some sort of gesture on this problematic issue? Sharett's response hardly answered their innermost hopes and expectations.

38   *The Lausanne Conference and the refugee problem*

Israel would be willing to consider the repatriation of a limited number of refugees and only as part of a comprehensive peace settlement. In an additional attempt to extract concessions from Israel on the issue, Sharett was asked whether his government would agree to recognize the refugees' right to return. The minister replied with a definitive no. According to Sharett, such recognition would grant each and every refugee the legal right to actualize the principle of repatriation. Towards the end of the meeting, the commission informed Sharett that it intended to confer again with representatives of Arab League nations, primarily in order to discuss the Palestinian refugee question. The foreign minister promised to transmit a memorandum to the commission with Israel's official position on the matter.[11]

On 14 March, during the new government's first working meeting, Sharett presented his cabinet ministers with the key points that would be included in the memorandum that his ministry would prepare to give to the commission:

> (a) place responsibility for the refugee problem on the Arab states;
> (b) convey our humanitarian sentiments regarding the plight of the refugees as people; (c) express our conviction that under current conditions as they've emerged, the main solution to the refugee problem is resettlement in other countries; (d) should returning a portion be discussed – it's possible to talk about this only in negotiation, as part of negotiation of peace; (e) should the matter of return be accepted – the scope of return would hinge on the character of the peace.

The proposed wording was passed by the cabinet without dissent. Minister of Supply and Rationing Dov Yosef (who also held the Agriculture portfolio), along with Prime Minister David Ben-Gurion, recommended that the last clause be dropped, without clarifying their reasons. It appears that they did not want to leave the impression that in the framework of a lasting peace with its Arab neighbors Israel was prepared to return masses of refugees.[12]

On 17 March, the Ministry of Foreign Affairs delivered the memorandum containing the Israeli position on the refugee problem to the Conciliation Commission. It stated: "When the whole matter comes up for discussion, in the context of general peace talks, the Israeli Government will consider whether conditions are stable enough for a certain number [of refugees] to come back without creating a security problem." At the same time it clarified that "the main solution is not repatriation, but resettlement elsewhere." In order to justify this statement, Israel pointed out the substantial physical changes, both economic and demographic, that had transpired on the ground: thousands of Arab refugees' homes had been destroyed during the war, and those still standing were now serving as temporary shelter for masses of Jewish immigrants; moveable assets left behind had "disappeared"; livestock had been slaughtered or sold; middle-class refugees – Mandatory civil servants, free professionals, small merchants – would have to begin their lives anew as a result of the termination of British rule and the demographic changes that had taken place in Mandate

Palestine. Besides these factors, the State of Israel was not in a position to allocate funding to absorb Palestinian refugees at a time when it was moving huge budgets to cover absorption of masses of Jewish immigrants.

"But even if repatriation were economically feasible," the authors of the memorandum continued, "is it politically desirable?" Was it logical, they asked rhetorically, to recreate the same binational society that was so internally at odds for such a long time, until things deteriorated into a state of war?

Israel did not suffice with presenting its reasons for rejecting repatriation. Rather, it also presented a complete tractate of arguments in support of the principle of resettlement. Geographic data was presented to the Conciliation Commission, proving that, Israel argued, three Arab nations – Iraq, Syria, and Trans-Jordan – were capable of absorbing relatively easily the entire refugee population and even deriving economic and social benefit from this. To illustrate the matter, examples of sparsely settled areas that from an agricultural perspective could support a sizable increase in population were presented: the Al-Habbaniyah Lake valley in central Iraq; the Jezirah region in northern Syria; and the Jordan Valley in Trans-Jordan.[13]

It was evident that the memorandum put major emphasis on the economic-social facets. The end of the 1948 war and the signing of armistice agreements with several of the Arab states forced Israel to broaden the scope of its arguments and to found its opposition to repatriation of the refugees on arguments that weren't on the whole or even primarily based on security-military factors.

In a 21 March meeting in Beirut between the Conciliation Commission and the foreign ministers of the seven Arab League states, the commission again encountered a stance on the refugee problem totally contrary to Israel's. According to the Arab states, the core issue in any future political deliberations with Israel was the refugee problem, and any discussion on that should be based, first and foremost, on the principle of repatriation.[14] Several days earlier, the League's council passed a decision demanding the right to repatriation for all refugees who desired to do so.[15]

Despite the fundamental differences in approach between the rival parties, and perhaps in light of them, the commission concluded that it was advisable to halt its diplomatic tour of Middle Eastern capitals and convene an international conference in Europe under its auspices where Israel and its neighbors could clarify all the problems (borders, refugees, and Jerusalem) that prevented a political settlement between them.[16]

On 7 April the Conciliation Commission met with Prime Minister Ben-Gurion and senior officials from the Ministry of Foreign Affairs to report to them, among other things, the conference concept. The Turkish delegate on the commission, Huseyin Yalcin, told his hosts that the Arabs were unwilling to meet directly with Israeli representatives and would parley only through the commission; moreover, the planned talks would not be called "peace talks," although in practice they would be such. It was clarified to the Israelis that the primary topic that would occupy the conference would be the refugee issue. The American delegate on the Conciliation Commission, Mark Ethridge, believed that

40 *The Lausanne Conference and the refugee problem*

resolution of the refugee problem was the key to peace, and that key was in Israel's hands (i.e. through some implementation of the principle of repatriation). The prime minister's response to these tidings did not go beyond Israel's official position:

> When peace will come, we will settle the refugee problem [...] For many reasons, political, humanitarian, economic and so forth, it would be advisable to settle the refugees in the Arab countries. But I don't exclude the possibility that we contribute to settling a portion of them among us.[17]

Despite the attention that the Conciliation Commission invested in the repatriation issue in its talks with Israeli representatives, its delegates judged that Israel would not need to absorb all the refugees, probably not even the majority of them. Their thoughts in this spirit were voiced by de Boisanger in his discussions with Dov Yosef in early February. Towards the close of the same month, Ethridge reported to Sharett that the Arab states did not expect Israel would absorb all the refugees. While he didn't know the percentage that would need to be repatriated, Ethridge claimed that "maybe it won't be a high percentage."[18] In an overview that Ethridge sent to the American secretary of state, Dean Acheson, he stated that successful negotiation between Israel and the Arabs would be impossible, unless the Arabs understood that not all the refugees would returned.[19]

High-echelon officials in the United Nations supported the commission's evaluation of the issue[20] and at the outset of 1949 discussed the possibility of resolving the refugee problem primarily through resettlement. Bayard Dodge, an advisor to the United Nations secretary-general, expressed his opinion that resolution of the problem rested on integrating masses of refugees in an initiative of wide-scale public works in the Arab states. Such an initiative, he emphasized, may lead to their resettlement. Thus, a kind of "transfer of populations" between the Palestinian refugees and hundreds of thousands of Jews who would emigrate to the State of Israel from Arab countries would materialize. At the same juncture, an activist in an American welfare agency that provided assistance to Palestinian refugees reported from Geneva to his colleagues in the United States that people dealing with the refugee question, including UN personnel, generally disregarded the principle of repatriation as a solution.[21]

The assessment that took form gradually in the United States in the spring months of 1949 was that about a quarter of the Palestinian refugee population should be allowed to repatriate, between 200,000 to 250,000 souls. The others would have to resettle in Arab territories. At the same time, Washington began to increase its efforts to solve the refugee problem after it became clear to the administration (particularly through America's representative on the Conciliation Commission) that this issue was a substantive obstacle on the road to achieving a political settlement between Israel and the Arabs. Without a political settlement, American diplomats feared, instability in the Middle

East would continue. The Cold War stood behind their apprehensions; from an American perspective, Soviet-style communism could easily penetrate a region like the Middle East so plagued by violence. Moreover, the Americans felt that masses of refugees, due to their wretched state, could become a vector for the spread of communism and could threaten the stability of pro-western governments in their host countries.[22]

At the end of February, the director of the United Nations Affairs office of the State Department, Dean Rusk, requested State Department official George McGhee visit the Middle East to investigate what could be done to resolve "in the long term" the complex refugee problem, which he viewed as "the key to war and peace in the Middle East." McGhee agreed and at the beginning of March embarked on his mission as the American coordinator on the Palestinian refugee question.[23] In a letter to Under-Secretary of State James Webb, Rusk wrote in regard to McGhee's mission that, according to a rough estimate, a quarter of the refugees, at the most, would be able to return to their former homes in Israel. Rusk added that in the framework of a final peace settlement, the majority of the refugees would have to be resettled in the Arab portion of Palestine and in neighboring Arab countries; therefore, he emphasized, it would be imperative to design special economic projects that would assist rehabilitation plans, and it would be necessary to allocate funding for this from various sources.[24] On 29 March, in the midst of his diplomacy tour in the Middle East, McGhee sent President Harry Truman and Secretary of State Acheson a special letter on the refugee issue that he wrote with Ethridge. The pair recommended putting pressure on Israel to agree to absorb all refugees that originated from areas occupied by the IDF that were not within the borders of the Jewish state under the Partition Plan – at least 250,000 persons according to their estimates. As for the rest, it was implied that they should be settled in Arab countries. In their opinion, the Arabs would refrain from absorbing a large number of refugees, if Israel wouldn't do so.[25] Washington didn't take issue either with this assessment or the number suggested, and the American ambassador in Tel-Aviv was quick to press the Israelis, albeit unofficially, to agree to the return of 250,000 refugees originating from parts of the Jewish state not allocated to the Jews under the Partition Plan.[26] Acheson clarified to Sharett in a 5 April meeting between the two in New York that the administration expected the repatriation of a quarter of the refugees, whose total numbers stood at 800,000 persons.[27]

On 22 April, at the close of his tour of the Middle East, McGhee submitted a comprehensive memorandum to Acheson with his recommendations for resolving the Palestinian refugee problem. According to his appraisals, the number of refugees in the Arab states was 950,000. Among these, 700,000 persons needed to be rehabilitated, according to the following distribution: half a million in the Arab countries (all told, 750,000 refugees would remain in Arab territories) and 200,000 within the State of Israel's domain. McGhee stated that the rehabilitation plan would succeed only if the economies of recipient Arab states would enjoy the fruits of investment in the refugee

42 *The Lausanne Conference and the refugee problem*

population. He judged that the projects that would be part of the rehabilitation plan would last three years and would require close collaboration between the United States and Britain – collaboration that, among other things, would be directed towards mobilization of capital from governments, international organizations, and private companies. In McGhee's opinion, the overall rehabilitation of the refugees would cost between 250 and 300 million dollars, of which 50 million dollars would be compensation paid by Israel.[28]

To a large extent, the American approach that took form, which held that the majority of Palestinian refugees would need to be rehabilitated in the Arab countries, emanated from recognition that Israel was determined not to allow mass repatriation. Remarks by Israeli representatives on the issue, and a wave of sweeping steps on the ground and legal measures taken by Israeli authorities from the second half of 1948 concerning abandoned Palestinian property, clarified this intention.

Already in the closing days of July 1948, the American consul-general in Jerusalem, John McDonald, judged that in light of Israel's attitude towards the refugee issue, "there is only a slim possibly, if at all, for repatriation of the Arabs to their homes in Israel or areas of Palestine held by the Jews." In a similar fashion, a senior diplomat in the American embassy in Cairo reported at the beginning of August that "it may be that only scanty prospects appear for hundreds of thousands of Arab refugees from Palestine to return to their former homes."[29] A number of months later, Resolution 194(3) was passed in the United Nations. Washington assessed that this would not make Israel change its rigid position on the repatriation issue. Two weeks after the resolution passed, Acting Secretary of State Robert Lovet argued that:

> Although this Government [the United States government] will use its best efforts to promote the purposes envisaged in this resolution, account must be taken of the possibility that the Government of Israel will be reluctant to accept the return of all those Arabs who fled from territory under Israeli control.[30]

In December 1948, William Burdett, John McDonald's successor, judged that the Emergency Regulations Relating to Absentees' Property published in Tel-Aviv was a kind of "negative answer" by Israeli authorities to UN Resolution 194(3). In his opinion, one should view the decree as "another cue that Israel's provisional government does not [...] intend to allow repatriation of a significant number of Arab refugees."[31] A number of weeks later, Burdett said that, from a political perspective, the best way to make peace in the region was through the resettlement of the refugees in the Arab countries and particularly in areas of Mandate Palestine that were held by the Arabs:

> Since the US has supported the establishment of a Jewish State, it should insist on a homogeneous one which will have the best possible chance of stability. Return of the refugees would create a continuing "minority

problem" and form a constant temptation both for [inner] uprisings and intervention by neighboring Arab States.

Burdett's approach was shared by the United States' representative in Jedda, Saudi Arabia, and he wrote in late January 1949 to the secretary of state: "One shouldn't strive to create another large and rebellious minority in one of the Middle East states."[32]

On 22 February, Ambassador James McDonald submitted a comprehensive report on the Palestinian refugee issue to Secretary of State Acheson. The report left the impression that in light of the dramatic physical realities developing on the ground, the chances of mass repatriation were slim:

> Though the Israeli spokesmen do not say so, the unprecedentedly rapid influx of Jewish refugees during 1948 and the plan to admit a quarter of million more in 1949 will, if carried out, fill all or almost all of the houses and business properties previously held by Arab refugees. Arab unoccupied farms will similarly, though not to quite the same degree, be occupied by the recent or expected Jewish refugees. Hence, there will be almost no residence or business property and only a limited number of farms to which the Arab refugees can hope to return.

The ambassador's conclusion in light of this state of affairs was clear:

> Comprehensive but general recommendations by the Palestine Conciliation Commission of an Arab refugee resettlement program is the obvious next step. Any plan to be acceptable in Tel Aviv must make provision for resettlement of the larger proportion of the refugees outside of Israeli territory.[33]

Indeed, the State Department intended to take to heart the insights of its representative in Tel Aviv. It told McDonald that "this timely and objective report has had an important influence upon the formulation of the Department's long-range policy towards the Palestine refugee question [...] the Department is in accord with your recommendations."[34]

Thus, a position paper prepared by the State Department in mid March 1949 expressed McDonald's outlook on the issue:

> In view of the stated position of Israel towards the question of repatriation, and the large-scale preemption of Arab lands and housing by Jewish immigrants, who are entering Israel at the rate of 25,000 monthly, it would be wholly unrealistic to expect Israel to agree to the repatriation of all those so desiring.

In the opinion of the position paper's authors, more than 80 percent of the refugee population (which in their estimates numbered 725,000) – that is,

44 *The Lausanne Conference and the refugee problem*

600,000 persons – would need to resettle in the Arab states, and the rest would return to Israel.[35]

In his memorandum, McGhee also noted Israel's strident objection to the principle of repatriation, and its plans to utilize abandoned Arab lands to implement the "Jewish immigration scheme."[36]

Israel's unyielding position was only one factor, although a very important one, that prompted the United States to base its position on the principle of resettlement. Other factors accompanied this.

The Americans understood that from a purely economic perspective, successful absorption of refugees could not be accomplished in Israel – a tiny and poor country grappling with a huge wave of immigration; rather, this could be achieved in the vast, fertile and sparsely populated expanses of Arab states such as Iraq and Syria.[37]

The policy of Trans-Jordan on the refugee question also influenced the United States' position on resettlement.[38] In closed discussion with American diplomats, Amman expressed its willingness to absorb the hundreds of thousands of refugees within its domain, who constituted 55 percent of the entire refugee population.[39] The Trans-Jordanian regime's approach reduced, at least theoretically, the acuteness of the refugee problem, and with it the demand that Israel repatriate masses of refugees within its territory.

The United States' view that resettlement was the desirable solution was completely acceptable to Britain. London was even willing to go farther and on numerous occasions its representatives clarified that a solution should be adopted whereby *all* the refugees would be resettled in the Arab states. Like the Americans, they also realized that the chances were slim that Israel would agree to receive back masses of refugees, and therefore it would be best to find other places to settle them. Since the British were very familiar with the promising economic potential of several of the countries in the region, first and foremost Iraq and Syria, London surmised that it would be possible to implement the principle of resettlement in full. The British view of the issue was important to the Americans for a number of reasons: first, the British had special status in Trans-Jordan, where, as noted, half the refugees were situated. Second, there were British forces in Egypt under contract, while Egypt controlled the Gaza Strip teeming with refugees. Third, the British had very close relations with Iraq, which the western powers viewed as a preferred destination for many refugees. In addition to this, due to their lengthy control as a colonial power of various parts of the region, the English were well versed in the twists and turns of the Middle Eastern arena, inside and out, making Britain a natural ally for Washington in solving the problem.

The British position regarding the refugee issue had already begun to take concrete shape in the summer months of 1948. A senior British diplomat who visited a refugee camp near Ramallah at the end of July reported to the Foreign Office in London about the terrible misery of masses of refugees and the urgent need to send them assistance, yet he stated that the solution in the long term hinged on their rehabilitation in the places where they were now to be

The Lausanne Conference and the refugee problem   45

found. John Troutbeck, head of the British Middle East Office in Cairo (BMEO), responded to this message saying that while he had always opposed the transfer of populations, under the present state of affairs, it seemed that the solution to the Palestinian refugee problem rested with their transfer to Iraq and Syria.[40] In late August, the British commander of the Arab Legion, John Glubb, estimated that out of 400,000 Palestinian refugees at the time, some 200,000 who originated from areas the United Nations had allotted to the Jewish state had no chance to return to their homes. The other half, stated Glubb, came from Arab areas under Israeli military control that according to the original United Nations Partition Plan were delineated as Arab. "In the worst case," the United Nations won't succeed in removing the Jews also from these areas, "and then we'll have to deal" with 400,000 refugees that won't be able to return, said Glubb. However, even if the refugees could return, they would find upon their return only shells of their former houses. In other words, according to Glubb, the refugees had nothing to return to in Israel.[41] Parallel to this, a report submitted to the secretary of state in Washington by the American embassy in London reveals that the British Foreign Office thought that Israeli authorities must choose one of two paths: to permit repatriation of the refugees or pay compensation for their abandoned property.[42] That is to say, Israel's agreement to pay for the abandoned property of the Palestinians would release Israel from all obligations to absorb refugees into its territory. British Assistant Under-Secretary of State Michael Wright reiterated this position in a large British-American conference convened in mid April 1949 to address the refugee question. He noted that in London's appraisal, the chances were slim that Israel would choose one of these two possibilities.[43]

In Tel Aviv, the British attitude towards the refugee question could already be discerned at the outset of August 1948. In a discussion that Ministry of Foreign Affairs official Leo Cohen conducted with the British vice-consul in Jerusalem, John Sheringham, the latter said that in his opinion it was clear that the refugees would not be able to return to Israel. Sheringham suggested to Cohen that Israel purchase abandoned Arab lands and transfer the monetary proceeds to an agency that would take care of resettling the refugees elsewhere.[44] Sentiments in a similar vein were voiced by a senior British government official at the beginning of April 1949 in a conversation with Israel's representative to the United Nations, Abba Eban.[45]

In keeping with this position – that it would be possible to apply the principle of resettlement to the entire refugee population – already in the fall of 1948 the British began to examine various plans to rehabilitate the refugees in the Arab states. In the Foreign Office's appraisal, evidenced in a special memorandum penned in September, resettlement plans would require "great effort or organization and broad-scoped funding."[46] At the end of December of the same year, British Foreign Secretary Ernest Bevin stated that Iraq could, based on various investment projects, absorb up to 150 percent of its population, and this could enable the resettlement of many Palestinian refugees in its territories.[47] Three and half months later, Bevin told US Secretary of State

46 The Lausanne Conference and the refugee problem

Acheson that he was pressuring the Syrian government to absorb between 200,000 and 300,000 refugees in the north of the country, and he hoped that the rest could be absorbed in Trans-Jordan.[48] Bevin's declarations were accompanied by actions. Michael Wright reported to the Americans that "the [British] Foreign Office has carefully examined all of the developments projects in the area [the Middle East] and has selected three short-range schemes which they feel could be put into effect very quickly." These projects, stated Wright, would make possible the absorption of a quarter of a million refugees in Trans-Jordan and in Syria.[49]

Thus, the two leading western powers approved of the Israeli position that rejected founding resolution of the refugee problem on repatriation. While the United States demanded that Israel absorb a very large number of refugees, still, according to the Americans, the majority of this population (about three-quarters) was supposed to be rehabilitated in the Arab countries. Britain went even farther than America, adopting in practice the Israeli position on the issue. In a 21 April 1949 cabinet meeting, Foreign Minister Sharett noted this state of affairs:

> On the refugee question, England has decided to envision things in a different fashion, and from its government's representatives things are heard in favor of settlement of the refugees in neighboring countries, without emphasizing the matter of their return. The United States [on the other hand], continues to champion the principle of partial repatriation, and tries all sorts of ways to extract from us some sort of commitment for return of a portion of the refugees.[50]

The Gaza Plan

On 27 April 1949 the conference to settle the Arab-Israeli conflict opened in Lausanne, Switzerland, under the auspices of the Conciliation Commission. The delegates were for the most part senior civil servants in their respective ministries of foreign affairs. The level of the delegations was a sign of the importance the parties assigned to this gathering. The Israeli delegation was headed by Director-General of the Ministry of Foreign Affairs Walter Eytan. The other members were the director of the Political Division and adviser on special affairs, Reuven Shiloah; the director of the Middle East Division, Eliahu Sasson; the director of the Western Europe Division, Gershon Avner; and the advisor to the Government of Israel on Land Issues, Zalman Liff.

In the fortnight prior to the convergence on Lausanne, Israeli statespersons and senior officials conducted several meetings at which Israeli policy at the conference was delineated. Participating in meetings were Ben-Gurion, Sharett, senior officials in the Ministry of Foreign Affairs and the defense establishment, and experts in Arab affairs. The participants were largely of the opinion that the approach that had begun to solidify in past months regarding the Palestinian refugee problem, that held the solution to the problem lay primarily in resettlement, needed to be adhered to. The discussants also agreed that Israel needed, in addition, to express its willingness to pay compensation for abandoned Arab lands. Ben-Gurion said in one of the meetings that Israel would not object that the monies would be directed to a "general fund" (that would care for rehabilitation of the refugees).[51]

One could hear a clear expression of Israel's position on the resettlement issue in a 26 April message that President Chaim Weizmann wrote to President Truman, 24 hours before the Lausanne Convention convened. Other than repatriation of "a limited degree," Weizmann stated, the refugee problem needed to be resolved through resettlement:

> As a scientist and a student of the [refugee] problem, I know the possibilities of development of the Middle East. I have long felt that the underpopulated and fertile areas in the river valleys of Iraq constitute [...] a massive opportunity for development and progress [...] Similar opportunities exist also in northern Syria and western Trans-jordan.[52]

When Sharett appeared before the Knesset Foreign Affairs and Defense Committee, days after the opening of talks in Lausanne, he reiterated and emphasized that Israel would not allow significant repatriation of refugees. On the question of compensation, he revealed, the government had not yet riveted this down, but several rudiments guided its policy on the issue: (a) agreement in principle to pay compensation for the abandoned property of the Palestinians; (b) the compensation would be given for land only, and there would be no compensation for houses or movables; (c) it was advisable that the compensation be transferred "to a central fund or central funds" from which settlement of the refugees in the Arab countries would be financed; (d) the payment of compensation to the Palestinian refugees would be linked to the issue of compensation that the Arab states would pay to Israel for war damage.[53]

In regard to the compensation issue, in a meeting that took place at the beginning of May, Walter Eytan clarified to the Conciliation Commission that this question would be discussed and solved only when a comprehensive and final political settlement between Israel and its Arab neighbors would be achieved.[54]

At the outset of deliberations at Lausanne, it became clear that the Arab states demanded that the refugee problem be the first item on the agenda. Israel, on the other hand, insisted that the issue be discussed together with all the other problems subject to controversy, among them the question of borders. "The Gaza Plan" that both sides raised on the agenda at the beginning of the conference created a direct linkage between these two items.

The seeds of this Plan were planted in what Prime Minister Ben-Gurion told the American representative on the Conciliation Commission, Mark Ethridge, in a discussion that took place between the two in Tiberias on 18

48 *The Lausanne Conference and the refugee problem*

April 1949. Ben-Gurion said that if Egypt doesn't want the Gaza Strip within its territory due to the refugees situated there, Israel would accept the Strip and allow the refugees to return to their homes.[55] Four days later, the prime minister declared in a political consultation that "if Gaza will be transferred to us, we won't decline and then it is clear [that] we will accept it with all of its inhabitants. We won't expel them."[56] Ben-Gurion's approach encouraged Ethridge and in a 30 April discussion with Walter Eytan, he raised the question of the Gaza Strip. In Ethridge's appraisal, the Egyptians were not interested in holding Gaza, and therefore there was nothing to prevent it being transferred to Israel. Ethridge believed that if Israel would receive within its territory the Strip's refugees, whose numbers he estimated were between 150,000 and 200,000, Israel would thus make an important contribution to the solution of the refugee problem.[57] After Eytan requested an urgent decision on the issue, Foreign Minister Sharett brought the matter to the cabinet on 3 May.[58] The foreign minister believed that Israel should oppose the addition of the Gaza Strip to the Jewish state on demographic grounds:

> There [in the Gaza Strip] out of 150,000 to 170,000 Arabs; among them 50,000 or perhaps a few less [were] local Gazans, and more than 100,000 [were] refugees. The refugees came from [settlements] throughout the south of Eretz Yisrael, from the Negev, from the southern Sharon up to Jaffa. The minute we inherit this Strip and inherit these Arabs, the following problems will arise: By our own hand, we more than double the Arab population in the State of Israel; consequently we will face an Arab minority of close to 300,000 souls within the State of Israel [...] We can't digest such a thing [...] I see this as a catastrophe.

When the foreign minister finished speaking, the prime minister presented the opposite position, affirming annexation of the Gaza Strip. Ben-Gurion envisioned the geopolitical advantages for Israel that could develop from such a step. "I don't know," he said, "if this thing [annexation of the Strip] is practical, If such a thing will be offered to us, but if it will be offered – we ought to accept it." It was dangerous to leave the Strip in Egyptian hands, he stated, since "it's impossible that a large state will sit [that an Egyptian enclave will exist] within our country." He also rejected the possibility of turning Gaza over to the Jordanians due to the complications this was liable to raise when the Jordanians would want to establish a corridor from the West Bank to Gaza through Israel. When Israel would receive the territory with its refugees inside, he added, Israel could claim before the world that it had done its part in settling the Palestinian refugee question. The demographic demon did not bother Ben-Gurion at all:

> I'm not so pessimistic about the refugee matter as Mr. Sharett is. I accept his factual description but [not] his philosophy regarding this matter. We

The Lausanne Conference and the refugee problem 49

are used to absorption woes, and we can absorb the Arabs as well [...] If you look at the map you'll see that in the south there are many empty places and nothing horrifies me more than this emptiness [...] They [the international community] won't leave empty places in our hands, and there's enough room for both us and the Arabs. If we were ready to accept the state – we must be ready to also accept the Arabs within it. There is enough land in Eretz Yisrael.

In animated deliberations that followed within the cabinet, it became apparent that the majority of the ministers supported Ben-Gurion's view. Consequently, the cabinet decided by a large majority, without any opposition, that "if annexation of the Gaza region to the state (of Israel) with all of its inhabitants will be offered, our reply will be affirmative." Sharett himself abstained.[59]

The remarks made by the parties in favor of annexation indicate that their positions were based on two erroneous assumptions. First, they estimated there were only 150,000 to 180,000 persons in the Strip, 50,000 to 60,000 of them permanent residents (e.g. Gazans) and some 100,000 to 120,000 refugees.[60] However, this number was close to half the *actual* population of the Gaza Strip: some 300,000 persons. Second, contrary to widespread assumptions during armistice negotiations that Egypt was interested in maintaining its control of the Gaza Strip,[61] during the Lausanne talks, the Israelis assumed that Cairo sought to rid itself of the Gaza Strip and the refugee yoke it entailed.[62] In fact, as will subsequently become clear, this time as well, Egypt didn't want to give up the Gaza Strip. It's possible that the eagerness of Ben-Gurion and his colleagues to annex Gaza would have cooled had they been cognizant of this two-fold miscalculation.

The idea of annexing Gaza to Israel didn't capture many hearts in the weeks that followed the floating of this idea. The Israeli delegation at Lausanne awaited an official American appeal on the matter, directly or through the Conciliation Commission, but this failed to surface. Washington, it seems, didn't address the issue at all at the start; consequently, Israel decided to raise the matter on its own initiative. On 19 May, after receiving authorization from Sharett,[63] Eytan told Ethridge that Israel was prepared to accept the Gaza Strip into its hands.[64] The next day, Eytan repeated the offer orally to the Conciliation Commission. The Israeli diplomat argued that such a step would be a substantial contribution towards resolving the refugee problem.[65] Three days later, Israel's representative at the United Nations, Abba Eban, sent a letter to UN Secretary-General Trygve Lie with the Gaza Plan.[66] On 29 May, Eytan submitted a detailed written proposal to the Conciliation Commission.[67]

The Israeli government strove not to go public on its decision to accept annexation of the Gaza Strip if it was offered. Ben-Gurion and his colleagues who supported annexation surmised that adoption of a scheme that would double the Arab population of the Jewish state would inevitably engender strong resentment among the Jewish public at large, particularly in right-wing

50 *The Lausanne Conference and the refugee problem*

circles. Yet attempts by the government to conceal the Plan were only partially successful. Most of the party newspapers refrained from writing about it, but two party organs nevertheless addressed the issue, albeit in a limited fashion, and all the non-party papers followed suit.

On 25 May, *Herut* (the party organ of the right-wing opposition party, Herut) published a prominent headline: "Dr. Eytan spurs the Arabs to precede the Jewish immigrants." In the body of the text it was reported that the Arabs demanded that Israel absorb 300,000 refugees. The paper, it became evident, knew that the government was willing to accept a sizable number of refugees, but it still didn't know the linkage between this willingness and the question of the future of the Gaza Strip.[68] The Herut movement – a party that called for establishment of a Jewish state on both sides of the Jordan River[69]– had difficulty publicly opposing a plan that championed adding new territory to the State of Israel. Thus, even after the linkage between annexation of Gaza and acceptance of Arab refugees was clarified, the paper sufficed with slamming the government for what it viewed as a conciliatory approach to the refugee issue, without specifically addressing the issue of the Gaza Strip.[70]

Ha-Boker, the party organ of the General Zionists (a right-center opposition party), was more explicit. On 30 May it published an exclusive and sensational headline that claimed, "Israel denies its willingness to return 300,000 refugees in exchange for annexation of the Gaza Strip to Israel."[71]

In an 11 May meeting of the Knesset Foreign Affairs and Defense Committee, the head of the General Zionist faction, Yosef Sapir, stated his opposition to annexing the Gaza Strip: "We are not interested in increasing the Arabs within the existing territory of the State of Israel, nor in the remaining part of Eretz Yisrael." The committee member from the Progressive Party (a center-oriented coalition party), Izhar Harari, presented a different position saying that the Gaza Strip should be incorporated into Israel's territory because when the number of Jews in the country would grow, "we'll be sorry we gave up this territory [the Gaza Strip] due to 100,000 [Arab] refugees." He added that "it should be stipulated that [we] are not prepared to accept Arab refugees without supplementary territory, be it in Gaza, in the Triangle[72] or elsewhere." Mapam, which was in the opposition, thought the same. It presented an 11-point document to the committee designed to guide Israel's negotiators at the Lausanne talks. In regard to the Gaza Plan, Mapam wrote:

> The State of Israel demands annexation of the Gaza Strip even if this requires Israel to accept [...] the inhabitants and the Arab refugees concentrated there. This will also be a weighty contribution of the State of Israel towards solving the refugee question as a whole.[73]

Mapam's position stemmed from its firm worldview that sanctified the idea of "Greater Israel" (i.e. an Israeli state that encompasses all of Mandate Palestine).[74]

Non-party papers were divided over annexation of Gaza. On 29 May, *Yedioth Ahronoth* ran the story on the front page, without any commentary.[75]

The Lausanne Conference and the refugee problem   51

The Palestine Post published an editorial the same day, presenting both sides of the issue: on one hand, Israel in its dire economic situation would find it difficult to absorb masses of wretched Arab refugees; on the other hand, such a move would add an important stretch of coastline to Israel. It was also possible that the move would set in motion negotiations with Egypt and enable Israel to sign a peace treaty with Cairo.[76] A 1 June editorial in *Ma'ariv* came out vehemently against the Plan. The Egyptians, argued the editorial, wouldn't agree to the idea; and even if they would agree, Israel couldn't accept tens of thousands of Arab refugees.[77]

The idea of annexing the Gaza Strip and its inhabitants to Israel was, in general, acceptable to Washington, except for one reservation. A 27 May State Department memorandum stated that Israel would have to offer territorial compensation to the Arabs in exchange for any territory it expected to receive from them that was not within the borders of the Jewish state delineated in the UN resolution of 29 November 1947 (the Partition Plan). According to the memorandum, the Israeli delegation at Lausanne had already raised with Ethridge the possibility that Israel would relinquish certain terrain from the Negev in exchange for the Gaza Strip, but it was not specified which Arab country would receive such territory.[78] On 4 June the State Department announced in a secret telegram to the American delegation at Lausanne that the American government supported annexation of the Gaza Strip to Israel as part of a final territorial settlement, provided that the settlement would be achieved through negotiation with Egypt and with its full consent, and provided that the Egyptians would receive territorial compensation if they were interested in such. The State Department added that if the Gaza Strip would be handed over to Israel, Israel would have to give guarantees in regard to the civil status of residents of Gaza who were refugees – in other words, to guarantee that they would not be discriminated against after the transfer.[79] Four days later, American diplomats were permitted to update the Israelis on Washington's position. The only change in the American position that took place in the interim was the stipulation that the issue must be settled through discussion between Israel and "Interest Governments" and with their full agreement.[80] This, apparently, referred to Jordan (besides Egypt), which had long coveted the Gaza Strip, primarily because of the outlet to the Mediterranean it would give them.[81] On 9 June, Ambassador James McDonald met with Sharett and updated him on the official American position on Israel's annexation proposal. Sharett expressed his satisfaction at Washington's position, which necessitated territorial compensation only if the Arabs were interested in such.[82] At the same time, Ben-Gurion was conducting political consultations on the issue together with Sharett and senior officials in the Ministry of Foreign Affairs. The prime minister, it became apparent, was ready and willing to offer Cairo "a strip in the western Negev [on] the border with Egypt in place of the Gaza Strip."[83]

Egypt, however, refused to accept the Gaza Plan. The head of the Egyptian delegation at Lausanne, Abd al-Mun'im Mustafa, told Eliahu Sasson, a

52 The Lausanne Conference and the refugee problem

member of the Israeli delegation, in a discussion that took place between the two on 1 June that "not only wouldn't Egypt relinquish the Gaza area, it would firmly reserve the right that it receive the southern Negev, along a line that would extend from Majdal [Ashkelon] to the Dead Sea."[84] On 8 June, Ethridge himself told the secretary of state that the Arabs viewed the Israeli offer as unacceptable since it "trades refugees for territory."[85] Things in a similar spirit were voiced by the Egyptian ambassador in Washington, who branded the Israeli proposal a "cheap barter." He argued that Israel must first allow the refugees from the Gaza Strip who wished to return to their former homes to do so.[86] The Conciliation Commission didn't reject outright the Egyptian ambassador's demand. In a 27 May meeting between Eytan and the Commission, Ethridge had told Eytan that the commission now expected a declaration from Israel on the number of refugees it was willing to absorb, if the Gaza Strip wouldn't be turned over to Israel.[87] In Ethridge's opinion, as expressed in a memorandum to the State Department, the very willingness of Israel to annex the Gaza Strip with its population was proof that it possessed the ability to receive within its domain, with outside assistance, between 200,000 and 250,000 refugees, even if Israel didn't receive Gaza.[88]

In a 21 June cabinet meeting, Sharett reported to the ministers that Ethridge suggested Israel inform the commission "what is the number of refugees we are prepared to accept: (a) in the case that we receive Gaza; (b) in the case we won't receive Gaza." According to the foreign minister, Ethridge believed "that in the latter case – the reasonable figure is 200,000." By contrast, in the first case more than 300,000 persons would arrive in Israel and, as a result, the number of Arabs in Israel would rise to approximately half a million persons. Sharett further clarified that Washington was liable to demand the city of Eilat (Israel's southernmost point and its outlet to the Red Sea) as territorial compensation. The prime minister was not deterred by the high price tag attached to the Gaza Strip. He preferred to underscore the economic importance embodied in the Gaza coastline and its fertile soil, and the security imperative to remove the Egyptians from that area. He also reiterated his opposition to transferring the territory to the Jordanians. On the basis of these considerations, Ben-Gurion concluded that Israel must continue to insist that it receive the Gaza Strip.[89]

Despite the Egyptians' hostile response, from the second half of June the Americans intensified their endeavors to take the Gaza Plan forward. Washington hoped that Egypt would agree to open political discussions with Israel on the basis of the Plan, thus paving the way for the rest of the Arab world, just as Egypt had done when it was the first to sign an armistice agreement with Israel. Officials within the administration surmised that a settlement between Israel and Egypt on the fate of the Gaza Strip could bring a comprehensive settlement between the two countries and thus assist in resolution of the Palestinian refugee problem.[90]

On 24 June, the Americans submitted a proposition to Israel that recommended embarking on diplomatic discussions with Egypt on the basis of the

The Lausanne Conference and the refugee problem   53

Gaza Plan. A week later, Israel expressed its consent to the American administration[91] and even suggested the talks be held in New York.[92] The Israeli government appointed Abba Eban to head the Israeli delegation to the projected negotiation with Egypt.[93]

Yet Tel Aviv anticipated that the American initiative would fail as long as Egypt felt that it could gain significant territorial compensation from the Jewish state.[94]

In informal talks that Israel's representatives held with representatives from the Egyptian delegation at Lausanne, it became apparent that the territorial issue was a critical matter from the Egyptian leadership's perspective, and the fate of the Palestinian refugees was only secondary in its eyes. The Egyptians demanded to receive all of the Negev, or at least most of it. This demand emanated from Egypt's desire to ensure territorial contiguity with the Arab world to the east.[95] In truth, as Israel's representatives learned in a meeting they held in Lausanne with the Lebanese delegation, the issue of borders was the top priority of the entire Arab camp:

> Although [the Arabs] primarily embraced the refugee problem [as the heart of the conflict], in practice it occupied only second place [...] Pressure [from the Arabs] on the refugee question is tactical. The main thing is the size of our country [...] Everyone [i.e. the Arab countries] agrees to 47 [the UN Partition Plan of November 1947]. Ready to compromise that leaves in our hands Jaffa, the Ramle area with adjustments in the Sharon, but resolutely demand part of the Galilee as well as part of the southern Negev in order to create territorial contiguity between Egypt and Trans-Jordan.[96]

Eliahu Sasson, who spent days and nights in Lausanne conducting informal talks with Arab diplomats,[97] underscored in his dispatches to Tel Aviv that the borders issue was the first in Arab eyes, not the refugee question.[98] Even the refugees' delegations that came to the conference to present their interests directly, without the mediation of the Arab states, thought this was the Arab states' real interest. Sasson reported to Sharett on 5 June:

> I met today for two hours with [...] members of the delegation of propertied refugees. They are furious at the Arab states who use their [the Palestinian refugees'] problem as an instrument in order to divvy-out among themselves the Arab parts of Eretz Yisrael.[99]

It became clear that when the Arab states firmly declared, on the eve of the Lausanne Conference, that the fate of the Palestinian refugees had to stand at the core of the talks, they were simply paying lip service to this issue.

The feeling that their affairs were being cynically exploited and that they were no more than "a political pawn" in the hands of the Arab states[100] accompanied the refugees and their leaders throughout the period of the

54 *The Lausanne Conference and the refugee problem*

study at hand (and even afterward). A senior representative of UNRWA stated in this context that "Arab leaders don't give a damn whether the [Palestinian] refugees live or die."[101] More than once, the refugees' leaders shared this feeling with the Israelis.[102] Thus, having been disappointed by the behavior of the Arab states, the refugees' delegations in Lausanne sought to arrive at a separate settlement with Israel that would resolve the problems of the public they represented.[103] On 7 June, Sharett reported to the cabinet:

> The refugees offer us, with bitter hearts, all sorts of far-reaching proposals: that we declare we are prepared for direct negotiation with the refugees, that we invite a delegation or delegations of refugees to the country [to Israel] to conduct negotiation with them, that they will stir-up a movement among the refugees that will demand annexation of all of Eretz Yisrael to Israel.[104]

Such overtures were not rejected outright, and Israeli policymakers even considered support for the establishment of an independent Palestinian entity in the Arab sectors of the country currently under Trans-Jordanian control (the West Bank) and Egyptian control (the Gaza Strip) that would be tied to the State of Israel. Such a plan could have served Israeli objectives: it would inevitably have solved the refugee problem (approximately 80 percent of the refugees lived in these areas), and adjacent to Israel a weak and obedient Palestinian entity would have arisen. What's more, merely raising the idea could have served as leverage to extort more concessions from Trans-Jordan, which held the West Bank and wanted to annex it. Yet in the end Tel Aviv took no concrete steps towards parleying with the refugees' delegations. It understood that the genuine desire was to return to their former homes within Israel, and that resolution of their problem would still leave the conflict between Israel and its neighbors unchanged. Moreover, it was widely held that those who claimed to represent the refugees only represented a small portion, and primarily themselves.[105]

The little interest that the Egyptians exhibited in the future of the refugees in the Gaza Strip, in contrast to the great importance they assigned the territorial issue, did not escape the eyes of the Americans. In a report to Acheson, Stuart Rockwell, a member of the American delegation to the Lausanne Conference, cited that along with far-reaching territorial demands, Abd al-Mun'im Mustafa demonstrated "complete indifference [to the] fate [of the] Gaza refugees."[106] In mid June, Egyptian Foreign Minister Khashaba Pasha announced to the American ambassador in Cairo that Egypt "would consider" giving up the Gaza Strip only if it would receive in exchange *all* of the Negev on a line extending from Gaza to Beersheva and from there to the Dead Sea. Such an "offer" was the height of impudence. After all, the Egyptians were demanding, in essence, Israel's entire south – an expanse of about 10,000 square kilometers (which constitutes no less than 50 percent of Israel's territory) almost void of population in exchange for the 330 square kilometer Gaza

The Lausanne Conference and the refugee problem 55

Strip teeming with Arab refugees. Khashaba Pasha claimed that the British had advised Egypt to raise this demand. Washington labeled the Egyptian position "not politically feasible" and ordered its ambassador in London to approach the British government and to request that they influence Egypt to give up its "unrealistic" demands.[107] The British didn't do what they were asked to do. Quite to the contrary, on 9 July, they floated a plan for a settlement between Israel and the Arabs that was to a large extent in line with the Arab position: if the Gaza Strip would be handed over to Israel, part or the whole southern Negev would be given "as a prize to Jordan or to Jordan and to Egypt."[108] This scheme particularly suited British interests in the Middle East, for had it been implemented, it would have created territorial contiguity between the Suez Canal, which was under British control, and Trans-Jordan, where British forces were stationed (in the area of Aqaba).[109] The Americans understood Great Britain's strategic perspective, but in light of Israel's adamant opposition to conceding a significant part of the Negev,[110] they requested that London not "coerce" the Arab states into accepting territorial compensation if they were not interested in it.[111]

Despite Washington's indulgent attitude, when July arrived, the feeling in Israel was that the question of territorial compensation was making inroads and commanding a central place in the marketplace of ideas. British Foreign Secretary Bevin mentioned in talks he conducted with the Israeli minister in London, Mordecai Eliash, that Israel would need to relinquish an overland corridor in the Negev in order to create Jordanian-Egyptian contiguity.[112] In Egypt, voices calling for Israel to relinquish Eilat intensified. In a telegram to Sharett, Eban remarked with sarcasm that such a demand was as groundless as an Israeli demand for Alexandria or the Suez. Nevertheless, Eban recommended that Israel consider relinquishing territory adjacent to the border with Egypt equal in magnitude to that of the Gaza Strip.[113]

In a 19 July cabinet meeting Sharett addressed the territorial compensation issue:

> [Should] it become clear that we will not be able to receive the Strip only at the price of the refugees that we absorb, rather we will have to enter negotiation on border adjustments – then I believe we must be prepared to talk about relinquishing certain terrain along the desert border between us and Egypt [...] but very far from Gaza, so that [the terrain ceded] won't touch it and won't impair our status there. It might also be possible to talk about relinquishment in the eastern part of the Negev, on a certain strip beginning south of Beit Guvrin and further on.

In his opinion, it was possible to give Jordan the terrain in the eastern Negev that Israel would relinquish, and "this would shorten the route of Trans-Jordan to Gaza." Israel would also grant the Jordanians the right to use the Gaza port, as it had offered them the Haifa port. Sharett emphasized that, in any case, compensation that included Eilat should be firmly opposed. From

56   *The Lausanne Conference and the refugee problem*

the territorial issue, the foreign minister went on to discuss the question of the Gaza population. He requested that the cabinet hinge its agreement to annex the Gaza Strip on a set number of its inhabitants that Israel would need to absorb. "We thought that this related to 150,000 or 160,000 Arab residents. Now we face figures that change the picture entirely," clarified Sharett. Moreover, the final tally could be much larger:

> There are 120,000 refugees in Lebanon, and The Lebanon is situated on the sea and Gaza is also situated on the sea. What is to prevent Egypt or Lebanon from calling on the French and the English and from transferring in a few ships thousands or tens of thousands of refugees to Gaza? If such a thing should be [come about], it is [also] possible to transfer refugees to Gaza from Syria, Trans-Jordan and the Triangle, and this hole we bought could turn out to contain many more [refugees], and [they] could continue to pour more [refugees] into it [Gaza] while we endlessly pump and pump [them out].

The foreign minister's conclusion was that Israel needed to stipulate that the maximum number it agreed to absorb through annexation of the Gaza Strip was 200,000 Arabs.

Prime Minister Ben-Gurion advocated this position,[114] and the cabinet decided to announce that "our readiness to accept Gaza with its inhabitants hinged on the number of Arabs in Gaza would not exceed 200,000 souls."[115]

Israel did not have to sit very long on the horns of the demographic and territorial dilemma that the Gaza Plan invited. On 20 July, Abd al-Mun'im Mustafa again rejected the Gaza Plan in an American official's hearing and again raised the Egyptian demand to receive all of southern Israel – that is, the entire Negev along a line extending from Gaza to Beersheva to the Dead Sea.[116] On 29 July Egypt formally rejected the Gaza Plan.[117] Two days later, on 1 August, Washington conceded that it was impossible to bring Egypt and Israel to discuss the Plan as a foundation for a broader political settlement. The Americans expressed hopes that the Plan would be integrated into regular discussions taking place in Lausanne, and perhaps there it would enjoy more success.[118] The failure of the Lausanne Conference in September 1949 sealed the fate of such hopes, as well.

"The 100,000 Proposal"

In the wake of the deadlock that prevailed at the Lausanne Conference in the first two months of its existence, the Conciliation Commission agreed to the State Department's initiative to recess the talks at the end of June and reconvene on 18 July. The pause was designed primarily to enable the delegations to carry out consultations in their respective capitals after which, Washington hoped, they would return to the negotiation table more prepared for painful concessions on the refugee and borders issues.[119] Yet the United

The Lausanne Conference and the refugee problem   57

States did not rest its fate solely on the good will of the rival parties to reach an accord, and even before talks were temporarily suspended, it increased pressure on both sides to moderate their stands on the various issues at hand, and did the same all the more intensively during the break in the talks.

Already on 29 May, Truman sent Ben-Gurion a forceful message, piqued at Tel Aviv's refusal to repatriate a large number of refugees. The United States government, Truman clarified unequivocally, "relies upon" the Israeli government "to take responsible and positive action concerning Palestine refugees." If the Israeli government continued to reject the fundamental principles set forth in UN Resolution 194(3), he warned, "the United States Government will regretfully be forced to the conclusion that a revision of its attitude toward Israel has become unavoidable."[120] The American president's appeal, harsh as it may have been, did not lead Ben-Gurion to change his fundamental approach regarding mass repatriation of refugees. In a lengthy 8 June telegram in reply, Ben-Gurion again presented the main Israeli positions on the issue and stated that "the wheel of history cannot be turned back." At the same time, Ben-Gurion understood that he could not totally turn down flat the president of a superpower such as the United States, and therefore he noted his government's readiness to pay compensation for abandoned Arab lands, to repatriate a limited number of refugees, and to reunite families of refugees who had been separated by the war.[121] Things in a similar vein were voiced by foreign minister Sharett on 15 June with the opening of deliberations in the Knesset on Israel's foreign policy.[122] Yet, as one could expect, such gestures from Tel Aviv did not satisfy Washington. After Israel agreed to annex the Gaza Strip and its 300,000 Arabs, it seemed to the Americans that it would not be hard for Israel to absorb a similar number, not to mention a smaller number of refugees, even if this was not part of the Gaza Plan.[123] The slow waning of the Plan from late June led the United States to intensify its tone towards Israel on the refugee question. Other international entities such as the UN and the Conciliation Commission now joined forces with the United States in order to rebuke Israel for its policies on this matter.[124]

The need for an Israeli "gesture" on the repatriation issue was the main subject of a 22 June telegram from Abba Eban to Sharett. In Eban's appraisal Israel faced a fierce and unprecedented crisis in its relations with the United States. Eban warned: "We may have [to] face choice between some compromise [in Israel's stance regarding] principle non-return [of refugees] before peace and far-reaching rift [with the] U.S.A."[125]

The next day, the acting American representative at Lausanne, Raymond Hare, delivered a message to Eytan from the United States government that expressed Washington's "disappointment" with Israel's lack of responsiveness to Resolution 194(3) on the repatriation question.[126] Hare clarified to his interlocutor that President Truman would request congressional approval of financial aid to the refugees only if Israel and its Arab neighbors would put their shoulders into resolving the problem.[127]

58 The Lausanne Conference and the refugee problem

In light of the fact that the United States was supposed to underwrite approximately half the international financial assistance earmarked for easing the distress of the refugees,[128] one could appreciate the tremendous distress into which this population was liable to be thrust, if this aid was not be approved by the Congress. It was not in Israel's interests, politically or defensively, for such a humanitarian calamity to be placed on its own threshold.

American pressure on Israel on the repatriation question escalated during the break in the Lausanne talks. The first secretary at the Israel embassy in Washington, Uriel Heyd, aptly described the atmosphere in the United States:

> The refugee problem is, no doubt, the main cause for the present tension in our relations with this country [the United States]. In the White House, the State Department, and American public opinion we have so far failed to put our case across. While the press, and I dare to venture also the [State] Department, consider the territorial question as a secondary problem, they consistently say and – maybe – believe that our handling of the refugee problem constitutes the main stumbling block in the present Israeli-Arab negotiations for peace. From Justices of the Supreme Court [...] down to the man in the street, most non-Jewish Americans place the onus [for not solving the refugee problem] on Israel.

Israel's offer to annex the Gaza Strip and its population, stated Uriel, did not contribute to improving attitudes towards Israel since Israel demanded to receive terrain in exchange for refugees.[129]

The growing pressure from the Americans and from the UN on the refugee question began to have an impact on the leadership in Tel Aviv. In a telegram to Eban at the end of June, Foreign Minister Sharett said he planned to ask Ben-Gurion to issue a public statement saying that Israel was prepared to absorb 25,000 refugees as part of the family reunification plan. In addition, Sharett also vacillated in his own mind "whether [to] urge [the] Government [to] [... add ...] 50,000 [refugees] as further final maximum contribution without Gaza [Plan]." Will this, he asked Eban, "pacify U.S. [and induce her to] turn scales [in] our favour?"[130] Eban sent him a reply the same day. In Eban's judgment, fixing the number at 100,000 refugees or more would placate the Americans, but putting the number at 75,000 would only evoke anger and it would be advisable not to cite such a low number at all.[131]

Sharett arrived at the 5 July cabinet meeting with Eban's advice in his bag. "The pressure on the refugee matter," he told his colleagues, "continues on-and-on," and Israel must "do something in order to relieve the tension [with the United States]." Washington, said Sharett, believed that Israel ought to numerate a large number of refugees that it would repatriate. The Americans noted three reasons for that:

> (a) our arguments [against mass repatriation] aren't genuine, after we said we are prepared to receive Gaza with its refugees; (b) we are not enabling

them [the Americans] to pressure the Arab states to also set a number of refugees that they are prepared to settle in their countries; (c) this doesn't enable the President to go to the Congress and receive approval for a large program [to rehabilitate the refugees].

Although according to the foreign minister Israel did not have to respond in the affirmative to every American request, in this instance it was imperative to compromise with them. "I don't think we can withstand the pressure and substantiate the justice of our stand," argued Sharett. The government must, therefore, "agree to a certain change in the position we took to date, not by saying that now we are prepared to return the refugees, rather by giving an idea of what we are prepared to return in peacetime." The figure the minister provided was 100,000, and this was comprised of three groups:

> We have, in effect, returned 25,000 to 30,000 refugees [...] in the Negev we permitted Bedouin tribes to return after our conquest, also in the north there were several villages that we allowed them to return, there were also a lot of cases of infiltration that we don't intend to remove them [...] We announced that we will accept [separated] families [...] According to our people's estimates this will be approximately 10,000 persons [...] We arrive at [the total approaching] 35,000 or maybe 40,000 souls. I recommend that we express willingness to return a total of 100,000 Arabs [...] [Yet] let it be clear that other than those who have already returned, the rest can return in peacetime.

In other words, "the 100,000 Proposal" was actually "a 70,000 Proposal". In order to embellish the offer and capture the hearts of the Americans, Sharett included in his calculations, in an arithmetic trick of sorts, tens of thousands of refugees who had already returned to the country, some illegally, over the past year. This scheme won the support of most of his colleagues in the cabinet, but there were those who expressed apprehensions that parties at Lausanne would exploit this number to extract even larger concessions from Israel on the repatriation issue. Prime Minister Ben-Gurion and Minister Dov Yosef were the only cabinet members who expressed categorical opposition to "the 100,000 Proposal". The prime minister raised several arguments to justify his negative position:

> (a) I am not sure that the number we will state now will satisfy American opinion, particularly if we speak of this figure and [America] will pressure us and we won't be able to say why not more [...] (b) we don't have any assurance that if we satisfy America – [and] I am sure that this number will not satisfy America – if this will satisfy the Arabs [...] (c) I am not sure that by this we will achieve peace with the Arabs.

Moreover, Ben-Gurion warned of the grave security risk to the state that repatriation of so many refugees would present. In order to prevent "a

60 *The Lausanne Conference and the refugee problem*

majority vote against the Prime Minister's opinion" Sharett suggested that Israel first check whether if and when it would declare [its willingness] to settle 100,000 refugees, the Americans would lift their pressure on Israel and direct it towards the Arabs. The government accepted the foreign minister's suggestion and authorized him, after he investigated the utility of this step, to announce that Israel agreed to raise the number of Arab refugees that would be repatriated to 100,000 after peace reigned between Israel and the Arab states.[132] At the next cabinet meeting, Sharett updated the government, saying he had concluded that "the 100,000 Proposal" would not only hinge on establishment of peace, but also on a comprehensive and final settlement of the refugee problem.[133]

Already in the second week of July the Americans could gain a vague sense from Israeli sources about intentions in Israel to compromise on the repatriation issue. Sharett transmitted a message to McDonald in which he stated that Israel was taking a "cardinal" interest in the refugee problem, believed that "something" should be done about the matter, and "desire[d]" to assist. He added a broad hint, saying "we may not have said the last word regarding our proposals [on the subject]."[134] McDonald duly observed the frenzied diplomatic activity in Israel and wrote to Secretary of State Acheson that the authorities in Israel were now giving "intensive consideration" in regard "to the repatriation of a large number of Arab refugees without involving additional territory for Israel."[135] Reuven Shiloah, who stood to replace Eytan at the head of the Israeli delegation, told the American ambassador in a discussion the two conducted on 15 July that he would be "taking with him a more elastic program" to the second round of talks in Lausanne. The next day, Eytan revealed to the ambassador that the Israeli delegation was prepared to make more progress in the talks. Even Ben-Gurion reported to an American diplomat (and did this as if driven by the devil) that Israel was preparing itself for a more reconciliatory approach in Lausanne.[136]

On 6 July, Sharett ordered Eban to make contact with a third party, preferably a UN figure, who could check the reaction among officials in the American administration to the idea that Israel would absorb 100,000 refugees as part of the terms of an Arab-Israeli peace treaty. The "third party" feeling out the administration, stressed the minister, should appear as if acting on the messenger's own volition, not at Israel's request.[137] Despite the host of hints spread by policymakers in Israel, Sharett did not intend for it to appear at this stage that there was an official link between "the 100,000 Proposal" and his government. Sharett wanted to avoid a situation in which the Americans would reject the figure floated, while at the same time using it as a reliable base figure and departure point for negotiation, and try to extract additional concessions from Israel. In keeping with the minister's directives, Eban made contact with a senior UN official and asked him to raise the idea with the Americans.[138] Several days later, the official returned to the Israelis with disappointing tidings: the Americans considered the figure too low.[139] John Hilldring, one of President Truman's aides, told Arthur Lourie, the Israeli

The Lausanne Conference and the refugee problem   61

consul-general in New York, that while the president thought the offer could break the stalemate at Lausanne, he still thought that Israel must absorb about a quarter of a million refugees. In Lourie's opinion, Truman's intention was "to bargain" over the final figure.[140] Sharett concluded from the American response that the State Department was not prepared to answer in the affirmative to unofficial feelers, "in [the] hope we might increase [the] figure." They would not, however, dismiss "the 100,000 Proposal" if it was officially presented to them.[141]

Based on this appraisal, Sharett suggested to the government in a 19 July cabinet meeting that Israel officially announce (to the Americans and the Conciliation Commission) that if the Arabs were "willing to negotiate peace," Israel was prepared to make the refugee issue a top priority and even agreed to "define" its contribution "to resolution of this problem in people [in 'people-terms']." Realization of Israel's contribution would hinge on establishment of a comprehensive peace settlement and resolution of the refugee problem. The response of the prime minister to his foreign minister's request was a firm "no". "Such a thing won't give us anything," argued Ben-Gurion, "It will bring one result: Increased pressure on us to raise the number." Yet Ben-Gurion again found himself a lone voice, and the government decided to adopt Sharett's strategy.[142]

Two days later, on 21 July, Sharett ordered Israel's ambassador to the United States, Eliahu Elath, to establish contact with Secretary of State Acheson without delay and to convey "the 100,000 Proposal" to him.[143] The secretary, however, had urgent parliamentary obligations, and therefore Elath requested a meeting with the president himself. The two met on 28 July, and the Israeli ambassador delivered his government's proposal on the refugee issue. Truman expressed his appreciation of Israel's willingness to participate in resolving the refugee problem.[144] However, when Elath presented the proposal to members of the State Department's Middle East Desk, their response was quite reserved. McGhee requested to know what would be Israel's position if it turned out that the Arab states were unable to absorb all the hundreds of thousands of refugees that would remain. Elath replied emphatically that 100,000 was the maximum that "we can take without destroying [a] new state and that even this figure [is] considered disastrously high by our experts." As to McGhee's question, how this position sat with the Gaza Plan in which Israel committed itself to absorb more than 200,000 Arabs, Elath replied that annexation of the Gaza Strip would have altered significantly Israel's security situation and thus eased absorption of the Gaza Strip's refugees.[145] In two telegrams that Elath sent to Sharett on 29 July, the ambassador judged that the State Department would wait for the time being and wouldn't officially respond to the Israeli proposal regarding the refugees. Only when a crisis broke out at Lausanne due to the anticipated refusal of the Arabs to take upon themselves the resettlement of the rest of the refugees would the State Department increase pressure on Israel and on the Arabs to close the gap between them, surmised Elath.[146]

62   *The Lausanne Conference and the refugee problem*

Just before "the 100,000 Proposal" became public knowledge, Sharett decided to update the Knesset and the public at large about the initiative. Prior to that, on 28 July and 1 August, a closed meeting at which the proposal was presented was held by the Mapai faction of parliament. The general reaction was opposition to the proposal, out of fear for the fate of the Jewish state.[147] A similar position was evidenced in the meeting of the Knesset Foreign Affairs and Defense Committee, held on 1 August to discuss the government's proposal.[148]

In his 1 August speech before the Knesset plenum, Foreign Minister Sharett sought to calm the fury that began to bubble up in the political arena in opposition to the government's initiative. First of all, he stressed that implementation of Israel's contribution to resolution of the refugee problem "would hinge on achievement of peace and would constitute part of a comprehensive and final solution of the refugee problem as a whole." Second, Sharett refrained from mentioning the explicate number "100,000" and at the same time said that the number of returnees would include "the refugees who already returned and resettled in Israel, whose numbers reach 25,000," as well as "the thousands who in the meantime would be returned to the country [...] in the course of implementation of the Arab family reunification."

The minister's explanations did not satisfy his audience in the legislature. In the political debate held in the Knesset on 1 and 2 August, representatives from both opposition and coalition factions, including Mapai parliamentarians, scathingly criticized the government's initiative. Speakers from the right and the center focused on the grave consequences – from a defense, economic, and settlement perspective – that in their opinions were liable to emerge from the repatriation of masses of Arab refugees to the Jewish state. They believed that the Arab states alone must bear responsibility for solving the problem. The Israeli Communist Party, Maki, and Mapam (which had a communist-socialist orientation) took the government to task for agreeing to return the refugees due to American pressure. They, however, didn't reject the concept of repatriation itself. Maki parliamentarian Shmuel Mikunis clarified to members of the legislature that his party sided with the rights "of peace-loving Arab refugees who did not participate in the war against us, to return to their homes and their homeland."[149] Mapam also agreed with the return of "peace-loving" refugees, but on condition that a peace settlement would be achieved between Israel and the Arabs.[150] This constituted to some extent a toughening of the party's position. Mapam, as already noted, since the summer of 1948 had held that the refugees should be allowed to repatriate immediately once hostilities ended.

The battle against "the 100,000 Proposal" also took place in the newspapers, party papers and non-partisan independent papers alike. The security dimension led the debate, but economic arguments weren't absent. The importance of the economic factor intensified in the face of the huge waves of Jewish immigration arriving in the country, which put unprecedented pressure on the country's limited fiscal resources.

The organ of the General Zionists party, *Ha-Boker*, expressed concern regarding the ramifications of the return of tens of thousands of refugees on the sense of security in the country and the stability of the local economy.[151] The mouthpiece of the religious Zionists, *Ha-Tzofe*, stated that even in peacetime, the Jewish state must not "contain a large number of Arabs," all the more so in wartime.[152] The right-wing *Herut* paper labeled the proposal "an act of suicide"[153] and gave prominent coverage to mass gatherings that the Herut movement organized to protest the government's initiative.[154] The Mapam party organ, *Al Ha-Mishmar*, viewed the proposal as an American dictate, reason enough to oppose it.[155] The paper of the Communist Party, *Kol Ha-Am*, placed itself beyond the general consensus; it declared that resolution of the refugee problem would be achieved by absorbing a portion of the refugees within an Arab sovereign polity that would be established in the Arab section of Mandate Palestine, and through the Israeli government's agreement to declare, without any tie to American pressure, the right of "peace-loving" refugees to return to Israel.[156]

Wholesale opposition to "the 100,000 Proposal" was also expressed by the independent press. A 1 August headline in *Ha'aretz* raised the question: "Who will provide the means to absorb tens of thousands of Arabs that will return to Israel?"[157] *Yedioth Ahronoth* asked rhetorically: "Can a young state under such [severe] security conditions allow itself such a large Arab minority, particularly facing the fact that this state is surrounded by [Arab] polities [...] that have yet to 'complete' their score [with Israel] for their defeat in the Middle East?"[158] The editor-in-chief of the paper called upon the Israeli government to "flee from Lausanne" since, in his opinion, this was "the only way to evade the plan for the return of one hundred thousand enemies."[159] *Ma'ariv* stated that "the 100,000 Proposal" wouldn't forward the talks one iota. Israel should retreat from the offer, for if it would not, American pressure would increase both in the territorial domain and on the refugee question, the paper clarified.[160]

Sharett didn't view the sweeping opposition to "the 100,000 Proposal" in the political arena and in the press as necessarily harmful. In a letter to Israeli representatives in Lausanne, he wrote:

> One should note that the flurry of emotions undermined my standing a bit, but in essence was beneficial externally, and it should be employed to nail-down that this proposal [is] the outer limits of concession for our part.[161]

That is to say, the slamming of the proposal at home should've clarified to the Americans, to the Conciliation Commission, and to the Arabs that Israel's leadership could not allow more than 100,000 refugees to repatriate. Yet Washington and the Arabs refused to get excited by the tempest aroused in Israel.

On 28 July, Shiloah presented an unofficial report to the Conciliation Commission on "the 100,000 Proposal".[162] A week later, on 3 August, he formally submitted it to the commission, with the emphasis on conditions of peace and linkage to comprehensive resolution of the refugee problem.[163] The Conciliation Commission informed the Arab delegations about the initiative, and they responded, as expected, with a blanket rejection. In their opinion, Israel's contribution to resolution of the Palestinian refugee problem was much too small,[164] and some considered it even "less than a token."[165]

The Americans, as already noted, also considered the Israeli proposal unsatisfactory. Paul Porter, who replaced Ethridge on the Conciliation Commission, talked to Shiloah and Sasson for two hours, attempting to extract from the Israelis "a commitment to a larger figure."[166] McGhee explained to Ambassador Elath that now, after the Arabs had rejected the Israeli proposal, he could allow himself to say that the proposal was insufficient to achieve peace or an overall solution to the refugee problem. He reiterated the view that if Israel expressed its willingness to accept the Gaza Strip with its 230,000 refugees, then it could offer repatriation of more than 100,000 refugees. Elath replied that this figure was the maximum concession that Israel would make. According to Elath, no government in Israel could obtain parliamentary consent for a figure larger than this.[167]

The inevitable collapse of "the 100,000 Proposal" didn't leave much residue in Tel Aviv. From the outset, Sharett had been forced to raise the idea against his own best judgment due to American pressure, and the scathing criticism with which the Proposal was met at home only further clarified how united Israel was in its opposition to the principle of repatriation. The Ministry of Foreign Affairs even believed the political move had brought a nice dividend: the diplomatic pressure of the Americans and the United Nations on Israel's leadership to make decisive and painful concessions on the repatriation question was frozen.[168]

Since the Arabs rejected the Gaza Plan as well as "the 100,000 Proposal" and since Israel refused to compromise on the number of refugees that would be repatriated, it appeared that "nothing remained of a viable foundation to reach a compromise," as Secretary of State Acheson put it.[169] On 15 September 1949, four and a half months after the Lausanne Conference opened, the Conciliation Commission decided to close its doors.

A host of reasons were given for the failure of the conference. Ministry of Foreign Affairs official Walter Eytan believed that the fact that the Arab states arrived at the conference as a bloc and not as individual countries led to radicalization of their positions in negotiation with Israel to such an extent that it caused the failure of the Lausanne Conference.[170] Historian Avi Shlaim claimed that the conference failed, among other reasons, due to the unbridgeably deep gaps between the positions of the sides and the absence of a sincere willingness to compromise.[171] The flawed performance of the Conciliation Commission, in part due to the unsuitability of its members to fulfill their functions, also contributed to the political fiasco, added Shlaim.[172] Abba Eban had expressed similar thoughts in his memoirs, noting that "none of the three governments composing the Conciliation Commission extended itself in

The Lausanne Conference and the refugee problem   65

the choice of its representative."[173] Neil Caplan, who has delved deeply into this historic episode, reinforces Shlaim's arguments.[174] Historian Yemima Rosenthal judged that the success of armistice talks was the primary reason for the failure of the Lausanne Conference; the armistice agreements provided arrangements that satisfied the two sides and suppressed the drive and the desire to arrive at an immediate peace settlement. Moreover, armistice agreements talks exacted the maximum concessions that the sides were willing to make, which were exhausted through that channel.[175] Rosenthal's colleague Shaul Zeitune viewed the failure of the conference as the biggest missed opportunity of the era, since the momentum achieved in the wake of the signing of the armistice agreements had tremendous potential that was not properly exploited. Zeitune argued that the failure at Lausanne harmed peace efforts that came later, since this conference "institutionalized" the collective opposition of the Arabs to the existence of Israel.[176]

Notes

1 George J. Tomeh (ed.), *United Nations Resolutions on Palestine and the Arab-Israeli Conflict, 1947–1974*, vol. 1, Washington, DC: Institute for Palestine Studies, 1975, pp. 15– 17.
2 David P. Forsythe, *United Nations Peacemaking – The Conciliation Commission for Palestine*, Baltimore, MD: The Johns Hopkins University Press, 1972, p. 29.
3 FRUS, 1949, VI, pp. 761–2, The Special Representative of the United States in Israel (McDonald) to the Secretary of State, 22 February 1949.
4 Muhammad Abu Massara, "The Refugees Issue in Israeli Policy in 1948–49," *International Problems, Society and Politics* 28(53/3–4), 1989, p. 54 (Hebrew).
5 DEPI, Vol. 2, Document 365, D. Joseph to M. Sharett, 1 February 1949.
6 DEPI, Vol. 2, Document 379, M. Sharett to A. Eban, 9 February 1949.
7 Neil Caplan, *The Lausanne Conference, 1949*, Tel Aviv: Tel Aviv University Press, 1993, pp. 23–4; Ruth Ninburg-Levy, "The Arab Position at Lausanne Conference, 1949," MA thesis, University of Haifa, 1987, p. 62 (Hebrew).
8 See the reports of American diplomatic representatives in Arab capitals: FRUS, 1949, VI, pp. 750–1, The Chargé in Egypt (Patterson) to the Secretary of State, 15 February 1949; FRUS, 1949, VI, pp. 756–7, The Chargé in Iraq (Dorsz) to the Secretary of State, 19 February 1949; FRUS, 1949, VI, pp. 757–8, The Chargé in Iraq (Dorsz) to the Secretary of State, 20 February 1949; Neil Caplan, *Futile Diplomacy: The United Nations, The Great Powers and Middle East Peacemaking, 1948–1954*, Portland, OR: Frank Cass, 1997, pp. 61–2.
9 FRUS, 1949, VI, p. 746, The Consul at Jerusalem (Burdett) to the Secretary of State, 12 February 1949.
10 DEPI, Vol. 2, Document 400, Meeting with Members of the Conciliation Commission (Tel Aviv, 24 February 1949); ISA, Government Meeting, 27 February 1949, p. 23.
11 DEPI, Vol. 2, Document 400, Meeting with Members of the Conciliation Commission (Tel Aviv, 24 February 1949).
12 ISA, Government Meeting, 14 March 1949, pp. 4–8.
13 DEPI, Vol. 2, Document 443, Memorandum on the Refugee Problem, 16 March 1949.
14 Caplan, *The Lausanne Conference*, p. 32.
15 Caplan, *The United Nations*, p. 64.

66 *The Lausanne Conference and the refugee problem*

16 ISA, MFA 2444/19, The Conciliation Commission's Statement, 5 April 1949.
17 DEPI, Vol. 2, Document 479, Meeting of the Conciliation Commission with the Prime Minister and Ministry for Foreign Affairs Staff (Tel Aviv, 7 April 1949).
18 DEPI, Vol. 2, Document 400, Meeting with Members of the Conciliation Commission (Tel Aviv, 24 February 1949).
19 Caplan, *The Lausanne Conference*, p. 26.
20 UN officials involved in the Palestine issue had already estimated in the summer and fall of 1948 that most refugees could not or would not want to return to their homes in the Jewish state. See Benny Morris, *The Birth of the Palestinian Refugee Problem, 1947–1949*, Tel Aviv: Am Oved, 1991, pp. 210–11 (Hebrew).
21 Benjamin N. Schiff, *Refugees unto the Third Generation: U.N. Aid to Palestinians*, Syracuse, NY: Syracuse University Press, 1995, pp. 16–17.
22 FRUS, 1949, VI, p. 831, Policy Paper Prepared in the Department of State, 15 March 1949.
23 George McGhee, *Envoy to the Middle World: Adventures in Diplomacy*, New York: Harper and Row, 1983, p. 28.
24 FRUS, 1949, VI, p. 788, Memorandum by the Assistant Secretary of State for United Nations Affairs to the Under Secretary of State, 3 March 1949.
25 Morris, *The Birth*, p. 345.
26 ISA, MFA 2447/3, Minutes of Consultation Concerning Peace Negotiations with the Arab Countries, 12 April 1949.
27 DEPI, Vol. 2, Document 477, M. Sharett to W. Eytan, 5 April 1949; FRUS, 1949, VI, p. 891, Memorandum of Conversation by the Secretary of State, 5 April 1949.
28 FRUS, 1949, VI, pp. 934–43, Memorandum by the Coordinator on Palestine Refugee Matters (McGhee) to the Secretary of State, 22 April 1949.
29 Morris, *The Birth*, p. 202.
30 FRUS, 1948, V, pp. 1696–7, The Acting Secretary of State to Certain Diplomatic and Consular Offices, 29 December 1949.
31 It seems that Secretary of State Acheson also assessed that these regulations were designed to block the repatriation of a significant number of refugees. In his opinion the Conciliation Commission should "express its concern to Israeli Government in light of absentee property ordinance that no party take unilateral action in advance of negotiations contemplated by General Assembly resolution [194(3)] which would prejudice achievement of agreed settlement on such questions as return of refugees to their homes and return of property to refugee owners." FRUS, 1949, VI, p. 725, The Secretary of State to the Consulate General at Jerusalem, 4 February 1949.
32 Morris, *The Birth*, pp. 342–3.
33 FRUS, 1949, VI, pp. 762–3, The Special Representative of the United States in Israel to the Secretary of State, 22 February 1949.
34 FRUS, 1949, VI, pp. 762–3, The Special Representative of the United States in Israel to the Secretary of State, 22 February 1949, Note 2.
35 FRUS, 1949, VI, p. 831, Policy Paper Prepared in the Department of State, 15 March 1949.
36 FRUS, 1949, VI, p. 935, Memorandum by the Coordinator on Palestine Refugee Matters (McGhee) to the Secretary of State, 22 April 1949.
37 McGhee wrote in this connection that "[a]part from political considerations [i.e. from economic considerations only] Syria, Iraq and Trans-Jordan offer significant possibilities for resettlement or employment of refugees." FRUS, 1949, VI, p. 935, Memorandum by the Coordinator on Palestine Refugee Matters (McGhee) to the Secretary of State, 22 April 1949. The understanding that from an economic standpoint it was preferable to rehabilitate the refugees in the Arab countries led the Americans to plan, from the spring of 1949, a variety of economic plans to absorb the refugees in the Arab states. No such plans were prepared with respect

The Lausanne Conference and the refugee problem   67

to the absorption of refugees in Israel. DEPI, Vol. 2, Document 494, M. Comay to M. Sharett, 15 April 1949; DEPI, Vol. 2, Document 525, M. Comay to M. Eliash, 29 April 1949.

38 On Jordan's policy concerning the refugee problem, see Chapter 4.

39 FRUS, 1949, VI, p. 837, Policy Paper Prepared in the Department of State, 15 March 1949; FRUS, 1949, VI, p. 935, Memorandum by the Coordinator on Palestine Refugee Matters (McGhee) to the Secretary of State, 22 April 1949; FRUS, 1949, VI, p. 963, The Chargé in Trans-Jordan to the Secretary of State, 1 May 1949.

40 Amitzur Ilan, *Bernadotte in Palestine 1948: A Study in Contemporary Humanitarian Knight-Errantry*, Basingstoke: Macmillan, 1989, pp. 171–2.

41 UKNA, FO 371/68822, Note by Glubb Pasha, 19 August 1948; UKNA, FO 371/68859, E12069, Glubb to Burrows, 7 September 1948.

42 FRUS, 1948, V, p. 1344, The Ambassador in the United Kingdom to the Secretary of State, 25 August 1948.

43 FRUS, 1949, VI, pp. 907–8, Memorandum of Conversation, Prepared Presumably by the First Secretary of the Embassy in the United Kingdom (Jones), 13 April 1949.

44 DEPI, Vol. 1, Document 423, L. Kohn to M. Shertok, 5 August 1948.

45 DEPI, Vol. 2, Document 489, A. Eban to M. Eliash, 11 April 1949.

46 UKNA, FO 371/68379, E12211, FO Minute, 8 September 1948.

47 FRUS, 1948, V, p. 1682, The Chargé in the UK to the Acting Secretary of State, 22 December 1948.

48 FRUS, 1949, VI, p. 51, Memorandum of Conversation, by the Secretary of State, 4 April 1949.

49 FRUS, 1949, VI, p. 907, Memorandum of Conversation, Prepared Presumably by the First Secretary of Embassy in the United Kingdom, 13 April 1949.

50 ISA, Government Meeting, 21 April 1949, p. 6.

51 DEPI, Vol. 2, Document 505, D. Ben-Gurion and M. Sharett Speaking at a Political Consultation in the Ministry for Foreign Affairs, 22 April 1949.

52 DEPI, Vol. 2, Document 509, C. Weizmann to President Truman, 26 April 1949.

53 ISA, MFA 2451/18, From the Foreign Minister's Remarks to the Knesset Foreign Affairs Committee, 2 May 1949.

54 DEPI, Vol. 4, Document 8, W. Eytan to M. Sharett, 5 May 1949.

55 FRUS, 1949, VI, pp. 926–7, The Consul at Jerusalem (Burdett) to the Secretary of State, 20 April 1949.

56 DEPI, Vol. 2, Document 505, D. Ben-Gurion and M. Sharett Speaking at a Political Consultation in the Ministry for Foreign Affairs, 22 April 1949.

57 DEPI, Vol. 2, Document 526, W. Eytan to M. Sharett, 30 April 1949.

58 DEPI, Vol. 4, Editorial Note, p. 10.

59 ISA, Government Meeting, 3 May 1949, pp. 10–18.

60 ISA, 7561/3 A, Foreign Affairs and Defense Committee Meeting, 1 June 1949, p. 12.

61 Jacob Tovy, "David Ben-Gurion, Moshe Sharett and the Status of the Gaza Strip, 1948–1956," *Iyunim Bitkumat Israel* 13, 2003, pp. 140–41 (Hebrew).

62 ISA, 7561/2 A, Foreign Affairs and Defense Committee Meeting, 2 May 1949, p. 12.

63 Shimon Golan, *Hot Border, Cold War: The Formulation of Israel's Security Policy, 1949–1953*, Tel Aviv: Ma'arachot, 2000, p. 42 (Hebrew).

64 FRUS, 1949, VI, p. 1036, The Minister in Switzerland to the Secretary of State, 20 May 1949.

65 DEPI, Vol. 4, Document 32, W. Eytan to A. Eban, 21 May 1949.

66 DEPI, Vol. 4, Document 32, W. Eytan to A. Eban, 21 May 1949, Note 3.

67 DEPI, Vol. 4, Document 41, W. Eytan to C. de Boisanger, 29 May 1949.

68 *Herut*, 25 May 1949.

69 Benyamin Neuberger, *Political Parties in Israel*, Tel Aviv: The Open University, 1997, p. 94 (Hebrew).

68   *The Lausanne Conference and the refugee problem*

70 *Herut*, 1 June 1949.
71 *Ha-Boker*, 30 May 1949.
72 The "Triangle" is a concentration of Arab-Palestinian settlements, located in the eastern plain among the Samarian foothills. The region was originally designated to fall under Trans-Jordanian jurisdiction, but at the 1949 armistice agreement Israel insisted on having it within its side, due to military and strategic reasons. To achieve this, a territorial swap was negotiated between the two countries.
73 ISA, 7561/2 A, Foreign Affairs and Defense Committee Meeting, 11 May 1949, pp. 2–3, 8–11.
74 Yossi Amitay, *The United Workers' Party (Mapam), 1948–1954: Attitude on Palestinian-Arab Issues*, Tel Aviv: Tcherikover, 1988, pp. 20–4 (Hebrew); Neuberger, *Political Parties*, p. 51. See, in this context, Mordechai Gazit, "Ben-Gurion's Proposal to Include the Gaza Strip in Israel, 1949," *Zionism* 12, 1987, p. 316 (Hebrew).
75 *Yedioth Ahronoth*, 29 May 1949.
76 *The Palestine Post*, 29 May 1949.
77 *Ma'ariv*, 1 June 1949.
78 FRUS, 1949, VI, p. 1060, Memorandum by the Acting Secretary of State to the President, 27 May 1949.
79 FRUS, 1949, VI, p. 1090, The Acting Secretary of State to the Legation in Switzerland, 4 June 1949.
80 FRUS, 1949, VI, pp. 1095 – 6, The Acting Secretary of State to the Embassy in Israel, 8 June 1949.
81 DEPI, Vol. 3, Document 186, E. Sasson to M. Sharett, 1 February 1949; DEPI, Vol. 3, Document 245, E. Sasson to W. Eytan, 21 March 1949.
82 FRUS, 1949, VI, p. 1111, The Ambassador in Israel (McDonald) to the Secretary of State, 10 June 1949; DEPI, Vol. 4, Document 67, M. Sharett to W. Eytan, 10 June 1949, Note 4.
83 BGA, BGD, 6 June 1949.
84 DEPI, Vol. 4, Document 48, E. Sasson to M. Sharett, 1 June 1949.
85 FRUS, 1949, VI, pp. 1096–7, Mr. Mark Ethridge to the Secretary of State, 8 June 1949.
86 FRUS, 1949, VI, p. 1116, The Acting Secretary of State to the Embassy in Egypt, 11 June 1949.
87 FRUS, 1949, VI, pp. 1070–1, The Minister in Switzerland to the Secretary of State, 28 May 1949.
88 FRUS, 1949, VI, p. 1139, Memorandum by Mr. Mark F. Ethridge to the Deputy Under Secretary of State, 15 June 1949.
89 ISA, Government Meeting, 21 June 1949, pp. 12–13, 21–2.
90 FRUS, 1949, VI, p. 1191, The Secretary of State to the Embassy in Egypt, 28 June 1949.
91 FRUS, 1949, VI, p. 1195, The Secretary of State to the Embassy in Egypt, 1 July 1949.
92 DEPI, Vol. 4, Document 122, A. Eban to M. Sharett, 4 July 1949, Note 1.
93 Morris, *The Birth*, p. 363.
94 FRUS, 1949, VI, p. 1197, The Ambassador in Israel (McDonald) to the Secretary of State, 3 July 1949.
95 Ilan Asia, *The Core of the Conflict: The Struggle for the Negev, 1947–1956*, Jerusalem: Yad Izhak Ben-Zvi, 1994, p. 220 (Hebrew).
96 DEPI, Vol. 4, Document 46, E. Sasson and Z. Liff to M. Sharett, 31 May 1949.
97 See, in this context, Yemima Rosenthal, "Shaping Israeli Policy for the Palestine Conciliation Conference," *Zionism* 13, 1988, p. 55 (Hebrew).
98 DEPI, Vol. 4, Document 51, E. Sasson to M. Sharett, 2 June 1949; DEPI, Vol. 4, Document 81, E. Sasson to S. Divon, 16 June 1949.

The Lausanne Conference and the refugee problem 69

99 DEPI, Vol. 4, Document 56, E. Sasson to M. Sharett, 5 June 1949.
100 Stian Johansen Tiller and Hilde Henriksen Waage, "Powerful State, Powerless Mediator: The United States and the Peace Efforts of the Palestine Conciliation Commission, 1949–51," *The International History Review* 33(3), 2011, p. 507.
101 Alexander H. Joffe and Asaf Romirowsky, "A Tale of Two Galloways: Notes on the Early History of UNRWA and Zionist Historiography," *Middle Eastern Studies* 46(5), 2010, p. 655.
102 At meetings held throughout the period under discussion between Israeli officials and representatives of the refugee organizations, the latter did not hesitate to criticize the Arab countries sharply; these countries, they asserted, sought to exploit the refugee problem for their own gain. Gideon Rafael, in a report to the Ministry of Foreign Affairs on a talk held on 5 June 1954 with the heads of the "General Refugee Congress for Palestine," remarked that "the Palestinian Arabs are disappointed by the Arab countries' actions and positions. Not only are they not coming to the aid of the Palestinians, they are actually taking advantage of their tragedy, both in an economic sense and in terms of both domestic and international politics." DEPI, Vol. 9, Document 239, Y. Palmon to G. Rafael, 5 June 1954.
103 Moshe Sasson, *Talking Peace*, Or Yehuda: Ma'ariv, 2004, pp. 52– 3 (Hebrew).
104 ISA, Government Meeting, 7 June 1949, p. 6.
105 ISA, Government Meeting, 7 June 1949, pp. 6–7; Golan, *Hot Border, Cold War*, pp. 55–61; Yemima Rosenthal, "David Ben-Gurion and Moshe Sharett Facing Decisions on Israeli Foreign Policy, 1949,", *Monthly Review* 25 (11), 1988, p. 20 (Hebrew); Avi Shlaim, *Collusion Across the Jordan – King Abdullah, The Zionist Movement and the Partition of Palestine*, Oxford: Clarendon Press, 1988, p. 495.
106 FRUS, 1949, VI, pp. 1238–9, Mr. Stuart W. Rockwell to the Secretary of State, 20 July 1949.
107 FRUS, 1949, VI, pp. 1179–80, The Secretary of State to the Embassy in the United Kingdom, 25 June 1949.
108 UKNA, FO 371/75350, E8393/31, Suggested Basis for New Approach by the Conciliation Commission to the Parties on Their Resumption of Work on the 18th of July, 9 July 1949.
109 For more on the British position concerning the Gaza plan, see Asia, *The Core of the Conflict*, pp. 96–7; Morris, *The Birth*, p. 362.
110 Asia, *The Core of the Conflict*, p. 93.
111 FRUS, 1949, VI, pp. 1223– 4, The Secretary of State to the Embassy in the United Kingdom, 13 July 1949.
112 DEPI, Vol. 4, Document 140, Meeting: M. Eliash – E. Bevin, 19 July 1949.
113 DEPI, Vol. 4, Document 122, A. Eban to M. Sharett, 4 July 1949.
114 ISA, Government Meeting, 19 July 1949, pp. 11–15, 21, 52.
115 ISA, Government's Resolutions, Government's Resolution from 19 July 1949.
116 FRUS, 1949, VI, pp. 1238 – 9, Mr. Stuart W. Rockwell to the Secretary of State, 20 July 1949.
117 Morris, *The Birth*, p. 366.
118 FRUS, 1949, VI, pp. 1275–6, The Secretary of State to the Embassy in the United Kingdom, 1 August 1949.
119 FRUS, 1949, VI, p. 1155, The Acting Secretary of State to the Legation in Switzerland, 18 June 1949; FRUS, 1949, VI, pp. 1164–5, The Acting Secretary of State to the Legation in Switzerland, 21 June 1949.
120 DEPI, Vol. 4, Document 42, J. McDonald to D. Ben-Gurion, 29 May 1949.
121 DEPI, Vol. 4, Document 64, M. Sharett to J. McDonald, 8 June 1949.
122 *Knesset Minutes*, vol. 1, 15 June 1949, p. 721.
123 FRUS, 1949, VI, p. 1139, Memorandum by Mr. Mark F. Ethridge to the Deputy Under Secretary of State, 15 June 1949; FRUS, 1949, VI, p. 1161, The Acting Secretary of State to the Legation in Switzerland, 20 June 1949. According to

70 *The Lausanne Conference and the refugee problem*

Yemima Rosenthal, Israel's agreement to annex the Gaza strip and the refugees in it violated Israel's principled opposition to the return of large number of refugees: Rosenthal, "Decisions," p. 20.

124 DEPI, Vol. 4, Document 88, A. Eban to W. Eytan, 20 June 1949.
125 DEPI, Vol. 4, Document 92, A. Eban to M. Sharett, 22 June 1949.
126 DEPI, Vol. 4, Document 96, W. Eytan to M. Sharett, 23 June 1949.
127 DEPI, Vol. 4, Document 97, W. Eytan to M. Sharett, 23 June 1949.
128 FRUS, 1949, VI, p. 971, The Secretary of State to the Secretary of Defense (Johnson), 4 May 1949.
129 DEPI, Vol. 4, Document 115, U. Heyd to E. Herlitz, 1 July 1949.
130 DEPI, Vol. 4, Document 106, M. Sharett to A. Eban, 25 June 1949.
131 ISA, MFA 2181/3, Eban to Sharett, 25 June 1949.
132 ISA, Government Meeting, 5 July 1949, pp. 13–36.
133 ISA, Government Meeting, 12 July 1949, p. 2.
134 FRUS, 1949, VI, p. 1216, The Ambassador in Israel (McDonald) to the Secretary of State, 11 July 1949.
135 FRUS, 1949, VI, p. 1222, The Ambassador in Israel (McDonald) to the Secretary of State, 13 July 1949.
136 FRUS, 1949, VI, pp. 1237–8, The Ambassador in Israel (McDonald) to the Secretary of State, 19 July 1949, and Note 1.
137 DEPI, Vol. 4, Document 124, M. Sharett to A. Eban, 6 July 1949.
138 DEPI, Vol. 4, Document 127, A. Eban to M. Sharett, 8 July 1949.
139 DEPI, Vol. 4, Document 134, A. Lourie and G. Rafael to M. Sharett, 12 July 1949.
140 DEPI, Vol. 4, Document 139, A. Lourie to M. Sharett, 19 July 1949. Additional reports that arrived during the last week of July indicated that the White House was "generally" pleased with the proposal concerning the repatriation of 100,000 refugees. See DEPI, Vol. 4, Document 156, A. Eban to M. Sharett, 27 July 1949; DEPI, Vol. 4, Document 158, A. Eban to R. Shiloah, 28 July 1949.
141 DEPI, Vol. 4, Document 144, M. Sharett to E. Elath, 21 July 1949.
142 ISA, Government Meeting, 19 July 1949, pp. 5–8, 38–9, 52.
143 DEPI, Vol. 4, Document 144, M. Sharett to E. Elath, 21 July 1949.
144 DEPI, Vol. 4, Document 159, E. Elath to M. Sharett, 28 July 1949; DEPI, Vol. 4, Document 177, E. Elath to W. Eytan, 3 August 1949; FRUS, 1949, VI, p. 1272, Memorandum by the Secretary of State, 1 August 1949.
145 DEPI, Vol. 4, Document 160, E. Elath to M. Sharett, 28 July 1949.
146 DEPI, Vol. 4, Document 160, E. Elath to M. Sharett, 28 July 1949, Note 3.
147 ILPA, 2-11-1949-1, Parliamentary Party Meeting, 28 July 1949, pp. 3–4; ILPA, 2-11-1949-2, Parliamentary Party Meeting, 1 August 1949, pp. 1–20.
148 ISA, 7561/7 A, Foreign Affairs and Defense Committee Meeting, 1 August 1949, pp. 7–17.
149 Maki maintained this position throughout the period under discussion. See YTA, Maki, Conferences, Container 1, File 3. Political Report by the Central Committee, 21–24 October 1949; YTA, Maki, Knesset, Container 2, File 4. Information Pamphlet for the Second Knesset Elections, June 1951; YTA, Maki, Conferences, Container 1, File 4. Political Report by the Central Committee to the 12th Maki Conference, 29 May 1952; YTA, Maki, The Maki Program, 1 June 1952.
150 *Knesset Minutes*, vol. 2, 1 August 1949, pp. 1195–215; *Knesset Minutes*, vol. 2, 2 August 1949, pp. 1216–36.
151 *Ha-Boker*, 1, 3, 5 August 1949.
152 *Ha-Tzofe*, 1 August 1949.
153 *Herut*, 1 August 1949.
154 *Herut*, 14 August 1949.
155 *Al Ha-Mishmar*, 1 August 1949.
156 *Kol Ha-Am*, 2 August 1949.

157 *Ha'aretz*, 1 August 1949.
158 *Yedioth Ahronoth*, 2 August 1949.
159 *Yedioth Ahronoth*, 9 August 1949.
160 *Ma'ariv*, 31 July and 8 August 1949.
161 DEPI, Vol. 4, Document 187, M. Sharett to R. Shiloah and E. Sasson, 7 August 1949.
162 DEPI, Vol. 4, Document 162, R. Shiloah to M. Sharett, 29 July 1949.
163 ISA, MFA 2447/5, Statement by the Conciliation Commission, on 3 August 1949.
164 DEPI, Vol. 4, Document 184, E. Sasson to M. Sharett, 6 August 1949.
165 FRUS, 1949, VI, pp. 1287–8, Mr. Paul A. Porter to the Secretary of State, 5 August 1949.
166 DEPI, Vol. 4, Document 180, R. Shiloah to M. Sharett, 5 August 1949.
167 DEPI, Vol. 4, Document 194, E. Elath to M. Sharett, 9 August 1949; FRUS, 1949, VI, pp. 1297– 8, The Secretary of State to the United States Delegation at Lausanne, 11 August 1949.
168 DEPI, Vol. 4, Document 198, M. Sharett to R. Shiloah, 10 August 1949; DEPI, Vol. 4, Document 200, W. Eytan to R. Shiloah, 11 August 1949; DEPI, Vol. 4, Document 287, E. Elath to W. Eytan, 14 September 1949.
169 Morris, *The Birth*, p. 378.
170 Asia, *The Core of the Conflict*, pp. 91–2.
171 Shlaim, *Collusion across the Jordan*, pp. 465–9.
172 Shlaim, *Collusion across the Jordan*, p. 462.
173 Abba Eban, *An Autobiography*, New York: Random House, 1977, p. 149.
174 Caplan, *The Lausanne Conference*, pp. 131–8.
175 Rosenthal, "Decisions," p. 21. See support for this argument in Elad Ben-Dror, *The Mediator: Ralph Bunch and the Arab-Israeli Conflict, 1947–1949*, Sede Boqer: The Ben-Gurion Research Institute, 2012, p. 299 (Hebrew); Forsythe, *United Nations Peacemaking*, p. 36.
176 Shaul Zeitune, *Deterrence and Peace: Israel's Attempts to Arrive at a Settlement*, Tel Aviv: Tcherikover, 2000, p. 111 (Hebrew)

3 Shifting the emphasis for solving the refugee problem

From a political approach to an economic one

The United States adopts the economic approach

From the beginning of the summer of 1948, as the Palestinian refugee problem intensified, the United States administration began to assist masses of refugees. This was done in several ways: extending humanitarian aid (food, clothing, blankets, medicine, and tents); funding United Nations bodies assisting the refugee population (for example, in March 1949 the United States Congress budgeted 16 million dollars to cover all the initial expenditures of UNRPR);[1] and urging private American relief agencies (among them, the Near East Foundation, the American Red Cross, and the Church World Service Committee) to extend assistance to the Palestinian refugees.[2] By these actions, Washington sought to prevent the refugee problem turning into an even graver humanitarian crisis.

From the spring of 1949, the administration in Washington also began to examine the economic facets of permanent rehabilitation of the refugees, whether in Israel or in the Arab states. In March, as already noted, State Department official George McGhee embarked on a comprehensive tour of the Middle East to find out what options, diplomatic and economic, existed for resolution of the problem "in the long term."

At the same time Secretary of State Acheson directed the American consul-general in Jerusalem, William Burdett, to investigate whether it was possible to prod the Arab states to commit themselves to various projects which would utilize the refugees' labor.[3] At the end of April, Mark Ethridge told Walter Eytan that in accordance with the recommendations McGhee had brought back from his tour of the Middle East, the State Department would be preparing a comprehensive economic development program for the Middle East. In the framework of the program, the rehabilitation of the refugee population would also be settled. Ethridge reported that, as an initial step, the Conciliation Commission planned to send a small technical committee to the region to gather data on existing development options.[4] The committee, established in May, was headed by an American diplomat. Among its members were representatives from France, Turkey, and Britain.[5] On 20 August 1949, the committee published its findings and suggested several ideas for regional

Shifting the emphasis for solving the refugee problem   73

development projects that would be beneficial, among other things, for settling the refugee problem.[6]

Concurrent to the work of the committee, a number of civil servants in the State Department contemplated the idea of establishing an even larger body – an economic survey mission – whose investigative authority would be broader than that of the technical committee. Its mission would be "to examine the economic situation in countries affected by the recent hostilities" and to raise suggestions that would enable the governments of the region to take steps that would assist them in three ways:

> to overcome economic dislocations created by the hostilities; to reintegrate refugees from the hostilities into economic life of area on self-sustaining basis within minimum period of time; and to promote economic conditions conducive to maintenance of peace and stability in the area.[7]

Paul Porter, the United States' new representative on the Conciliation Commission, was one of the key figures behind the idea to establish an economic survey mission. In the face of the spasmodic character the Lausanne Conference had taken, Porter sensed that attempts to resolve the Arab-Israeli conflict solely, or even primarily, through political mediation formulas were doomed to failure. In his estimation, comprehensive economic development of the region would, in the end, make possible settlement of the political disagreements between the sides, first and foremost the refugee problem.

On 31 July, during a working meeting with Reuven Shiloah, the head of the Israeli delegation at Lausanne, Porter reported that he intended to bring about appointment of a mission of experts under United Nations' auspices that, with the assistance of Israeli and Arab experts, would examine programs for economic development and rehabilitation of the refugees.[8] Foreign Minister Sharett was quick to direct Shiloah to agree in principle to the concept, while making it clear that Israel opposed giving the United Nations' mission authority to set the absorption capacities of each of the nations in the region.[9] Sharett feared that in the wake of its tour of the region, the survey mission would conclude that Israel was able to absorb a large number of refugees within its domain. In such an event, in order not to appear as a country that flaunted a binding decision of a body established by the United Nations, Israel would be forced to accept such a finding.

On 12 August, Porter arrived in Washington for consultations at the State Department regarding the future of the Lausanne Conference. Porter believed that the conference, and the political approach to problem-solving that it reflected, had reached the end of the line, and it was now time to try and arrive at a solution to the conflict, and at its core the refugee problem, through an economic approach. He, therefore, recommended immediate implementation of the concept of an economic survey mission for the Middle East.[10] Similar sentiments were voiced by McGhee in a lengthy memorandum submitted to Acheson on 16 August.[11]

74 *Shifting the emphasis for solving the refugee problem*

This recommended course of action was warmly received both within the State Department and by the White House.[12] In a letter to American representatives in the Middle East and Europe, Acheson explained that the new policy was the product of the fact that "neither side [in the Arab-Israeli conflict] is prepared at this time to make concessions which would make settlement possible." Acheson stated that the State Department did not rule out more political deliberations in the future between the sides (along the lines of the Lausanne Conference) designed to reach solutions, even partial ones, but in the meantime the emphasis needed to be on the economic level.[13] The concept of using economic tools to achieve political objectives wasn't a one-time deal directed only towards the Middle East. The Truman administration had already implemented this course of action in various regions of the world, particularly in Europe (the Marshall Plan).[14]

On 15 August, the Conciliation Commission submitted a questionnaire to the Israeli and Arab delegations that dealt with the refugee and border issues, and requested their responses within eight days. In the first question, the sides were requested to express their views regarding the assumption that the solution to the refugee problem rested on repatriation to Israel and resettlement of others in the Arab states. The question that followed debuted in abbreviated form the idea of an economic survey mission. The two sides were asked whether they were willing to facilitate the workings of such a mission and accept its recommendations.[15]

The replies of the Israeli and Arab delegations to the Conciliation Commission questionnaire arrived at the end of the month. Israel again declared that resolution of the refugee problem rested, in the main, on resettlement, and the Arabs expressed willingness (with some reservations) "to examine" the commission's assumptions on this matter. As for the economic survey mission, the Arab representatives promised to recommend their respective governments facilitate its work and take all measures necessary to implement its recommendations. The Israeli delegation also promised to facilitate the work of the survey mission, but noted that Israel could not commit itself in advance to implementing its recommendations.[16] The refugees' delegations also sent a response to the questionnaire. As expected, they demanded that the refugees be able to decide whether they wished to repatriate to their former homes or not. As for the suggested economic survey mission, the refugees' delegations agreed to facilitate its work and assist in implementing its conclusions; nevertheless, they believed that the mission would not succeed if it didn't take into account the opinions of a special representative body that the refugees would elect by themselves in order to safeguard the rights of the refugee population. This position alluded to the refugees' dissatisfaction with the way the Arab states had represented their interests. They felt that the Arab states continued to exploit the Palestinians' case to advance their own aspirations in regard to an entirely different matter – the territorial domain.[17]

After the Conciliation Commission studied the responses, it decided to suggest that the sides sign a draft summary declaration regarding the refugee problem. In the commission's opinion, the proposed wording of the declaration was very close to areas of consensus between the two camps. According to the first clause, the refugee problem would find its solution in repatriation of the refugees and resettlement in the Arab countries of others who would not return to Israel. The next clause stated that the countries of the region would be able to absorb in their territories a large number of Palestinian refugees with only the technical and fiscal assistance of the international community. In the fifth clause, Israel and its Arab neighbors obligated themselves to take steps to implement the recommendations of the economic survey mission, at such time as they deemed suitable.[18] It seems that the Conciliation Commission sought to close the Lausanne Conference with a declaratory achievement on the refugee issue that would assist the economic survey mission to carry out its task.

The rival parties, however, refused to commit themselves to the solution offered regarding the refugee problem and declined to declare officially that, in the end, their governments would accept the economic survey mission's recommendations. In addition, the Arabs felt uncomfortable with the separation of the refugee issue from the borders issue, which they felt had been neglected.[19]

The failed attempt by the Conciliation Commission to cajole the sides into signing an agreed-upon declaratory draft symbolized all the more cogently the hopelessness of continuing down the Lausanne path. It was clear to the Americans that the conference, which championed the political approach over the new economic approach, should be brought to a close forthwith. Now, at the outset of September, the State Department urged the Conciliation Commission to close the Lausanne Conference as soon as possible. Breaking off talks, the commission was told, would emphasize even more the importance of the economic survey mission. Moreover, if the talks were drawn out, the rival parties were liable to stiffen their positions even more, thus making the work of the mission more difficult.[20]

The Americans' intention to try to solve the Palestinian refugee problem through economic means was acceptable to the British. The resounding failure of Lausanne strengthened opinions within the Foreign Office that the solution to the refugee problem was to be found in resettlement and that, to implement this principle, a comprehensive economic approach was needed. This orientation was voiced at a gathering that convened in London at the end of July 1949, at which senior government officials and senior military brass conferred with British representatives in the Middle East to examine developments in the region since 1945.[21]

Among the topics was the Arab-Israeli conflict, including the refugee problem. Discussion dealt primarily with two aspects: aid and resettlement. The question of repatriation was considered of marginal importance. The United Kingdom's minister in Amman, Sir Alec Kirkbride, reported on a plan for a British-funded survey that would examine the feasibility of irrigating vast stretches of the Jordan Valley to settle as many refugees as possible there. Deputy Director-General of the Foreign Office Michael Wright told the gathering that Foreign

76   *Shifting the emphasis for solving the refugee problem*

Minister Bevin hoped France would assist Britain in its efforts to convince Syria to resettle refugees in its domain. The British ambassador in Baghdad, Sir Henry Mack, related that his embassy had examined all sorts of options to settle refugees in Iraq, and presently the embassy believed that it was possible to settle tens of thousands of them in agricultural areas of Iraq. Wright closed discussion of the Palestinian refugee issue stating that "one of the primary missions of His Majesty's representatives in the Middle East would be to encourage the resettlement of the Arab refugees."[22]

At the outset of September, just before the economic survey mission was due to embark on its mission, the British reiterated and clarified to Washington their position on the refugee issue, as they had done on the eve of the Lausanne Conference. London argued that the Arabs needed to know that sooner or later they would have to absorb the overwhelming majority of refugees. They suggested to the Americans that the willingness of the western countries to provide financial aid for "resettlement programs" be emphasized to the states of the region (i.e. to the Arab states).[23]

Not surprisingly, the British approach to resolution of the refugee problem was well received in Israel. In a cabinet meeting held towards the close of August, Sharett expressed his support for British representatives participating in the economic survey mission, saying: "As strange as it may be, it is possible [...] that there may be parallel interests on this point [the refugee issue] between us and the English." The minister argued that the British were interested in reconstructing their stature in the Middle East, and promotion of large-scale development programs for (Arab) states in the region (that would include resettlement of refugees) was viewed as one of the avenues to achieving this goal.[24]

On 12 September, the Conciliation Commission took its final action at the Lausanne Conference, sending the delegations its response to their remarks made vis-à-vis the 15 August questionnaire. The commission believed that if the sides would continue to stand firm on their current political positions, it would be almost impossible in the future to make progress towards a settlement. In regard to the refugee problem, the commission clarified that it would be ineffective to formulate proposals on the issue at this stage, since the economic survey mission was slated to examine the issue in the near future.[25] The Israeli response to the commission's memorandum only arrived on 27 October. It contained nothing new. Israel reiterated and stated emphatically that it would assist in resolving the refugee problem only if a comprehensive peace settlement would be established in the region and as part of a permanent solution to the Arab refugee problem. Even if such conditions would arise, it was argued in Israel's letter of response, in light of security concerns, there would be no possibility of returning a large number of refugees to Israeli territory.[26]

The course of the Economic Survey Mission

On 23 August 1949, the Conciliation Commission officially established the Economic Survey Mission for the Middle East.[27] Three days later, on 26

Shifting the emphasis for solving the refugee problem 77

August, the United Nations Secretariat at Lake Success and the White House in Washington announced that Gordon Clapp, chair of the Tennessee Valley Authority executive, had been appointed director of the mission.[28] Three deputy-directors were appointed – one British, one Turkish, and one French – accompanied by a team of engineering, agriculture, and economics specialists.[29]

On 1 September, the Economic Survey Mission received its letter of appointment from the Conciliation Commission, detailing its objectives. According to the document, the mission had been established to examine the economic situation among the states that had participated in the 1948 war and to offer recommendations that would make it possible (a) to advance development programs that would assist the countries of the region to overcome the economic damages caused by the war; (b) to assuage the refugees' repatriation and resettlement, as well as their rehabilitation from an economic and social perspective, and arrange the matter of compensation; (c) to promote economic conditions that would help keep peace and stability in the Middle East. The mission was also instructed to recommend a course of action that would delineate the way to realize all the projects it recommended. Likewise, it was requested to estimate the overall cost of the projects.[30]

On 11 September, the Economic Survey Mission set out for the Middle East. Its first stop was Beirut, where the mission established its headquarters. During the first four weeks of its work, the mission's members visited Syria, Lebanon, Jordan, Egypt, and Iraq, conducting meetings with the political and professional echelons to assess the economic and social state of each country.

On 9 October, the mission met for the first time with members of the Israeli government. The latter viewed the Economic Survey Mission's visit to Israel as a suitable opportunity for promoting the position that favored resettlement of the overwhelming majority of Palestinian refugees in the Arab states. Those participating in the talks from the Israeli side were Foreign Minister Sharett, Minister of Finance Eliezer Kaplan, and several officials from their ministries. Clapp reported to his hosts that the distress of the refugees was great, and it was imperative to quickly find a solution.

A political solution, which was liable to take a long time to be implemented, did not answer this necessity. It was therefore suggested that assistance continue, parallel to formulation of a program that would provide employment opportunities for as many refugees as possible "in the places where they are situated at present." Clapp knew that, in practice, this plan of action constituted realization of the principle of resettlement. However, in its letter of appointment the mission had been mandated to address the principle of repatriation as well. Consequently, Clapp was forced to point out to the Israelis that this program did not cancel out the validity of UN Resolution 194(3) and the principle of repatriation it entailed. In light of the above, he requested that Sharett detail the Israeli leadership's position on this issue in order to ascertain whether there had been any change in the Israeli position. The foreign minister's reply clarified that Israel's position stood firm: for its part, Israel held that resolution

78 *Shifting the emphasis for solving the refugee problem*

of the refugee problem didn't rely on repatriation; it rested on resettlement. Sharett promised Clapp that the director-general of the Ministry of Finance, David Horowitz, would expand on this in the second session between the parties.

Following these remarks, and directly linked to them, the minister pointed to the Israeli government's proposal two and a half months earlier regarding the return of 100,000 Arabs to the State of Israel and told Clapp that this offer was no longer valid. The government, he explained, raised this offer in order to try and achieve a breakthrough in talks during the Lausanne Conference, which had reached an impasse. The offer, however, had met fierce criticism in Israel, both among the public at large and particularly among specialists in the field. Implementation of the proposal, he added, would create "unending difficulties and complications" inside the State of Israel: it would lead to perpetual friction (between the Jews and the Arabs citizens), a sense of insecurity, and financial problems. Moreover, the contribution of "the 100,000 Proposal" to the permanent resolution of the refugee problem would be marginal since it addressed only several tens of thousands that would be absorbed in Israel out of the hundreds of thousands of refugees who would still remain in the Arab countries. Besides this, Israel linked its contribution to resolving the refugee problem to a comprehensive peace settlement, which would solve the entire refugee problem. If this proviso (that is, peace) still didn't exist, Israel had no obligation to try and bring about a solution to the refugee problem.

At the end of his comments, Sharett touched briefly on the question of compensation. He reiterated that Israel was willing to pay compensation for abandoned Arab lands but preferred to pay a lump sum to a fund that would deal with resettlement of the refugees. Having said that, Israel also demanded compensation for the war damage the Arabs caused Israel.[31]

On 10 October, the Economic Survey Mission and Israeli representatives held their second session. Director-General of the Ministry of Finance David Horowitz presented select demographic, geographic,and economic data substantiating Israel's argument that Iraq, Jordan, and Syria could absorb all the Palestinian refugees relatively easily. Clapp responded that in the eyes of the survey mission it was secondary whether the program that it was outlining for employment of refugees would impact on their final place of settlement.[32] The subtext of this remark, along with Clapp's statement the previous day that the refugees would be employed "in the places where they are situated at present," indicated that the conviction had taken root among members of the mission that the refugees would be forced by economic realities to rehabilitate themselves in the Arab countries. Further evidence of this orientation can be seen in the fact that during all of its sessions in Israel, the survey mission didn't raise the idea of or a proposal for a refugee employment plan within Israel even once.

The third session between Israeli representatives and members of the Economic Survey Mission took place several hours after the second one and focused primarily on the number of internal refugees situated within Israeli territory. Family reunification and refugees' blocked bank accounts were also briefly discussed.[33]

A week after the Economic Survey Mission's visit in Israel, the mission's secondary committee of specialists arrived in order to continue to discuss the refugee issue.[34] In a meeting with Israeli representatives headed by Horowitz, they requested to know whether "the 100,000 Proposal" still stood. It is possible that Clapp had not updated them regarding the negative response he had already received from Sharett; on the other hand, it is possible that they sought to determine whether Israel had indeed decided to bury the initiative once and for all. Horowitz replied that the Israeli public was adamantly opposed to the plan. Besides that, security and economic factors indicated that it would be best to settle the 100,000 in the territory of the Arab states, and not in Israel.[35]

Thus a mere three months after "the 100,000 Proposal" was first floated, the most far-reaching concession ever offered by the State of Israel regarding the repatriation issue was taken off the political agenda. This was a signal of things to come. A number of weeks later, on the eve of 1950, Israeli officials ceased completely to voice any Israeli willingness to discuss repatriation of a small number of refugees "in the framework of a peace settlement." According to the Israelis, from this point onward, the rehabilitation of the whole Palestinian refugee population was supposed to be implemented solely in the Arab states. Israel was prepared to allow only a token number to enter, several thousand individuals at the most, within the framework of family reunification and on humanitarian grounds. One could hardly expect Israel to continue to adhere to the principle of repatriation when the American outlook on the issue was taking important steps in the direction of the Israeli position. By adopting an economic approach to solving the refugee problem, Washington entrenched the resettlement principle in practice, since it was clear to anyone that from a purely economic standpoint, rehabilitation of the refugees in the Arab states was far more viable than their rehabilitation in Israel. Against such a backdrop, one shouldn't be surprised that Washington didn't try to pressure Tel Aviv to retract its decision to withdraw and bury "the 100,000 Proposal," just as the administration discontinued its former demands that Israel absorb 200,000 to 250,000 refugees, as it had done during the Lausanne Conference.

On 16 November 1949, the survey mission submitted an interim report to the United Nations General Assembly. A considerable part of the report was dedicated to presenting development programs designed to employ refugees. At the same time, these programs dealt with small-scope infrastructure projects that, by nature, were designed to last only a short while. The mission claimed that the dire distress of the refugees required immediate employment initiatives that would not require lengthy preparations. Yet it also appears that the survey mission refrained from offering large infrastructure projects to the refugees in Arab states that could employ refugees for an extended period

80 *Shifting the emphasis for solving the refugee problem*

because it feared that Arab capitals would view such projects as an unofficial declaration vis-à-vis resettlement of the refugees. Clapp, however, updated the State Department that the survey mission believed that the employment programs, which at present were designed solely for the short term, would, in the future, be integrated into larger broad-scale economic development projects.[36]

According to the interim report, *all* the economic enterprises proposed (most in the agricultural and transportation domain) would be carried out in the Arab states: first and foremost in Jordan, but also in Syria, Lebanon, and Egypt (the Gaza Strip). Not one project was tied to Israel. Thus, the position that crystallized among members of the survey mission – an assessment that the refugee problem could be resolved only in Arab territory – was officially expressed in the projects that the mission recommended. In this spirit, the mission stated that "the opportunity to work will increase the number of practical options before the refugees, and therefore will encourage a more realistic view as to the type of future they desire and can achieve." In other words, the minute the refugees would find a livelihood (in the Arab countries) they would conclude by logic that their future lay there.

To implement the relief and works programs in the Arab states, the Economic Survey Mission proposed the following actions be taken:

1 Relief for the refugees through the auspices of UNRPR would continue until 1 April 1950. The number of persons eligible for relief would be reduced, once bogus refugees were weeded out and refugees entered the work force. Relief aid would cease completely on 31 December 1950, unless the United Nations stipulated otherwise at the 5th General Assembly;
2 By 1 April 1950, a new United Nations agency would be established to replace UNRPR, and it would handle the relief and works program for the Palestinian refugees. The new agency, which was to be located in the Middle East, was supposed to be a fully independent body mandated to make its own decisions within its operational domain. Likewise, the personnel and equipment of UNRPR would be put at the disposal of the new body;
3 On 1 April 1950, the new agency would begin to operate work programs for refugees. These would continue until 30 June 1951 (unless the 5th General Assembly would decide otherwise). The cost of the relief and work programs would be 53.7 million dollars – 19 million allocated to relief, 34.7 million to work initiatives.[37]

On 30 November 1949, the Ad Hoc Political Committee of the United Nations began to discuss the interim report of the Economic Survey Mission. At the end of three days of consultations during which minor changes were made in the document, the committee confirmed and accepted the report with an absolute majority of 48 states in favor, none against, and 6 abstentions.[38]

The revised draft was brought before the General Assembly, which ratified it on 8 December with the support of 47 states in favor, none against, and 6 abstentions. Resolution 302(4) established the United Nations Relief and

Works Agency for Palestine Refugees in the Near East (UNRWA). The duties of the new agency were: (a) to execute, in collaboration with local governments, relief and work programs such as those suggested by the Economic Survey Mission; and (b) to discuss with interested Middle Eastern governments steps they could take for the future, when international assistance for relief and work would no longer be offered. The resolution also mandated the establishment of an advisory commission that would assist the UNRWA in its operations. The advisory commission was comprised of representatives from the United States, Britain, France, and Turkey and was authorized to add three more members from states contributing to the UNRWA's maintenance.[39] The UNRWA's director was required to submit an annual report to the United Nations General Assembly on the agency's operations and accounts.[40]

On 18 December 1949, the Economic Survey Mission completed its final report, and ten days later the Conciliation Commission authorized its publication. The report repeated, without detail, the development and employment programs that were already cited in the interim report and emphasized the linkage that existed between economic development of the states in the region and peace and stability in that area.[41]

At the outset of March 1950, the Secretary-General of the United Nations announced the appointment of Canadian Colonel Howard Kennedy as director of the UNRWA, and on 17 April the agency staff held its first meeting in Geneva. A week later, the UNRWA established its Middle East headquarters in Beirut, and on 1 May – a month later than planned – the UNRWA began to operate.

The Palestinian refugees were the only group in the world with a United Nations agency of its own. Tens of millions of other refugees around the world – members of various races, religions, and nationalities, who had been uprooted by wars and natural disasters – were the responsibility of one single body, the United Nations High Commissioner for Refugees (established in December 1950).[42] Such unique treatment of the Arab-Palestinian refugees reflected the complexity of the Arab-Israeli conflict and the political, religious, and emotional powder keg it constituted in the eyes of the international community.

The role of the UNRWA from a British perspective

A short time after publication of the interim report recommending establishment of the UNRWA, the Foreign Office and British Treasury in London opened discussions designed to determine what would be the financial contribution of the United Kingdom to the new body. Officials at the British Treasury recommended that two-thirds of the sum (that had yet to be set) would be transferred only if the funds would be dedicated to plans designed to resettle the refugees. Officials at the Foreign Office, who already sided with rehabilitating the Palestinian refugees in Arab territories, gave their blessings

82 *Shifting the emphasis for solving the refugee problem*

to this proposal.[43] Moreover, they believed that it had to be emphasized to the Arab governments that the refugees would receive no international financial assistance after June 1951. Such a statement of intent, they believed, would force Arab rulers to agree to the execution of broad-scale development projects in their territories that could solve the refugee problem.[44] In this context, Clapp updated British officials that the UNRWA would hammer out agreements with Arab governments that would lead to the gradual transfer of responsibility for relief and work programs from the agency to the governments themselves. This transfer of responsibility, said Clapp, would prepare the Arab governments for implementation of long-term economic development programs in their territories.[45]

In contrast to the British, the Americans refrained from establishing a clear-cut linkage between the financial aid that the United States would be giving the UNRWA and advancement of resettlement programs. Secretary of State Acheson sought to clarify to his colleagues in London that it was illogical that contributing states insist that a certain sum out of their contribution be earmarked for a specific objective – for example, resettlement. It would be best, Washington argued, for the UNRWA's director and its advisory commission decide how to allocate the money.[46]

At the same time, Acheson and his people in the State Department understood that the approach they championed – that is, resolution of the refugee problem via economic means – was in itself, in essence, what truly drove the principle of resettlement, and the UNRWA had, in practice, been assigned the task of realizing this principle.

Towards the end of February 1950, following completion of the Economic Survey Mission's work, and the pending establishment of the UNRWA, a report was composed at the State Department that sought to examine, among other things, the Palestinian refugee issue. According to the report the concept of resettlement gained momentum due to:

> [the] growing realization in the Arab states that the return to their homes of the majority of the refugees is physically impossible and [due to] the acceptance by the Arab states of the refugee relief and works program recommended by the United Nations Economic Survey Mission.

The works program that the UNRWA was to operate would bring about the resettlement of many of the refugees:

> While the program envisaged by this resolution [Resolution 302(4)] does not furnish a political solution of the Arab-Israeli dispute concerning repatriation and resettlement of refugees, it does foresee the end of international assistance for direct relief and, by assisting the Arab countries to integrate the refugees into the local economy, it paves the way for future resettlement for many of these people.[47]

Shifting the emphasis for solving the refugee problem   83

Washington was well aware of the UNRWA's role in advancing the resettlement principle, but it sought to play this down so as not to arouse the anger of the Arabs who were committed, at least in theory, to the concept of repatriation.

In mid March 1950, the British Foreign Office completed preparation of a comprehensive report that examined the planned operations of the UNRWA. In the report, the British representative on the UNRWA's advisory commission, Sir Henry Knight, was given directives concerning the approach the new agency should take in its contacts with Arab governments. In public declarations, the document said, the UNRWA would emphasize that it did not engage in political aspects of the refugee problem, but in private talks with leaders in Arab capitals the agency could cite that, in its opinion, a solution that called for the repatriation of a large number of refugees was clearly unrealistic. Even if Israel would agree to the principle of repatriation, after all "there is no longer enough living space for them in Israel." Therefore, "the Arab statesmen have [...] to think in terms of resettlement." Resettlement, the document stated, could succeed only if the economies of the Middle East would be developed. This development must be done by the Arab governments themselves. The UNRWA, for its part, would assist them with technical advice and financial help. The agency, Knight was instructed, must explain to these governments that it cannot promise in the name of the UN or in the name of any member-state of the organization that financial assistance would continue after June 1951. The agency must clarify that, in its personal opinion, the probabilities were slim that assistance would continue after this date. Arab governments must therefore understand that at the close of this period, the refugees would be their full responsibility. Consequently, every effort must be made to ensure that the development programs (in the Arab countries) would include projects that would ensure opportunities for resettlement of the refugees. In London's opinion, projects of this kind could be implemented in the Kingdom of Jordan right away, but they should aspire to implement similar projects in Iraq and Syria as well.[48]

In May, the British Foreign Office approached several western leaders and requested that their countries contribute to the UNRWA. All the letters were worded in a similar fashion and, in the opening, presented a short overview of the agency and its objectives. Among other things, the letter said that the UNRWA marked a passage from relief programs to employment programs directed towards the absorption of Palestinian refugees in the economies of the countries where they were currently situated. The UNRWA should be encouraged in regard to such operations, London told western leaders.[49] Thus, despite the apprehensions of the United States, Britain continued to work vigorously to harness the UNRWA to implementation of the principle of resettlement.

Notes

1 Sarah Lillian Botsai, *The United States and the Palestine Refugees*, Ann Arbor, MI: University Microfilms, 1972, p. 55.

84 *Shifting the emphasis for solving the refugee problem*

2 FRUS, 1948, V, pp. 1324–5, Memorandum by the Department of State to President Truman, undated; FRUS, 1948, V, pp. 1332–3, The Secretary of State to the Legation in Lebanon, 20 August 1948; FRUS, 1948, V, pp. 1465–6, Mr. Wells Stabler to the Secretary of State, 10 October 1948; FRUS, 1948, V, pp. 1477–8, The Secretary of State to the Acting Secretary of State, 14 October 1948; FRUS, 1948, V, pp. 1478–80, Memorandum by the Department of State to President Truman, 15 October 1948; FRUS, 1948, V, pp. 1486–7, The Special Representative of the United States in Israel (McDonald) to President Truman, 17 October 1948; FRUS, 1949, VI, pp. 663–5, The Acting Secretary of State to the President, 14 January 1949.

3 FRUS, 1949, VI, p. 806, The Secretary of State to the Consulate General at Jerusalem, 9 March 1949.

4 DEPI, Vol. 2, Document 526, W. Eytan to M. Sharett, 30 April 1949. A representative from one of the American relief agencies providing assistance to the Palestinian refugees had already noted in March that the "general reports" he was hearing in diplomatic circles indicated that programs for the resettlement of refugees in Trans-Jordan and Iraq were being planned. "It has been my impression," he wrote, "that this type of solution to the problem is very appealing to [the] Americans especially." Benjamin N. Schiff, *Refugees unto the Third Generation: U.N. Aid to Palestinians*, Syracuse, NY: Syracuse University Press, 1995, p. 17.

5 DEPI, Vol. 4, Document 8, W. Eytan to M. Sharett, 5 May 1949, Note 7.

6 ISA, MFA 2441/10, A Report Submitted to the Conciliation Commission on 20 August 1949.

7 FRUS, 1949, VI, pp. 1064–5, The Acting Secretary of State to the Legation in Switzerland, 27 May 1949; FRUS, 1949, VI, pp. 1218–21, Memorandum by the Assistant Secretary of State for Near Eastern and African Affairs (McGhee) to the Secretary of State, 13 July 1949.

8 DEPI, Vol. 4, Document 164, R. Shiloah to M. Sharett, 31 July 1949.

9 ISA, MFA 2442/8, M. Sharett to R. Shiloah, 2 August 1949.

10 DEPI, Vol. 4, Document 226, Meeting: A. Feinberg – P. Porter (New York, 16 August 1949), 18 August 1949; DEPI, Vol. 4, Document 287, E. Elath to W. Eytan, 14 September 1949; ISA, 7561/11 A, Foreign Affairs and Defense Committee Meeting, 9 November 1949, p. 10; Rony E. Gabbay, *A Political Study of the Arab-Jewish Conflict – The Arab Refugee Problem (A Case Study)*, Geneve: Librairie E. Droz, 1959, pp. 262–3.

11 FRUS, 1949, VI, p. 1315, Memorandum by the Assistant Secretary of State for Near Eastern and African Affairs (McGhee) to the Secretary of State, 16 August 1949.

12 DEPI, Vol. 4, Document 177, E. Elath to W. Eytan, 3 August 1949; DEPI, Vol. 4, Document 211, U. Heyd to M. Sharett, 14 August 1949.

13 FRUS, 1949, VI, pp. 1317–18, The Secretary of State to Certain Diplomatic and Consular Offices, 16 August 1949.

14 M. Kolinsky, "The Efforts of the Truman Administration to Resolve the Arab-Israeli Conflict," *Middle Eastern Studies* 20(1), 1984, p. 81.

15 DEPI, Vol. 4, Document 213, E. Sasson to M. Sharett, 15 August 1949.

16 DEPI, Vol. 4, Document 249, E. Sasson to M. Sharett, 28 August 1949; DEPI, Vol. 4, Document 255, R. Shiloah to C. de Boisanger, 31 August 1949; Gabbay, *A Political Study*, pp. 259–60.

17 Ruth Ninburg-Levy, "The Arab Position at Lausanne Conference, 1949," MA thesis, University of Haifa, 1987, pp. 141–2 (Hebrew).

18 DEPI, Vol. 4, Document 264, E. Sasson to M. Sharett, 5 September 1949; DEPI, Vol. 4, Document 265, E. Sasson to M. Sharett, 5 September 1949.

19 DEPI, Vol. 4, Document 267, E. Sasson to M. Sharett, 6 September 1949; Neil Caplan, *Futile Diplomacy: The United Nations, The Great Powers and Middle East Peacemaking, 1948–1954*, Portland, OR: Frank Cass, 1997, pp. 119–20.

Shifting the emphasis for solving the refugee problem 85

20 FRUS, 1949, VI, p. 1369, The Secretary of State to the United States Delegation at Lausanne, 8 September 1949.
21 UKNA, FO 371/75072, E9366, From Foreign Office to Cairo, 29 July 1949.
22 UKNA, FO 371/75072, E9045, FO Minute, 23 July 1949.
23 FRUS, 1949, VI, pp. 1342–3, The British Embassy to the Department of State, 1 September 1949.
24 ISA, Government Meeting, 30 August 1949, p. 7.
25 DEPI, Vol. 4, Document 281, Note by the Conciliation Commission to the Israeli Delegation in Lausanne, 12 September 1949.
26 ISA, MFA 3011/19, 27 October 1949.
27 Article 12 of resolution 194 (3) allowed the Conciliation Commission "to appoint such subsidiary bodies and to employ such technical experts, acting under its authority, as it may find necessary for the effective discharge of its functions and responsibilities under the present resolutions." George J. Tomeh (ed.), *United Nations Resolutions on Palestine and the Arab-Israeli Conflict, 1947–1974*, vol. 1, Washington, DC: Institute for Palestine Studies, 1975, p. 16.
28 Gabbay, *A Political Study*, p. 263.
29 Edward H. Buehrig, *The U.N. and the Palestinian Refugees*, Bloomington, IN: Indiana University Press, 1971, p. 33.
30 UNESM, A/1106, p. 29.
31 ISA, MFA 2447/15, Meeting of Economic Survey Mission and Representatives of Government of Israel, 9 October 1949.
32 ISA, MFA 3011/19, Meeting with the Economic Survey Mission, 10 October 1949.
33 ISA, MFA 2447/15, Meeting with the Economic Survey Mission, 10 October 1949.
34 ISA, MFA 2442/1, Information to Israel Representatives Abroad, 21 October 1949.
35 ISA, MFA 2442/1, Minutes of Meeting held in Tel Aviv on 18 October 1949 between Members of the United Nations Economic Survey Mission and Representatives of the Government of Israel.
36 FRUS, 1949, VI, p. 1505, Memorandum by the Department of State to the President, undated; Schiff, *Refugees*, p. 19.
37 UNESM, A/1106, pp. 16–28.
38 Joseph B. Schechtman, *The Arab Refugee Problem*, New York: Philosophical Library, 1952, p. 53
39 In 1953, three Arab countries – Syria, Egypt, and Jordan – joined the advisory commission, bringing the total number of commission members to seven. See D. Alexander, "U.N. Aid to Palestine Refugees," *The New East* 5(1), 1953, p. 9 (Hebrew).
40 Tomeh, *United Nations Resolutions*, pp. 18–20.
41 FRUS, 1949, VI, pp. 1548–51, Editorial Note.
42 Avi Beker, *The United Nations and Israel: From Recognition to Reprehension*, Lexington, MA: Lexington Books, 1988, pp. 49–50; Arlene Kushner, "The UN's Palestinian Refugee Problem," *Azure* 22, 2005, pp. 57–77.
43 UKNA, FO 371/75452, E1821/31, Comments on the Conditions Which the Treasury Have Suggested Should Be Attached to Our Further Contribution to Arab Relief, 9 December 1949.
44 Ilan Pappe, *Britain and the Arab-Israeli Conflict 1948–1951*, New York: St. Martin's Press, 1988, p. 153.
45 UKNA, FO 371/75452, E1821/31, Relief for Arab Refugees, 20 December 1949.
46 FRUS, 1950, V, p. 670, The Secretary of State to the Embassy in the United Kingdom, 5 January 1950.

86 *Shifting the emphasis for solving the refugee problem*

47 FRUS, 1950, V, pp. 763–4, Memorandum by the Acting Secretary of State to the Executive Secretary of the National Security Council, 27 February 1950.
48 UKNA, FO 371/82245, E1825/88, United Nations Relief and Works Agency for Palestine Refugees in the Middle East, 3 March 1950.
49 UKNA, FO 371/82236, E1822/26, Evans to Person, 23 May 1950; UKNA, FO 371/82236, E1822/28, Bevin to Van Zeeland, 26 May 1950.

4 The refugee problem and Abdullah's Jordan

According to UNRWA statistics, in June 1950 there were 506,200 Palestinian refugees registered in the Kingdom of Jordan. This number constituted 55 percent of the entire refugee population in the Arab states at the time. This ratio remained stable throughout the period under study – that is, until 1956.[1] From the data, it is clear that Amman's position on resolution of the refugee problem had decisive weight in any political settlement on this issue. Consequently, it would be fitting to dedicate a chapter to an in-depth overview of Jordan's moves regarding the refugee problem, an overview that, understandably, is associated with the relationship that existed between Jordan and Israel.

The underpinnings of Jordanian policy vis-à-vis the Palestinian refugee problem were set down by Jordan's first ruler, King Abdullah, whose position on the issue was a byproduct of his own national aspirations. From the time of his appointment by the British as emir of Trans-Jordan in April 1921, Abdullah nurtured a political-diplomatic master plan known as "Greater Syria," whose final objective was unification of Syria, Lebanon, Palestine, and Trans-Jordan into one united kingdom (or federation) under his leadership.[2] Abdullah raised such thoughts among senior British officials, who for the most part categorically rejected the idea.[3] The king's pressure on Britain to support his territorial aspirations amplified after the outbreak of the Second World War, and particularly after the fall of France in June 1940 and the establishment of a Vichy regime in Syria. Abdullah hoped to achieve a political breakthrough following the turmoil and realignment of forces wrought by the war, but the British stood firm in their opposition.[4] Besides Britain, several Arab states disassociated themselves from the monarch's plan. Hence, from 1946, Abdullah focused his endeavors on realizing more limited territorial gains – the annexation of Palestine to Trans-Jordan. In his eyes, this move was the first attainable step on the road to eventual realization of the "Greater Syria" concept as a whole.[5]

The 1948 war presented Abdullah with the opportunity to embark on the actualization of his national aspirations in this regard. Within weeks, his army, the Arab Legion (with the aid of an Iraqi expeditionary force), gained

88   *The refugee problem and Abdullah's Jordan*

control of most of the interior of Mandate Palestine (the West Bank). In the two years that followed, Abdullah took a series of actions designed to bring about the full annexation of the West Bank to Trans-Jordan. Already on 19 May 1948 a Jordanian military government was imposed on the regions occupied by Jordanian forces, and the Palestinian population was ordered to follow only its orders. On 6 March 1949, the military government was replaced by a civilian administration. Two months later, Palestinian ministers were included in the Jordanian cabinet for the first time. In June, Trans-Jordan's name was changed to the Hashemite Kingdom of Jordan, a step that was designed to signify to Palestinians that the kingdom was no longer limited to "one side" of the Jordan River.[6] On 20 December 1949 King Abdullah took the most important step of all on the road to the full integration of Palestinians, both refugees and non-refugees: legislation that made the West Bank subject to governmental authorities on the East Bank from an administrative standpoint. Moreover, the law stipulated that, from this point hence, all Palestinians in the kingdom had equal rights from a political standpoint to Jordanian citizens: they were given the right to vote and to be elected to the parliament, to receive Jordanian citizenship, and to hold a Jordanian passport. Parallel to this, the Ministry of Refugee Affairs that had been established several months earlier became unnecessary and was abolished by decree. In its place, a new office was established, called the Ministry of Development and Reconstruction. Its name indicated the king's wishes to see the Palestinian refugees resettle in his kingdom and become Jordanian subjects. Publication of the December law made Jordan the only Arab state to offer the Palestinian refugees full citizenship.[7]

On 11 April 1950, elections were held for a new Jordanian parliament that would represent both sides of the Jordan River; in their wake Palestinian representatives entered the parliament. Some two weeks later, on 24 April, the united parliament ratified annexation of the West Bank by the Kingdom of Jordan, thus consummating unification of the two "banks". Unification of the two territories and granting of Jordanian citizenship to Palestinians tripled the population of the Hashemite kingdom from 400,000 citizens to 1.3 million; 900,000 were Palestinians, about half of them refugees.[8]

The monarch's efforts to assimilate the Palestinian population within the Jordanian state led him to work vehemently towards their full integration into all civil frameworks. As noted, Palestinians were elected to the Jordanian legislature and served as ministers in the government. They held a host of positions in the public sector, include senior posts in the economic domain. At the same time, Abdullah sought to ensure that the Palestinians would never become a majority in core political bodies such as the cabinet and the parliament, and he saw to it that the Palestinians who were elected or chosen to serve in important institutions within the kingdom were loyal to him and his policies. In the first years following unification of the two banks, the number of Palestinians allowed to serve in the security forces, particularly the Arab Legion, was limited.[9]

The refugee problem and Abdullah's Jordan 89

Abdullah's sense of obligation to the Palestinian population and its absorption within the Hashemite kingdom was expressed most distinctly in his attitude towards and treatment of the refugee population. From the outbreak of hostilities in Palestine, the Jordanian government tried to assist the masses of refugees who arrived in territories under its responsibility. The first waves of war refugees that arrived from the cities of Tiberias, Beit Shaan, and Haifa were transported in Arab Legion trucks to Trans-Jordan. Most of the refugees were housed in temporary camps,[10] some took shelter in mosques, schools, hostels, and unoccupied homes. The government took steps to provide them with water and basic food stuffs. The authorities also assisted UN-sponsored aid agencies and private humanitarian aid organizations to establish their machinery within the kingdom, and extended help to these bodies to ease their operations on behalf of the refugees.[11]

Once the battles came to a close, Amman began to divert most of its efforts towards rehabilitation of the refugees throughout the kingdom. Contrary to the other Arab states, Jordan was not interested in keeping the refugees in temporary camps in order to derive political capital in the international arena.[12] Quite the opposite, Jordan sought their permanent absorption within the social, economic, and political fabric of the state.[13] In the end, however, due to financial and technical constraints and due to refugees' opposition to their own rehabilitation so as not to loose their eligibility for free assistance from UNRWA, Jordan was forced to agree that there would be refugee camps within its domain as well. Nevertheless, this fact did not prevent Jordan from taking vigorous steps to take resettlement programs forward. Already in June 1949, Amman submitted to the United Nations a practical program for rehabilitation of the refugees: preparation of a feasibility study for resettlement in the Jordan Valley.[14] Jordanian hospitality was so ardent that there were Palestinian refugees who left other Arab states for the Hashemite kingdom.[15]

At the time, the Israeli Ministry of Foreign Affairs judged that "on the question of resettlement and rehabilitation, Trans-Jordan possesses a special and firmer position than among the rest of the Arab states." Tel-Aviv concluded that Trans-Jordan operated "from the assumption that the refugees would remain in it."[16] This conclusion was not just the product of observations of what was taking place beyond Israel's eastern border; it was also the fruit of things the Israelis heard from King Abdullah himself in political contacts that took place at the outset of 1949. The king clarified to his interlocutors that the refugee problem was not important right now and after peace came it would solve itself. He said nothing about repatriation of the refugees.[17] The main issue that occupied the Jordanians in these talks was the territorial issue; the king and his representatives demanded parts of the Negev, an outlet to the Mediterranean Sea, and even expressed interest in the cities of Lod and Ramle.[18] A short time later, at the beginning of May, the king and his prime minister, Tawfiq Abu al-Huda, met at the Jordanian city Shuneh with Foreign Minister Sharett and the commander of the Jerusalem sector, Lieutenant Colonel Moshe Dayan. This time as well, Abdullah refrained from raising the

90 *The refugee problem and Abdullah's Jordan*

repatriation issue. For the most part, the conversation revolved around the issue of borders and a bit about the question of Jerusalem. When the refugee issue was mentioned, Sharett was quick to report to his hosts that the Americans planned to allocate large sums of money towards resettlement of the refugees in the Arab countries. Sharett added that Israel was prepared to assist and to augment the sums the Americans would allocate to Trans-Jordan, to ensure that the refugee matter would serve as an impetus for the economic development of the country. Abdullah and his prime minister chose not to take issue with Sharett's remarks, even indirectly.[19]

During the Lausanne Conference in the spring–summer of 1949, it had become admirably clear to Israel diplomats and their western colleagues that the Jordanians were far from enthusiastic about adopting the public position of the Arab states that demanded realization of the repatriation principle, and in fact the Jordanians sought implementation of the resettlement principle.

At the outset of the conference, Prime Minister Abu al-Huda met with the American chargé d'affaires in Amman, Wells Stabler. Abu al-Huda reported to his interlocutor that unlike the meeting in Beirut (that took place on 21 March 1949 between representatives of the Conciliation Commission and representatives of the Arab states), where "he adopted common line with other Arab states regarding repatriation principle," in separate talks with American officials Ethridge and McGhee, "he expressed willingness and awareness regarding resettlement principle." Al-Huda felt that "such parallel approach was realistic as on one hand it did not work against common line of Arab states and on other hand it did provide positive line in assisting PCC [Palestine Conciliation Commission] work out overall solution to [refugee] problem."[20] At the same time, sentiments in a similar vein, expressing support for the idea of resettlement, were being voiced by the Jordanians in the ears of the British.[21]

In the course of the Lausanne Conference, against the backdrop of deliberations taking place on the refugee question, Stabler spoke a number of times with King Abdullah about the issue and heard from him very decisive words in favor of the resettlement concept. In one case, the king expressed his desire to conduct a survey that would help determine suitable projects for resettlement of the refugees in his kingdom.[22] In another talk, Abdullah stated that all the Arab refugees should be resettled in the Arab states. He remarked that if a large number of refugees would be repatriated to Israel, they would be a constant source of friction between the Arab states and Israel, and in the end this would lead to a dangerous situation.[23] Several days later, Abdullah told Stabler that he wanted to establish a new government ministry that "would be charged with formulation plan to resettle refugees in Trans-jordan and Arab Palestine [the West Bank]." In addition to that, "each Trans-jordan village would be requested [to] take 10 percent refugees living in Hebron and Samaria districts where resettlement possibilities difficult."[24]

The head of the Israeli delegation to the Lausanne talks, Walter Eytan, stated in a report submitted to Foreign Minister Sharett that all the signs indicated that Trans-Jordan and Syria were prepared to accept refugees; although the two states would continue to exhibit "righteous recalcitrance" on the refugee issue, in the end, they would agree to "make a great 'concession' by taking the refugees and the dollars that go with them."[25] Eliahu Sasson, who was also a member of the Israeli delegation, put things in a similar spirit: "Trans-Jordan and Syria," he said, "want to keep the refugees with them in order to enjoy the American or international aid to develop this way and to become strong states that are able to sustain themselves from every standpoint."[26]

In the course of the Lausanne deliberations, two senior members of the Jordanian cabinet raised a demand that Israel relinquish territories under its sovereignty that initially had been slated for an Arab state under Resolution 181, so that Jordan could settle some of the refugees there.[27] This demand, however, almost dissipated by the close of the conference, and it is unlikely that it reflected the king's position. Abdullah was prepared to absorb Palestinian refugees in his country whether or not Israel would relinquish territory, since he viewed the integration of the refugees in his kingdom (together with the permanent residents of the West Bank) as a national goal in its own right.

The economic approach to resolution of the refugee problem; the approach that the Americans adopted after the failure of the Lausanne Conference, meshed well with Jordan's aspirations to bring about implementation of the resettlement principle. The government in Amman was cognizant that it would require huge investments of capital by foreign governments to rehabilitate the refugees and provide them with housing and employment. In the second week of October 1949, after he met with the members of the Economic Survey Mission, Sharett updated his colleagues in the cabinet that Jordan was very interested in executing the employment schemes that the mission suggested and that the Jordanians had submitted a very comprehensive plan to employ the refugees within the kingdom.[28]

Amman had taken steps to inform the western powers and the United Nations of its complete support for the economic approach to resolution of the refugee problem,[29] and the Economic Survey Mission could, without any apprehension, offer in its interim report many diverse employment plans that would be executed on the kingdom's territory. In fact, according to the mission's report, the majority of employment programs in the Middle East were supposed to be implemented in Jordan, where over time, in the mission's estimations, some 75,000 out of 77,000 able-bodied male refugees were supposed to be employed.[30]

The stout commitment of Abdullah's Jordan to the principle of resettlement was manifested in the course of the political negotiations that took place between Jordan and Israel in the winter of 1949–1950. Many research papers have been devoted to this historical affair.[31] In terms of the discussion in the work at hand, we will examine this affair from the perspective of the refugee problem.

Between 27 November 1949 and 7 March 1950, twelve rounds of talks in three stages took place between Israeli and Jordanian representatives, all on

92   The refugee problem and Abdullah's Jordan

Jordanian territory. The first stage of the talks lasted a month, from the closing days of November until the end of December 1949. The kingdom was represented primarily by Minister of the Royal Court Samir al-Rifa'i, and Israel was represented by the Ministry of Foreign Affairs' adviser on special affairs, Reuven Shiloah and by the director of the Middle East Division, Eliahu Sasson (who was appointed in December 1949 to be the Israeli representative in Turkey).[32] The focus of deliberations was on territorial issues. The Palestinian refugee problem was not on the agenda at all.[33] On 13 December the two sides reached an agreement for a draft treaty that included four clauses, all relating to territorial issues.[34] Ten days later the agreement was dropped due to differences of opinion about the width and exact location of an overland corridor from the West Bank to the Mediterranean, a corridor that Israel was supposed to transfer to Jordanian hands.[35]

The two sides renewed their meetings towards the end of January 1950. Participating in the meetings were Shiloah and Moshe Dayan (the latter, the IDF general staff officer responsible for the armistice agreement), and al-Rifa'i and Jordan's defense minister, Fawzi al-Mulqi. This time, discussions focused on the future of Jerusalem. The intention of the United Nations to bring about the internationalization of the city pressed the two countries to try and reach an agreement on dividing the city between them.[36] Among the topics discussed in this context was the question of the fate of Arab neighborhoods in Jerusalem that were in Israeli hands, and whose Arab residents had abandoned them during the 1948 war. The Jordanians demanded that several of those neighborhoods be handed over to them, and that residents of the others (that would remain in Israeli hands) receive compensation.[37] The Israelis clarified to the Jordanians that these neighborhoods would remain forever under Israeli sovereignty, but they expressed willingness to discuss giving compensation for abandoned property.[38]

At this juncture it became more and more apparent that Jordan very much wanted to receive compensation from Israel for property abandoned by Arab residents who had lived in Jerusalem and in the rest of the country. This issue occupied the Jordanians both in their contacts with officials in the State Department in Washington and in discussions they conducted with the Israelis. Abdullah raised this topic, apparently for the first time, in April 1949 in a telegram he sent to President Truman. The monarch brought to the president's attention the harsh economic straits of the Arab refugees and requested that Truman use his influence to return their abandoned property. At the same time, Abdullah refrained from mentioning the principle of repatriation.[39] In the second week of January 1950, in a discussion on the future of Jerusalem, the Jordan Minister in Washington, Yusuf Haikal, tried to interest George McGhee and other officials in the Middle East Department in the fate of Palestinian abandoned property.[40] Two weeks later, in another discussion Haikal held with American officials, the Jordanian delivered a message from Abdullah, expressing Amman's concern in light of reports in the Arab media that Israel intended to pass a law that would enable it to sell

The refugee problem and Abdullah's Jordan   93

the abandoned lands of Palestinian Arabs.[41] The media reports were referring to the Absentees' Property Law, subsequently passed by the Knesset on 14 March 1950.

The second stage of talks between the two states, as the previous one, came to naught. In a 17 February meeting that included King Abdullah, al-Rifa'i, Dayan, and Shiloah, Abdullah suggested that Israel and Jordan reach a temporary agreement, valid for a number of years, that would serve as a bridge between the armistice agreement, which didn't fulfill all the needs of the sides, and a peace agreement. The Jordanian monarch suggested Israel and Jordan sign a five-year non-aggression pact. The treaty he proposed contained seven clauses; two of them, five and seven, dealt with the compensation issue. In Clause 5, it was suggested that special compensation for their property be given to Arab residents of Jerusalem who become refugees in Jordan. In addition, it was stipulated that if Israel agreed to relinquish several Arab neighborhoods in Jerusalem, this "could render the attainment of the ultimate goal – a comprehensive peace – easier." In the seventh clause it was stated that every refugee or his representative would be allowed to enter Israel to make arrangements for (the disposal of) his abandoned property, whether by selling it or by another means.[42]

On 22 February, the Israeli cabinet discussed the draft treaty. Ben-Gurion and Sharett were in favor of the draft proffered, but remarked that there were still outstanding problems between the two states, such as the question of Israeli access to Mount Scopus and the Wailing Wall, that needed to be resolved through negotiation.[43] At the close of deliberations, the cabinet passed a decision approving the draft non-aggression pact.[44]

Two days latter, Shiloah and Dayan met with King Abdullah and two of his ministers, al-Rifa'i and al-Mulqi. The Israelis presented to their interlocutors the version that had been presented by the Jordanians on 17 February, in which several Israeli changes had been entered. The most important alteration was that the non-aggression pact would be subordinated to the armistice agreement between Israel and Jordon. In the section that dealt with compensation, the Israelis had entered several inconsequential changes. Discussion between the sides was tense. The king was eager to sign the draft, while his two ministers had many reservations and expressed their dissatisfaction with the document. In the end, the representatives of the two countries initialed the draft, which was defined as the "Preliminary Outline for a Non-Aggression pact."[45]

A harsh controversy took place in the Jordanian government in regard to the proposed pact. Many of the ministers repudiated it, primarily due to two aspects: the need to sign a new treaty in lieu of the existing armistice agreement; and the requirement, in light of the proposed agreement, to forge commercial ties between the two countries (a step that was totally contrary to the decisions of the Arab League). On the other hand, the ministers had no grievances with the king's conduct on the refugee issue – neither in general nor on the repatriation question in particular.

94   *The refugee problem and Abdullah's Jordan*

On 28 February, the Israelis and the Jordanians met again in order to discuss the draft of the non-aggression pact. Here again, Shiloah and Dayan represented the Israelis; al-Mulqi and Jamal Tuqan (the latter, Amman's former governor of the West Bank) represented Jordan, although Abdullah and al-Rifa'i were present during part of the meeting. The version that the Jordanians presented to the Israelis expressed the inability of King Abdullah to ignore the opposition he was encountering at home, and thus it reflected the reservations of the Jordanian ministers. In the clauses that dealt with compensation, the Jordanians had made one addition: a demand that the rights of land and property owners in the "Triangle," who had been separated from their property and lands as a result of the armistice lines ("economic refugees"), would be upheld. The changes (except for that about compensation) were totally unacceptable to Israel, and it refused to accept the new version. When no concurrence could be reached, the sides decided to adjourn and meet again at the beginning of March.[46] The strident opposition to the non-aggression pact. Abdullah had initiated, both within Jordan and in the Arab world in general, led the king to declare in a 7 March meeting with Dayan and Shiloah (also attended by al-Mulqi and Jordanian Interior Minister Sa'id al-Mufti) that the talks between the two countries would have to be postponed for the time being.[47]

Negotiations that took place between Amman and Tel Aviv from November 1949 until March 1950 proved without a shadow of a doubt that Abdullah was not interested in repatriating the Palestinian refugees in Jordan to Israel. The very fact that the king and his representatives did not demand even one discussion with the Israelis on this issue, and in any case didn't demand a repatriation clause be entered into the 13 December and the 24 February drafts, demonstrates that this was not the orientation of the Hashemite ruler. Abdullah and his envoys were riveted on the territorial question. Parallel to that there was the demand to receive compensation from Israel for the abandoned property of the Palestinians. The objective of the compensation was to ease Amman's burden rehabilitating the refugees who had found shelter in the Kingdom and to placate the refugees who had left considerable property behind and were pressuring the Jordanian government to work towards its return.[48]

Israel was prepared to expedite payment of compensation for abandoned property because it knew that this step could contribute to the achievement of a political settlement with the Hashemite kingdom that would solve, among other things, the refugee problem in the kingdom (through resettlement). Such an agreement, the Israelis judged, would deal a fatal blow to the idea of repatriation.[49] In a meeting of the Foreign Affairs and Defense Committee that took place at the end of January 1950, Sharett told the gathering that a settlement with the Kingdom of Jordan that would not include terms for repatriation would benefit Israel since "the Arab state closest [to Israel] and most crowded with this burden of the refugees [...] totally didn't insist that one of the terms would be what number of refugees we will accept." In the foreign minister's view, that would lead to the weakening of American pressure on Israel "to receive a considerable number of refugees."[50] Things in a similar spirit were written by Ben-Gurion in his diary, three weeks after the beginning of talks between Israel and Jordan.[51]

The halt in negotiations between the two states in March 1950 did not bring contact between them to an end, only their character changed. They no longer dealt with an attempt to reach a comprehensive peace between the countries; rather they focused on solving particular points of conflict – mostly territorial – and preventing the threat of war.[52] When the refugee issue was discussed, the Jordanians continued to demand, all the more forcefully, that Israel give them compensation for the refugees' property, first and foremost the property of the wealthy among them. The repatriation principle remained absent from the political agenda of the two countries. A host of remarks made by Jordanian officials, or at least attributed to them, testified that this absence was a bona fide pillar in Jordan's foreign and domestic policy, not a passing whim.

On 16 April 1950, Jerusalem District Commissioner in the Israeli Ministry of Interior Avraham Biran met with the United Nations press officer in Jerusalem, Hamilton Fisher. Fisher reported to Biran on the Conciliation Commission's impressions of its visit to Jordan. He related that Abdullah aspired to gain certain territorial concessions from Israel, but it would be possible to "work things out" with him on this issue. Also, the refugee problem wasn't as bad it seemed, since "it is known that Abdullah not only objects to repatriating the refugees to Israel, [he] will actually prohibit the return of the refugees."[53]

Ten days later, Abdullah met with Shiloah and Dayan in Amman. The king said to the Israelis that since the talks between the two countries last winter, he had come to the realization of how crucial an agreement that would settle relations between the two peoples was. In regard to the refugee problem, he clarified that he would stand firm on his decision not to allow any one of them to return to Israel. He stressed that the issue of compensation to property owners was extremely important in his view, since if compensation were to be paid, one of the factors that was liable to pull on the heartstrings of the refugees to return to Israel would be eliminated once and for all.[54]

In al-Rifa'i's opinion, as it was related to Israeli officials at the outset of May, Jordan would be able to negotiate a settlement with Israel and ignore the pressure Egypt was putting on Amman to cut off contact, only on condition that Israel was willing to make progress on two issues: territorial concessions (including an overland corridor between the West Bank and the Mediterranean Sea) and full payment of compensation to the refugees.[55]

On 2 October, on the eve of the 5th General Assembly, Abdullah met with Walter Eytan and Deputy Commander of the IDF Intelligence Department Lieutenant General Yehoshafat Harkabi. He told the two that he was sending a Jordanian delegation to the UN gathering to discuss two topics on which he was at odds with the all-Arab position: one of them was the Palestinian

96 *The refugee problem and Abdullah's Jordan*

refugee issue. In that context, Abdullah emphasized that he was opposed to repatriation of the refugees to Israel.[56]

At the end of the assembly, a member of the Israeli delegation, Gideon Rafael, sent a report to Eytan with an analysis of the Jordanian position as it had been presented by Jordan's education minister, Ahmad Tuqan, who served as a Jordanian observer at the 5th General Assembly. Rafael reported that in regard to "the refugee problem and the peace, [Ahmad Tuqan] was forced to take the traditional Arab position, but didn't express himself with excessive extremism." In addition, Rafael related a conversation he himself and Israel's ambassador in Washington, Abba Eban, had conducted with Tuqan after the close of the UN gathering. They clarified several points raised in the assembly's discussions, including the issues of Jerusalem and the refugees. In regard to the Jerusalem question, Eban reiterated to Tuqan Israel's consent to discuss payment of compensation for some of the Arab neighborhoods. As for the refugee problem, he pointed out Israel's willingness to pay compensation for abandoned Arab lands. Tuqan said that in his opinion a two-fold model needed to be found through which monies for such extensive assets would be funneled to each and every owner, but a lump sum would also be given (to the Jordanian government), earmarked for resettlement of masses of property-less refugees.[57]

The fate of the wealthy refugees also concerned the Jordanian representative on the Israeli-Jordanian Armistice Commission, Ahmad al-Khalil. In his estimation, the number of such (wealthy) refugees was only 15,000 to 20,000 persons, and Israel should allow them to return to its territory, he argued. At the same time, Israel should pay compensation so that Jordan could resettle the rest of the refugees who were property-less.[58]

Ambassador Eban believed that Israel should acquiesce to the Jordanian request and compensate wealthy refugees. Such a move, he argued, could contribute to a settlement between the two countries: the wealthy Palestinian refugees in Jordan, who carried much political clout, would assist in achieving an Israeli-Jordanian peace settlement if they would be promised they would receive fair compensation for the large amount of abandoned property left in Israel. In a telegram to the Ministry of Foreign Affairs Eban elaborated:

> I have the distinct impression that if we found it possible to pay compensation to [Palestinian] members of the Jordanian government and [Palestinian] members of the parliament for their abandoned estates in the State of Israel, we would encounter an entirely different attitude [towards Israel] from the one that exists today among such circles. It's possible that our own tendency to look at political affairs according to a general view leads us astray. [It is] the manner of Arab statesmen to see such affairs from a personal viewpoint, and to favor [their] private [personal] fate over the fate of the general public. In any case [...] it would be wise to cast this bread upon these waters. It is clear that this mission is very delicate and its execution demands no small measure of

diplomatic artistry, but you can be confident that you will find the way, if the decision is taken.[59]

Eban's appraisal received reinforcement from the Belgian consul in Jerusalem. The consul said to Avraham Biran that the attitude towards Israel of Azmi al-Nashashibi, a Jordanian of Palestinian origins who served as undersecretary of state in Amman, "emanated 70 percent from the fact that he had houses in Hebrew Jerusalem, and only 30 percent [from] objective hatred of Israel." He added that "Nashashibi, like other Arab officials, can be bought," and it would be worthwhile for Israel to take steps of this kind since al-Nashashibi wields much influence in government circles, and in the absence of a foreign minister in the kingdom, the undersecretary determined "many things on his own."[60]

Wealthy Palestinian refugees, including many who lived within the Hashemite kingdom, appealed daily to Israeli representatives, requesting their considerable assets be returned to them. In one such request, a long and emotion-filled appeal was submitted by Muhammad al-Taji to the counselor in the Israeli Legation in London, Mordecai Kidron. The minute the issue of compensation was arranged, wrote al-Taji, "nothing will stand in the way to peace." It was in Israel's interest to pay compensation as soon as possible to this group of refugees of great wealth. "Members of this group," explained al-Taji, "now hold or will hold in the future important political and economic positions in a number of important Arab states, and it is [in] Israel's interest to well placate them." At the end of the memorandum a list was appended of several refugee families who had left considerable assets behind in Israel and who were party to al-Taji's appeal.[61] In response to the appeal, Kidron commented that most outstanding in the appeal was the "lack of scruples and the greediness of the large land owners," but nevertheless he suggested that the Ministry of Foreign Affairs examine whether there was room to exploit "these weaknesses" in Israel's compensation policies. "There is no question," he said, "that a 'private' arrangement so to speak with land owners will contribute significantly to a settlement with the Arab states which suffer from ongoing pressure from these notables." But Kidron added that compensation to wealthy refugees would not solve the problem of the Palestinian refugee population, which was, for the most part, truly destitute.[62]

Eliahu Elath, Israel's Minister in London, like Counselor Kidron, thought that it was advisable that Israel weigh al-Taji's offer in a positive light. In a telegram to the Ministry of Foreign Affairs he wrote:

> The truth is that the primary disturbers for peace between us and Abdullah are not the refugee masses, but rather the functionaries [political hacks] operating among them, sitting in Jordan and exploiting their position as Jordanian subjects in order to undo the King's efforts to make peace with us. Isn't it worthwhile for us to pay compensation to a number of [wealthy refugee] families so that they will help us to arrive at an agreement with Abdullah?[63]

98 *The refugee problem and Abdullah's Jordan*

The idea of compensation for wealthy refugees did not sit well in the eyes of the Middle East Division of the Ministry of Foreign Affairs, which was responsible for the refugee issue. In the division's view, Israel should concentrate on mobilizing international assistance, particularly American and British, for the resettlement of the refugees in the Kingdom of Jordan. The division held that such an action on the part of Israel, and other actions besides this, would assist in easing the tensions between the two countries that had prevailed since talks between them were cut off in March 1950.[64] Ben-Gurion also did not believe in "compensation of the wealthy." In his estimation, all the Arabs, regardless of their socioeconomic status, were hostile to the Jewish state, and therefore nothing useful would be gained from compensating the rich and most respected among the refugees.[65]

On 23 January 1951, Foreign Minister Sharett announced in the Knesset that Israel was prepared to pay only collective compensation.[66] This announcement caused a major uproar among the wealthy refugees in Jordan who had hoped Israel would agree to give personal compensation. Moshe Sasson, an official in the Middle East Division, reported to Sharett on a conversation he held with King Abdullah's personal secretary, Abd al-Ghani al-Karmi. Sasson related that the Jordanian secretary had expressed great bitterness towards the Israeli minister's declaration and said that it constituted a blow to the chances of success in negotiations between Israel and Jordan, which had just been renewed. Al-Karmi also told Sasson that the Jordanian ministers who were supporting a peace settlement, and with whose knowledge and consent meetings between representatives of the two countries were now taking place, claimed that giving personal compensation could have been a very important achievement for Israel since it would have brought the support of the wealthy refugees for such a settlement. Now just the opposite was happening: a delegation of wealthy refugees that in recent weeks had more than once demanded that the government reach a peace settlement with Israel had now announced to the government that it did not intend to continue to demand this as long as the government of Israel didn't retract its stand on payment of collective compensation.[67] In an appendix to this report, Sasson placed in writing a number of his own comments regarding Israel's compensation policy. Among other things, he suggested "to personally and partially compensate a very limited number of wealthy [refugees] so the rest of the wealthy would see that all [anyone] who operate in keeping with Israeli interests is liable [likely] to receive his due."[68]

Suggestions of this nature were raised from time to time by different governmental elements. Thus, a governmental commission established in the summer of 1953 to examine the compensation issue as a whole suggested this in its conclusions.[69] However, the idea and its various ramifications were never discussed in depth in Israel, let alone carried out in practice. The rapid deterioration that took place in relations between Israel and its Arab neighbors weakened chances that the two sides would reach a settlement on one of the core issues that kept them apart, such as the question of compensation. In

The refugee problem and Abdullah's Jordan   99

addition, the great complexity of this issue (the scope of the abandoned property, its valuation, and identification of its owners) hardly contributed to the feasibility of implementing compensation.

Jordan's unqualified support of the resettlement principle was expressed as well in its behavior towards the UNRWA. A short while after its establishment, the UNRWA inaugurated intensive contacts with the government in Amman with the objective of taking the refugee employment programs forward. The American legation operating in Beirut, the location of the UNRWA's head-quarters, reported that King Abdullah suggested that the agency focus its operations in the Hashemite kingdom. The logic of the offer was clear: most of the refugee population resided in Jordan, and the royal house was an ardent supporter of the principle of resettlement. The UNRWA itself treated Jordan as a spearhead, with the best chances to begin work programs. The agency, however, judged that the absorptive capabilities of the country were likely to constrict its work.[70] The State Department in Washington thought the same. In its opinion, Jordan didn't have the economic resources to absorb hundreds of thousands of refugees within its domain. Nevertheless, the State Department hoped that the UNRWA's development projects would assist in the permanent resettlement of the largest number of refugees possible in Jordon.[71] The British representative on the UNRWA's advisory commission, Henry Knight, argued that although Amman "is eager to collaborate," it now understands that it cannot absorb all the half-million refugees that are situated on its soil.[72] Knight, however, quickly learned that this prognosis was fundamentally erroneous. In late May 1951, in a discussion he held with al-Rifa'i (who had become prime minister of Jordan), Knight stated that arrangements should be made for the transfer of 350,000 refugees from Jordan to Syria or Iraq since Jordan was unable to settle so many refugees in its territory. The earlier that Jordan, Egypt, Syria, and perhaps also Iraq would agree on resettlement plans and transfer of refugees among them, the better things would be. Al-Rifa'i, much to Knight's surprise, rejected hands down the idea of a transfer. In his opinion, this idea was not practical on two counts:

1 The refugees in Jordon were "Jordanian citizens," thus it would be hard to request that a foreign country such as Syria accept in its territory Jordanian citizens. Furthermore, it was unreasonable to expect that King Abdullah would agree to changing the citizenship of "Jordanian refugees" (term in the original) for Syrian citizenship.
2 Since the refugees in Jordan hoped that one day they would be able to return to their abandoned homes, they preferred to remain in Jordon, as close as possible to the border with Israel.

After hearing al-Rifa'i's remarks, Knight wrote to his superiors that it appeared the Hashemite monarch believed that his country could absorb an unlimited number of refugees.[73]

100 *The refugee problem and Abdullah's Jordan*

The UNRWA's first periodic report to the 5th General Assembly, submitted on 15 September 1950, praised Jordan for operating in full cooperation with the agency, without any unnecessary delays. Thus, Jordan was the first Arab state that began to implement work programs. Yet, despite all the good will, the kingdom still could not provide work for all the refugees in its realm, said the report.[74] According to the data, in mid September 1950, close to 14,500 refugees were employed in a host of UNRWA works in Jordan, Syria, Lebanon, and the Gaza Strip: 43 percent of them (6,216) were employed in Jordan. Another 3,125 refugees in Jordan worked paving roads throughout the country, thanks to a loan from the British government.[75]

At the outset of 1951, another chance of achieving a settlement between Israel and Jordan arose, albeit a more limited one. This opportunity was made possible, among other things, due to changes in the Hashemite kingdom's government. On 3 December 1950, Prime Minister Sa'id al-Mufti resigned, and the next day a new government was formed headed by Samir al-Rifa'i (who also served as foreign minister). Al-Rifa'i, a Palestinian by origin (born in Safed), was a seasoned statesperson of stature in the royal court who was considered a loyal supporter of the Hashemite dynasty. Unlike many others among Jordan's governing elites, al-Rifa'i took a conciliatory attitude regarding relations with Israel.[76]

Al-Rifa'i established a stable and moderate government that was not supposed to place obstacles in Abdullah's path to a political settlement with its western neighbor. Nevertheless, public pressure, primarily from Palestinians in the kingdom, against a settlement with Israel led al-Rifa'i to adopt a neutral stance towards Abdullah's peace efforts.[77]

Discussions designed to achieve a settlement between Israel and Jordan at the time began in the second week of January 1951 with a meeting between al-Rifa'i and Shiloah. These talks continued intermittently until the beginning of May of the same year. The objective of the talks was to achieve a limited political settlement within the framework of the armistice agreement. Talks between the two sides dealt primarily with territorial issues. In regard to the refugee question, the Jordanians sufficed with repeating their demand to receive compensation from Israel for Palestinian abandoned property in Jerusalem. Likewise, they requested that Israel free all the blocked Arab bank accounts in Israeli banks. Israel expressed willingness to free monies from the blocked accounts, but only after the talks on implementation of the armistice agreement's clauses made satisfactory progress. In the end, this attempt to reach an accord, the last during Abdullah's lifetime, came to naught.[78]

During the nine months since the last round of talks between Israel and Jordan were cut off in March 1950, until this point in time – the outset of 1951 – when the sides made another attempt to reach an accord, less ambitious than the previous one, the room to maneuver that the Hashemite monarch enjoyed had diminished considerably. Trans-Jordan's control over the Arab parts of Palestine and the absorption of hundreds of thousands of Palestinians in Abdullah's kingdom gave the Palestinians tremendous political clout, and

The refugee problem and Abdullah's Jordan 101

they exploited their power to rein in the king's attempts to arrive at a settlement with Israel that was liable to bring to an end their dreams of returning to their former homes. The Palestinians, who repudiated the king's peace polices, aligned themselves with opposition forces on the East Bank, and together they challenged Abdullah and his actions.[79] In March 1950, the king's opposition forces at home were strengthened from abroad; various details on the content of talks between Israel and Jordan began to leak out to the world press, leading Syria, Saudi Arabia, and first and foremost Egypt to attack Abdullah for his willingness to reach a peace with Israel.[80] The verbal attacks on Abdullah and his policies reached a peak in a meeting of the Arab League's council in Cairo, which opened on 25 March 1950 and closed on 13 April. The council rebuked Jordan for its secret ties with Israel, and for its intentions to annex the West Bank. King Abdullah did not want relations between Jordan and the Arab states to be overly tense, and he also sought to moderate their opposition to pending annexation of the West Bank. Consequently, he joined the League decision of 1 April that forbids members of the League to negotiate separately with Israel on a peace agreement, not to mention sign such an accord.[81]

Nevertheless, Abdullah and his followers continued to conduct (secret) contacts with Israel, and in the first months of 1951, as noted above, there was an attempt to take a settlement forward, although a partial one. Abdullah maintained a consistent approach not only with regard to a political settlement with Israel, but also with regard to the desired solution to the Palestinian refugee problem (i. e. resettlement). He did not retreat from this position concerning the refugee question even in the face of criticism he was subject to from some Arab states.[82] A series of remarks from members of his own government in the first half of 1951 demonstrated this consistency.

Thus, during a visit to Jordan by the head of the Iraqi government, Nuri al-Sa'id, in mid January 1951, Prime Minister al-Rifa'i urged his Iraqi colleague to see the importance of "reeducating the refugees to the idea that they could not return to their homes in Israel" and the need to convince other Arab states to agree to absorb the Palestinian refugees in their countries.[83] In a conversation that the French representative in the Conciliation Commission, de Boisanger, conducted with al-Rifa'i, the Jordanian argued that the United Nations could not force Israel to return the refugees to its territory. Moreover, al-Rifa'i underscored to de Boisanger that, if he had stood in the Israeli government's shoes, he would also have refused to accept the refugees. The primary role of the Conciliation Commission, al-Rifa'i clarified, was to achieve compensation for abandoned property.[84] The Jordanian finance minister expressed similar sentiments in talks that he held in late February and early March 1951 in London with British leaders. He told his British counterpart that monetary efforts should focus on the reintegration of refugees and not on extension of relief.[85] Later on, he expressed to the British foreign minister his discontent that the UNRWA had not yet executed a number of resettlement projects for refugees in the Kingdom of Jordan that had already been planned.[86]

102 *The refugee problem and Abdullah's Jordan*

In a lengthy conversation with Hamilton Fisher three weeks before his assassination (by a Palestinian on 20 July 1951), King Abdullah summed up his attempts to reach an accord with Israel. In his opinion, it would have been possible to achieve peace with Israel, had Israel agreed to make a few concessions on his behalf. Fisher commented that on the eve of elections in Israel (that were to take place on 30 July 1951), it was highly unlikely that the Israelis would offer concessions more far-reaching than those offered in the winter of 1949–1950. Abdullah hoped that the discussion (with Israel) would be renewed after the elections, but underscored that his people would not support his efforts to achieve an accord with the Jewish state if it would not agree to make several concessions: territorial adjustments on behalf of the kingdom in the "Triangle" or "somewhere else," and a corridor to the Gaza Strip "which then would become Jordan territory." As for the refugee issue, the Hashemite ruler said he understood that repatriation of the refugees or even full compensation was not possible. Yet, he said, the feelings of bitterness would be diminished if propertied refugees would be allowed to come to Israel for a limited period of time in order to arrange their affairs, and if they could at least receive the proceeds from their assets, if not their assets themselves. Such a solution, argued Abdullah, and a fair settlement of blocked Arab bank accounts in Israeli banks would enable many refugees to rehabilitate themselves elsewhere, outside Israel, and overcome their feelings of bitterness.[87]

Notes

1 More than 70,000 of the refugees settled on the eastern bank of the Jordan River, and the rest settled on its western bank. Maan Abu Nowar, *Jordanian-Israeli War, 1948–1951: A History of the Hashemite Kingdom of Jordan*, Ithaca, NY: Reading, 2002, p. 342; UNRWA, A/3686, p. 12.
2 Clinton Baily, *The Participation of the Palestinians in the Politics of Jordan*, Ann Arbor, MI: University Microfilms, 1972, p. 51; Yoav Gelber, *Jewish-Transjordanian Relations, 1921–1948*, London: Frank Cass, 1997, p. 15; Avi Plascov, *The Palestinian Refugees in Jordan, 1948–1957*, London: Frank Cass, 1981, p. 1; Dan Schueftan, *A Jordanian Option: The Yishuv and the State of Israel vis-à-vis the Hashemite Regime and the Palestinian National Movement*, Tel Aviv: Yad Tabenkin, Hakibbutz Hameuhad, 1986, pp. 38–9 (Hebrew).
3 Gelber, *Relations*, pp. 60–1; Joseph Nevo, *King Abdallah and Palestine: A Territorial Ambition*, Oxford: Macmillan, 1996, pp. 44–6.
4 Gelber, *Relations*, pp. 166–70; Schueftan, *A Jordanian Option*, p. 39.
5 Baily, *The Participation*, p. 61; Gelber, *Relations*, pp. 194–5; Nevo, *King Abdallah*, p. 56; Plascov, *The Palestinian Refugees*, p. 1.
6 Shaul Mishal, "The Conflict between the West and East Banks under Jordanian Rule and Its Impact on the Government and Administrative Patterns in the West Bank (1949– 1967)," PhD thesis, The Hebrew University, 1974, pp. 132–6, 151–6 (Hebrew); Plascov, *The Palestinian Refugees*, pp. 10–37.
7 Plascov, *The Palestinian Refugees*, pp. 44–5.
8 Mishal, "The Conflict," p. 122.
9 ISA, MFA 2402/9, Problems Regarding the Economic Rehabilitation of the Arab Refugees from Palestine, undated, p. 67; Mishal, "The Conflict," pp. 142–6; Baily, *The Participation*, pp. 89, 94.

The refugee problem and Abdullah's Jordan 103

10 Nevo, *King Abdallah*, p. 128.
11 Abu Nowar, *Jordanian-Israeli War*, p. 256; Robert L. Jarman (ed.), *Political Diaries of the Arab World: Palestine and Jordan, 1948–1965*, vol. 10, Slough: Archive Editions, 2001, p. 295; Nevo, *King Abdallah*, p. 148; Plascov, *The Palestinian Refugees*, pp. 42–3.
12 John Glubb, the commander of the Arab Legion, provided instructive commentary on the issue: "The fact remained that, eight years after the 1948 disaster, the number of refugees was still increasing [...] The excuse put forward for this failure was that the Arab governments wished to keep the refugees destitute, in order to maintain the Palestine problem as a live political issue. This charge may or may not have been true of some Arab governments in whose countries the number of refugees was negligible. It was certainly not true of the Jordan government as long as I knew it." John Bagot Glubb, *A Soldier with the Arabs*, London: Hodder and Stoughton, 1957, p. 324.
13 Amnon Kertin, "The Program for Rehabilitating Palestinian Refugees in the Eastern Ghor in the Kingdom of Jordan," *Studies in the Geography of Israel* 13, 1992, p. 51 (Hebrew).
14 UKNA, FO 371/75072, E9045, Minute, 23 July 1949; Laurie Brand, "Building the Bridge of Return: Palestinian Corporate Mobilization in Egypt, Kuwayt and Jordan," PhD thesis, Columbia University, 1985, p. 320.
15 Bulent Gokay (ed.), *British Documents on Foreign Affairs: Near and Middle East, 1951*, Vol. 2, London: Lexis Nexis, 2005, p. 90.
16 ISA, MFA 2566/13, News from Middle East Countries, 20 April 1949.
17 James G. McDonald, *My Mission in Israel, 1948–1951*, New York: Simon and Schuster, 1951, pp. 135–6.
18 Schueftan, *A Jordanian Option*, pp. 167–72.
19 DEPI, Vol. 4, Document 15, Meeting: M. Sharett – King Abdallah, 9 May 1949.
20 FRUS, 1949, VI, p. 963, The Chargé in Transjordan to the Secretary of State, 1 May 1949.
21 FRUS, 1949, VI, p. 969, The Ambassador in the United Kingdom to the Secretary of State, 3 May 1949. See, in this connection, George McGhee, *Envoy to the Middle World: Adventures in Diplomacy*, New York: Harper and Row, 1983, p. 40.
22 FRUS, 1949, VI, p. 1186, The Secretary of State to Certain Diplomatic and Consular Offices, 27 June 1949, Note 3.
23 FRUS, 1949, VI, p. 1231, The Secretary of State to Certain Diplomatic Offices, 16 July 1949, Note 2.
24 FRUS, 1949, VI, pp. 1247–8, The Chargé in Jordan to the Secretary of State, 23 July 1949.
25 DEPI, Vol. 4, Document 13, W. Eytan to M. Sharett, 9 May 1949.
26 DEPI, Vol. 4, Document 81, E. Sasson to S. Divon, 16 June 1949.
27 FRUS, 1949, VI, p. 963, The Chargé in Transjordan to the Secretary of State, 1 May 1949; DEPI, Vol. 4, Document 113, W. Eytan to M. Sharett, 1 July 1949.
28 ISA, Government Meeting, 11 October 1949, pp. 18–19.
29 King Abdullah asserted before the Economic Survey Mission that he "endorsed resettlement in Transjordan": FRUS, 1949, VI, p. 1416, The Minister in Lebanon to the Secretary of State, 1 October 1949. In a conversation that Clapp and his British deputy, Desmond Morton, held with British Foreign Office officials, Morton told those present that the Jordanian government was certainly prepared to cooperate with the Economic Survey Mission and with its (resettlement) plans: UKNA, FO 371/75092, E1103, FO Minute, 21 December 1949. A British Foreign Office memorandum, containing instructions for Henry Knight, the designated British representative on the UNRWA advisory commission, noted that Jordan had openly expressed its willingness to accept the principle of resettlement:

104 *The refugee problem and Abdullah's Jordan*

UKNA, FO 371/82245, E1825/88, United Nations Relief and Works Agency for Palestine Refugees in the Middle East, 14 March 1950.

30 ISA, MFA 2402/9, Problems Regarding the Economic Rehabilitation of the Arab Refugees from Palestine, undated, p. 19.

31 See, for example: Itamar Rabinovich, *The Road Not Taken: Early Arab-Israeli Negotiations*, New York: Oxford University Press, 1991, pp. 111–67; Schueftan, *A Jordanian Option*, pp. 190–200; Avi Shlaim, *Collusion across the Jordan – King Abdullah, the Zionist Movement and the Partition of Palestine*, Oxford: Clarendon Press, 1988, pp. 513–50; Shaul Zeitune, *Deterrence and Peace: Israel's Attempts to Arrive at a Settlement,* Tel Aviv: Tcherikover, 2000, pp. 123–75 (Hebrew).

32 For a review of the development of events during the first month of the talks, see: Rabinovich, *The Road Not Taken*, pp. 120–30; Schueftan, *A Jordanian Option*, pp. 195–202; Shlaim, *Collusion across the Jordan*, pp. 519–36; Zeitune, *Deterrence and Peace*, pp. 123–49.

33 Alec Kirkbride, *From the Wings: Amman Memoirs, 1947–1951*, London: Frank Cass, 1976, pp. 112–13; Zeitune, *Deterrence and Peace*, p. 134.

34 DEPI, Vol. 4, Editorial Note (p. 716).

35 BGA, BGD, 24 December 1949; Shlaim, *Collusion across the Jordan*, p. 530.

36 For a review of the development of events during the second phase of the talks see: Rabinovich, *The Road Not Taken*, pp. 130–3; Schueftan, *A Jordanian Option*, pp. 203–5; Shlaim, *Collusion across the Jordan*, pp. 537–40; Zeitune, *Deterrence and Peace*, p. 151.

37 FRUS, 1950, V, p. 729, The Ambassador in Israel (McDonald) to the Secretary of State, 7 February 1950.

38 DEPI, Vol. 5, Document 40, Meeting: M. Dayan and R. Shiloah – F. al-Mulqi (Shuneh, 24 January 1950).

39 FRUS, 1949, VI, p. 916, Editorial Note.

40 FRUS, 1950, V, pp. 681–2, Memorandum of Conversation, by the Assistant Secretary of State for Near Eastern, South Asian and African Affairs (McGhee), 11 January 1950.

41 FRUS, 1950, V, p. 702, Memorandum of Conversation, by Mr. Stuart W. Rockwell of the Office of African and Near Eastern Affairs, 24 January 1950.

42 ISA, MFA 4374/1, Ninth Meeting between Israel and Jordan, Held in Shuneh on 17 February 1950.

43 DEPI, Vol. 5, Document 100, M. Sharett to A. Eban, 19 February 1950, Note 4.

44 ISA, Government Meeting, 22 February 1950, p. 23.

45 ISA, MFA 2453/3, Compensation and Property in Arab Countries, 24 February 1950; DEPI, Vol. 5, Editorial Note (p. 139).

46 DEPI, Vol. 5, Document 112, Drafts of a Non-Aggression Agreement between Israel and Jordan, 28 February 1950, and Note 1.

47 DEPI, Vol. 5, Document 130, Meeting: R. Shiloah and M. Dayan – King Abdallah (Shuneh, 7 March 1950); Rabinovich, *The Road Not Taken*, pp. 140–3; Shlaim, *Collusion across the Jordan*, pp. 545–6; Zeitune, *Deterrence and Peace*, pp. 154–7.

48 DEPI, Vol. 5, Document 213, Meeting: R. Shiloah and M. Dayan – King Abdallah (Amman, 27 April 1950); ISA, Government Meeting, 8 February 1950, pp. 9–10.

49 See, in this context, Zaki Shalom, "Positions of Israeli Leaders Regarding the Territorial Status Quo – A New Perspective," *Iyunim Bitkumat Israel* 8, 1998, p. 132 (Hebrew).

50 ISA, 7562/1 A, Foreign Affairs and Defense Committee Meeting, 31 January 1950, pp. 12–13.

51 BGA, BGD, 14 December 1949.

52 Rabinovich, *The Road Not Taken*, pp. 111–12; Shlaim, *Collusion across the Jordan*, p. 550.

The refugee problem and Abdullah's Jordan   105

53 ISA, MFA 2441/3, Cable from A. Biran to the Foreign Minister, 16 April 1950.
54 DEPI, Vol. 5, Document 213, Meeting: R. Shiloah and M. Dayan – King Abdallah (Amman, 27 April 1950).
55 ISA, MFA 2565/11, On the Chances of an Agreement between Israel and Jordan, 6 May 1950.
56 DEPI, Vol. 5, Document 400, W. Eytan to the Israel Delegation to the United Nations, 2 October 1950.
57 DEPI, Vol. 5, Document 519, G. Rafael to W. Eytan, 28 December 1950.
58 DEPI, Vol. 6, Document 102, A. Biran to M. Sharett, 2 April 1951.
59 DEPI, Vol. 6, Document 12, A. Eban to W. Eytan, R. Shiloah, and S. Divon, 10 January 1951.
60 ISA, GL 17108/39, A. Biran to the Director-General of the Ministry of Foreign Affairs, 6 May 1952.
61 ISA, MFA 36/10, Compensation for Arab Land and Property in Israel, 20 November 1950.
62 ISA, MFA 36/10, Subject: Compensation to the Arab Refugees, 27 November 1950.
63 ISA, MFA 2445/A, Israel Minister to Great Britain to M. Comay, 11 April 1951. A cabled response sent by the British Commonwealth Division in the Ministry of Foreign Affairs to Kidron stated that al-Taji's property "no longer existed." The counselor was therefore asked to turn al-Taji away empty-handed. "When he comes to Israel [in order to have his property returned]," the division explained, "he will no doubt complain of theft and stir up a scandal." ISA, MFA 36/10, Subject: Compensation to al-Taji, 11 April 1951.
64 ISA, MFA 2565/22, On Arab-Israel Relations, 18 January 1951.
65 Zaki Shalom, *David Ben-Gurion, the State of Israel and the Arab World, 1949–1956*, Brighton: Sussex Academic Press, 2002, pp. 7–9.
66 *Knesset Minutes*, vol. 8, 23 January 1951, pp. 850–1.
67 DEPI, Vol. 6, Document 40, M. Sasson to M. Sharett, 31 January 1951.
68 DEPI, Vol. 6, Document 40, M. Sasson to M. Sharett, 31 January 1951, appendix.
69 On the circumstances of its establishment, see Chapter 9.
70 FRUS, 1950, V, p. 893, The Legation in Lebanon to the Secretary of State, 16 May 1950.
71 FRUS, 1950, V, p. 1097, Policy of the United States with Respect to Jordan, 17 April 1950.
72 UKNA, FO 371/82248, E1825/182, Knight to Evans, 24 August 1950.
73 UKNA, FO 371/91402, E1821/80, Knight to Evans, 28 May 1951.
74 UNRWA, A/1451/Rev. 1, p. 7.
75 UNRWA, A/1451/Rev. 1, p. 9.
76 Yaacov Shimoni and Evyatar Levine, *Political Dictionary of the Middle East in the Twentieth Century*, London: Weidenfeld and Nicolson, 1972, p. 328; Shlaim, *Collusion across the Jordan*, pp. 589–90; Zeitune, *Deterrence and Peace*, p. 125.
77 Shlaim, *Collusion across the Jordan*, p. 590.
78 DEPI, Vol. 6, Introduction, pp. XIV–XV; Schueftan, *A Jordanian Option*, pp. 221–4; Shlaim, *Collusion across the Jordan*, pp. 590–6.
79 Miriam Joyce Haron, *Palestine and the Anglo-American Connection, 1945–1950*, New York: Peter Lang, 1986, pp. 158–9; Shlaim, *Collusion across the Jordan*, p. 551; Zeitune, *Deterrence and Peace*, pp. 157, 168. See also on this subject: Mordechai Gazit, "The Israel-Jordan Peace Negotiations (1949–1951): King Abdallah's Lonely Effort," *Journal of Contemporary History* 23(3), July 1988, pp. 409–24.
80 Leaders in the Arab World already knew of the talks between Israel and Jordan in November of 1949, but they did nothing to stop them so long as the general public was unaware that they were being held. Rabinovich, *The Road Not Taken*, p. 153; Shlaim, *Collusion across the Jordan*, pp. 550–2.
81 Shlaim, *Collusion across the Jordan*, p. 554.

106 *The refugee problem and Abdullah's Jordan*

82 There were demands to sever relations with Abdullah's Jordan, "the country which betrays Islam and the Arab unity." Ronen Yitzhak, "The Assassination of King Abdallah: The First Political Assassination in Jordan: Did It Truly Threaten the Hashemite Kingdom of Jordan?"*Diplomacy and Statecraft* 21(1), 2010, p. 70.
83 UKNA, FO 371/91399, E1821/16, Kirkbride to Bevin, 18 January 1951.
84 ISA, MFA 2566/13, Samir al-Rifa'i's Comments During his Conversation with de Boisanger on 26 February 1951, 27 March 1951.
85 Gokay (ed.), *British Documents*, pp. 94–5.
86 UKNA, FO 371/91400, E1821/35, Evans to Knight, 1 March 1951.
87 FRUS, 1951, V, pp. 735–6, The United States Representative on the Palestine Conciliation Commission (Palmer) to the Secretary of State, 28 June 1951.

5 An exchange transaction

Paying compensation in exchange for the resettlement of the refugees

The Geneva talks

On 19 October 1949, a month after the failure of talks in Lausanne, the Conciliation Commission renewed its operations in New York. The Arabs demanded that the commission not limit itself, as it had in the past, to ferrying messages from side to side; rather, it should raise its own proposals for the parties to study. Israel, on the other hand, argued that the differences between it and the Arab states should be solved through direct negotiations, not through a third party.[1] After several weeks of clarifications with the Israelis and the Arabs, the commission decided to move its operational base to Europe and opened talks there with the two rival camps.

On 16 January 1950, the commission established itself in Geneva and invited the representatives of Israel, Egypt, Jordan, Syria, and Lebanon to join it. The parties had no great expectations from the new diplomatic enterprise, and consequently they were represented by relatively low-echelon officials from their foreign ministries. The talks opened on 30 January.

In order to bridge the gap between the Israeli demand to conduct direct negotiations and the Arab demand that the Conciliation Commission serve as an active broker, in late March the commission proposed that a number of committees be established in which Israeli and Arab representatives would participate. Each committee would be headed by a representative from the Conciliation Commission. The commission would reserve the right to determine what joint committees would be established – that is, what questions would be raised for discussion (for example: borders, refugees, and Jerusalem). The parties could propose a list of topics to the commission about which they felt a joint committee should be established. The Conciliation Commission would decide if discussion of a given topic that had been proposed was warranted.[2]

The Arabs' response, submitted in mid April, was mostly negative. They demanded that Israel agree to take upon itself to implement Clause 11 of Resolution 194(3) that dealt with the Palestinian refugee problem (and according to the Arab interpretation – that is, unfettered repatriation). If Israel would respond positively to this demand, the Arab states would be

108   *An exchange transaction*

willing to sit with Israel on a joint committee whose deliberations would be limited to one issue: ways to implement Clause 11. As for other outstanding problems between the sides, the Arabs believed in preservation of the status quo, except for one substantive change: the Conciliation Commission must serve as a "mediator" besides its work as a "conciliator."[3]

Israel, for its part, told the commission it was willing to begin talks with any Arab state that would declare its willingness to arrive at a peace settlement in which all outstanding problems between the sides would be resolved. Israel did not demand any concessions or commitments from the Arabs in advance for such negotiations, holding that all political claims should rightly be discussed only in the course of negotiations. The commission was also told that Israel would be willing to carry out the talks with the Arabs, either with the Conciliation Commission in attendance (that is, within the format of a joint committee) or without the commission's presence. However, if the commission would participate in talks, its role should be very limited. In contrast with the commission, which viewed itself as responsible for setting the topics that would be raised for discussion within the joint committees, Israel proposed that the commission only be "a harmonizing agent between the parties with a view to inducing a friendly atmosphere and extending its good offices to the parties with their consent."[4]

The reservations and conditionals in both the Israeli and Arab replies to the joint committees' proposal led the commission to the conclusion that it must take a more forceful position – inform the sides what would be the principles upon which negotiations would be conducted within the framework of the joint committees. The commission hoped that such a clarification would enable both sides to accept its proposal as written, without any provisos.[5] From the clarification letter submitted to members of the delegations on 11 May, it is evident that the commission endeavored to satisfy everyone: it declared (in the spirit of the Arab demand) that United Nations resolutions on the Palestine question – that is, Resolutions 181 and 194(3) – were what guided the commission when it envisioned the concept of joint committees; on the other hand, it took into consideration the position of the Israeli and Arab governments in regard to the implementation of these decisions. The sides were told that the Conciliation Commission's objective in establishing joint committees was to achieve a comprehensive and final settlement between them. In the commission's opinion, the outstanding questions between Israel and the Arabs were interlinked. This remark was directed towards the Arab side, which had sought to separate the refugee issue from the rest of the issues. In the close of its letter, the Conciliation Commission proposed the joint committees begin their deliberations without delay, on 23 May.[6]

On 19 May, the Arabs' response to the clarification letter arrived. They repeated their demand that Israel commit to implementing Clause 11 of Resolution 194(3) as a precondition to their agreement to sit with Israel in a joint committee whose deliberations would be limited solely to implementation of that clause.[7] A day later, the Israeli response arrived. It recommended that before attempting to convene the sides together on 23 May, the commission should await additional clarifications from the Arabs regarding direct talks.[8]

The fact that the Arabs held steadfastly to their position regarding the refugee issue did not weaken the hand of the Conciliation Commission. On 30 May, the commission sent an additional clarification letter to the Israeli and Arab delegations. At the outset, the commission declared (targeting the intransigent position of the Arabs) that it believed that the sides would recognize the fruitlessness of appending preconditions to renewal of negotiations between them. Further on, the commission again sought to satisfy everyone: in accordance with the Arab demands, it declared that Israel and its neighbors must honor UN resolutions, but it negated (in keeping with the Israeli demand) attempts by the Arabs to deal solely with the refugee question, since such an agenda "would impair the balance" of Resolution 194(3), which demanded settlement of all aspects of the conflict, without exception.[9]

The Arabs' response, which arrived in mid June, failed to show substantial change in the position the Arabs had held since the concept of the joint committees was raised. They declared that if Israel would agree, totally and without any reservations, to allow the repatriation of those refugees who wished to do so, then the Arabs would be willing to sit in a joint committee that would be devoted to this issue. Only after this matter was resolved would the Arabs be prepared to discuss the other points of disagreement between the sides.[10]

This reply sealed the fate of the concept of the committees and, in essence, the fate of the entire political process that the commission hoped to set in motion in Geneva. At the outset of July 1950, the Conciliation Commission announced that it had reached an impasse in its attempts at conciliation between Israel and the Arabs and that it would finish up its discussions in Geneva on 15 July. The commission decided to reconvene at the beginning of August in Jerusalem in order to continue its diplomatic activity.[11]

Israel changes its policy on the compensation issue

From the mid 1950, the Palestinian refugee problem stood at the hub of the Conciliation Commission's operations. The Arab states' insistence in the Geneva talks, and prior to that during the Lausanne Conference, that the refugee issue be dealt with before all the other issues that divided the sides, gave the commission no choice, forcing it to devote most of its time and efforts to trying to settle this issue. Nevertheless, one should keep in mind that, in many ways, this insistence by the Arabs was merely a charade, designed primarily to ram Israel in the international arena. The main issue that interested counties such as Egypt, Jordan, and Syria was the territorial issue.

In any case, the commission was unable, in practice, to address the settlement aspects of the refugee problem: repatriation and resettlement. As for the first component – repatriation – Israel had doggedly rejected it every time it was raised, systematically employing a broad range of physical and legal steps to

110 *An exchange transaction*

foil repatriation, and had garnered the support of the western powers behind this position. The second ingredient – resettlement – had been placed virtually in the hands of the UNRWA. This United Nations agency was allotted monetary and human resources and the authority to initiate refugee employment ventures in the Arab states that in essence took forward the concept of resettlement. In light of this state of affairs, the Conciliation Commission decided to deal mostly with the refugees' primary economic problem: compensation for their abandoned property. The commission quickly learned, as did the UNRWA and the western powers, that resolution of this problem would make it easier for states such as Jordan and Syria to resettle refugees among themselves. As a result, from the middle of 1950, the commission, along with the UNRWA and the western powers, began a pressure campaign to gain Israeli willingness to make progress on this issue.

At this point in time, Israel's position vis-à-vis the compensation issue was based on several principles: (a) the compensation issue was an integral part of the refugee problem, and therefore should be dealt with and be resolved, together with the other core aspects of the conflict, only in the framework of a comprehensive peace settlement; (b) Israel was, in principle, prepared to pay compensation for "abandoned Arab property"; (c) compensation would only be for cultivated lands; (d) Israel "preferred" that the full sum earmarked for monetary compensation would be channeled to a central fund that would deal with resettlement of the refugees; (e) compensation of Palestinian refugees was tied to and inseparable from compensation that Israel deserved from its Arab neighbors for war damages.[12]

These principles were not the fruit of in-depth political consultations, nor were they the product of recommendations by experts who had seriously studied the compensation issue. The principles had not even been formally adopted by the government. Sharett had presented them in abbreviated form in a 16 June 1948 cabinet meeting,[13] and over time, they simply consolidated into declared policy.

Until the summer of 1950, Israel was not required to delve into or seriously mull over the compensation issue, since the western powers and the United Nations focused solely on the settlement dimension (of resettlement and repatriation), and compensation was almost entirely sidelined. As a result, Israeli officials could allow themselves to make general and passing references regarding compensation, no more. This situation changed following the Conciliation Commission's decision to focus on the issue, and against the backdrop of the increasing frequency with which the UNRWA and the western powers were raising the issue. Thus, the Israeli Ministry of Foreign Affairs and the Israeli government were now forced to deal with that monetary aspect in a thorough and intensive manner.

In fact, the first move by the government on the compensation matter took place prior to the middle of 1950. In the course of the Economic Survey Mission's visit to Israel, it had requested to examine the compensation issue with its hosts in depth. In light of this, Minister of Finance Eliezer Kaplan recommended in the 11 October 1949 cabinet meeting that the government formulate an official position regarding compensation. As a preliminary step, Kaplan proposed that a committee of experts be established that would seriously study the compensation issue in depth and produce a working paper that could assist the cabinet to establish its position on the matter.[14] The cabinet adopted the proposal, and on 20 October, the Committee to Examine the Question of Compensation for Absentees' Property was established. The committee was headed by Zalman Liff, the government of Israel's advisor on land issues. On 17 March 1950 the committee submitted a report, summing up its findings.[15] In its conclusions, the Liff committee suggested a thorough revision of Israel's compensation policy, the crux of which was that Israel would be willing to discuss the compensation issue and pay compensation outside the framework of a comprehensive peace settlement, but on the condition that compensation money would be used solely for resettlement of the refugees.[16] From Israel's standpoint such a transaction was a worthwhile deal. While Israel would be forced to pay compensation before peace was achieved, at the same time, this payment would contribute to implementation of the solution it sought with all its might: the resettlement solution. Put another way, in exchange for conceding a secondary issue of the refugee problem – compensation – Israel would see the implementation of its position on the core issue – the place where the refugees would go.

On 8 June 1950, a short time prior to the conclusion of contacts at Geneva, the Conciliation Commission sent Foreign Minister Sharett a letter that dealt with compensation. The commission reminded the Israeli foreign minister that his government had indicated on several occasions its willingness to pay compensation for the property of Arab refugees. The Conciliation Commission told Sharett that it "believes that this question should now be examined more closely with a view to determining ways and means for settling it as soon as possible." The commission requested to know the Israeli government's opinion regarding the best way to clarify this matter.[17] The government's response, delivered by Foreign Minister Sharett, was disappointing from the Conciliation Commission's perspective. The commission was told that the Israeli government would agree to discuss the compensation issue only in the framework of comprehensive peace negotiations, in which all the outstanding questions among the parties would be deliberated.[18]

At the same time, the British had begun to feel their way through the compensation maze. Their interest emanated, among other things, from the impasse that the Conciliation Commission had reached at Geneva, but there were other factors at work. The British Foreign Office had come to the realization that huge sums of money were needed, far more than what had been envisioned at first, if the UNRWA was to implement its work programs. One of the ways of obtaining such sums was compensation from Israel.[19] Moreover, London believed that an Israeli concession on the compensation issue could accelerate resolution of the refugee problem as a whole (primarily by their resettlement) and perhaps even lead to a breakthrough in Arab-Israeli

112　*An exchange transaction*

relations.[20] Besides these dividends, if the compensation issue could be resolved, it could significantly assist Jordan, a faithful British ally in the Middle East. The British were concerned with the economic crisis that the Hashemite Kingdom faced due to the flow of refugees into the country. They found it hard to believe that Jordan would be able to absorb all the hundreds of thousands of refugees that had settled in it, and they believed that settlement of the compensation issue would pave the way for rehabilitation in Iraq and Syria of most of the refugees in Jordan at the time.[21]

The British position received the support of the UNRWA. Its director, Howard Kennedy, said in a meeting with several British officials that if the compensation issue would be settled, it would be the most important step that could be taken to solve the refugee problem. Without settlement of the compensation issue, it would be impossible to convince the refugees to settle permanently outside Israel.[22] In a similar spirit, the British representative on the UNRWA's advisory commission, Sir Henry Knight, told the British Foreign Office that if Israel agreed to pay compensation, the Arabs were likely to be reconciled "and then it will be possible to say to the refugees, without hesitation, that they won't ever return home."[23] Yet the road to this end was still long. Knight reported to his superiors in London that the Conciliation Commission complained that it could not deal with the compensation issue as long as Israel linked it to a peace settlement.[24]

In the meantime, against the backdrop of the upcoming convention of the 5th General Assembly on 19 September 1950, which was scheduled to discuss, among other things, the issue of Palestine, the Israeli Ministry of Foreign Affairs began to devote far more attention to the refugee problem, including the compensation issue.

During the third week of July, Israeli representatives from the world's capitals convened with the foreign minister and his senior staff, a number of officials from other ministries, the IDF chief of staff and senior brass, and the head of the Knesset Foreign Affairs and Defense Committee for a comprehensive discussion of Israel's foreign policy. In the third session on 18 July, the participants discussed questions tied to Arab-Israeli relations. Zalman Liff warned that the Palestinian refugees would not forget their property, which had fallen into the hands of Israel during the 1948 war, and at some point there would be the need to solve this problem. He highlighted the fact that the State of Israel had not yet set an official policy on the compensation question; rather, it had sufficed with stating that the question would be resolved only in the framework of a comprehensive peace settlement. In Liff's opinion, it was undesirable to tie the compensation question unconditionally to a peace settlement between Israel and its neighbors. He argued that it might be more convenient as a prelude to a peace settlement, to settle – one way or another – the problem of the refugees and their property. Thus, Liff reiterated the conclusions of the cabinet-appointed committee he had headed. Israel Minister to Italy Shlomo Ginossar opined that the refugee problem was liable to surface all the more forcefully when United Nations funding for maintaining the refugees ran out.

An exchange transaction 113

In his view, the nations of the world understood that for security and other reasons, Israel could not allow the refugees to return to their former homes, but all believed that Israel must contribute its part to easing their distress. Ministry of Foreign Affairs' advisor on special affairs Reuven Shiloah, who chaired the third session, closed deliberations on the refugee problem saying that the State of Israel must make haste to find a solution to this problem in order to enhance the chances of peace.[25]

In a 30 July letter to Foreign Minister Sharett, Shiloah detailed his position on the matter. "I am very concerned," he wrote, "that in the coming weeks, or at most the coming months, we are liable to face a renewed and heightened political attack against us on the Arab refugee issue." Israel must take a political initiative on this issue in order to "take this card out of the hands of our opponents and dull the severity of any attack of this kind that will come." Shiloah, it turned out, had an idea for just such an initiative, which could be presented to the United States, Britain, and the United Nations. In Shiloah's mind, Israel must contribute the compensation money for the Palestinian abandoned property to a central fund, and that fund would promote the resettlement of the Palestinian refugees in the Arab countries. He was even prepared to transfer to the fund compensation that Israel demanded from the Arab states for war damages. Israel's consent to compromise on the compensation question would hinge not only on resettlement of the refugees, stated Shiloah, but also on the "readiness [of] the Arab states for a peace settlement with Israel."[26] Shiloah refrained from saying that the initiative would be implemented only if a comprehensive peace agreement would be achieved or, at the least, that peace talks would take place; he sufficed with vague wording that coupled compensation of the refugees with an expression of the Arabs' "readiness" to arrive at a peace settlement, no more than that. In other words, Shiloah, like the Liff committee, recommended that Israel detach the compensation issue from a comprehensive peace settlement, but maintain a clear affinity between compensation and the implementation of the resettlement principle.

On 7 and 8 August, the Knesset Foreign Affairs and Defense Committee convened to discuss Israel's preparations for the United Nations' 5th General Assembly. Sharett, Shiloah, and Israel's ambassador in Washington, Eban, were invited to the meeting to update the Knesset committee members. Eban reported that the UNRWA had been unsuccessful in curtailing the scope of the refugee problem, and in the United Nations there were already parties suggesting international assistance should cease, leaving the burden to Israel and the Arab states to bear. This issue was to be clarified at the upcoming meeting of the General Assembly, and Eban was hardly a bearer of good tidings: "I see clouds in the sky from the standpoint of this problem, clouds that at any time and at any hour are liable to pour upon us [flood us] with international criticism and international strife."[27] Sharett assured the gathering that Israel was not about to change its policy in regard to the repatriation principle. However, he stressed "that doesn't mean we need to sentence

114 *An exchange transaction*

ourselves not to take any initiative to solve the refugee problem." This problem exists, poisons the atmosphere, serves as one of the sources of insecurity surrounding Israel and as an obstacle on the path to achieving a settlement with the Arab countries. The government, clarified the foreign minister, certainly can't ignore this problem because it is liable to serve as a whip in the hands of the Arabs against Israel at the upcoming assembly.[28]

At the same time, the Conciliation Commission had returned and set itself up in Jerusalem, having decided to once again try and convince Israel to find a solution to the compensation issue.[29] The commission considered it very important to achieve substantive progress on this issue at this point in time in order to present some sort of political achievement in its annual report, which was scheduled to be presented to the 5th General Assembly. In talks commission members conducted with Israeli officials, they clarified that Israel's chances of successfully promoting the resettlement principle and deflecting international pressure on Israel to implement repatriation hinged on Israel's readiness to carry out a revision of its compensation policy. Thus, when the American representative on the commission, Ely Palmer, met with Abba Eban on 9 August, he recommended that the Israeli government reconsider the possibility that the compensation question be dealt with separately. Palmer argued that settlement of the compensation issue held a tremendous advantage for Israel, since this would, in essence, put the repatriation issue on the back burner.[30]

Approximately a week later, the commission's members presented to Foreign Minister Sharett a preliminary working plan for resolution of the compensation problem. They told him that "in light of the fact that the Israeli government recognizes the principle of compensation," and out of understanding that differences of opinion that exist between the Israeli government and the commission rest on the timing and the conditions for payment of the compensation, a technical committee would be established that would begin to assess the worth of Palestinians' abandoned property. This plan, according to the commission, would be implemented even if a solution to the remaining issues of the Arab-Israeli conflict were not reached. The foreign minister didn't categorically reject the suggestion and replied that the government would weigh it seriously.[31] Thus it appears that Sharett began to internalize that Israel's compensation policy would need to undergo a substantive change, along the lines of Shiloah's and the Liff committee's proposals.

In the cabinet meeting on 21 August, the foreign minister reported the commission's proposal to try and find a solution to the compensation issue without coupling it to the other outstanding questions between Israel and the Arabs. In his appraisal, such a move would push aside the repatriation concept:

> I view it as a move in the Commission's position that it bases the discussion with us about the solution of the refugee problem on the basis of compensation and not on the basis of their repatriation. It is a Commission

tied to the United Nations resolution from 1948 [Resolution 194(3)], and that 1948 resolution calls for repatriation. By its new proposal, it says in effect: For us, the question of repatriation doesn't exist, but the question of compensation exists; You yourselves always said you admit this obligation, so let's march [let's take] this matter forward. If we rebuff them on this matter, it's as if we are releasing them from this approach [i.e. compensation], and the Commission can go back to where it was before [i.e. repatriation].

Sharett, however, did not end with this line of reasoning. He told his colleagues that they must also take into account the possibility that Israel will not arrive at a peace with the Arabs in the coming years. Would Israel, he asked rhetorically, prefer that the refugees would stay where they were, without any solution, and in "an atmosphere fraught with demands" to implement the repatriation principle and to receipt compensation? "Wouldn't we be interested that at least the compensation issue will be resolved ?" Sharett summed up his position:

> If we put the question this way, it is clear to me that it would be better for us to separate [the compensation issue from other issues] and march this thing forward [.] hence, I suggest [that we] not yet clarify the matter with them in detail, but to try and find out, at the crux, what kind of arrangement with them is possible on this matter, that we begin to discuss payment of compensation under the clear premise that [we're] not talking about repatriating the refugees.

The foreign minister's proposal reflected a significant alteration in Israel's fundamental position that had linked in an iron-clad manner clarification of the compensation issue (and its implementation) with a comprehensive peace settlement. After Sharett's overview of the situation, an animated discussion in the presence of all the cabinet commenced. This was the first time that the Israeli government examined in depth its policy on the issue of compensation for refugees. Four ministers supported Sharett's proposal. Some held that, along with discussion of the compensation issue, Israel should, at the same time, raise the demand to receive compensation from the Arab world for war damages. Six ministers, including Prime Minister Ben-Gurion, took issue with the proposal raised before the cabinet. Several of them expressed apprehensions that if at this point Israel began to exhibit flexibility in its position, demands for further concessions would follow.[32]

At the close of deliberations, the cabinet set about deciding between two proposals: the foreign minister's and the proposal of the Minister of Religious Affairs, Yehuda Leib Maymon. Five voted in favor of Sharett's proposal, six voted in favor of Maymon's proposal. The foreign minister's suggestion that "Israel enter a preliminary clarification with the Commission on the principles of payment of compensation for Arab refugee property, without committing

116   *An exchange transaction*

to any arrangement until a comprehensive peace settlement, and without waiving payment of compensation to us [to Israel]" was dropped. The decision that was passed by the cabinet, and this was the first time since the refugee problem was created that the Israeli government took an official decision on the compensation issue, stated that "as long as there is no comprehensive peace, there will not be any negotiation on the principles for payment of compensation or any other partial negotiation." In addition, it was decided, according to Maymon's proposal, "to announce to the Conciliation Commission that if there would not be negotiations on peace soon, Israel would be forced to withdraw from the principle of payment of compensation."[33]

Ben-Gurion strictly upheld the line that the cabinet passed. On 23 August, he met with the Turkish representative on the commission, Tevfic Rustu Aras. Aras requested that the government of Israel stand behind the commission, particularly in anticipation of the 5th General Assembly, by demonstrating a positive attitude towards the compensation issue. In his opinion, a positive attitude would impact favorably on the commission's endeavors to hasten peace. Ben-Gurion, unwilling to comply, told him that Israel was prepared to contribute to resolution of the refugee problem, including compensation, only in the framework of a comprehensive peace settlement. The prime minister warned that if the Arabs would continue, as in the past, to reject Israel's offers to negotiate a peace with them, Israel was liable to cancel promises to pay compensation for the abandoned property of the refugees.[34] In a talk that Ben-Gurion held with Palmer, he expressed things in a similar vein.[35]

In a telegram to Sharett, Abba Eban judged that the government's decision was deficient. While he agreed with the principle "no compensation without peace," there was room in Eban's opinion for a "more flexible tactical line." The ambassador gave three reasons for his stand: first, Israel should take steps to ensure that the upcoming United Nations General Assembly would be conducted calmly in all aspects of the Palestine issue. In his opinion "some sort of negotiation on compensation, even if not successful finally, would keep General Assembly quiet now;" Second, the United States was interested that Israel deal with the compensation issue now; and third, Palmer had argued lately that compensation was an "antithesis" to the principle of repatriation, and therefore Israel had a special interest to discuss it.[36] In another telegram to the foreign minister, Eban stressed that giving compensation to the refugees was one of the ways of transferring [western] money to the Middle East, including to Israel, because after all no one imagined that Israel was able to bear alone the burden of compensation from its own resources.[37]

A month prior to the opening of the 5th General Assembly signs began to appear that Israel would face unprecedented pressure from the western countries and the Arab states on the Palestine question, including the refugee problem. A Ministry of Foreign Affairs' document noted: "From the various reports we have read of late, it has become more and more clear that the Arabs and their friends are preparing a general attack on us in the United Nations Assembly." In addition, the document said that government officials in Washington and

An exchange transaction 117

London often bring up the refugee problem, particularly the compensation issue, with Israeli representatives. Discussions on this topic, it was clarified, were more frequent now than prior to the 4th General Assembly at the close of 1949.[38] According to another document prepared for the 30 August cabinet meeting, the Arab states intended to work vigorously to raise the Palestine question in the 5th Assembly's agenda, and with it the host of UN resolutions on the issue.[39]

In a meeting with Avraham Biran, the French representative on the Conciliation Commission, de Boisanger issued a sharp warning of what Israel could expect if it persevered in its refusal to discuss the compensation issue. In de Boisanger's opinion, Israel was not taking into account at all the huge change that had taken place in the Arab position regarding the refugee problem. That is, that the Arab states were now willing to settle the Palestinian refugees in their territories. The Conciliation Commission, said de Boisanger, would cite this Arab willingness in its report, and if it was forced to the commission would also cite Israel's refusal to collaborate on the compensation issue, and this would not be in Israel's best interests. De Boisanger made it clear that the commission and even the United Nations General Assembly could decide that the compensation issue would be examined without Israel's consent, and in such a case, Israel would have no influence on the outcome.[40]

In a 30 August cabinet meeting, the foreign minister discussed the latest developments in the political arena. The picture he described wasn't at all encouraging from Israel's perspective. According to information that reached the Ministry of Foreign Affairs, American diplomats on the Conciliation Commission believed that "the rights of the Palestinian refugees to compensation was a decisive right that was inalienable." The State Department in Washington also felt the same way. Sharett hinted that this position was liable to be expressed by the Americans during the 5th Assembly. Moreover, the Arab states themselves were liable to launch a diplomatic offensive against Israel on the refugee issue during the 5th Assembly. In light of this state of affairs, the foreign minister sensed that the government must show "a positive initiative" on the issue. Sharett, however, quickly added reservations to his words, saying that he was not seeking "to awaken the controversy of the previous [cabinet] meeting [on 21 August]" and was not interested in "suggesting any revision of the decision that was adopted." His suggestion was that the government give the Ministry of Foreign Affairs authority "to appear in the Assembly with a constructive program [...] on the refugee problem, [one] that would be founded and built entirely on a plan for resettlement [of the refugees] in neighboring [Arab] countries and based entirely on a program for peace." In Sharett's view, if the Arab states would agree to accept the program, Israel should immediately make a gesture and announce that it was prepared to relinquish the compensation it deserved from the Arab countries for war damage during the 1948 war. An idea in a similar spirit had been voiced by Shiloah to Sharett a month earlier, and it turns out that the foreign minister was open to the idea. The response of the cabinet ministers to the course of

118 *An exchange transaction*

action Sharett proposed was hardly enthusiastic, and they questioned what practical utility could be derived from it. The remarks of Immigration Minister Moshe Shapira (who also held the Interior portfolio) reflected prevailing opinion in the cabinet:

> One needs to grasp that gentiles [i.e. the Arabs] also have brains. We'll bring them a proposal based entirely on such [an idea] that the refugee will remain with them, that their settlement will be arranged among them; they will say that that's a "good proposal" [...] I doubt whether this is likely to weaken to any extent atrocity propaganda going on against us.

In response, Sharett clarified that it was clear to him that the program would not fundamentally change Israel's international standing, but this was not the intention. The plan's objective was to try to "improve" – even a little bit – Israel's political standing in regard to the refugee issue. At the end of Sharett's remarks, the government decided to give the Ministry of Foreign Affairs permission to prepare a plan for the resettlement of the refugees that would be presented to the 5th Assembly at the ministry's discretion.[41]

After the cabinet meeting, Sharett met with members of the Conciliation Commission. He related Israel's existing position to them, reiterating that it would agree to enter discussions on the compensation problem only in the framework of comprehensive peace negotiations. Yet Sharett immediately added and underscored that payment of compensation would be Israel's contribution "to the cost of resettlement." This statement constituted a political innovation. Up until this point, Israel had sufficed with expressing its "preference" that compensation be channeled into rehabilitation of the refugees in the Arab states; now it required this. For the first time in the history of its exchanges with international parties, Israel tied payment of compensation to and made it inseparable from resettlement of the refugees. The commission chair, Palmer, did not reject out of hand the linkage between the two. After all, he himself had reasoned that there was a connection between giving compensation and shelving the repatriation principle. Yet Palmer was still considerably annoyed that Israel continued to object to resolution of the compensation issue outside the framework of a comprehensive peace settlement. His colleague de Boisanger tried to explain to Sharett the magnitude of Israel's miscalculation in this regard. As he has told Biran, there had been a change in the approach of several Arab governments on this issue, and now they believed that the Arab refugees needed to settle in Arab territory. The approach of these governments, stated the French representative, was exactly the same as the Conciliation Commission's approach. "Hence," de Boisanger argued with Sharett, "when Arab governments tell us that they envision resettlement of the refugees with the Commission's assistance, and particularly that this assistance needs to include compensation [from Israel], we wonder what are we supposed to reply to them."[42]

An exchange transaction 119

The foreign minister had no answer to this argument. He was caught in the middle: he had to back the political position of his government even if he opposed it. In an attempt to present a more flexible Israeli position, he told the commission that the government in Jerusalem was prepared to shelve its demand for war damages from the Arab states, if they would agree to settle the refugees in their territories. As noted, up until now, Israel had tied war compensation together with refugee compensation. In the last meeting of the cabinet, Sharett had proposed that this linkage be cut. The government had not rejected the suggestion, and Sharett anchored it in Israel's compensation policy.[43]

Such flexibility, however, didn't satisfy the international parties dealing with the refugee issue at all. Among UNRWA and Conciliation Commission personnel, as well as officials in the British and American governments, opinions strengthened that in light of growing signs testifying that countries such as Jordan and Syria were willing to settle refugees in their territories, and in light of the agreement of the United Nations and the western powers to sideline the repatriation principle, Israel must immediately begin to try and resolve the compensation problem.

In a meeting with UNRWA personnel, the members of the Conciliation Commission clarified that they planned to dedicate all of their efforts to the compensation issue, leaving on the back burner the repatriation principle. Palmer reported the commission's intentions to establish an auxiliary body that would be charged with examining the technical aspects of compensation. The new body would try to clarify the number of refugees with abandoned property, and the scope and value of their assets. UNRWA director Howard Kennedy declared that it must be recognized that implementation of Resolution 194(3) in full was impossible. In his opinion, the Arabs' expectations, particularly those regarding implementation of Clause 11, could not be realized. The UNRWA and the Conciliation Commission must report to the 5th General Assembly that over the past two years, it had become evident that the approach to resolution of the refugee problem upon which Resolution 194(3) was based [i.e. through repatriation] was not practical.[44] Kennedy's position reflected the viewpoint of several members of the UNRWA's advisory commission.[45]

The British Foreign Office assumed that at the 5th General Assembly, the Arabs would try to achieve reconfirmation of Clause 11. London believed that after they achieved "their diplomatic satisfaction," beyond the limelight, one could expect them to quietly make progress on the resettlement road.[46] Palmer was of a similar mind. To the best of his knowledge, underneath their intransigent public stand, the Arab states were prepared to make far-reaching concessions. Palmer reported to the American secretary of state that although the Arab states continued to view the refugee problem as "a natural and effective basis" for condemning Israel, they understood that their public insistence on the repatriation principle was pointless, and therefore they must try and ensure compensation and assistance for resettlement programs.[47] The

120   *An exchange transaction*

American representative on the UNRWA's advisory commission, John Bland-ford, also believed that winds of change could be felt emanating from Arab capitals in the direction of acceptance of the principle of resettlement.[48]

In the face of these appraisals, Israel, by standing firm on an inflexible policy vis-à-vis the compensation issue, appeared to be the primary obstacle in the path to resolving the refugee problem. In a joint meeting in late September of State Department officials with their counterparts in the British Foreign Office, strong criticism was voiced regarding Israel's refusal to make progress on the compensation issue.[49] Several days later, the head of the Eastern Department, Geoffrey Furlonge, met with the principle secretary of the Conciliation Commission, Pablo de-Azcarate. De-Azcarate related that the commission urged the Arabs to be more realistic regarding the possibility that a large number of refugees would return to Israel, and that the commission believed there had been some tempering of the Arab stand regarding repatriation. Israel, on the other hand, was not prepared to compromise at all regarding compensation, de-Azcarate complained.[50]

In order to prod Israel to moderate its position on the issue, Conciliation Commission officials together with representatives of the western powers again stressed to their Israeli interlocutors the marked change they sensed in the stand of several Arab states vis-à-vis the resettlement principle.[51] In a 7 September cabinet meeting, Sharett reported to his colleagues that according to the Conciliation Commission:

> Trans-Jordan recently renounced any serious demand for the return of the refugees, and its King in particular espouses this [...] [and] in Syria they were told explicitly that the Syrian government would compel settlement of refugees in its country as a matter beneficial to the state.

The commission held that Israel had the ability to assist in taking this process forward, said Sharett paraphrasing their sentiments:

> Here, we see progress on the part of Arab states in this direction [towards resettlement] [...] We thought there would be progress from your side as well, and that you would be prepared, in the meantime, to enter with us into a parliamentary investigation of the compensation issue – something that could ease continued progress from the Arab side.[52]

A short time after the opening of the 5th General Assembly, the State Department began to increase its pressure on Israel to agree to moderate its position regarding compensation. Washington hoped to achieve a break-through on the refugee question and, as a byproduct, progress on resolution of the Arab-Israeli conflict as a whole. The vigorous United States' intervention in the Middle East conflict was fueled to a large extent by the Korean War. From the armed struggle that broke out in the Korean Peninsula in June 1950 the Americans concluded that a new war did not have to break out in Europe necessarily, a prognosis that had been widely held up until then. Soviet penetration into Asia, including the Near East, was now a reasonable probability and a threat that must be countered.[53] The Americans and the British, as already noted, believed that effective self-defense against penetration of the Middle East by communism was possible, provided peace and security could be achieved in the region. A tranquil Middle East void of conflicts and bloodshed, the western powers judged, would make it possible to consolidate the various forces in the region as a fortified wall to fend off the Soviet threat.[54] Moreover, Arab diplomats had expressed more than once grievances towards the United States, charging that it exhibited a lack of evenhandedness in the international arena: Washington was quick to respond to impose the United Nation's decisions in regard to the Korean conflict, but was in no haste to do so in Palestine.[55]

On 30 September, Reuven Shiloah met with Deputy Assistant Secretary of State for Near Eastern, South Asian and African Affairs Burton Berry to discuss Arab-Israel relations. In Berry's mind, Israel needed peace more than the Arab states, and in order to prepare the ground for peace talks, Israelis must make a conciliatory gesture towards the Arabs. Such a gesture could be on the compensation issue. The United States knew that Israel was unable to pay large sums of money as compensation at the present time, said Berry, but Israel could now enter discussion with the Arabs on the details of a settlement for such a payment.[56] Approximately a week later, Ambassador Eban, the Israeli delegation's advisor at the United Nations, Gideon Rafael, and Israeli consul-general in New York, Arthur Lourie, met with the deputy United States representative on the security council, John Ross. Ross stated that "the majority of people" believed that resettlement, not repatriation, was the only answer to the Palestinian refugee problem. Israel, however, would need to contribute its share to the resolution of this problem. The Israeli diplomats were asked whether their government would be prepared to discuss the compensation question outside a comprehensive peace agreement. The reply that came from the Israelis was negative. Eban reiterated his government position, which coupled compensation with a peace settlement.[57] The minister at the Israel embassy in Washington, Teddy Kollek, said things in a similar vein in a talk with Burton Berry on 11 October.[58]

Towards the end of October, a large Israeli-American gathering convened to discuss the refugee problem. Among those present were Eban, Rafael, Shiloah, Blandford, and Ross. Ross believed that Israelis' intense desire for peace required them to try and break through the impasse in their relations with the Arabs, that is, to adopt a more elastic position on the compensation question. Eban clarified that Israel agreed in principle to pay compensation, but at the same time it hadn't received any sign that compensation would contribute somehow to resolving its relations with the Arab states.[59]

In a long letter to Walter Eytan, Eban summed up the messages that had been passed on to him on the refugee issue in talks in Washington with "various and sundry government circles":

122 *An exchange transaction*

It is clear-cut that Israel can't absorb Arab refugees, [it is] clear also that the one and only solution to the refugee problem is their settlement in the Arab countries and all efforts should be focused on this. Israel is being demanded to contribute a contribution to solving this problem because without the refugee problem being solved, there is no possibility of making progress towards peace. It is known that Israel doesn't have the requisite monetary means to participate in the endeavor [of] settling the Arab refugees and this is not demanded of Israel - what is demanded is that the government of Israel will repeat and affirm its political and moral commitment to pay compensation to Arab refugees for the property they left in the country without hinging this commitment on negotiation on peace.[60]

At the outset of October the Conciliation Commission published a report reviewing its operations between December 1949 and October 1950. The commission said that the compensation question received "special attention" in contacts it established with "interested governments" during its sojourn in the Middle East in August 1950. The report added that, during this period, in the course of a host of meetings it carried out with relevant Arab governments, the commission had also dealt with the issue of resettlement. The commission's conclusion, worded diplomatically with caution, was that despite the Arab states' official and public stand on the repatriation issue they understood that there must be a considerable implementation of the principle of resettlement.[61]

Two weeks later, on 19 October, the UNRWA published its own report on the agency's first six months of operation, from May to October 1950. The UNRWA report refuted most of the optimistic forecasts of the Economic Survey Mission from November 1949. For example, the survey mission forecasted that in the third quarter of 1950, only 492,000 refugees would still be in need of relief, while the UNRWA reported that during the corresponding period, in reality, 860,000 persons had received relief – a 75 percent gap.[62] The second half of the UNRWA report contained recommendations made by the advisory commission. In the committee's evaluation, the refugee problem would not end on 30 June 1951, as forecasted in the Economic Survey Mission's report. Since the problem involved great human suffering and peril to the peace and stability of the Middle East, the committee recommended that direct aid to the Palestinian refugees be continued after 31 December 1950. In addition, it recommended that the works programs continue after the original 30 June 1951 cut-off date. The wording of the advisory commission's third recommendation alluded to preference for the resettlement principle. "Some time in the future," it stated, "a huge task of rehabilitation and re-establishment awaits." According to its suggestion, a special fund would be established that would be called the Reintegration Fund. The contributions that would be deposited in this fund would be channeled, when needed, towards execution of "reintegration plans for refugees, conduct of surveys and technical assistance" that governments of the region would propose. The committee recommended that from 1 July 1951 to 30 June 1952, 30 million dollars would be allocated to the Reintegration Fund. Another 20 million dollars would be allocated to direct relief for the refugees. The advisory commission held that "establishment of the 30 million dollar fund, was a first step [...] in [...] reintegrating the majority of more than three-quarter of a million refugees."[63]

The Reintegration Fund, in truth, was oriented towards realization of the resettlement concept. A telegram to the British delegation at the United Nations from the Foreign Office in London stated that "the Arabs will probably view this proposal [establishment of a Reintegration Fund] as an attempt to divert them from their declared goal, that is to say, repatriation of the refugees to Palestine."[64]

Thus, the reports of the Conciliation Commission and the UNRWA promoted, almost openly, the principle of resettlement. Consequently Israel was demanded now, more than ever, to pay for the willingness of the western powers, the United Nations, and, no less so, a number of Arab states (first of all Jordan) to embrace the principle that Israel had championed since the summer of 1948.

In the meeting of the cabinet on 24 October, Foreign Minister Sharett presented a political review following his return to Israel from United Nations headquarters in New York. In his appraisal, when the issue of the Palestinian refugees would be raised for discussion in the Ad Hoc Political Committee and in the General Assembly plenum, Israel could expect a difficult battle, since several parties, including the Americans, claimed Israel had not fulfilled Resolution 194(3) at all. He told the members of the government that State Department official McGhee said: "It's clear to us and clear to everyone that this problem won't be resolved without major settlement of refugees in neighboring states," but Israel must make some sort of gesture towards the Arabs.[65]

The fact that, during this cabinet meeting and several others that had preceded it, Sharett had focused particularly on Washington's position on the refugee issue was pinned to the fact that, at the time, Israel had begun to develop increasing economic dependence on the American superpower. During its first two years of independence, Israel tried to apply a policy of nonalignment towards both global blocs, neither taking sides with the western block led by the United States nor with the eastern bloc led by the USSR. There were a number of reasons for that: concern for the welfare of the large Jewish diaspora communities in both the west and in the east; gratitude towards the rival powers for their support of the establishment of a Jewish state; and the desire to avoid creating a rift within the Israeli labor movement between those who supported socialism and others who sided with the west.[66] At the same time, during those first two years of statehood, Israel, in practice, had established closer ties with the western bloc, first and foremost with the United States.[67] Under pressure from Washington, Israel sided with the west following the outbreak of the Korean War, the beginning of a process that brought to a close Israel's endeavors to remain neutral in the Cold War.[68] One of the

124   An exchange transaction

primary reasons for the change in policy that began in the summer of 1950 was economic. Almost from the start, Israel was economically dependent on the United States. In 1949, 30 percent of Israel's imports originated in the USA, and in the first four months of 1950 this percentage rose to 40 percent. In 1949, Israel was on the verge of economic collapse when the American administration approved a 100 million dollar loan to Israel for economic development. Within a year, this influx of capital was augmented by another 35 million dollars in loans earmarked for agricultural development. Moreover, American tax authorities eased the transfer of monies from the wealthy American Jewish community to Israel. Thus, American economic assistance, direct and indirect, helped Israel deal with the tremendous economic difficulties it faced in its first years of statehood – difficulties stemming from the 1948 war, ongoing security problems in its aftermath, and the flood of destitute immigrants that flooded the country. Israel's economic dependence on the United States, which grew over the years, undermined the young state's ability to maintain an independent foreign policy.[69]

Foreign Minister Sharett's pressures since mid August on the government on the compensation issue, parallel to endeavors by the Conciliation Commission, the American State Department, and the British Foreign Office to convince Israel to moderate its position on this matter, finally took effect. In its 30 October cabinet meeting, the Israeli government decided to change its position. Before the decision was passed, Sharett had updated members of the government on the latest input his ministry had received regarding the refugee problem in general and the compensation question in particular. Sharett opened his update with the Conciliation Commission's report. In his opinion, the report was very positive from Israel's perspective. "They put strong emphasis," he explained, "on the question of the refugees' settlement in neighboring [Arab] countries, which is a considerable progress." Nevertheless, Israel would have to pay for this diplomatic achievement with the compensation coin. The State Department, Sharett reported, is increasing pressure and demanding that the Israeli government commit to pay compensation, separate from all other issues. They propose to establish a Reintegration Fund that will deal with finding work and housing for the refugees [in the Arab states]. It would be worthwhile for Israel, Sharett stated, to commit to pay compensation through the new fund: first of all, because Israel has always preferred to pay compensation to a centralized fund, not "to each and every individual." Second, the monies would not be wasted on relief for the refugees, but rather on their final settlement in the Arab countries. The Americans, Sharett said, request three specific things from Israel: the first, to reiterate Israel's willingness to pay compensation; the second, to express agreement that payment of compensation would be transferred to the Reintegration Fund; third, to pay the first installment towards the compensation account to this fund. But more than anything else, "they are begging us not to demand a preliminary declaration from the Arabs that any discussion of this question [compensation] be part of discussion on peace."

An exchange transaction   125

They hinted, added Sharett, that if Israel would not accept the approach they proposed to resolve the compensation problem:

> It will be impossible to prevent increase in bitterness against Israel among world opinion because it will be impossible to hide the terrible state of the refugees from the eyes of the world, and Israel will appear in an uneasy position [when] it both refuses to repatriate refugees and also refuses to contribute its part to their resettlement elsewhere.

The Israeli delegation to the United Nations, Sharett related, supported the American proposal, but suggested a clarification be appended: that Israel's agreement to transfer compensation to the Reintegration Fund was "the first chapter in the process of a final settlement." The foreign minister closed his overview saying he viewed positively the American proposal, as well as the addition that the Israeli delegation at the United Nations had raised. He added that the minister of finance, Eliezer Kaplan, and the minister of labor, Golda Meir, who were absent from the cabinet meeting, had sent a telegram supporting the American proposal. Nevertheless, they requested that Israel declare that it had counter claims against the Arab side.[70]

The government didn't discuss the issue at all and immediately embarked on summarizing a decision, as follows:

> It was decided to give the delegation at the United Nations authority to announce the Government of Israel's position on the question of [...] [the] Arab refugees, as follows:
>
> 1. Our agreement to the continuance of aid and to the creation of a special fund for permanent absorption [of the refugees].
> 2. Our readiness [...] to pay fair compensation for abandoned property.
> 3. Our agreement to pay such compensation to an absorption fund under United Nations auspices.
> 4. Our agreement to negotiation with authorized United Nations institutions on the mode of payment arrangements.
> 5. We view arrangement of compensation payments for Arab abandoned property as the first stage in a final peace settlement process between us and the Arab states.
> 6. We declare a claim for compensation owed us due to the [1948] war, without linking the two reciprocal claims to one another.[71]

The above decision testifies to three substantive changes in existing policy: (a) Israel retreated from its position that discussion of the compensation issue and its resolution hinged on resolving all the other aspects of the conflict; (b) Israel officially anchored the principle that to date had been defined as a "preference" that the purpose of compensation monies was resettlement of the refugees (the "absorption fund" that appears in Clause 3 refers to the

126 *An exchange transaction*

Reintegration Fund that the UNRWA was scheduled to establish and that Israel viewed as a resettlement fund); (c) the proviso was dropped that handing over compensation to the refugees hinged on receipt of compensation from the Arab states for war damages. One could say, in general, that Israel agreed to moderate its policy extensively on the compensation issue, but it took care to link compensation to taking the resettlement principle forward.

The government's decision satisfied officials in the British Foreign Office, although they were doubtful whether Israel could mobilize the necessary money. A memorandum prepared by Head of the Eastern Department Furlonge said that the decision of the Israeli government regarding compensation should be attributed great importance in the context of a settlement between Israel and the Arab states, more than the importance it should be attributed in the context of the Arab refugees. In Furlonge's opinion, Israel's decision was also "a wise political move" since it enabled Israel to claim it had taken an initiative for a settlement with the Arabs and made a genuine gesture. If the Arabs didn't respond positively to the Israeli initiative, the Israelis could place the blame on their shoulders for the impasse that would be created. At the same time, it was likely that even if the Arabs would respond positively to the offer, there were still three difficult problems on the road to resolution of the compensation issue: the way the scope of compensation would be set; the economic capabilities of Israel to pay compensation in foreign currency; the way in which compensation monies would be allocated to refugees.[72] Britain's minister in Israel, Alexander Knox Helm, was of similar opinion and surmised that most probably the sum of compensation that Israel could mobilize would be small and therefore would not succeed in making any substantive change in the lives of the refugees. In his opinion, the Americans' appraisal was similar, and they understood that Israel was incapable of compensating the refugees with a large enough sum to make a serious impact.[73]

The comprehension that Israel would find it difficult to mobilize the full amount for compensation from its own resources was derived from the country's shaky economic state. As already noted, mass immigration and the grave security situation left the State of Israel on the edge of a fiscal abyss in its first years of existence. Various economic indexes testified clearly to the very limited abilities of Israel to withstand extra expenditures in hard currency: the country's current balance of payments faced a huge deficit (288 million dollars in 1950, and 362 million in 1951); and foreign currency reserves dwindled (in December 1950, they stood at 30 million dollars, and in December 1951 the treasury was near empty). The state of the economy only began to gradually improve towards 1953, but in terms of financial robustness, the situation hardly enabled Israel to pay the full sum of compensation. Thus, the western powers, and with them the Conciliation Commission and the UNRWA, continued throughout the period under study to maintain that Israel could not bear on its own the brunt of the compensation burden. The conclusion was that it was imperative to extend foreign aid to Israel in the form of loans, so that it would be able to pay compensation. Israeli leadership was a full partner in this conclusion.[74]

The principle of resettlement takes center stage in the international arena

In the first week of November 1950, the Palestinian refugee problem was put on the table of the General Assembly's Ad Hoc Political Committee. The UNRWA's interim report constituted the basis for deliberations. On 7 November, Abba Eban reported to the committee the change that had taken place in the position of his government in regard to the compensation issue. He added that Israel's readiness to pay compensation related to, as stated previously, abandoned Arab lands, and that a collective method of payment of compensation should be adopted, not an attempt to resolve the problem through individual compensation.[75]

The UNRWA's recommendations, as they appeared in its report submitted on 19 October, including the recommendation that a Reintegration Fund be founded, served as a foundation for a draft resolution that the United States, Britain, France, and Turkey jointly submitted on 6 November to the Ad Hoc Political Committee. In an initiative by the Arab bloc, Pakistan proposed an amendment be entered which would underscore that the draft resolution did not contravene Clause 11 of Resolution 194(3). Pakistan's proposal was accepted, and on 27 November the Ad Hoc Political Committee voted to adopt the amended draft with 43 member states in favor, none against, and 6 abstentions.[76]

On 2 December, the General Assembly passed the resolution adopted by the Ad Hoc Political Committee. Resolution 393(5) garnered the support of 46 countries (including the Arab delegations) with no opposition and 6 abstentions. In Clause 2 of the resolution, the UNRWA was directed to continue to provide direct aid to refugees in need. For this purpose the United Nations budgeted a sum of 20 million dollars for the period between 1 July 1951 and 30 June 1952. In Clause 5 establishment of a Reintegration Fund was stipulated, mandated to underwrite plans recommended by states in the region that would be approved by the agency. These plans were supposed to enable the reintegration of the refugees in the economic life of states of the region and extricate them from dependence on welfare. Clause 6 granted the new fund 30 million dollars for the period between 1 July 1951 and 30 June 1952. The monies for aid and for the Reintegration Fund were supposed to come primarily from contributions by member states.[77]

A day prior to approval of the resolution in the General Assembly, the Israeli government decided to budget a sum of one million Israel pounds (equivalent to three million dollars) to the Reintegration Fund.[78] Three weeks later, Ambassador Eban publicly announced the decision;[79] in doing so, Israel sought to signal its full support behind establishment of the new fund.

In his meeting with members of the Knesset Foreign Affairs and Defense Committee, the director-general of the Ministry of Foreign Affairs, Walter

128 *An exchange transaction*

Eytan, stated that the decision to establish a Reintegration Fund was a positive move from Israel's perspective on two counts: "(a) the emphasis in this decision was on absorption elsewhere and non-return [without repatriation] of the refugees to Israel; (b) also, this time the main sum wasn't budgeted for aid, rather for more practical things." The advantage of the resolution, according to Eytan, stemmed also from its very foundation "on the idea of sums and collective compensation, that is, not every individual would be entitled to claim compensation, rather everything would be paid to a fund," as Israel preferred.[80]

Besides discussion of providing aid to the refugees and rehabilitating them, the Ad Hoc Political Committee addressed the political aspects of the refugee problem and resolution of the Arab-Israeli conflict as a whole. Discussion of these issues began on 29 November and continued until 6 December. The Conciliation Commission's report from the beginning of October was before the committee. In deliberations, delegates from the Arab states harshly attacked Israel's refusal to allow refugees to return to their former places of residence. They demanded that a resolution be passed that would require Israel to do so and obligated Israel to pay compensation to those who were not interested in repatriation. Likewise, the Arab delegates demanded that the refugee problem, including the compensation question, be separated from comprehensive settlement issue. In its response, Israel reiterated its argument that resolution of the problem lay in resettlement of the refugees in the Arab states, and that Israel was willing to pay compensation for abandoned land.[81] While Israelis and Arabs continued to argue, in the meantime, the United States, Britain, France, and Turkey presented a joint draft resolution. The draft called for the sides to begin direct negotiations without delay to settle all outstanding problems between them and directed the Conciliation Commission to establish a special office that would deal, among other things, with all the aspects of the compensation issue, primarily estimation of the refugee property. The joint draft was put to a vote in the Ad Hoc Political Committee and was passed by a large majority on 6 December.[82]

Due to the emphasis the new resolution put on Clause 11 of Resolution 194 (3), as will be detailed below, Israel chose to abstain from the vote. Nevertheless, Sharett saw a genuine advantage in the draft resolution, since it called upon the rival sides to discuss all the problems outstanding between them and not to focus first and foremost on the refugee issue (as the Arabs had demanded).[83] Moreover, Israel felt that, in the final analysis, the resolution identified the compensation issue and not the repatriation question as the primary and most practical issue in need of settlement, in order to take a comprehensive solution to the refugee problem forward.[84] On 14 December, the General Assembly plenum passed the joint draft resolution that had been approved by the Ad Hoc Political Committee a week earlier. Resolution 394 (5) was passed with 48 in favor, 5 against, and 4 abstentions. The resolution called upon the governments concerned to reach a final settlement of all points of disagreement between them through negotiations that would be managed by the Conciliation Commission or directly between the parties. Clause 2 directed the Conciliation Commission to establish a new office that would operate under its authority and deal with the compensation issue according to Clause 11 of Resolution 194(3), parallel to execution of the other goals stipulated in this clause. At the same time, the new office would consult with the relevant parties (that is Israel and its Arab neighbors) about the various means that should be employed to protect the refugees' rights, property, and interests.[85]

On 22 January 1951 Foreign Minister Sharett appeared before the Knesset Foreign Affairs and Defense Committee to sum up the 5th General Assembly from an Israeli viewpoint. He addressed Resolution 394(5) and updated the committee members about attempts by the Arab states to separate the refugee problem from all other aspects outstanding between the sides and their endeavors to advance a resolution that would call for the repatriation of the refugees to Israel. The minister summed up the results of these anti-Israel offensives, declaring:

> In both these objectives, to use an understatement, one needs to say that the Arabs didn't succeed. One could [even] say they were defeated, at least compared to what they planned to achieve [...] In terms of the goals they presented to themselves, one could mark it up to a defeat for the Arab side.

Sharett pointed out to his audience the absence of the word "return" in Resolution 394(5) – that is, there was no clear call for the refugees' return – explaining, "This was the product of much bargaining." He also revealed that in the first draft of the resolution (in Clause 2), it was proposed that a new office be established that would care first and foremost for the return of the refugees to Israel, but this demand was dropped during deliberations. The practical part (in Clause 2) of the resolution focused, therefore, on the compensation issue and not on repatriation. Sharett elaborated the positive side of the resolution from Israel's perspective, saying:

> That is, the departure point of the operative part [of the resolution] is that people won't return. Emphasis on the matter of compensation can be grave on one hand, but [on the other hand] it means retreat from the demand for a return. About compensation it speaks explicitly and solidly [as a matter of fact]. Afterwards it was said that this Committee [i.e. the new office] would also examine other aspects of the refugee problem. One could say they mean also to return them, but this was said between the lines, not [said] explicitly.

In the foreign minister's opinion, if one compared Resolution 394(5) with Resolution 194(3) passed two years earlier "there is no question that the retreat from the demand to return the refugees is clearly obvious to the eye."

130 *An exchange transaction*

While one still can't say that the demand for return has been eliminated in the 5th Assembly, "it has received a critical blow."

Afterwards, the minister began to address the 2 December Resolution 393 (5). The establishment of the Reintegration Fund, said Sharett, hides within it "a number of welcome elements": first, there will be separation between monies allocated to relief and monies allocated to the fund that will be used to resettle the refugees; and second, the permanent resettlement of the refugees and their rehabilitation will begin immediately. Nevertheless, he said, on the road to success, the Reintegration Fund still faces difficult problems: (a) the UNRWA would need the approval of the Arab governments to operate the [resettlement] plans, and there was no assurance that these governments would indeed cooperate; (b) it would take some time until one could see whether the countries, primarily the United States, indeed would contribute the necessary amounts to activate the plans; (c) it wasn't certain that sufficient practical and effective programs to settle the refugees could be found.[86] Against such a backdrop, Sharett warned that "the campaign to eradicate the Arab refugee problem" would, in the end, continue some years.[87]

Prime Minister Ben-Gurion, like his foreign minister, concluded following the 5th General Assembly that the international community had begun to accept the solution founded on the resettlement principle. In a speech in Tel Aviv before the Commercial and Industrial Club, Ben-Gurion argued that "the Arab states as well are already inclined towards rehabilitation in place of relief."[88] In a meeting with Jerusalem journalists, in response to a question about the refugee problem, he clarified:

> There are few people, if there are any people, who believe that we need to return [the Palestinian refugees]. And even less believe we will return refugees. This matter has begun to take root in the mind of the general public, [people are] beginning to comprehend that on this there is nothing to talk about.[89]

The American State Department, the British Foreign Office, and the Conciliation Commission were party to the Israeli assessment that the 5th General Assembly's resolutions had center-staged the resettlement principle in the international arena at the expense of the repatriation principle. A report prepared by the State Department in the first week of February 1951 on American policy in the Middle East cited that the UNRWA "has concluded that the only hope of reintegration for any substantial number of these people [the Palestinian refugees] lies in resettlement in the Arab countries." The authors of the report stated that the Reintegration Fund would work to implement this conclusion.[90] At the outset of January, Foreign Office Eastern Department official in London Trefor Evans argued that in voting in favor of Resolution 393(5) the Arab governments expressed their support of the principle of resettling the refugees.[91] Similar assessment was voiced by the American under-secretary of state, James Webb, in a memorandum sent at the end of January to the

National Security Council, designed to examine the changes that had taken place in the Middle East in the course of 1950. In describing the Arab refugee issue, the memorandum stated: "By their public acceptance of this resolution [Resolution 393(5)], and by private statements, Arab representatives have indicated that they regard resettlement of most of the refugees in Arab territory as inevitable."[92] In talks between Avraham Biran and the secretary of the Conciliation Commission, de-Azcarate, the secretary claimed that according to the mood prevailing at the 5th General Assembly and in light of the resolutions that were adopted there, the impression was that the Palestinian refugees could never return to the Jewish state. In de-Azcarate's opinion, it was time to direct all endeavors towards their settlement in their present places of residence.[93]

Party to de-Azcarate's opinion were his colleagues in the UN agencies dealing with the refugee problem. In two joint meetings at the beginning of 1951 between the UNRWA's advisory commission and members of the Conciliation Commission, including the UNRWA's director, it was decided to split work between the organizations. The two sides agreed that the UNRWA would execute the reintegration programs, that is, resettlement. The Conciliation Commission, for its part, would place the issues of compensation and repatriation in the hands of the new office: henceforth, the Refugees Office, whose establishment was anchored in Resolution 394(5).[94]

In the course of the joint meetings, however, the two bodies judged that if the Conciliation Commission dealt with the repatriation issue, even in a limited way,[95] it would surely lessen the refugees' readiness to adopt the resettlement principle. In order to avoid this situation the two agencies resolved that they must be very careful not to mislead the refugees with false hopes regarding the chances they would ever return to Israel. Thus, it was agreed that the Conciliation Commission's discussions with the Arab governments regarding repatriation would be played down.[96]

The division of labor between the two United Nations agencies was carefully maintained. Over time, the more the Conciliation Commission's status and relevance declined, the more the solution placed in its hands (that is, repatriation) dissipated. Parallel to this, the UNRWA's foothold among the Palestinian refugee population deepened, strengthening international consciousness of the resettlement principle.

Notes

1 UNPCC, A/1255, pp. 12–13.
2 ISA, MFA 2441/2, A Memorandum from the Conciliation Commission to Gideon Rafael, 29 March 1950.
3 UNPCC, A/1255, p. 14.
4 DEPI, Vol. 5, Document 228, M. Sharett to the Chairman of the United Nations Conciliation Commission for Palestine, 6 May 1950.
5 UNPCC, A/1288, p. 19.
6 ISA, MFA 2441/3, Text of Note Handed to Dr. Kahany by P.C.C., 11 May 1950.

132   *An exchange transaction*

7 UNPCC, A/1288, p. 20.
8 ISA, MFA 2441/3, M. Kahany to E. Palmer, 20 May 1950.
9 DEPI, Vol. 5, Document 262, M. Kahany to W. Eytan, 30 May 1950, appendix.
10 UNPCC, A/1288, pp. 20–21; FRUS, 1950, V, p. 928, The United States Representative on the Palestine Conciliation Commission to the Secretary of State, 13 June 1950.
11 UNPCC, A/1288, p. 21.
12 ISA, MFA 2451/18, Initial Steps on the Question of Compensation, December 1949.
13 ISA, Provisional Government Meeting, 16 June 1948, pp. 19–47.
14 ISA, Government Meeting, 11 October 1949, p. 26.
15 For minutes of the Liff Committee's meetings, see ISA, GL 17109/28.
16 ISA, MFA 3743/12, Report of the Committee Examining the Question of Compensation for Absentees' Properties, undated.
17 ISA, MFA 2447/1B, Information to Israel Missions Abroad, 10 July 1950.
18 ISA, MFA 2447/1B, Information to Israel Missions Abroad, 10 July 1950.
19 UKNA, FO 371/82247, E1825/138, Knight to Evans, 12 June 1950.
20 UKNA, FO 371/82257, E18213/3, FO Minute, Sheringham, 15 June 1950; UKNA, FO 371/82196, E10110/26, From Foreign Office to Washington, 12 July 1950.
21 UKNA, FO 371/82247, E1825/138, Knight to Evans, 12 June 1950; FRUS, 1950, V, p. 210, Record of Informal United States – United Kingdom Discussions, 21 September 1950; Ilan Pappe, *Britain and the Arab-Israeli Conflict 1948–1951*, New York: St. Martin's Press, 1988, pp. 160–1.
22 UKNA, FO 371/82237, E1822/46, Minutes of Meeting Held in the Foreign Office on 3 July 1950.
23 UKNA, FO 371/82248, E1825/163, Knight to Evans, 25 July 1950.
24 UKNA, FO 371/82248, E1825/168, Knight to Evans, 8 August 1950.
25 ISA, MFA 2384/15, Third Meeting: Israel-Arab Countries, 18 July 1950.
26 ISA, MFA 2491/5, R. Shiloah to M. Sharett, 30 July 1950.
27 ISA, 7562/4 A, Foreign Affairs and Defense Committee Meeting, 7 August 1950, pp. 7–8.
28 ISA, 7562/5 A, Foreign Affairs and Defense Committee Meeting, 8 August 1950, p. 17.
29 UNPCC, A/1367/Rev. 1, p. 17.
30 ISA, MFA 2441/3, A. Eban to the Director-General, 9 August 1950.
31 DEPI, Vol. 5, Document 341, Meeting: M. Sharett – Members of the United Nations Conciliation Commission for Palestine (Tel Aviv, 17 August 1950.
32 ISA, Government Meeting, 21 August 1950, pp. 6–25.
33 ISA, Government's Resolutions, Government's Resolution from 21 August 1950.
34 ISA, MFA 2441/3, Dr. Tevfic Rustu Aras' Meeting with the Prime Minister, on 23 August 1950; BGA, BGD, 23 August 1950.
35 ISA, MFA 4372/3, The Prime Minister's Conversation with Mr. Palmer, 30 August 1950; BGA, BGD, 30 August 1950; FRUS, 1950, V, p. 989, The United States Representative on the Palestine Conciliation Commission to the Secretary of State, 31 August 1950.
36 DEPI, Vol. 5, Document 365, A. Eban to M. Sharett, 31 August 1950.
37 DEPI, Vol. 5, Document 365, A. Eban to M. Sharett, 31 August 1950, Note 2.
38 ISA, MFA 2424/24I, Subject: The Arab's Attacks against Us at the Next General Assembly, 27 August 1950.
39 ISA, MFA 2424/24I, Information for Cabinet Members, 28 August 1950.
40 ISA, MFA 4372/3, A. Biran to the Foreign Minister, 29 August 1950.
41 ISA, Government Meeting, 30 August 1950, pp. 6–25.
42 ISA, MFA 2447/1II, Information to Israel Missions Abroad, 6 September 1950.

An exchange transaction 133

43 In his remarks to the Knesset Foreign Affairs and Defense Committee, Foreign Minister Sharett asserted that the solution of the refugees' problem required their resettlement and that Israel would make its contribution by waiving the reparations owed to it by the Arab countries for damages suffered during the war: ISA, 7562/5 A, Foreign Affairs and Defense Committee Meeting, 1 September 1950, pp. 2–3.
44 ISA, MFA 4372/3, Joint Meeting between the UNPCC and the UNRWA, in Jerusalem, on 1 September 1950.
45 UKNA, FO 371/82249, E1825/204, Knight to Evans, 19 September 1950.
46 UKNA, FO 371/82249, E1825/204, Evans to Knight, undated.
47 FRUS, 1950, V, p. 993, The United States Representative on the Palestine Conciliation Commission to the Secretary of State, 9 September 1950.
48 UKNA, FO 371/81922, E10213/10, FO Minute, 22 September 1950.
49 UKNA, FO 371/81922, E10213/10, The Palestine Question, the Role of the PCC in the General Assembly and the Tripartite Declaration, 22 September 1950.
50 UKNA, FO, 371/82197, E10110/59, Record of Conversation between Furlonge and Azcarate, 26 September 1950.
51 See, for example, ISA, MFA 2441/3, A.S. to M. Sharett, 8 September 1950.
52 ISA, Government Meeting, 7 September 1950, pp. 2–3.
53 FRUS, 1950, V, p. 182, Memorandum of Conversation, by Mr. Arthur Z. Gardiner of the Bureau of Near Eastern, South Asian and African Affairs, 1 September 1950; Meir Avidan, *Main Aspects of Israel-United States Relations during the 1950's*, Jerusalem: The Hebrew University, 1982, p. 13 (Hebrew).
54 FRUS, 1950, V, p. 299, Memorandum of Informal United States – United Kingdom Discussion, 19 September 1950; FRUS, 1950, V, p. 999, The Secretary of State to the Embassy in Egypt, 11 September 1950.
55 FRUS, 1950, V, p. 1213, The Minister in Syria to the Secretary of State, 19 July 1950; FRUS, 1950, V, p. 1106, Memorandum of Conversation, by the Officer in Charge of Lebanon-Syria-Iraq Affairs, 1 August 1950.
56 ISA, MFA 2460/9, A Report on a Conversation at the State Department Held on 30 September of that Year between Mr. Shiloah and Mr. Berry, in the Presence of Mr. Rockwell and Mr. Keren, 12 October 1950.
57 FRUS, 1950, V, p. 1026, Memorandum of Conversation by Mr. Wells Stabler, 9 October 1950.
58 ISA, MFA 2460/9, A Report on a Conversation at the State Department Held on 11 October of that Year between Mr. T. Kollek and Mr. Berry, in the Presence of Mr. S. Rockwell and Mr. M, Keren, 13 October 1950.
59 FRUS, 1950, V, p. 1037, Memorandum of Conversation, 26 October 1950.
60 DEPI, Vol. 5, Document 415, R. Shiloah to W. Eytan, 12 October 1950.
61 UNPCC, A/1367/Rev. 1, pp. 17–18.
62 UNRWA, A/1451/Rev. 1, p. 6.
63 UNRWA, A/1451/Rev. 1, pp. 7–13.
64 UKNA, FO 371/82250, E1825/220, From Foreign Office to New York, 28 October 1950.
65 ISA, Government Meeting, 24 October 1950, pp. 22–4.
66 Uri Bialer, *Between East and West: Israel's Foreign Policy Orientation, 1948– 1956*, Cambridge: Cambridge University Press, 1990, pp. 206–7; Shimon Golan, *Hot Border, Cold War: The Formulation of Israel's Security Policy, 1949–1953*, Tel Aviv: Ma'arachot, 2000, p. 359 (Hebrew); Yemima Rosenthal, "Israel's Foreign Policy: Between Security and Diplomacy," in Hanna Yablonka and Zvi Zameret (eds), *The First Decade: 1948–1958*, Jerusalem: Yad Izhak Ben-Zvi, 1997, pp. 181–3 (Hebrew).
67 Rosenthal, "Israel's Foreign Policy," p. 183.
68 Bialer, *Between East and West*, p. 220; Golan, *Hot Border, Cold War*, pp. 383–4; Rosenthal, "Israel's Foreign Policy," p. 183.

134   *An exchange transaction*

69 Bialer, *Between East and West*, pp. 197–202; Golan, *Hot Border, Cold War*, pp. 377–9, 383; Zach Levey, *Israel and the Western Powers, 1952–1960*, Chapel Hill, NC: University of North Carolina Press, 1997, p. 4; Rosenthal, "Israel's Foreign Policy," pp. 183 –5.

70 ISA, Government Meeting, 30 October 1950, pp. 8–15.

71 ISA, Government's Resolutions, Government's Resolution from 30 October 1950.

72 UKNA, FO 371/82257, E18213/14, FO Minute, Furlonge, 4 November 1950.

73 UKNA, FO 371/82257, E18213/18A, Knox Helm to Furlonge, 14 November 1950.

74 For various details concerning the Israeli economy during those years, see: Haim Barkai, *The Beginnings of the Israeli Economy*, Jerusalem: Bialik Institute, 1990 (Hebrew); Don Patinkin, *The Israel Economy: The First Decade*, Jerusalem: The Falk Institute for Economic Research in Israel, 1967.

75 ISA, MFA 2491/5, Appendix, undated; ISA, MFA 2581/7, Israel Service of Information, 10 November 1950.

76 Rony E. Gabbay, *A Political Study of the Arab-Jewish Conflict – The Arab Refugee Problem (A Case Study)*, Geneve: Librairie E. Droz, 1959, pp. 386–8.

77 George J. Tomeh (ed.), *United Nations Resolutions on Palestine and the Arab-Israeli Conflict, 1947 – 1974*, vol. 1, Washington, DC: Institute for Palestine Studies, 1975, pp. 21–2.

78 ISA, Government's Resolutions, Government's Resolution from 1 December 1950.

79 Gabbay, *A Political Study*, p. 393.

80 ISA, 7562/6 A, Foreign Affairs and Defense Committee Meeting, 12 December 1950, pp. 4–5.

81 ISA, MFA 2402/9, Problems Regarding the Economic Rehabilitation of the Arab Refugees from Palestine, undated, pp. 24–5.

82 DEPI, Vol. 5, Editorial Note, p. 690.

83 DEPI, Vol. 5, Document 493, M. Sharett to W. Eytan, 7 December 1950.

84 See Shelly Fried's analysis: Shelly Fried, "Precious Land – Israel's Policy on Compensation for Abandoned Palestinian Property, 1947–1951: From the UN Partition Resolution to the Paris Conference," MA thesis, Tel Aviv University, 1998, p. 73 (Hebrew).

85 Tomeh, *United Nations Resolutions*, pp. 22–3.

86 ISA, 7562/7 A, Foreign Affairs and Defense Committee Meeting, 22 January 1951, pp. 4–9; similar remarks were made by the foreign minister in a political discussion held the next day in the Knesset: *Knesset Minutes*, vol. 8, 23 January 1951, p. 850. And see also Zalman Aranne's comments: *Knesset Minutes*, vol. 8, 23 January 1951, p. 866.

87 *Knesset Minutes*, vol. 8, 23 January 1951, p. 850.

88 BGA, Correspondences, The Prime Minister's Speech at the Commercial and Industrial Club in Tel Aviv, 6 April 1951.

89 BGA, Minutes of Meetings, Ben-Gurion's Meeting with Jerusalem Journalists, 12 June 1951.

90 FRUS, 1951, V, p. 574, Department of State Policy Statement, 6 February 1951.

91 UKNA, FO 371/91399, E1821/1, Evans to Knight, 4 January 1951.

92 FRUS, 1951, V, pp. 18–19, Memorandum by the Under Secretary of State to the Executive Secretary, National Security Council, 26 January 1951.

93 ISA, MFA 2441/4, Conversation with Dr. Azcarate, 14 January 1951.

94 UKNA, FO 371/91410, E1826/15, Summary Conclusions Reached at the Meeting of the Advisory Commission and the Director with the Conciliation Commission, 26 January 1951.

95 Michael Fischbach, who studied the activity of the UN bodies with respect to the issue of compensation to Palestinian refugees, argues that throughout its lifetime

the Conciliation Commission acted on the basis of the American assumption that repatriation was not practicable and that efforts should instead be directed at obtaining compensation from Israel for the abandoned Arab property. Michael R Fischbach, "The United Nations and Palestinian Refugee Property Compensation," *Journal of Palestine Studies* 31(2), 2002, p. 36.
96 UKNA, FO 371/91410, E1826/16, Summary of the Decisions Reached at the Informal Meeting of the Advisory Commission and the Director with the Palestine Conciliation Commission, 6 February 1951.

6 Israel and the compensation issue prior to the Paris Conference and during its proceedings

The Refugees Office

After the close of the 5th General Assembly, members of the Conciliation Commission went to the Middle East and, at the end of January 1951, again settled into their Jerusalem offices at "the Government House." In the first five months of 1951, members of the commission devoted themselves to establishing the Refugees Office.[1] During this period, and in essence up until the Paris Conference convened in the fall, no official negotiations took place on the refugee problem between Israeli representatives and representatives of the Arab states, neither direct talks nor talks with the commission's mediation.[2]

On 15 May the Conciliation Commission announced to the Arab and Israel governments the official establishment of the Refugees Office.[3] The new body was headed by a Danish national, Holger Andersen. The other staff included an economic advisor, Rene Servoise; land expert, John Berncastle; legal counsel, Beck Erim; and an assistant and a secretary. After they moved into their offices in Jerusalem, members of the Refugees Office began carrying out talks on refugee issues with representatives of Israel, Egypt, Jordan, Syria, and Lebanon; with a spokesperson for the refugees; and with experts in issues related to the Palestinian abandoned property.

It became clear to Israel that the new office would deal solely with "professional questions concerning the compensation problem." One should keep in mind that Resolution 394(5) stated that the Refugees Office would deal with all matters mentioned in Clause 11 of Resolution 194(3), including repatriation. The office's focus only on the question of compensation reflected the Conciliation Commission's inclination to invest a considerable part of its mediation efforts in solving this issue.

In the first stage of its work, the Refugees Office intended to address assessment of the total abandoned property of Palestinians and its value. The sources upon which it sought to base its calculations were: documents from the British Colonial Office; the files of Israel's state custodian for absentees' property; interviews with officials who dealt with the issue; and questionnaires that were filled out by the refugees themselves regarding their property. In the next stage, the Refugees Office was supposed to examine what means for paying compensation were at Israel's disposal. Nevertheless, Andersen and his colleagues had no intention of setting the sum total of compensation that the State of Israel must pay. The range of their authority was solely technical, and the magnitude of compensation was a political issue that was supposed to be hammered out in negotiations between the Conciliation Commission and the Israeli government.[4] In any case, in the end, the operation of the Refugees Office had an impact only on the first stage of this process.

In the course of June and July, Andersen and his people conducted a number of meetings with Israeli representatives in order to obtain information regarding the Palestinian abandoned property. Israel, however, refrained for the most part from cooperating with the Refugees Office. It appears that in light of Israel's dire economic state at the time, Jerusalem feared that should the Refugees Office fulfill its mission, its success would place Israel in a position where it would be forced to begin paying compensation that it could ill afford.[5] Andersen and his colleagues did not intend to give up, however. They stuck to their undertaking in Israel, and at the end of August completed their work. The office's appraisal of the extent of abandoned property left by Palestinians and its value was turned over to the Conciliation Commission. The commission decided to use the data at the Arab-Israeli conference convened in Paris in the fall of 1951.[6]

Moves towards convening another Arab-Israeli conference

Establishment of the Refugees Office was the only concrete step taken by the Conciliation Commission to forwarding solution of the Arab-Israeli conflict during its first six months of operation in Jerusalem. Such an achievement was exceedingly thin, particularly since the new body had addressed only one aspect of the conflict: the compensation issue. The commission's idleness frustrated its members. Such feelings were expressed in a lengthy letter, dated 9 May, penned by the American representative on the commission, Ely Palmer, to Secretary of State Acheson. Palmer complained that "during past three months there has been no progress made on compensation, repatriation, blocked accounts or peace negotiation as envisaged in General Assembly resolution of 14 December 1950." In Palmer's opinion, in order to break the impasse it would be appropriate to embark on a new political initiative. A precondition to this was that the American representatives on the commission take a more decisive approach. Yet, Palmer added, American representatives could not do so since they had no clear comprehension of the State Department's objectives at this point in time on the various aspects of the Arab-Israeli conflict, mainly the refugee problem. When Palmer addressed this issue, he reported that the compensation question was liable to remain "academic" until sources of funding could be found, and from the perspective of the Conciliation Commission, repatriation was no more than lip service. Besides these points, Israel was not willing to unfreeze blocked bank accounts. The State Department must therefore support two steps: first, preparation of a "realistic" plan for

138 Israel and the compensation issue

compensation that would suggest funding possibilities for the sum that Israel would be forced to pay. "This in itself," wrote Palmer, "would be [an] important contribution toward [a] political settlement in [the] area." Second, direct talks between Israel and Jordan and between Israel and Syria, both under UN auspices on topics covered by the armistice agreements. Palmer closed his letter cautioning that if Washington would not actively support the Conciliation Commission, the commission would turn into a symbol of the United Nation's failure in solving the Middle East conflict, and in the eyes of the Arabs would be viewed as a sign of American apathy towards events in the region.[7]

Acheson's response to Palmer's appeal came on 12 June, in which the secretary of state addressed primarily the refugee problem. In the State Department's appraisal, the prospects were small that a large number of refugees could realize the concept of repatriation; but despite this State Department officials thought that it was appropriate for the Conciliation Commission to try to encourage Israel to publish a statement expressing its willingness to allow repatriation of a certain number of refugees to its territory. Washington believed that in regard to compensation, the commission must make an effort to achieve an agreement on the issue between Israel and its Arab neighbors, although it felt the chances were faint that Israel could pay any significant sum. Apparently, the money for compensation would, in the last analysis, have to come from outside (non-Israeli) sources. Aside from the refugee issue, the Arab states and Israel must weigh issuing a non-aggression declaration, which hopefully would dampen the hostility between them. Israel could also contribute to the matter, if it would adopt several confidence-building measures, such as allotting an area in Haifa Port for the use of the Arabs, opening a land corridor to make passage between Jordan and Egypt, and unfreezing the blocked bank accounts of Palestinian refugees.[8]

The State Department had no intention of leaving these proposals solely "on paper." Less than a month after sending this response, Secretary of State Acheson suggested to Palmer that the Conciliation Commission initiate a conference where members of the commission would meet separately with representatives of Israel and with representatives of the Arab states, to discuss the proposals raised by the State Department. The State Department judged that beyond what had already been achieved over the past six months, there was little to be gained by doggedly sticking to the current format of personal informal meetings between members of the Conciliation Commission and Israeli and Arab representatives.[9]

In the following weeks, the State Department continued to mold the concept of a conference, and by the end of July, Acheson was in a position to send a formulated and detailed memorandum on the subject to Palmer. Washington held that the conference should deal with four primary issues:

1 a non-aggression declaration or treaty between the rival sides: this step could significantly dampen the hostility between Arabs and Israelis and

create a positive atmosphere for treatment of the multitude of other problems pending;

2 repatriation: an issue that could be dealt with by designating certain categories of refugees whose return to their homes would be perceived by Israel as economically beneficial. In addition, it would be possible to permit wealthy refugees to return to Israel. This step would remove several of the largest compensation claims on the books;

3 compensation: an agreement between Israel and the Arabs on the principle of compensation could take forward payment that Israel would have to pay. Settlement of this issue would assist the Conciliation Commission in convincing the Arab states to ease the economic restrictions they had imposed on Israel;

4 the Mixed Armistice Commissions: the willingness of the rival sides to expand the topics treated by the Mixed Armistice Commissions would improve day-to-day relations between them.[10]

Thus, despite the resounding failures of the Lausanne Conference and the Geneva talks, the United States sought to try this diplomatic course of action again. Two main factors stood behind this decision: The impasse that the Conciliation Commission encountered when it sought to bring about a comprehensive Arab-Israeli settlement had, to a large extent, rendered its own existence useless. Washington sensed that what was needed was another mediation initiative before the 6th General Assembly convened (in late 1951), when the commission was scheduled to submit a report of its operations. The Americans were apprehensive about the future of the commission if it would be unable to demonstrate that its operations in the region had produced positive results;[11] A series of events – the outbreak of conflict between Syria and Israel over the draining of the Hula Valley in the spring of 1951,[12] diplomatic sparring the summer of that year between Israel and Egypt over freedom of navigation through the Suez Canal,[13] and the assassination of King Abdullah in July – all threatened to collapse the armistice agreements and sweep the entire region into a state of chaos. The western powers could ill afford to wait for such a scenario to emerge, since such a development would jeopardize their efforts to establish an anti-Soviet pact. Consequently, the administration in Washington was prepared to do everything in its power to cool down the hot lava bubbling just below the surface in the Middle East, by finding solutions to several of the problems that divided Israel and its Arab neighbors.[14]

It should be kept in mind that both Palmer and the State Department focused first and foremost on efforts to resolve the Palestinian refugee problem.[15] There were two reasons for this: first of all, the Arab insistence on discussing the Palestinian refugee problem; second, the American assumption that the refugee issue was one of the core problems of the Arab-Israeli conflict.[16] The British Foreign Office in London shared this assumption.[17]

140   *Israel and the compensation issue*

At the outset of August, Palmer updated the French representatives on the Conciliation Commission, de Boisanger and his new replacement, Leon Marchal, as well as the secretary of the commission, de-Azcaratel, about the State Department initiative. The French representatives responded favorably and even proposed that the conference be convened in Paris.[18]

The invitation to the conference submitted to Foreign Minister Sharett cited that the Conciliation Commission was willing to again offer its assistance to the rival sides in the search for a solution to the issues in dispute. The letter called upon Israel to decide who would be its representatives at the talks, which would open in Paris on 10 September (and, in fact, opened after a short delay, on 13 September).[19]

Sharett requested two clarifications from the commission before the Israeli government could give its answer: first, would the meetings between Israeli representatives and Arab representatives be direct or would they be carried out with the commission serving as a go-between? second, what would be the conference's proposed agenda and, if it had yet to be set, by what method would it be laid down?[20] Sharett's queries to the invitation reflected Israel's traditional apprehensions regarding the even-handedness of the Conciliation Commission's "mediation services." In a 14 August cabinet meeting, the foreign minister reminded the cabinet that already in the winter of 1949, after the failure of the Lausanne Conference, he had told the Conciliation Commission that the format of indirect negotiations wasn't effective and that the commission must stop submitting its own proposals for Israel and the Arab states to study, since they immediately became bargaining points in the eyes of the Arabs, even if they are unacceptable to Israel.[21] In internal correspondence among officials in the Ministry of Foreign Affairs and in formal meetings that Sharett and senior officials in his ministry conducted with foreign diplomats, it was underscored that it was imperative that meetings between the rival sides be direct. Likewise, members of the Ministry of Foreign Affairs also expressed their concern regarding proposals that the Conciliation Commission might raise on the Paris Conference's agenda, particularly in regard to repatriation.[22]

On 22 August the government again discussed the Conciliation Commission's invitation. The foreign minister predicted that the commission's proposals during the conference would be "in the middle" – that is "between our demands and the demands of the Arabs." Yet since the Arabs had nothing to offer Israel in terms of territory and refugees, in the last analysis, the proposals would be directed towards gaining some sort of concessions from Israel. Opposition to the Conciliation Commission's proposals on Israel's part would be viewed as opposition to the United Nations itself.

Despite this stark forecast, Sharett asked the government to give the Ministry of Foreign Affairs authority to answer the invitation in the affirmative. He explained that commission members sought to calm apprehensions in Jerusalem by assuring Israeli diplomats of the commission's good intentions in regard to the nature of the meetings and the pending agenda of the conference.

Israel and the compensation issue 141

Furthermore, Sharett added, he could not foresee any way of avoiding discussion of the disputed issues. Even if these issues were not discussed at the Paris Conference, they were liable to be raised on the agenda of the 6th General Assembly, which would open the coming winter. Closing discussion of the issue, Prime Minister Ben-Gurion gave the Ministry of Foreign Affairs permission to answer the commission's invitation in the affirmative, provided the ministry would consult with him on the wording of the response.[23]

In the course of the next three weeks, senior officials in the Ministry of Foreign Affairs conducted consultations on the conference issue. The conclusions they arrived at were expressed in the response letter that Israel submitted to the Conciliation Commission.[24] In the response, Foreign Minister Sharett expressed his government's agreement to participate in the proposed talks, but requested to note several conditions that, the Israeli government estimated, would enhance the chances of the gathering's success: first of all, at the outset, the Conciliation Commission should gain the agreement of the two sides to the assumption that the objective of the Paris Conference was to achieve a final settlement of all questions pending between Israel and its Arab neighbors. Second, problems should not be discussed as isolated issues, rather only as part of a comprehensive settlement. Third, separate meetings of the commission with each party were not a suitable substitute for direct talks between the adversaries themselves, even if such direct talks would take place under the commission's auspices. Sharett suggested that meetings between the Israel delegation and each of the Arab delegations be conducted separately, so in each meeting issues that interested both parties could be discussed. Apart from these suggestions, Israel opposed the idea that the Conciliation Commission would raise its own proposals for the delegations to study. At the close of the response letter, Sharett informed the commission of the names of the Israeli representatives to the talks: Israel Minister in Paris Maurice Fischer, who would head the delegation; counselor at the Israel legation, Emile Najar; and the director of the Middle East Division in the Israeli Ministry of Foreign Affairs, Shmuel Divon.[25]

Like the Israelis, the Arabs also appended many comments to their response. Despite their agreement to participate in the conference, they objected to direct contacts between their representatives and members of the Israeli delegation. Beside that, they demanded that the commission's proposals be in line with United Nations resolutions related to the conflict, including Resolution 194(3). Finally, they reiterated their public demands that Israel allow the Palestinian refugees to return to their abandoned homes.[26]

The impending convention in Paris was discussed at length by the UNRWA. It became apparent that the new head of the UNRWA, John Blandford, and the members of the agency's advisory commission were worried about the negative effect that the conference would have on the readiness of Arab rulers to make progress on resettlement plans.[27] Their concern testified to the great importance that senior UNRWA officials assigned the resettlement principle as *the* solution to the refugee problem. Blandford told Palmer in a

142   *Israel and the compensation issue*

meeting between the two that there were two paths to solving the Arab-Israeli conflict: one was through diplomatic negotiations to achieve a comprehensive settlement, as was attempted at Lausanne and Geneva; the other was to address certain problems that arose from the conflict one by one, similar to what the UNRWA had been doing for over a year in regard to the refugee issue. It was impossible to put both into action at the same time without each jeopardizing the other, he argued. As proof Blandford noted the initial response of the Arab states to the Conciliation Commission's invitation: Syria was inclined to put off cooperation with the UNRWA until the results of the Paris Conference clarified, and Egypt and Lebanon feared that the suggested conference would postpone talks on resettlement programs for an unlimited time.

Besides this, the ideas floated in the memorandum that the State Department sent to Palmer at the end of July raised Blandford's ire. The proposal that repatriation be put on the Paris Conference's agenda could, in his judgment, fan false hopes among Palestinians and a number of Arab states that the masses would be able to return to Israel, while there were clear signs that they had begun to acclimate to the fact that this solution was impossible. Furthermore, the proposal that refugees who were designated "economically useful" be allowed to return to their homes was both unfeasible and undemocratic. He compared this to the actions of the Nazis, who postponed the extermination of Jews who were designated "economically useful" to the Third Reich's war machine (!). This proposal would leave all the economically inferior refugees in the Arab states and evoke bitterness among the Arabs towards the United Nations and the United States. Blandford summed up his case, expressing hopes that the State Department would ensure that deliberations at the Paris Conference would not unintentionally undermine the UNRWA's work.[28]

Things in a similar vein were voiced by Henry Knight from the UNRWA's advisory commission in his reports to the British Foreign Office.[29] His supervisors in London indeed were worried about the negative influence that the conference was liable to have on the UNRWA, and therefore they endeavored to convince the State Department and the Conciliation Commission to play down as much as possible sensitive issues like repatriation.[30]

On 12 September 1951, a day before the formal openings of the Paris Conference, Foreign Minister Sharett presented the cabinet with his ministry's appraisal of the position Israel should take in the talks. Sharett said that the Americans would do everything in their power to bring about resolution of the conflict and establishment of stability in the region, and therefore one could expect pressure on Israel and its Arab neighbors to make political concessions. However, from all standpoints, it was easier to pressure Israel: "We are few and they [the Arabs] are many"; Israel is dependent on the United Nations more than the Arabs; Israel is more sensitive to the international arena; and its economic state is fragile. Consequently, the Israeli delegation would adopt a two-fold move: on one hand, it would attack the Arabs for their unwillingness to sit with Israel in direct talks and argue that this was a sign that they didn't truly and genuinely want to make peace with the Jewish state. Likewise, Israel would express its opposition "to all sorts of things that we can't accept" such as concessions in the territorial or demographic domain (repatriation). On the other hand, to avoid Israel itself appearing as if it rejected peace, which was liable to create a rift between Jerusalem and Washington, Israel would be willing to make significant progress on one of the core issues on the agenda. The Ministry of Foreign Affairs believed such progress could be made on the compensation issue. If Israel would present the issue as a bone of contention between it and the Arab states, there would be no chance of solving the issue since the Arabs were likely to try to tie compensation to the overall resolution of the refugee problem. Therefore, Israel should present compensation as a joint responsibility of Israel and the United Nations and "as a problem that should be solved irrespective of other problems." Yet Israel should demand that an agreement with the United Nations on compensation would hinge on Israel not being required to make any other contribution to resolution of the refugee problem, first and foremost not to implement the repatriation principle. At the end of his statement, the foreign minister requested that the cabinet allow the delegation in Paris to clarify, without making any commitments in the meantime, "the matter of compensation for Arab lands, provided [there would be] cancellation of the demand for return [repatriation]." Sharett concluded that if this matter could be arranged, and following this, the refugee problem settled as a whole, Israel would be freed from "all this nightmare." The majority of the cabinet supported the course of action that Sharett suggested.[31]

A day after the cabinet meeting, Foreign Minister Sharett updated members of the Israeli delegation to the Paris Conference regarding the position they should present in the talks. The delegation should be prepared to compromise with the Conciliation Commission on one central question – compensation for abandoned lands – while at the same time hinging this on cancellation of demands for repatriation.[32]

Thus, less than a year after the Israeli government agreed to a new compensation policy on 30 October 1950, the cabinet made a significant declaratory amendment in the policy designed to remove in an unequivocal manner the repatriation issue from the agenda. This new position, in fact, had been hanging in the air for months. In the last week of February, Sharett had conducted a lengthy discussion on the compensation question in conjunction with the prime minister's advisor on Arab affairs, Yehoshua Palmon; the former Middle East Department official in the Ministry of Foreign Affairs, Ezra Danin; and the director of the Jewish National Fund's Land and Forests Department, Yosef Weitz. In his diary, Weitz wrote that the participants had all supported several fundamental assumptions that Sharett had presented, including the stipulation that after Israel paid the compensation, the United Nations and the Arab states would declare that they had no more financial claims or other demands from Israel in regard to the refugee problem.[33]

144 *Israel and the compensation issue*

From the foreign minister's remarks in the cabinet, it appears that he was eager to receive the United Nations' approval of Israel's position on the compensation issue. There were several reasons behind this aspiration: the prestige of this international institution around the world was growing; its involvement in the Arab-Israeli conflict, through various UN bodies, was deep; and the Palestinian refugee problem was often on the General Assembly's annual agenda. For his part, Sharett felt that the United Nations was indeed a body with clout in all aspects of resolution of the Arab-Israeli conflict, and therefore it was imperative to take its opinion into account. Lastly, one should note that, in his remarks, the foreign minister refrained from making any sort of linkage between compensation and peace;[34] in the cabinet's decision of late October 1950, while the government expressed its willingness to resolve the compensation question separate from all other aspects of the conflict, it added, even without hinging one thing to another, that it viewed "arrangement of compensation payments [...] as the first stage in a final peace settlement process between us and the Arab states."

Israel and the compensation issue at the Paris Conference

On 13 September 1951, the Paris Conference opened; participating were Israel and four of its Arab neighbors: Egypt, Jordan, Syria, and Lebanon. The chair, Ely Palmer, held two separate meetings: the first with the Arab delegations, the second with the Israeli delegation. In the meetings, he presented a similar declaration to each side: the objective of the Paris Conference was to find, with the mediation of the Conciliation Commission, solutions to the various problems, in two categories. The first, problems that impact primarily on the rights and the status of individuals such as repatriation, resettlement, compensation, blocked bank accounts, and claims for war damage; the second, problems that impact primarily on the rights of states, their obligations and relations between them, such as demarcation of borders and disengagement lines, demilitarized zones, free port arrangements, water rights, and fishing and navigation issues. In the Conciliation Commission's view, it was impossible to treat the various problems pending between the sides as if there were no connection between them. For example, economic development would be impossible in a region where hundreds of thousands of refugees resided, unsure about their future and their place in society. According to this approach, if Israel did not receive guarantees from its Arab neighbors regarding its national and economic security, it would not be able to withstand the obligations demanded of it to solve the refugee problem. In the commission's opinion comprehensive resolution of the refugee problem hinged on repatriation of some refugees to Israel and resettlement of others in the Arab states. Yet before the parties began to hammer out a solution to this problem, and others on the agenda, they must declare their determination "to honor the rights of the other side to security and freedom from aggression, to refrain from belligerent acts or hatred towards the rival side, and to promote the return of a lasting peace in Palestine."[35]

Israel and the compensation issue 145

At the end of the separate meetings, the delegations were requested to submit to the commission by 17 September their responses to the opening declaration; immediately afterwards, they were supposed to receive a working paper with detailed proposals of the issues on the agenda.[36]

The next day, the head of the Israeli delegation, Fischer, met with Palmer and informed him that Foreign Minister Sharett was surprised to find a demand in the declaration that Israel repatriate refugees to its territory. Raising this issue, warned Fischer, would make progress on payment of compensation difficult. In any case, Israel's response would be received only after the cabinet discussed the declaration during its weekly meeting, to be held on 19 September.[37]

By contrast, the response of the Arabs was submitted on schedule, but was primarily in the negative. They rejected the idea that the parties would, at the opening of deliberations, declare publicly their determination to refrain from all acts of aggression against the other side, arguing that this matter was already anchored in the armistice agreements. In addition, they demanded that the conference give top priority to resolution of the refugee problem. The refugees' rights shouldn't hinge at all on Israel's position on the issue, the Arabs claimed. Moreover, Israel's agreement to honor these rights shouldn't place any obligation that is not covered by international law on the Arab states. As they perceived it, "To ask the Arab states to provide assurances for the economic security of Israel in return for respecting the rights of the refugees is a novelty in international dealings."[38]

After the Arabs' response was received, the commission submitted its working paper to their delegations for study. In the introduction to the document, the Conciliation Commission underscored the importance it saw in a public declaration of non-aggression and offered wording that was identical to that in the opening declaration. Immediately after that, the commission presented its proposals for solving the Arab-Israeli conflict:

1 Israel and the Arab states would cede their demands for compensation for war damages from the 1948 war.
2 The Israeli government would agree to accept within its territory a certain number of Arab refugees who could integrate into the "economic life" of the country and were interested in returning and living in peace with their Jewish neighbors.
3 The Israeli government would agree to pay compensation for abandoned property of refugees who would not return. The sum would be a lump sum, based on the Refugees Office's appraisal. The United Nations would establish a committee of economic and monetary experts that would prepare a payment schedule, taking into account Israel's economic capabilities.
4 The Israeli and Arab governments would agree to unfreeze all blocked bank accounts in their countries.
5 The Israeli and Arab governments would agree to consider revision or amendment of the armistice agreements they had signed, particularly

146 *Israel and the compensation issue*

regarding the following points: (a) territorial adjustments; (b) water issues; (c) the future of the Gaza Strip; (d) creation of a free port in Haifa; (e) legislation regarding the borders between Israel and its neighbors; (f) supervision of health, narcotics, and smuggling; (g) arrangements that would ease economic ties between the two sides.[39]

Already on 15 September, these proposals were leaked to Israel, before being formally presented. Ben-Gurion got wind of them from Shiloah and was furious. In his diary he wrote:

> I asked Aharon to telegraph Moshe [Sharett] that he explain to the State Department that no Israeli government will discuss these proposals, and the mere bringing of these proposals [constitutes] incitement of the Arabs and prevention of peace, and perhaps anarchy in the Near East. I requested that Fischer say that he would leave the Conference if these proposals will be put forward by Palmer or his colleagues.[40]

Several hours after the Conciliation Commission submitted its working paper to the Arab delegations, Palmer and his deputy, James Barco, met with Shiloah (who went to Paris at Ben-Gurion's bidding to assist in the diplomatic battle) and members of the Israeli delegation. Shiloah told the American representatives that the commission's mediation proposals, the content of which had reached Israeli ears, were biased against Israel, and thus only stiffened the Arabs' stand and reduced chances of peace. The commission, he said, must only discuss with the rival sides a list of topics that should be raised on the agenda, then let the parties conduct direct negotiations on the topics that had been set out, to arrive at solutions. Regarding the non-aggression declaration, Shiloah stated that Israel and its Arab neighbors must *sign* such a declaration, and no other issues should be discussed until this matter was solved. Thus, Israel was not only willing to obligate itself orally to non-aggression; it also demanded that a formal non-aggression treaty be signed.

Although the Israeli delegation did not submit its official response to the opening declaration, Palmer and Barco asked Shiloah that the Israeli delegation study the commission's working paper in a non-committal manner. The Israelis refused and even expressed anger at the very submission of the working paper to the Arab delegations.[41]

During the 19 September cabinet meeting, in the absence of Foreign Minister Sharett (who was in New York for the opening of the 6th General Assembly), the director-general of the Ministry of Foreign Affairs, Walter Eytan, presented to the cabinet an overview of developments at the Paris Conference. He related Palmer's opening declaration and the contents of the working paper that had been submitted to the Arab delegations. Eytan reported that the Ministry of Foreign Affairs recommended that Israel go along with the Conciliation Commission for appearances' sake, while at the same time doings its best to undermine the commission's five proposals. The ministers, however, took a dim view of the notion of discussing the proposals with the commission, and some members of the cabinet even demanded Israel leave the Paris Conference if the proposals were submitted to the Israeli delegation. Minister of Labor Golda Meir suggested that the delegation put off responding to the opening declaration as long as possible; yet the minute the Israeli delegation had to submit its response and receive the commission's working paper, it should leave negotiations. Several ministers supported this suggestion. Eytan responded, saying that the delegation couldn't put off giving its response any longer. He raised a counter suggestion that was less drastic: "After giving our answer, we can draw [things out] and drag [our feet]. We'll give our answer now, but afterwards there will be a demand from our side to set an agreed-upon agenda [...] This is a matter of weeks." Moreover, he added, it was possible to hinge the beginning of deliberations on signing the non-aggression declaration first "and this will again be a long struggle with the Arabs." At the end of his remarks, Eytan requested that the government authorize the Ministry of Foreign Affairs to word a general response to the opening declaration. The answer would not address the various issues, such as war damages, compensation, and a comprehensive settlement, since the Israeli response to these issues would be set only afterwards, according to developments.

The prime minister rejected the Ministry of Foreign Affairs' approach. Foot-dragging tactics wouldn't be effective, he said, since in the end this tactic would run out – that is, it would merely be a stop-gap measure. "We have to 'kill' these proposals," claimed Ben-Gurion, and since the source of these proposals is the State Department, the Ministry of Foreign Affairs must concentrate the battle on Washington. In the prime minister's opinion, it would be more appropriate to answer the commission's opening declaration and address each issue clearly. "The answer has to be such that they won't be able to submit proposals to us." He suggested, for example, tying Palestinian blocked bank accounts in Israel with the frozen accounts of Iraqi Jews. In the unbending approach that the prime minister took there was no room for compromise on the compensation issue as Sharett had proposed on the eve of the Paris Conference. Ben-Gurion concluded:

> I want to study the compensation issue again, because when we discussed it, we lacked information. If at the time of our deliberations we had had the information we have today, it's possible that we would have reached different conclusions.

In his opinion Israel could announce to the commission that it was willing to give compensation to take care of the refugee problem on condition that the Arab states would also agree to give money "to take care of the Jewish refugees who fled and were forced to leave the [Arab] countries." Thus, Ben-Gurion sought to annul Sharett's original suggestion of disengaging the compensation issue from the other problems that separated Israel from its neighbors. At the close of the cabinet meeting, the ministers decided, contrary to Eytan's

148   *Israel and the compensation issue*

proposal, to authorize the prime minister himself to word the government's reply to the opening declaration.[42]

On 21 September, Fischer submitted Israel's reply to the opening declaration, and immediately afterwards he was given the commission's working paper. At the beginning of the reply, Israel set forth several preliminary steps that could bring peace, first of all the signing of a non-aggression treaty. The second part of the response dealt with the refugee problem. Again, Israel accused the Arabs of responsibility for the problem, but despite this agreed to allocate money for their resettlement, provided the Arabs would give a similar sum for the resettlement of 200,000 Jews who had fled to Israel from the Arab states. Israel also expressed willingness to discuss the question of the refugees' blocked bank accounts, but hinged this on settling the issue of the bank accounts of Iraqi Jews who immigrated to Israel.[43]

The wording of Israel's reply demonstrated that despite his remarks in the cabinet, Ben-Gurion had internalized the ruse that the Ministry of Foreign Affairs had initiated – to raise the non-aggression treaty issue in order to put off or even prevent entirely any substantive discussion of the Conciliation Commission's five proposals.[44]

The unwillingness of the Israeli leadership to compromise on the questions at the heart of the Arab-Israeli conflict, and at the core of the refugee issue, along the lines proposed by the Conciliation Commission won the sweeping support of the Israeli political system. This was clearly reflected in the political periodicals of the period.

The Mapai party daily, *Davar,* warned that the Israeli government's agreement to go to the Paris Conference should not be interpreted "as willingness to accept every procedure and every proposal."[45] Mapam's daily, *Al Ha-Mishmar*, stated, in regard to the clauses that dealt with the refugee issue, that under no circumstances should the solution to this question be separated from the issue of a comprehensive peace.[46] The party paper of the General Zionists, *Ha-Boker*, felt that some adjustment of the state's borders and return of a small number of refugees, as the Conciliation Commission called for, would not solve these issues, since the Arab states demanded return to the Partition Plan borders and full repatriation of the refugees. Yet the paper believed that it was possible to discuss compensation for "Arab runaways" while clarifying that "they should not be viewed as refugees in the conventional sense."[47] The party organ of religious Zionist circles, *Ha-Tzofe*, argued that Palmer's opening declaration could be interpreted "as excessive and danger[ous] appeasement of the Arabs." The paper explained that the Conciliation Commission sought to award the Arabs "various discounts" [i.e. bonuses] without the latter committing to reach a peace settlement with their Jewish neighbor.[48] In a similar tone, *Ha-Modia,* the party organ of the ultra-Orthodox Agudat Israel party, said that the overwhelming majority of the commission's proposals were aimed at trying "to furnish the core Arab demands on the refugee and the compensation issues."[49]

Israel and the compensation issue 149

The non-partisan print media held similar positions. The editor-in-chief of *Ma'ariv* stated that one could not find even one person in Israel who would agree to return "any number of Arabs [i.e. Palestinian refugees] at all," since "every Arab that would enter would occupy the place of a Jew who needed to be absorbed." In regard to the compensation proposal, he stated emphatically that "we don't have any[thing for which] to pay them and we don't have what to pay them with."[50] *Yedioth Ahronoth* recommended the government of Israel "flee from" the Paris Conference. "If we don't knock on the door [kick in the door] [and flee] now," the paper explained, "after it is proposed to us [to] return refugees without signing a final peace, the difficulty that awaits us tomorrow will be all the greater, because then we won't even be able 'to knock'."[51] *The Jerusalem Post* also felt that the question of repatriation must be linked to the issue of a peace settlement between Israel and its neighbors.[52] *Ha'Aretz*, in contrast with all the other papers, saw one ray of light in Paris. It noted favorably the willingness of the Conciliation Commission to limit the number of refugees returning to economic criteria.[53]

In the meantime, in Paris the Israelis stood firm on the non-aggression issue. This approach proved a wise choice. Weeks and weeks of wrangling between the Israeli and Arab delegations over procedures and wording ensued. The Israel delegation demanded that, before any discussion of the commission's five proposals, the rival parties should sign a non-aggression treaty in the same spirit as that proposed by the Conciliation Commission, or even broader and more binding. The Arabs adamantly refused. They were not interested in any such signing, certainly not such a binding document. At the beginning of October, they suggested a version of an oral declaration in which their commitment to refrain from acts of violence was even narrower than the one in the Conciliation Commission's version. During the first five weeks of the conference, the Conciliation Commission was bogged down in a futile, last-ditch attempt to bridge the gaps between the parties on this issue.[54]

During the last third of October, the Conciliation Commission began, with American support, to pressure Israel to discuss topics other than the non-aggression issue. Fischer updated Eytan that in the coming days, the commission was interested in summoning the Israeli and Arab delegations to explain to them its five proposals. The commission warned the Israelis that if the Paris Conference ended without any results, it would submit the five proposals to the 6th General Assembly for approval and place the blame for the failure of the entire diplomatic move on Israel's shoulders.[55]

In a meeting between Fischer and Palmer on 22 October, Palmer reported Acheson's discontentment with Israel's refusal to deal with issues other than the non-aggression issue. The State Department, Palmer notified the Israelis, believed that the Israeli stance was "hasty and ill advised." The American diplomat pressed Israel to retreat from its refusal to discuss the commission's proposals and again warned that Israel would be blamed for the failure of the conference. He also said that if Israel agreed to meet with the commission so

150 *Israel and the compensation issue*

that the latter could explain the five proposals, he was prepared to accept the Israeli argument that it could not accept any proposal for negotiation with the Arabs, as long as they didn't agree to an appropriate version of non-aggression.[56]

Washington's pressure made it imperative for Israel to modify and update its ruse regarding the non-aggression treaty. Fischer explained to Eytan that Israel had only two choices: first, to refuse to accept the commission's explanations of its five proposals – in essence, "to torpedo the Conference over the non-aggression dispute and be prepared to be blamed for the failure of the Conference"; the second, to find a way to maintain decent relations with the commission. "This requires accepting the [explanations to the] proposals, with all the dangers they entail," Fischer said. In the Israeli delegation's opinion, if it decided to prefer the second option, Israel must refuse to discuss issues emanating from Arab-Israeli relations, as long as the Arabs were unwilling to sign a non-aggression treaty acceptable to Israel. This path would enable Israel to discuss the compensation issue with the commission and perhaps also the question of blocked bank accounts.[57]

Israel's ambassador to the United States, Abba Eban, was in agreement with the delegation's position. In a conversation with McGhee, Eban had argued that the Arab refusal to sign a non-aggression declaration in the spirit of the Conciliation Commission's proposal forced Israel to discuss only those issues between Israel and the United Nations – that is, "financial aspects [of the] refugee question." Eban suggested to Sharett that Israel demand that the commission note the attitude of the two opposing parties toward the non-aggression issue. Parallel to this, he suggested Israel and the commission take the compensation issue forward.[58]

Thus, under intense American pressure, Israel's diplomatic envoys came to the conclusion that the time was now ripe for rolling out the revised compensation initiative that the government had agreed upon on the eve of the Paris Conference. Sharett stood behind this recommendation, but he now had to persuade Ben-Gurion to shelve his reservations and support this move. In the cabinet meeting of 25 October, Sharett told the government:

> There is a way [that will assist Israel] to extricate [itself] in one piece from the straits [in Paris]. This path is not new, I took it when I suggested to the government [on 12 September] before my trip, to give authority [give a green light] to open a new approach on the compensation matter.

Under the prevailing circumstances of increasing diplomatic pressure from the United States and the Conciliation Commission, Israel must adopt this course, claimed Sharett. This time Ben-Gurion was convinced and expressed again his agreement with Sharett's compensation initiative.[59]

Israel softened its position, and on 26 October, the Conciliation Commission succeeded for the first time in putting its five proposals on the conference's agenda. It explained them to each side separately.[60]

Despite this progress, members of the American delegation felt that the Paris talks had reached an impasse. In a 27 October telegram to Acheson, Palmer expressed great pessimism regarding the future of the conference. He reported that from informal talks the American representatives had conducted with Israeli diplomats, it became clear that Israel was prepared to discuss only the question of compensation with the commission. Palmer said that this Israeli stance, a derivative of the Arabs' attitude towards the non-aggression issue, greatly diminished the changes of conducting a discussion of the five proposals by the two sides.[61] In talks that members of the Israeli delegation conducted with Barco, the American diplomat clarified that the Conciliation Commission did not expect that the Arabs would view its proposals favorably, even after they were elaborated, and that the commission had no hopes that the sides could arrive at an agreement. He argued that if the Conciliation Commission discussed the compensation issue with Israel alone, the Arabs were liable to raise political difficulties. In his estimation, if such a discussion did not bring concrete results, the commission would come out all the poorer for it.[62]

On 31 October a last attempt was made to resuscitate the slowly dying conference. In a letter that Palmer sent to the Israeli and Arab delegations, he wrote that in the commission's opinion the explanations of the five proposals that the two sides had received made it possible to open discussion on all the topics and issues. The delegations were requested to inform the Conciliation Commission by 6 November whether they were prepared to conduct such a discussion.[63]

The secretary of state's assistant on United Nations affairs, John Hickerson, advised Eban that Israel embrace, for tactical considerations, a policy that would not categorically reject discussion of the five proposals that the commission had raised.[64] The French representative on the Conciliation Commission, Leon Marchal, believed the same; in his opinion, the Arabs would reject in any case the commission's proposals and therefore, from a tactical standpoint, it would be advisable for Israel to agree to discuss all the proposals (and not just the one that dealt with the compensation issue).[65]

In the 4 November cabinet meeting, Israel's response to the latest appeals from the Conciliation Commission was discussed. The foreign minister updated the cabinet on the commission's remarks regarding the five proposals. He assessed that the commission now stood on Israel's side regarding the clause dealing with repatriation of the refugees. Sharett justified his prognosis on the differences in wording between the commission's explanations of this clause and the wording submitted in its 21 September working paper: in its elaboration of this clause, the commission maintained that whether returning refugees could be integrated into the "*national* life" of the State of Israel must be examined, while the version submitted to the Israeli delegation on 21 September talked of the integration of the refugees into the "*economic* life" of the state. Sharett judged that the change hinged on the desire of the commission to demonstrate to Israel that it was interested in making repatriation of the

152   Israel and the compensation issue

refugees difficult, since "there will be few [Arab refugees] that one could say about them that they can integrate into the national life of Israel [i.e. of a Jewish state]."

In Sharett's view, the clause dealing with the compensation issue was very important. According to him, the Conciliation Commission demanded that Israel commit to pay a lump sum of compensation based on the value of unmovable abandoned property set by the Refugees Office. Then "the question will stand how to pay." The Conciliation Commission "will take into account that there isn't peace between us and the Arabs, that we have a large defense budget, that there are emergency needs." While Israel would agree to make progress on the compensation issue, Sharett stated, it had made no commitment to accept the appraisal of the Refugees Office regarding the worth of Palestinian abandoned property. After all:

> There wasn't a commercial transaction here. The State of Israel didn't come out and say: Let's buy all the land [of Palestinian Arabs] with the houses and the trees [...] This [the abandoned property] is one of the legacies from this [1948] war [...] One shouldn't approach this matter as if we must pay as if we had bought this property under peacetime conditions.

The compensation question, Sharett again underscored, was completely tied to the repatriation issue. That is, compensation that the State of Israel would pay, meant the refugees wouldn't return. The minister told the government that he intended to voice this position again and even detail it in a political debate that was to take place the same day in the Knesset. At the close of his political overview Sharett presented the wording of his suggestion for Israel's reply to the Conciliation Commission. According to his version, Israel would express its agreement to open a discussion with the Arab states, "if they will declare [but not sign] a non-aggression declaration in keeping with the position of the Security Council, or if they announce that they view this discussion as a stage for a peace settlement."

The cabinet, and first and foremost Ben-Gurion, objected to Sharett's wording of the response to the commission. Israel should not retreat from its previous position regarding the signing of a non-aggression treaty, stated the prime minister emphatically, a position that was followed by similar sentiments from the other ministers. On the other hand, the cabinet approved once again Sharett's stance on the compensation issue.[66]

At the close of the cabinet meeting, the foreign minister appeared before the Knesset, where he made a statement on behalf of the government, regarding Israel's foreign policy. A considerable part of his Knesset speech was devoted to the chain of events at the Paris Conference and Israel's position on the compensation issue. Sharett declared that the refugee problem was a matter whose resolution "should fittingly serve as a topic for a joint responsibility of the two sides [Israel and the Arab states] with the United Nations."

According to Sharett, the Arabs must absorb masses of refugees in their countries, and Israel must pay compensation for abandoned lands. The government decided "to activate this responsibility" and it was willing to enter "without delay" into negotiations with the Conciliation Commission or with any other authorized United Nations organization, on the compensation issue.

Israel's willingness to discuss compensation "as a separate question that should be dealt with immediately" hinged on several conditions:

1 The scope of the Israeli commitment – that is, the magnitude of payment and the conditions for its fulfillment – needed to be set in an agreement with the government.
2 Israel's ability to pay was affected by the "war legacy" – that is, the physical and human damage inflicted on Israel by the 1948 war. This "legacy" continued to this day, through the Arab boycott and Egyptian maritime blockade. In light of this, "Israel should not be demanded [to pay] more than a fair contribution [a fair share], in keeping with circumstances and within the framework of its realistic capabilities."
3 Israel would need international aid in order to withstand payment of the compensation.
4 The sum that would be set in agreement with the government would be the final payment in full of Israel's obligation of compensation for the abandoned property.
5 Israel's responsibility is vis-à-vis United Nations institutions, not the Arab states or the landowners. The fund that the United Nations would establish to coordinate the compensation would distribute the money "according to plans that would be determined – whether to cover the cost of settlement and absorption, or to remove financial claims of certain owners."
6 The sum that Israel deserved for frozen Jewish property in Iraq would be deducted from the sum of compensation for [Arab] refugees.
7 Israel would be prepared to obligate itself but only after it was agreed that with this [payment of compensation], Israel's debts to resolution of the Palestinian refugee problem would be completed, and the question of their repatriation would never again be placed at its door.

Thus, Sharett made public the position of the government, which completely separated the compensation issue from the issue of a comprehensive peace settlement, while at the same time hinging payment of compensation on dropping the repatriation principle from the United Nations' agenda (and that of the United States) as far as Israel was concerned.

The foreign minister's announcement regarding the compensation issue passed relatively quietly in the Knesset plenum.[67] The political system as a whole adopted the change in Israel's position on the compensation issue that Foreign Minister Sharett led without controversy. One could assume that linking resolving this question with dropping implementation of repatriation

154   Israel and the compensation issue

convinced Israel's politicians to support the new policy, whether wholeheartedly or with reservations.

Sharett, as one can ascertain, considered it suitable to link settlement of the compensation question with two political-economic matters that did not appear in the government's decision of 30 October 1950: Arab economic warfare and the frozen property of Iraqi Jews. Their inclusion now was a byproduct of significant developments that took place in both realms in the previous year, events that had a negative impact on Israel's economy (discussed in detail in the next chapter).

On 7 November, Israel submitted its answer to the Conciliation Commission's 31 October letter. After addressing in brief the non-aggression issue, Israel expressed its readiness to offer in coming days its response to the five proposals of the Conciliation Commission.[68] The Arabs also expressed their willingness to study the Conciliation Commission's proposals.[69] Despite these seemingly positive answers, now with the failure of the conference only a matter of time, the two sides busied themselves in an attempt to shake off their responsibility for the Paris Conference's collapse.[70]

Palmer did not consider Israel's reply to the Conciliation Commission's letter a harbinger of readiness to enter a substantive discussion of the five proposals. In his appraisal, the commission had no choice but to report the outcome of the talks to the 6th General Assembly. Sharett was apprehensive that Israel would be presented in the commission's report as responsible for the Paris Conference's failure.[71] On 12 November Fischer rushed, at Sharett's request, to tell Palmer and Barco that Israel would provide a forthright response to the commission's five proposals.[72] Indeed, on 14 November, the Israeli delegation met with the Conciliation Commission in order to submit its comments. At the beginning of his remarks, the head of the delegation, Fischer, again chose to remind his interlocutors that in contrast to the Arabs' opposition, Israel had agreed to take upon itself the commission's version of the non-aggression declaration. His comments to the five proposals were as follows:

1   Since the Arabs were responsible for the outbreak of the 1948 war, they bore the moral and material responsibility for its effects. Israel, therefore, did not see any possibility of canceling its demands for war damages.
2   Defense, economic and political considerations prevented Israel from allowing Arab refugees to settle in its territories.
3   The compensation issue needed to be dealt with between Israel and the Conciliation Commission or any other United Nations body that would be established for this purpose. In this context, Israel had some fundamental provisos: (a) it was imperative to set the value of abandoned Arab lands, prior to any discussion of the subject; (b) the economic capabilities of Israel [to pay] were limited due to the 1948 war forced upon it, the Arab boycott, and the flight of tens of thousands of Jewish refugees to Israel from the Arab countries; (c) one must address abandoned Jewish property left in the Arab states and particularly in Iraq; (d) the agreement between

Israel and the compensation issue 155

Israel and the United Nations regarding the compensation issue must absolve Israel of all additional obligations regarding the refugee problem.

4 In any settlement of the blocked bank accounts question, the bank accounts of Iraqi Jews who immigrated to Israel must be taken into account.

5 Israel was willing to consider revision or amendment of the armistice agreements. At the same time, for various reasons, it took issue with any discussion of territorial matters and water. Giving Arab states transport access to Haifa port needed to be part of discussion of economic agreements between the two sides.[73]

Within hours of its meeting with the Israeli delegation, the Conciliation Commission met with the Arab delegations. Their response to the commission was also loaded with reservations. They held:

1 The war damages issue did not need to be discussed with the commission's mediation.

2 Each and every refugee had the right to return to their home if they desired, and no limitations whatsoever could be appended to this right.

3 Each and every refugee who was not interested in returning to their home was entitled to receive compensation for their abandoned property. There should be no linkage between the compensation issue and the economic capabilities of Israel to withstand payments.

4 The commission's proposal regarding the blocked bank accounts issue was acceptable to the Arab states.

5 The Arabs did not view the commission as authorized to mediate between the Arab states and Israel in the economic sphere.[74]

After the Conciliation Commission examined the Israeli and Arab comments to its proposals, it came to the conclusion that the gap between the sides was so great that it was impossible to bridge them. In its report to the United Nations General Assembly, the commission stated that it had failed in its efforts to convince the two sides to discuss its proposals as a whole "in a fair and realistic spirit of give-and-take" because "neither party had indicated a willingness substantially to recede from its rigid position and to seek a solution through mediation along the lines set forth in the comprehensive pattern of proposals." On 19 November, the commission sent a letter to the Israeli and Arab delegations informing them of its decision to close the Paris Conference.[75]

The failure of the Paris Conference rested on two main factors: first, in terms of the circumstances prevailing at the time in the Middle East, its timing was poor. In Egypt, the largest and most important Arab state, nationalism was on the rise, accompanied by an anti-western and anti-Israeli mood.[76] In Jordan, the assassination of King Abdullah, two months prior to the opening of the conference, strengthened the Palestinian wing of Jordanian

156 *Israel and the compensation issue*

politics, which rejected any settlement with Israel.[77] The military-political clash between Israel and Syria in the spring of 1951 over Israel's draining of the Hula Valley also created an atmosphere of tension between the sides. Thus, the leaders of the Arab states had no desire or ability to reach any kind of compromise with Israel. In talks between the United Kingdom minister in Amman, Sir Alec Kirkbride, and the former Jordanian foreign minister, Ahmad Tuqan, now Jordan's observer at the United Nations, Tuqan claimed that the Arab states didn't feel there was any rush to reach a settlement with the Jewish state. The Arab states wanted to preserve the conflict in its current state, as a vehicle to promote their own national objectives, and the interests of the Palestinians didn't occupy them at all.[78] On the other side, the Israel leadership felt that the United States was trying, through the auspices of the Conciliation Commission, to squeeze political concessions out of Israel in order to calm the situation in the region.[79] Israel, however, was not under any circumstances willing to make serious concessions.

The other factor behind the failure of the conference was the State Department's insistence that a conference be convened urgently under a format that had already failed at Lausanne and Geneva. Preparations for the conference were inadequate,[80] and the parties came unwillingly and with a strong sense that the conference's failure was ensured.[81]

Notes

1 UNPCC, A/1985, p. 1.
2 Pablo Azcarate, *Mission in Palestine, 1948–1952*, Washington, DC: The Middle East Institute, 1966, p. 166.
3 UNPCC, A/1985, p. 1.
4 ISA, MFA 2455/13, Refugee Office, May 1951.
5 ISA, MFA 2477/1, Refugee Office, 20 June 1951; ISA, MFA 339/7, Second and Third Meetings with Refugee Office, 5 July 1951; ISA, MFA 2445/1, Fourth Meeting with Refugee Office, 26 July 1951.
6 For the Refugees Office's estimates of the scope and value of the refugees' property, see Chapter 1, Blocking the feasibility of repatriation.
7 FRUS, 1951, V, pp. 671–3, The United States Representative on the Palestine Conciliation Commission to the Secretary of State, 9 May 1951. On 28 May Palmer sent a letter with a similar theme to the State Department. He noted with concern that there were increasing calls in the press for the dissolution of the commission because of its inefficiency and irresponsibility: FRUS, 1951, V, p. 673, The United States Representative on the Palestine Conciliation Commission to the Secretary of State, 9 May 1951, Note 4.
8 FRUS, 1951, V, pp. 714–16, The Secretary of State to the United States Representative on the Palestine Conciliation Commission, 12 June 1951. The proposals mentioned in the letter had already been discussed during March and April, in conversations between State Department officials and representatives of the British Foreign Office: see Mordechai Bar-On, *Of All the Kingdoms: Israel's Relations with the United Kingdom during the First Decade after the End of the British Mandate in Palestine, 1948–1959*, Jerusalem: Yad Izhak Ben-Zvi, 2006, p. 119 (Hebrew).
9 FRUS, 1951, V, pp. 753–6, The Secretary of State to the United States Representative on the Palestine Conciliation Commission, 7 July 1951.

10 FRUS, 1951, V, pp. 799–801, The Secretary of State to the United States Representative on the Palestine Conciliation Commission, 27 July 1951.

11 ISA, MFA 2441/4, Subject: American Proposals Regarding Measures to Be Taken by the Conciliation Commission, 1 August 1951; UKNA, FO 371/91365, E1071/12, The British Embassy in Washington to Foreign Office, 8 August 1951; UNPCC, A/1985, p. 2.

12 Aryeh Shalev, *The Israel-Syria Armistice Regime, 1949–1955*, Boulder, CO: Westview Press, 1993, pp. 49–88.

13 Shimon Golan, *Hot Border, Cold War: The Formulation of Israel's Security Policy, 1949–1953*, Tel Aviv: Ma'arachot, 2000, pp. 349–55 (Hebrew).

14 ISA, Government Meeting, 14 August 1951, p. 9; DEPI, Vol. 6, Document 322, E. Najar to W. Eytan, 12 August 1951; Shaul Zeitune, *Deterrence and Peace: Israel's Attempts to Arrive at a Settlement,* Tel Aviv: Tcherikover, 2000, p. 193 (Hebrew).

15 The State Department understood from the Conciliation Commission that "Settlement [of] refugee problem took priority over political negotiations [regarding] Palestine peace." See FRUS, 1951, V, p. 714, The Secretary of State to the United States Representative on the Palestine Conciliation Commission, 12 June 1951.

16 A few months before the conference idea was proposed, the State Department prepared a comprehensive document dealing with American policy toward Israel. Among other matters, it contained a comprehensive discussion of the refugee problem. The report noted that of all the issues separating Israel from its neighbors, the refugee problem was the most serious. See: FRUS, 1951, V, pp. 573–4, Department of State Policy Statement, 6 February 1951.

17 At a meeting between the British Foreign Secretary Anthony Eden and the UN Secretary-General Trygve Lie, at the end of November 1951, Eden commented that he viewed the issue of the Palestinian refugees as the "most serious" problem in the Middle East, and that there would be no peace between Israel and the Arabs until it was resolved. Bulent Gokay (ed.), *British Documents on Foreign Affairs: Near and Middle East, 1951*, Vol. 2, London: Lexis Nexis, 2005, p. 104.

18 FRUS, 1951, V, pp. 816–17, The United States Representative on the Palestine Conciliation Commission to the Secretary of State, 3 August 1951. Despite France's agreement to hold another conference for Israel and the Arab countries, the French and the Americans appear to have disagreed regarding the content of such a conference. Thus, for example, the French representative to the Conciliation Commission, Leon Marchal, did not want a discussion of the refugees' repatriation, on the grounds that Israel's leadership had long since rejected the concept. Azcarate, *Mission in Palestine*, p. 174; David P. Forsythe, *United Nations Peacemaking – The Conciliation Commission for Palestine*, Baltimore, MD: The Johns Hopkins University Press, 1972, p. 87.

19 ISA, MFA 341/50, The Conciliation Commission's Letter of Invitation, 10 August 1951.

20 ISA, MFA 341/50, The Foreign Minister's Answering Note, 13 August 1951. The Commission refrained from responding to Sharett's letter.

21 ISA, Government Meeting, 14 August 1951, pp. 8–12.

22 See, for example: ISA, MFA 2602/9, Comay to Elath, 17 August 1951; DEPI, Vol. 6, Document 347, M. Comay to the Bureau of the Minister of Foreign Affairs, 24 August 1951; DEPI, Vol. 6, Document 353, W. Eytan and G. Avner to the Israel Missions in Ankara and Paris, 28 August 1951; DEPI, Vol. 6, Document 362, Meeting: M. Sharett – M. B. Davis (Tel Aviv, 23 August 1951), 2 September 1951.

23 ISA, Government Meeting, 22 August 1951, pp. 5–9, 13.

24 ISA, MFA 2447/14, Our Position Regarding the Conciliation Commission's Invitation, 4 September 1951; ISA, MFA 2447/14, In Anticipation of the Paris Conference and the General Assembly, 9 September 1951.

158   *Israel and the compensation issue*

25 DEPI, Vol. 6, Document 375, M. Fischer to E. Palmer, 10 September 1951.

26 UNPCC, A/1985, p. 2; Rony E. Gabbay, *A Political Study of the Arab-Jewish Conflict – The Arab Refugee Problem (A Case Study)*, Geneve: Librairie E. Droz, 1959, p. 330.

27 At the same time, Blandford was attempting to obtain the Arab leaders' agreement regarding a broad program for the rehabilitation of the Arab refugees. See Chapter 8, The 6th General Assembly.

28 FRUS, 1951, V, pp. 842–3, The Chargé in Lebanon to the Department of State, 27 August 1951; UKNA, FO 371/91410, E1826/32, From Beirut to Foreign Office, 27 August 1951.

29 UKNA, FO 371/91410, E1826/33, Furlonge to Hood, 4 September 1951.

30 UKNA, FO 371/91365, E1071/30, FO Minute, Oliver, 7 September 1951. The British Foreign Office attempted to assist the UNRWA with regard to the Paris Conference even though Britain itself did not participate in the conference and was not a member of the Conciliation Commission. Because of this non-participation, Britain refused to support the conference, despite the efforts of the Americans and the French to obtain such support. See: UKNA, FO 371/91365, E1071/12, Burrows to Furlonge, 8 August 1951; UKNA, FO 371/91365, E1071/10, From Foreign Office to Amman, 11 August 1951; UKNA, FO 371/91365, E1071/30, FO Minute, 7 September 1951; UKNA, FO 371/91365, E1071/32, British Embassy in Paris to Attlee, 14 September 1951.

31 ISA, Government Meeting, 12 September 1951, pp. 18–33.

32 ISA, MFA 2602/9, Instruction to the Missions, 13 September 1951.

33 Joseph Weitz, *My Diary and Letters to the Children*, vol. 4, Ramat Gan: Massada, 1965, pp. 124–5 (Hebrew).

34 In this context, see Neil Caplan, *Futile Diplomacy: The United Nations, the Great Powers and Middle East Peacemaking, 1948–1954*, Portland, OR: Frank Cass, 1997, p. 172.

35 ISA, MFA 2447/1II, The Paris Conference, 16 September 1951.

36 ISA, Government Meeting, 19 September 1951, p. 2; Caplan, *The United Nations*, p. 173.

37 FRUS, 1951, V, p. 862, The United States Representative on the Palestine Conciliation Commission to the Secretary of State, 14 September 1951; DEPI, Vol. 6, Document 386, M. Fischer to W. Eytan, 14 September 1951.

38 FRUS, 1951, V, pp. 864–6, The United States Representative on the Palestine Conciliation Commission to the Secretary of State, 18 September 1951.

39 UNPCC, A/1985, pp. 3–4.

40 BGA, BGD, 15 September 1951; see also DEPI, Vol. 6, Document 387, W. Eytan to the Israel Delegation at the United Nations, 15 September 1951.

41 FRUS, 1951, V, pp. 867–9, The United States Representative on the Palestine Conciliation Commission to the Secretary of State, 18 September 1951; DEPI, Vol. 6, Document 390, W. Eytan to the Israel Embassy in Washington, 18 September 1951.

42 ISA, Government Meeting, 19 September 1951, pp. 2–21.

43 ISA, MFA 2447/1II, The Paris Conference, 20 September 1951.

44 ISA, MFA 2566/11, Subject: The Paris Conference – Divon and the Arabs, 25 September 1951; ISA, 7562/11 A, Foreign Affairs and Defense Committee Meeting, 27 September 1951, p. 5; DEPI, Vol. 6, Document 407, W. Eytan to the Israel Legation in Paris, 30 September 1951.

45 *Davar*, 19 September 1951.

46 *Al Ha-Mishmar*, 26 September 1951. At the same time, Mapam issued a paper dealing with the Arab-Israeli conflict, calling for the resettlement of most of the refugees in Arab countries. The paper took the position that it would be appropriate for Israel to absorb a limited number of "peace-seeking" refugees when full

peace was achieved: HHA, Mapam (4)1.90-k, Instructions to the Israel Delegation at the General Assembly, undated.

47 *Ha-Boker*, 26 September 1951.
48 *Ha-Tzofe*, 19 September 1951.
49 *Ha-Modia,* 26 September 1951.
50 *Ma'ariv*, 26 September 1951.
51 *Yedioth Ahronoth*, 19 September 1951.
52 *The Jerusalem Post*, 26 September 1951.
53 *Ha'aretz*, 26 September 1951.
54 Caplan, *The United Nations*, pp. 177–93; Zeitune, *Deterrence and Peace*, pp. 200–4.
55 DEPI, Vol. 6, Document 449, M. Fischer to W. Eytan, 21 October 1951.
56 ISA, MFA 2344/8, M. Fischer to W. Eytan and A. Eban, 22 October 1951; ISA, MFA 2447/11, M. Fischer to W. Eytan, 23 October 1951.
57 ISA, MFA 2447/11, M. Fischer to W. Eytan, 23 October 1951.
58 DEPI, Vol. 6, Document 451, A. Eban to M. Sharett, 23 October 1951.
59 ISA, Government Meeting, 25 October 1951, pp. 31–4, 40–1.
60 DEPI, Vol. 6, Document 454, Statement made by the Chairman of the Conciliation Commission to the Israel Delegation at the Paris Conference, 26 October 1951; Caplan, *The United Nations*, pp. 197–8.
61 FRUS, 1951, V, pp. 920–2, The United States Representative on the Palestine Conciliation Commission to the Secretary of State, 27 October 1951.
62 DEPI, Vol. 6, Document 458, M. Fischer to W. Eytan, 30 October 1951.
63 DEPI, Vol. 6, Document 462, E. Palmer to M. Fischer, 31 October 1951, and Appendix.
64 ISA, MFA 2447/1, A. Eban to W. Eytan, 1 November 1951.
65 DEPI, Vol. 6, Document 465, M. Fischer to W. Eytan, 2 November 1951.
66 ISA, Government Meeting, 4 November 1951, pp. 29–45.
67 *Knesset Minutes*, Vol. 10, 4 November 1951, pp. 277–89.
68 DEPI, Vol. 6, Document 470, M. Fischer to E. Palmer, 7 November 1951.
69 DEPI, Vol. 6, Document 478, M. Sharett to W. Eytan, 10 November 1951.
70 Caplan, *The United Nations*, pp. 198–9.
71 DEPI, Vol. 6, Document 478, M. Sharett to W. Eytan, 10 November 1951.
72 DEPI, Vol. 6, Document 483, M. Fischer to M. Sharett, 12 November 1951.
73 DEPI, Vol. 6, Document 488, Fischer's Statement before the Palestine Conciliation Commission (Paris, 14 November 1951).
74 UNPCC, A/1985, pp. 19–24.
75 UNPCC, A/1985, p. 10.
76 Geoffrey Aronson, *From Sideshow to Center Stage: U.S. Policy toward Egypt, 1946–1956*, Boulder, CO: Lynne Rienner Publishers, 1986, pp. 28–9; John C. Campbell, *Defense of the Middle East: Problems of American Policy*, New York: Harper and Brothers, 1960, pp. 43–6; Caplan, *The United Nations*, p. 201.
77 FRUS, 1951, V, p. 794, Memorandum of Conversation by the Acting Officer in Charge of Lebanon-Syria-Iraq Affairs, 24 July 1951; DEPI, Vol. 6, Document 289, M. Sharett to the Israel Missions Abroad, 24 July 1951; Zeitune, *Deterrence and Peace*, p. 209.
78 UKNA, FO 371/91367, E1071/59, Kirkbride to Furlonge, 3 November 1951.
79 ISA, Government Meeting, 12 September 1951, p. 19.
80 UKNA, FO 371/91365, E1071/23, Ankara Chancery to Eastern Department, 21 August 1951; DEPI, Vol. 6, Document 487, A. Eban to M. Fischer, 14 November 1951.
81 UKNA, FO 371/91365, E1071/32, The British Embassy in Paris to Attlee, 14 September 1951; ISA, MFA 2447/14, In Anticipation of the Paris Conference and the General Assembly, 9 September 1951.

7 Two political matters linked to the compensation issue

Arab economic warfare: the economic boycott and the maritime blockade

Already in the first years of the British Mandate in Palestine, Arab leaders called for imposing an economic boycott on the Jewish community of Palestine.[1] There were several attempts to establish such a boycott, for the most part by Palestinian Arabs, during the 1929 Disturbances and all the more forcefully in the course of the Great Arab Revolt (1936–39).[2] After the Second World War, the Arab campaign against the Zionist enterprise amplified. In the second meeting of the Arab League's council on 2 December 1945, it was decided to impose an Arab economic boycott on the Jewish community of Palestine.[3] In January 1946, boycott laws were published in Egypt, Syria, Lebanon, and Trans-Jordan, and a month later in Iraq and Yemen, and in December of the same year in Saudi Arabia. At the third meeting of the council in March 1946 it was decided to establish national boycott offices in each member state of the Arab League. Three months later, during the fourth gathering of the council, it was agreed that the national boycott offices would be tied to a central boycott committee, which would be established for this purpose somewhere in the future.[4] On 19 May 1951 the League's council decided to establish centralized machinery that would oversee organization and implementation of the economic boycott. Damascus was chosen to serve as the home of the head office, which would coordinate boycott machinery and handle contacts with the national offices.[5]

Parallel to this, at a convention of the Arab Chambers of Commerce it was proposed that a "blacklist" be prepared of all foreign companies trading with Israel. The proposal was accepted enthusiastically and, at the outset of July 1951, the head office in Damascus began to prepare the list.[6] Within a short time, there were already approximately one hundred foreign companies on the Arab League's blacklist.[7] This number swelled greatly in the first months of 1953. At the same time, the Arab states intensified their pressure on businesspeople and companies not to conduct commerce with Israel, and beyond threats to boycott-breakers, they stressed the tremendous trade potential of the Arab market compared to the limited opportunities Israel's small economy and population could offer.[8]

During the Mandate era, the Arabs held that their decision to impose a boycott on the Jewish community was the upshot of their desire to prevent the Zionist enterprise from establishing itself in Palestine.[9] After the outbreak of the 1948 war and the establishment of the State of Israel, the Arabs explained to the international community that they were fully within their rights to carry out economic warfare against a polity that they viewed as an enemy state.[10] Moreover, the Arabs made it clear that from their perspective the expulsion of hundreds of thousands of Arab brethren by Israel and the seizure of their property justified imposition of a boycott as a retaliatory measure.[11]

Another aspect of the Arabs' economic warfare against the State of Israel was the Egyptian maritime blockade. On 15 May 1948, concurrent to the military incursion of Egyptian forces into the Negev, Cairo imposed a blockade of Israeli shores and closed the Suez Canal to ships flying the Israeli flag or ships flying a foreign flag carrying cargo of any sort bound for or originating in Israel. Following the signing of the armistice agreement, Egypt cancelled its blockade of Israeli shores, but left in effect the closure of the Suez Canal.[12] On 6 February 1950, the Egyptian government published a Blockade Law that replaced wartime emergency regulations. The law forbade ships flying the Israeli flag from using the Canal, irrespective of their cargo. Israel was also forbidden from transporting cargo defined as "war materials" through the Canal on ships flying a foreign flag. The forbidden cargo included military equipment, aircraft, ships, vehicles, and fuel. This law prevented Israel from conducting ongoing and unrestricted commerce with countries in Asia and Africa.[13] Israel's efforts between 1949 and 1951 to remove the Egyptian maritime blockade through the Mixed Armistice Commission were to no avail.[14] Therefore, the Israeli Ministry of Foreign Affairs decided to request the assistance of the Security Council. At the beginning of September 1951 the Security Council ruled that the Egyptian blockade was in contradiction of the rights of all peoples to freedom of the seas.[15] Despite the unequivocal verdict of the Security Council, Cairo chose to persist with its embargo and even worsened it. In 1953 Egypt added more restrictions to the Blockade Law. The list of materials Israel was forbidden to transport through the Canal (in ships flying foreign flags) was broadened to include cotton, spare parts for vehicles, foodstuffs, and other trade items that in Egyptian parlance could "strengthen the war potential of the Zionists in Palestine."[16]

Besides the blockade that Egypt had imposed in the Suez Canal, it also disrupted passage of ships headed for Eilat, through the Straits at the mouth of the Red Sea. Such actions had already begun in the summer of 1951, and increased in the coming years. These harassments were in defiance of international law[17] and constituted one of the triggers behind the launch of Israel's October 1956 Sinai Campaign.[18]

It is difficult to quantify the impact of the economic boycott and the maritime blockade on Israel's economy. The economic warfare certainly undermined potential foreign investment that Israel sorely needed, particularly in its first

162 *Two political matters linked to the compensation issue*

years of statehood.[19] In March 1953, Israel estimated that Arab economic warfare had inflicted not less than 70 million dollars in damage.[20]

During the period covered in this volume, Israel conducted its struggle against the Arab economic boycott and the Egyptian maritime blockade solely in the diplomatic arena.[21] In the last analysis, however, it did not have any really effective tools at its disposal to defeat or bring about annulment of the Arab economic warfare, and it was forced to suffice with linking this matter to the compensation issue.[22]

The Jewish property in Iraq

The establishment of the Jewish State in May 1948 and the Arab-Israeli war that followed, in which Iraq participated, led the regime in Baghdad to adopt a harsh anti-Zionist domestic policy.[23] In mid July 1948, the Iraqi parliament defined Zionism as a crime (along with Communism and anarchism) carrying a penalty from seven years imprisonment to a death sentence. The new policy was bad news for the 140,000 Jews living in Iraq.[24] Against the backdrop of the war in Palestine, the thin veneer distinguishing "Zionism" from "Judaism" that had existed for years in Iraq dissolved almost completely, sparking brutal and sweeping anti-Jewish measures under the guise of anti-Zionism. Jews' freedom of movement was curtailed, an almost blanket prohibition on Jews leaving the country was clamped down, and heavy fines were imposed on wealthy members of the community. Hundreds of Iraqi Jews, primarily young people, were arrested and some sentenced to prison or fines for various and sundry Zionist activities. Jews employed in the civil service were fired, the commerce and financial dealings of members of the Jewish community suffered, and many families were left without a livelihood.[25]

In 1949, the attitude of the Iraqi regime towards its Jewish citizens escalated. Prime Minister Nuri al-Sa'id began to seek the expulsion of the Jews from Iraq. He mentioned this possibility at the end of January 1949 in a meeting that took place at the British Embassy in Amman between al-Sa'id and the prime minister of Jordan, Samir al-Rifa'i, in the presence of the United Kingdom minister in Amman, Sir Alec Kirkbride.[26] On 18 February, al-Sa'id voiced things in a similar vein to representatives of the Conciliation Commission visiting Baghdad.[27]

Britain, whose ties with Iraq, including al-Sa'id personally, were very close,[28] feared the ramifications such an idea could have on the Palestinian refugee issue. The expulsion of the Jews from Iraq, London claimed, would provide the Israeli government with "the perfect excuse" to refuse to pay compensation for the property of Palestinian refugees. In other words, acting on the threat was liable to weaken the prospect of solving the refugee problem. Consequently, Britain's minister in Baghdad was asked to advise al-Sa'id to drop the idea.[29]

London's opposition to the expulsion of the Jews had an impact on al-Sa'id, and he stopped raising this issue. Yet his heart's desire to see the Jewish

Two political matters linked to the compensation issue 163

community leave the country remained. In order that the exodus of Jews from Iraq would not appear to be a unilateral act under compulsion, in the course of the months May to July 1949, the Iraqi ruler proposed to American and British diplomats in Baghdad that "a voluntary exchange [of populations] on a proportional basis" be carried out between his country's Jewish citizens and the Palestinian refugees.[30] One can surmise that the linkage he created between the exit of Iraqi Jews and the refugee issue took place against the backdrop of animated talks taking place at the time in Lausanne on the refugee problem and parallel to ideas raised by the British suggesting resettlement of Palestinian refugees in the fertile regions of Iraq.

On 14 October 1949, when the Economic Survey Mission visited Baghdad, al-Sa'id raised the exchange-of-populations concept with them.[31] The details of the proposal leaked out and soon found their way into the Israeli press.[32] In a 25 October cabinet meeting, Sharett updated his colleagues regarding the Iraqi ruler's offer:

> We turned to the Survey Mission and asked about the degree of truth in this news. We received an official reply saying that following talks, Nuri al-Sa'id "threw out" such an idea, that perhaps it would be possible to exchange Iraqi Jews for Arab refugees.

The Economic Survey Mission, however, was quick to clarify to al-Sa'id that this matter was not within the limits of its authority. Sharett warned the members of the cabinet that Israel must object to the exchange since accepting it would mean:

> agreement on our part that the property of Iraqi Jews would be confiscated by the Iraqi Ministry of Finance in exchange for the Arab property we confiscated here, and then [thus] we take upon ourselves the responsibility to compensate the Jews of Iraq [...] It's also possible that the interpretation of this [will be] that each Arab country will commit to accept [Palestinian] refugees only to the extent that it has Jews. If we enter such negotiations, I fear very serious complications will be created.[33]

To sum it up, under Sharett's orchestration, Israel refused to accept the connection between the emigration of Iraqi Jews to Israel and the resettlement of Palestinian refugees in Iraq. The main concern was that such an exchange would establish a tie between the fate of abandoned Palestinian property and the fate of Jewish property in Iraq, and in a broader context also between the refugees' property and the assets of Jews living in other Arab states, first and foremost Egypt. Israeli leaders were unwilling to relinquish the huge assets of Jews in Arab countries, particularly those of Iraqi Jews, since this capital could assist in absorbing tens of thousands of Jewish immigrants from the Arab states and even help strengthen Israel's economy on the whole.

164 *Two political matters linked to the compensation issue*

The idea of a population exchange was dropped, however, much to Israel's dismay, the idea of confiscating the property of Iraqi Jews began to take shape. At the outset of March 1950, the Iraqi parliament passed the Denaturalization Law, which allowed any citizen interested the right to leave Iraq, provided they relinquished their citizenship and the right to return to Iraq in the future. The law would be in force for one year only, and its execution would be put in the hands of the Ministry of Interior.[34] A year after publication of the law, it became apparent that close to 105,000 Iraqi Jews had signed up to leave the country and approximately 35,000 had utilized this right during the prescribed period.[35]

On 10 March 1951, the parliament in Baghdad passed a government-sponsored bill "for the supervision and management of the property of Jews who have been deprived of their Iraqi nationality." According to the new law, the property of all Jews who had signed up to leave the country was frozen, rendering it unavailable for any commercial use. The same day, it was stipulated that a government custodian would be appointed and machinery for administration of the frozen Jewish assets would be established; the running costs of the work of the custodian and those employed in the administration machinery would be deducted from the Jewish assets. The Property Freeze Law related to all forms of property: land, homes (including their contents), vehicles, businesses, securities, bank accounts, and cash.[36]

From the moment the law came into effect, the Iraqi police embarked on a vigorous campaign to implement it: all shops owned by Jews were closed and sealed; all vehicles owned by Jews were confiscated; and police were sent to the homes of Jewish merchants to confiscate their goods.[37] Prior to passage of the law, Jews who had requested to emigrate from Iraq were allowed to sell their assets and exchange them for money. Yet since Iraqi foreign currency restrictions allowed Jews to take out only 200 dinar, émigrés sought to smuggle their capital out of the country by various devious means.[38] After promulgation of the law, it was impossible to sell assets at all, making attempts to detour the restrictions a moot question. Moreover, now the sum that the government allowed Jewish émigrés to take with them was reduced to 50 dinar.[39] Those worst affected by the new law to freeze all Jewish assets were some 30,000 Jews who had signed up in the first months of 1951 to leave the country and had not yet liquidated their assets.[40]

On 22 March 1951, the Property Freeze Law was expanded. According to government Ordinance 12 (1951), the property in Iraq of Jews who left the country legally since January 1948 was also frozen. Such property, stated Ordinance 12, would be returned to their owners only if they returned to Iraq within two months of the date the new ordinance was published abroad by the Iraqi diplomatic corps. The new directive impacted on several thousand wealthy Iraqi Jews who had emigrated to Europe, the United States, and Israel,[41] and who owned approximately 80 percent of all Iraqi Jewish assets, since many such émigrés continued to run their businesses in Iraq through relatives and friends. In light of the situation in Iraq, it was questionable whether anyone would want to return, even in order to try and save some of their wealth.[42]

Observers believed that al-Sa'id passed the Property Freeze Law in order to prevent the flight of capital in Jewish hands (drained primarily through smuggling).[43] Publicly, he justified the law, saying among other things that it was reprisal for Israel's attitude towards the Palestinian refugees and their abandoned property.[44]

By the end of 1951 a little more than 120,000 Iraqi Jews had arrived in Israel.[45] There is no exact data that can pinpoint the exact worth of the assets they left behind. Nevertheless, according to various estimates, the scope was enormous – several tens of millions of dollars –[46] immeasurably greater than the assets of Jewish communities in other Arab countries whose assets were seized by the authorities.[47]

The sheer measure of Iraqi Jews' assets prompted Israel to embark on a vigorous campaign against the Iraqi Property Freeze Law. On 15 March 1951, the cabinet in Jerusalem discussed the Iraqi law. At the close of discussion, it was decided to request the intervention of two western powers – the United States and Britain – in the Iraqi matter and at the same time to formally declare that there was a linkage between the compensation issue and the question of Jewish frozen assets in Iraq.[48] A public statement was issued by Sharett on 19 March, in a special announcement in the Knesset:

> By freezing the property of tens of thousands of Jews immigrating to Israel [...] the Iraqi government has opened an account [to solve] between itself and the State of Israel. There is already an account between us and the Arab world and it is the account for compensation owed to Arabs who left Israeli territory and abandoned their property in it due to the unleashed war of the Arab world against our state. The act that the Kingdom of Iraq has just perpetrated towards the property of Jews, who have not broken its laws and have not done anything to undercut its standing or undermine its security, forces us to couple the two accounts. Therefore the [Israeli] government has decided to inform the relevant United Nations institutions, and I hereby declare this publicly, that the value of Jewish property that has been frozen in Iraq will be taken into account by us in regard to compensation that we have committed to pay to Arabs who abandoned their property in Israel.[49]

The next day, Sharett sent letters to the American ambassador to Israel, Monnett Davis, and Britain's minister in Israel, Alexander Knox Helm, in which the foreign minister promised to rescind the linkage between the two accounts if the Baghdad government would allow Iraqi Jews requesting to emigrate to take their assets with them.[50] A letter in a similar vein was sent on 29 March to the chair of the Conciliation Commission, Ely Palmer. Palmer was also informed that Israel could not keep its December 1950 commitment to pay three million dollars to the Reintegration Fund. The

166   *Two political matters linked to the compensation issue*

expected arrival to Israel of more than 100,000 destitute Jews from Iraq, it was explained, will place a heavy, unexpected financial burden on Israel.[51]

A number of reasons led Israel to create a linkage between the two accounts: Israel hoped that the tie it created between them would prompt the western powers to take action against Iraq's seizure of Jewish property; would deter other Arab rulers from similar steps; would convince the large Jewish community in Iraq that the Jewish state was working to solve their difficulties; and finally would remove the possibility that the Israeli treasury would have to deal with two immense burdens: compensation of the Palestinian refugees and rehabilitation of tens of thousands of destitute Iraqi Jews.

The response of the two western powers to Israel's request that they intervene in the plight of Iraqi Jewry was disappointing from an Israeli perspective. Britain believed Iraqi policy and what had transpired in Palestine could not be separated, since one could not view the freezing of the assets of Jews in Iraq in a vacuum, unconnected to the fate of the Palestinian refugees. London argued that the seizure of the property of Iraqi Jews was a measure that, to a large extent, reflected the mood in the Arab world, angered by the suffering of the Palestinians. In Arab eyes, Israel was the guilty party for the fate of hundreds of thousands of refugees: their chances of ever returning to their homes were slim; they had received no compensation for their property; and their bank accounts had been frozen.[52] The freezing of the Arab refugees' assets had served as an excuse and as a model for Iraq.[53] While the British believed that the main objective of the Property Freeze Law was to block the flight of Jewish capital from the country,[54] there was no sense in Israel requesting the western powers intervene in events in Iraq as long as Israel refused to take effective steps of its own to alleviate the plight of the Palestinians, in other words, to free abandoned property or pay compensation.[55]

The American response was very close to that of the British. The administration in Washington replied that "constructive action" by Israel, aimed at resolving the problem of abandoned Palestinian property, would enable the United States to consider approaching the Iraqi government and requesting it resolve the problem of Jewish property in Iraq.[56]

The great powers' demand that Israel relinquish the Palestinians' abandoned property by either returning it to its owners or by paying compensation in order to take forward a solution to frozen Jewish assets in Iraq was unacceptable to Israel. Israel hoped to enjoy the best of both worlds: to receive the Iraqi-Jewish immigrants together with their assets, and to keep the abandoned property of the Palestinians for itself (and when the time came, to pay only partial compensation for their overall assets). Moreover, at this point – at the outset of 1951 – Israel was still linking (albeit in a vague manner) compensation and a comprehensive peace settlement. Israel did not want to lose this trump card for unfreezing the property of Jews in Iraq.

In the first years after mass immigration from Iraq, Israel continued from time to time to raise the question of confiscated Jewish assets and link it to the compensation issue. Yet, towards the mid 1950s, this changed, and Israeli

Two political matters linked to the compensation issue 167

diplomats ceased almost entirely to publicly link the two issues.[57] There is no unequivocal answer why it was decided to separate the two. Nevertheless, it would seem that the political use of confiscated Jewish assets did not sit well with Israeli public diplomacy; it was a bad fit since reference to Jewish assets carried a constant reminder of the Palestinian confiscated assets in Israeli hands.

Notes

1 Dan S. Chill, *The Arab Boycott of Israel: Economic Aggression and World Reaction*, New York: Praeger, 1976, p. 1; Yuval Elizur, *Economic Warfare: The Hundred-Year Economic Confrontation between Jews and Arabs*, Tel Aviv: Kinneret, 1997, p. 114 (Hebrew); Gil Feiler, *From Boycott to Economic Cooperation: The Political Economy of the Arab Boycott of Israel*, London: Frank Cass, 1998, p. 22; Aaron J. Sarna, *Boycott and Blacklist: A History of Arab Economy Warfare against Israel*, Totowa, NJ: Rowman and Littlefield, 1986, p. 5.
2 Elizur, *Economic Warfare*, pp. 115–16; Feiler, *From Boycott to Economic Cooperation*, pp. 22–4; Sarna, *Boycott and Blacklist*, pp. 5–7; Norman Vander Clute, *Legal Aspects of the Arab Boycott*, New York: Practising Law Institute, 1977, p. 11.
3 ISA, MFA 2427/7, The Arab Boycott, September 1958.
4 ISA, MFA 2566/9, Special Review: The Arab Economic Boycott of Israel, 6 December 1951.
5 ISA, MFA 2427/7, The Arab Boycott, September 1958.
6 ISA, MFA 2566/9, Special Review: The Arab Economic Boycott of Israel, 6 December 1951.
7 Shimon Golan, *Hot Border, Cold War: The Formulation of Israel's Security Policy, 1949–1953*, Tel Aviv: Ma'arachot, 2000, p. 344 (Hebrew).
8 ISA, Government Meeting, 8 February 1953, pp. 56–60; ISA, MFA 2427/5, The Arab Boycott, 11 January 1953; ISA, MFA 2452/1A, Subject: The Arab Boycott, 3 February 1953; Elizur, *Economic Warfare*, p. 127; Golan, *Hot Border, Cold War*, p. 344.
9 ISA, MFA 2427/7, The Arab Boycott, September 1958.
10 ISA, MFA 2566/9, Special Review: The Arab Economic Boycott of Israel, 6 December 1951.
11 Chill, *The Arab Boycott of Israel*, p. 5; Elizur, *Economic Warfare*, p. 123.
12 Golan, *Hot Border, Cold War*, p. 346.
13 ISA, MFA 3744/1, Special Review: History of the Egyptian Blockade, 24 February 1954; Golan, *Hot Border, Cold War*, p. 346.
14 ISA, MFA 3744/1, Special Review: History of the Egyptian Blockade, 24 February 1954.
15 ISA, MFA 3744/1, Special Review: History of the Egyptian Blockade, 24 February 1954; DEPI, Vol. 6, Editorial Note, p. 499.
16 ISA, MFA 3744/1, Special Review: History of the Egyptian Blockade, 24 February 1954.
17 David Tal, *Israel's Day-to-Day Security Conception: Its Origin and Development,1949–1956*, Sede Boqer: The Ben-Gurion Research Institute, 1998, p. 196 (Hebrew).
18 Motti Golani, *Israel in Search of a War: The Sinai Campaign, 1955–1956*, Brighton: Sussex Academic Press, 1998, pp. 175, 183.
19 Chill, *The Arab Boycott of Israel*, p. 23; Elizur, *Economic Warfare*, p. 150.
20 ISA, MFA 2477/21A, Memorandum from the Israeli Embassy in Washington, 30 March 1953.

168 Two political matters linked to the compensation issue

21 ISA, MFA 2452/1A, Subject: The Arab Boycott, 3 February 1953; Feiler, *From Boycott to Economic Cooperation*, p. 130.
22 ISA, MFA 2452/1A, The Foreign Minister to the Members of the Israel Delegation in Paris, 11 December 1951; ISA, MFA 2452/1A, Subject: The Suez Canal and the Arab Boycott, February 1953; ISA, MFA 2452/1A, Subject: The Arab Boycott, 3 February 1953.
23 Anti-Zionist policy by Baghdad began already at the close of the 1930s and amplified gradually. See in this connection: Esther Meir-Glitzenstein, "The Palestinian Dispute and Jewish-Muslim Relations in Iraq in the 1940s," *Pe'amim* 62, 1995, pp. 111–32 (Hebrew).
24 ISA, MFA 2563/8, The Persecution of Jews in Iraq, 16 November 1949.
25 Esther Meir-Glitzenstein, "The Riddle of the Mass Aliya From Iraq – Causes, Context and Results," *Pe'amim* 71, 1997, p. 32 (Hebrew).
26 Michael B. Bishku, "The Other Side of the Arab-Israeli Conflict: Great Britain and the Issue of Iraqi Jewry Prior to 'Operation Ezra and Nehemia'," *Studies in Zionism* 12(1), 1991, p. 34; Jacob Meron, "The Expulsion of the Jews from the Arab States and the Position of the Palestinians toward It," *State, Government and International Relations* 36, 1992, p. 31 (Hebrew).
27 Meron, "The Expulsion of the Jews," p. 32.
28 Fawas A. Gerges, *The Superpowers and the Middle East Regional and International Politics, 1955–1967*, Boulder, CO: Westview Press, 1994, p. 26; Moshe Shemesh, "The Kadesh Operation and the Suez Campaign: The Middle Eastern Political Background, 1949–1956," *Iyunim Bitkumat Israel* 4, 1994, p. 79 (Hebrew).
29 UKNA, FO 371/75182, E1571/93, From Foreign Office to Baghdad, 18 February 1949.
30 ISA, MFA 2447/15, Arab Governments' Position toward the Conciliation Commission, undated; Meron, "The Expulsion of the Jews," p. 32.
31 BGA, Correspondences, Shiloah to Sharett, 20 October 1949; DEPI, Vol. 4, Document 356, R. Shiloah to E. Elath, 19 October 1949.
32 Yehuda Shenhav, "Bringing Iraqi Jews to Israel," *Theory and Criticism* 12–13, 1999, p. 71 (Hebrew).
33 ISA, Government Meeting, 25 October 1949, pp. 17–18.
34 Dafna Zimhoni, "The Government of Iraq and the Mass Aliya of Jews to Israel," *Pe'amim* 39, 1989, p. 64 (Hebrew). For an analysis of the factors that motivated the Iraqi government to enact this legislation, see Itamar Levin, *Locked Doors: The Seizure of Jewish Property in Arab Countries*, London: Praeger, 2001, pp. 27–9.
35 Moshe Gat, *The Jewish Exodus from Iraq, 1948–1951*, London: Frank Cass, 1997, p. 144.
36 Gat, *The Jewish Exodus*, p. 144.
37 Gat, *The Jewish Exodus*, p. 145.
38 Gat, *The Jewish Exodus*, pp. 149–50; Zimhoni, "The Government of Iraq," p. 96.
39 Zimhoni, "The Government of Iraq," p. 98.
40 Zimhoni, "The Government of Iraq," p. 98.
41 Gat, *The Jewish Exodus*, p. 145.
42 Zimhoni, "The Government of Iraq," p. 99.
43 Gat, *The Jewish Exodus*, p. 150; Zimhoni, "The Government of Iraq," p. 99.
44 DEPI, Vol. 6, Document 99, S. Bendor: Report on the Visit of G.C. McGhee in Israel (27–28 March 1951), 1 April 1951; Zimhoni, "The Government of Iraq,", p. 98.
45 ISA, MFA 2014/11, Jewish Refugees from the Arab Countries, 31 August 1956.
46 See Itamar Levin's exhaustive survey of the many assessments that were prepared concerning this matter: Levin, *Locked Doors*, pp. 8–10; Gat, *The Jewish Exodus*, p. 149.

Two political matters linked to the compensation issue   169

47 Additional confiscations of Jewish property took place in Egypt, Lebanon, and Syria, but on much smaller scale than in Iraq. On this subject, see Levin, *Locked Doors*, pp. 87–210.
48 ISA, Government Meeting, 15 March 1951, pp. 2–10.
49 *Knesset Minutes*, vol. 8, 19 March 1951, p. 1359.
50 ISA, MFA 2451/11, Freezing of Jewish Property in Iraq, 20 March 1951.
51 ISA, MFA 2451/11, Payment of Compensation and the Freezing of Jewish Property in Iraq, 29 March 1951.
52 UKNA, FO 371/91692, E1571/50, Baghdad to FO, 4 April 1951; UKNA, FO 371/91692, E1571/66, FO Minute, Rhodes, 24 April 1951; UKNA, FO 371/91692, E1571/66, Morrison to Morgan, 7 May 1951.
53 UKNA, FO 371/91692, E1571/35, Helm to FO, 31 March 1951.
54 UKNA, FO 371/91692, E1571/30, Baghdad to FO, 14 March 1951.
55 UKNA, FO 371/91692, E1571/32, FO Minute, Rhodes, 22 March 1951.
56 DEPI, Vol. 6, Document 150, Aide-Memoire from the Government of the United States to the Government of Israel, 1 May 1951.
57 ISA, MFA 2603/4, Subject: Our Position Regarding Compensation to the Arab Refugees and the Issue of Jewish Property in Iraq, 3 June 1955.

8　The resettlement question following the 6th United Nations General Assembly

The 6th General Assembly

The 6th United Nations General Assembly opened in Paris on 6 November 1951 and continued, after recessing for Christmas and New Year's, until 5 February 1952. Palestine affairs, and particularly the Palestinian refugee issue, were discussed in the second half of the session, first in the Ad Hoc Political Committee, afterwards in the assembly plenum. On the agenda were the reports of the Conciliation Commission and the UNRWA. The western powers, the Arab states, and Israel had to study the recommendations that appeared in the two memorandums and adopt a position in their regard. The Conciliation Commission's failure to forward any Arab-Israeli settlement and the UNRWA's failure to bring relief to masses of refugees over the past year through the Reintegration Fund resonated in the background.

The Conciliation Commission's report, submitted at the end of November, surveyed its operations between 23 January and 19 November 1951, in particular the Paris talks. The commission noted the failure of the talks, stating that neither side in the conflict was willing to work towards peace through full implementation of the relevant United Nations resolutions. The report said that the (negative) attitude of the parties and the (physical) changes that had taken place in Palestine over the past three years nullified the commission's endeavors. The Conciliation Commission clarified that this state of affairs needed to be taken into account in any future discussion of the Palestine problem.[1]

At the same time the UNRWA submitted its own account. The account cited the agency's disappointment that so few refugees had been freed of dependence on the agency and that the Reintegration Fund had not succeeded in reducing the number of welfare recipients.[2] In light of the above, the agency recommended adoption of a new plan that had been formulated from the spring of 1951 by the UNRWA's director, John Blandford. The plan would focus almost exclusively on rehabilitation of the refugees and would try to mobilize much greater resources than those garnered to date. The primary objective would be to assist as many refugees as possible to obtain suitable housing and work, particularly in agricultural areas of the Arab states where

The resettlement question 171

they were situated, in order to reduce to a minimum the circle of welfare recipients among the refugees while enhancing the contribution of the refugees to local economies. The UNRWA was supposed to execute the proposed plan in close cooperation with the relevant governments. It expected the governments would propose housing and employment projects in their respective countries and allocate land and services for them. The proposed duration of the project was three years (from July 1951 to July 1954) and the overall cost was expected to be 250 million dollars, of which 200 million would be earmarked for rehabilitation and 50 million for relief.[3]

On 7 January 1952, the Ad Hoc Political Committee began to discuss the Conciliation Commission's report. On the table was a draft resolution sponsored by the United States, Britain, France, and Turkey stipulating that the Conciliation Commission "should continue to be available to the parties to assist them in reaching agreement on outstanding questions." This assistance, however, would be handled "remotely," from a distance. The Conciliation Commission's headquarters would be moved to the United Nations head-quarters in New York, leaving only one commission representative in Jerusalem. The four-states proposal, it became apparent, sought to minimize the presence of the Conciliation Commission in the Middle East and, in practice, to curtail its operations. This approach was the product of the commission's ongoing failures to narrow the gaps between Israel and its Arab neighbors.[4] Israel presented a draft resolution of its own that called for abolition of the Conciliation Commission and establishment of a new body – a Good Offices Committee – similar in composition to the Conciliation Commission. The Good Offices Committee would reside in New York and would remain at the disposal of the parties, stepping in only at the request of the two sides.[5] The Ad Hoc Political Committee rejected the proposal. Israel strove to dispose of the Conciliation Commission, since from the very establishment of this UN body Israel was displeased with its performance, primarily due to its mediation initiatives, which were perceived by Israel as too close to the Arab positions, thus discouraging any compromise on the part of the Arabs.

On the initiative of Columbia and Afghanistan, and with the encouragement of the Arabs, several substantive amendments were made in the draft resolution sponsored by the western powers and Turkey. One of the amendments said that the General Assembly notes "with regret" that previous United Nations resolutions regarding the Palestine question had still not been implemented, particularly those related to repatriation and compensation. Another amendment increased the number of members on the Conciliation Commission to seven. The amended draft was totally at odds with the position of the western powers and Turkey, not to mention Israel's proposal; instead of freezing the Conciliation Commission it sought to expand it, and it cited the repatriation principle. Thus, it is not surprising that the western powers and Turkey, who had initiated the original draft, voted in the Ad Hoc Political Committee against the amended version. Nevertheless, the draft resolution passed by a large majority.[6]

172 *The resettlement question*

On 16 January, a day after deliberations regarding the Conciliation Commission were closed, the Ad Hoc Political Committee convened in order to discuss the UNRWA's report, particularly its three-year plan, the Blandford Plan. The United States, Britain, France, and Turkey presented a draft resolution that called for adoption of the report's recommendations. Yet even before the committee could discuss it, the Egyptian representative demanded that the draft resolution be struck from the agenda, claiming that it undermined the sovereignty of the states in the Middle East. In essence, the Arabs wanted to cite Resolution 194(3) in the draft resolution, as well. The committee adjourned for informal consultations and reconvened on 21 January. The sponsoring nations submitted a revised draft resolution, which called for adoption of the UNRWA report's recommendations, but without detriment to certain terms adopted within previous United Nations resolutions regarding the refugees, including Clause 11 of Resolution 194(3). This amendment satisfied the Arabs, and the Ad Hoc Political Committee approved the revised resolution.[7]

Israel completely rejected the new version hands down. In an urgent letter to representatives of the western powers and Turkey at the General Assembly, Abba Eban detailed Israel's reasoning. First, the amendment was liable to create a situation in which, although reintegrated in the Arab states, the same refugees could still claim eligibility for repatriation. Second, reference to the repatriation principle would lessen Israel's willingness to make progress on the compensation issue. Third, the illusion that the refugees could, at some point, return to Israel was liable to undermine their desire to accept the UNRWA's rehabilitation plan. Fourth, the idea that nothing substantial had changed since 1948, and therefore it was still possible to talk about implementation of the repatriation principle, was incompatible with what members of the Conciliation Commission and the UNRWA had told Israeli diplomats during their conversations.[8]

The Israelis hoped that the western powers would introduce changes in the wording of the resolutions regarding the Conciliation Commission and the UNRWA. The western powers tried to do so in regard to the Conciliation Commission. Their efforts were reflected in the course of deliberations on Palestinian affairs in the assembly plenum session in late January. The Ad Hoc Political Committee's report, containing the resolutions passed by the committee regarding the future of the Conciliation Commission and the UNRWA report, were before the General Assembly plenum. Under American and British pressure, several revisions were made in the committee's wording, the most important from Israel's standpoint was omission of the part of the draft resolution regarding the Conciliation Commission – the part that had specifically mentioned the repatriation and compensation issues.[9] Thus, Resolution 512(6) cited, in general, in general terms, that the assembly "recalls all the resolutions adopted at previous sessions of the General Assembly on the Palestine problem." Besides this, the Conciliation Commission was not given any special or specific missions, as it had been in December

1950 when it was authorized to establish the Refugees Office. The commission was only requested to "continue its efforts to secure the implementation of the resolutions of the General Assembly on Palestine and accordingly should be available to the parties to assist them in reaching agreement on outstanding questions."[10] The same day, another resolution, Resolution 513(6), was passed, adopting all the elements of the UNRWA plan "without prejudice to the provisions of paragraph 11 of resolution 194(3)."[11]

In general, opinions in Israel held that the wording of the two resolutions adopted in the end was good for Israel. The advisor to the Israeli delegation at the United Nations, Gideon Rafael, wrote:

> The Commission was not given [in Resolution 512(6)] authority to appoint special representatives; [the resolution] did not talk of refugees, their repatriation or compensation; [...] the Conciliation Commission's five proposals [at the Paris Conference] [...] were not endorsed [by the General Assembly]; the Commission is released from submitting a report at the next session [of the General Assembly] and therefore the Palestine question will not automatically appear on the agenda.[12]

At a 27 January cabinet meeting, Sharett told his colleagues that "most of the bad things" for Israel that the Arabs succeeded in inserting during discussion about the Conciliation Commission in the Ad Hoc Political Committee were shelved in the General Assembly plenum vote. As for the resolution on the UNRWA, Sharett believed that one should not view the amendment, inserted under Arab pressure, as a great calamity, since "at this price, a resolution to resettle refugees in neighboring [Arab] countries was passed."[13] Several years later, the director-general of the Ministry of Foreign Affairs, Walter Eytan, wrote in his diary, in retrospect about Resolution 513(6) concerning the UNRWA, that:

> The intention of the General Assembly was plain. It did not wish the refugees to drag out an idle and demoralized existence on relief, but to be "reintegrated". "Reintegration" meant resettlement in the Arab countries – and as far as possible, those [Arab countries] to which the refugees had gone [during the 1948 war].[14]

The direction the two General Assembly resolutions were headed was also clear to the rest of the parties involved in the Middle East conflict. In a discussion between Avraham Biran and the chief of staff of the United Nations Truce Supervision Organization in Palestine and chairman of the Mixed Armistice Commissions, William Riley, the latter commented that now that the 6th General Assembly was over, the Conciliation Commission (according to the resolution passed) would no longer be present in place [in the Middle East] to influence the refugees and kindle in their hearts hopes of returning to their former homes.[15] From various reports in the Arab press that appeared

174 *The resettlement question*

already in December 1951, it was evident that the Palestinian refugees understood that the Blandford Plan led to their resettlement.[16]

Israel, indeed, had good reason to be pleased with the resolutions adopted regarding the Conciliation Commission and the UNRWA. On one hand, the Conciliation Commission had been neutralized (substantiated by its limited operations in coming years); on the other hand, the UNRWA had deepened its involvement in the region. As a byproduct of the two trends, the principle of resettlement was reinforced by the very nature of UNRWA activities – provision of housing and employment to refugees in Arab countries – in contrast to the decline of the repatriation principle anchored in the Conciliation Commission's mandate. Israel, which fervently hoped the new "distribution of power" mandated by the two resolutions could be a game changer giving resettlement the upper hand, watched with satisfaction as this orientation gained momentum.

The Arab states' position on UNRWA resettlement plans

Immediately after the close of the 6th General Assembly, the UNRWA began to take vigorous steps to implement the three-year Blandford Plan. Among other things, it conducted a host of working meetings with the heads of the regimes in Jordan, Lebanon, Syria, and Egypt, at which various economic projects were studied, most of them agricultural, designed to bring about the integration of Palestinian refugees into the life fabric of their host countries. In the next sub-chapter the attitudes of the Arab states to the UNRWA's refugee rehabilitation plans in general, and towards the Blandford Plan in particular, are discussed.

The Jordanian government was the first among the Arab governments to sign a refugee rehabilitation agreement with the UNRWA in the framework of the Blandford Plan. This step reflected the desire of Abdullah's heirs (Talal and, after him, Hussein) to continue Abdullah's political policy on the refugee issue. On 5 August 1952, an agreement was signed in which the UNRWA was supposed to allocate 11 million dollars to the Hashemite Kingdom to rehabilitate 5,000 refugee families. Most of the money was earmarked for the establishment of permanent agricultural settlements along the border between Israel and Jordan.[17] However, by June 1954, only 3.7 million dollars out of the sum total earmarked for the project had been utilized.[18] On 30 March 1953, the two parties signed a second agreement in which the agency committed to budget 40 million dollars to finance a large settlement project in the Jordan Valley. According to this plan, a large sector in the Jordan Valley would be irrigated with water from the Jordan River and its Yarmuk tributary. In scope, the project was designed to absorb 150,000 refugees.[19] Yet, by mid 1957, the UNRWA still could not report to the United Nations General Assembly that substantive progress had been made on that project.[20] Besides these two extensive initiatives the UNRWA was involved in carrying out a host of other projects on behalf of the refugees, much smaller ones, throughout the kingdom: construction of permanent housing, technical assistance to small land owners, extension of loans for the establishment of small businesses, occupational training, and the like.[21] Despite the willingness of the Jordanian Royal House to promote the UNRWA's resettlement plans,[22] the large projects and many of the smaller projects failed to materialize due to the lack of natural resources as well as the opposition of most of the refugees, fearing they would lose their rights to UNRWA relief and their (theoretical) right to return to Israel.[23]

The situation in Lebanon was diametrically opposed to the situation in Jordan. Since 1948, the leadership in Beirut had emphatically rejected the rehabilitation of the Palestinian refugees in Lebanon. It exhibited no signs of retreating from this stance, even after the Blandford Plan was adopted by the United Nations. First and foremost, the Lebanese government feared Palestinians would disrupt the delicate ethnic balance in their country. According to official demographic data, the Christians, from whom most Lebanese leaders were drawn, constituted about 50 percent of the population. The resettlement of more than 100,000 refugees, who constituted approximately 10 percent of the population of Lebanon – the overwhelming majority of them Muslims (approximately 90 percent) – would have totally unbalanced the prevailing ethic composition of the country. All the more so, structurally and economically, Lebanon was not in any position to absorb masses of destitute refugees: the size of the country is small, its natural resources are limited, opportunities for development were very slim, and the economic situation was grim.

It is not surprising that the Lebanese leadership, particularly the Christians in power, did everything they could to make integration of the refugees in Lebanon difficult. The refugees' legal status in the country was that of "foreigners": they were exempt from basic civic duties, but also were ineligible for most civil rights. In addition, their freedom of movement was limited and employment options greatly curtailed by law.[24] Almost every year, invariably, the UNRWA's report to the United Nations General Assembly said that rehabilitation projects were not being executed on Lebanese territory due to the government's categorical opposition to such projects.[25]

Syria, unlike Lebanon, could have absorbed the 85,000 Palestinian refugees that ended up in Syria relatively easily; its territory is large, blessed with rich natural resources, and it did not suffer from major economic straits at the time. Moreover, several tens of thousands of refugees could not jeopardize its social and political structure since the Palestinian refugees in Syria were a mere 3 percent of the overall population.[26] Such objective conditions enabled the Syrian regime to pass from 1949 a series of regulations that enabled the refugees in the country to enjoy all the civil rights existing in Syria for Syrian citizens.[27] The leadership in Damascus did not suffice with these steps and on several occasions even declared its intention to rehabilitate all the refugees in Syria, as well as a large number of Palestinian refugees situated in other states.

This proposal was first voiced by Husni Za'im. Za'im, who was the chief of staff of the Syrian army, seized the reins of government on 30 March 1949 in

176　*The resettlement question*

a military coup. His primary objective was to establish his own regime in Damascus and transform Syria into a unified, strong, and progressive nation that would command a prominent and independent role in the politics of the Middle East.[28] In realizing this goal he needed large-scale economic, military, and political assistance, which only the United States could provide. Za'im understood this and made concerted efforts to win the heart of the administration in Washington.[29] One of the far-reaching steps he took in this direction was a proposal to reach a peace settlement with the Jewish state.[30] Za'im's representatives raised this idea with the Israelis in mid April 1949, in the armistice talks that were taking place between the two countries. The Syrians proposed a peace treaty, economic and political cooperation, and even a joint army, in exchange for moving the international border to give Syria part of the Sea of Galilee.[31] Two weeks later, at the end of April, Za'im met with James Keeley, the United States' representative in Damascus, and expressed his willingness to absorb a quarter of a million Palestinian refugees in Syria as part of the political settlement with Israel. This hinged on receipt of large-scale assistance, beyond compensation for the refugees' abandoned property. On 1 May, Za'im raised this offer again with Keeley,[32] and on 17 May Colonel William Riley reported Za'im's offer to absorb refugees in Syria to the legal advisor of the Israeli Ministry of Foreign Affairs, Shabtai Rosenne.[33] Ben-Gurion and Sharett were hardly entranced by the offer, for a number of reasons. First and foremost, they had no wish to give the Syrians a foothold in the Sea of Galilee, an essential and irreplaceable natural resource slated to supply water to the country's national irrigation project and for development of the Negev – even if this would be in exchange for substantial realization of the resettlement principle.[34]

After Za'im, the idea of absorbing a huge number of Palestinian refugees was raised by the Syrian ruler, Colonel Adib al-Shishakli. On 19 December 1949, al-Shishakli led a military coup in Damascus. Although he only appointed himself deputy chief of staff and the parliamentary government continued to exist, in practice Syria had one-man rule. On 29 November 1951, al-Shishakli initiated a second coup d'etat, which transformed him into a dictator without pretences, although he appointed a straw man to serve as president and prime minister, Colonel Fawzi Selo. In July 1953 even this facade was abandoned, and al-Shishakli officially appointed himself president and prime minister.[35] After he seized power, particularly after the second coup, al-Shishakli worked vigorously to obtain massive economic and military assistance from the West, especially from the United States. He wanted to develop and strengthen his army and to undertake social-economic reforms to gain domestic stability and ensure the sustainability of his regime.[36] Therefore, he was prepared, like Husni Za'im before him, to adopt a pro-western orientation. In keeping with this strategy, in a number of talks, al-Shishakli presented a moderate stand vis-à-vis Israel[37] and even expressed a degree of readiness to reach a political settlement with the Jewish state.[38] Against this backdrop, it becomes understandable that Syria in the years when al-Shishakli's

The resettlement question   177

was in power agreed to assist in resolving the Palestinian refugee problem by implementing the UNRWA's resettlement programs.

From the summer of 1950 (as discussed in Chapter 5), and in an even more vigorous manner in the first half of 1951, the heads of the Syrian regime expressed in private talks with western diplomats and UNRWA officials Syria's readiness to discuss resettlement plans. They even hinted that they might agree to absorb Palestinian refugees currently located in other Arab countries. The primary proviso the Syrians presented was that the United Nations finance the cost of resettlement and absorption.[39] Therefore, it was rather surprising that in the summer and fall of 1951, Syrian leadership expressed reservations regarding the Blandford Plan. It said that it was apprehensive of public opinion at home.[40] Yet after the Plan was ratified in the United Nations General Assembly and won the support of the Arab bloc, Damascus again signaled its desire to discuss with the UNRWA implementation of rehabilitation projects.[41] The Syrian regime's readiness to contribute to resolution of the refugee problem reached its peak in mid April 1952: Prime Minister Selo, with authorization from al-Shishakli, offered to absorb in Syria half a million Palestinian refugees from Jordan, Lebanon, and the Gaza Strip, in addition to the 85,000 refugees already in the country.[42] In exchange, the Syrians now demanded international capital that would be invested not only in financing resettlement and absorption of the refugees, but also in development and strengthening of the local economy so that Syria's citizenry would not feel "left out" in the face of such large investments in the refugee population.[43]

The Syrian offer astounded and enthralled both the UNRWA and the western powers. The British Foreign Office wrote its representatives in Beirut that this opportunity should not be missed and that the offer could strengthen the UNRWA approach (the resettlement approach).[44] The Americans expressed a similar position. The State Department viewed the Syrian proposal as an important contribution towards improving the political climate in the Middle East. This in itself could promote resolution of the refugee problem.[45] The State Department surmised that if the offer were acted on (and with it the Jordan Valley settlement plan), a genuine breakthrough could be achieved in resolution of the problem.[46] The British, the Americans, and the UNRWA had for some time viewed resettlement of Palestinian refugees in Syria (in addition to Iraq) as the most practical solution, since Syria's geographic conditions made it the best choice for rehabilitation of the refugees.[47]

Hopes and realities, however, were two different things. Al-Shishakli hinged his readiness to absorb half a million refugees on receipt not only of massive economic assistance, but also significant military aid.[48] Washington, which was the chief address for such requests, declined to accept the terms as set forth by the Syrians (particularly regarding supply of military equipment),[49] and in response, the Syrians withdrew their dramatic offer. But even had al-Shishakli received everything he demanded, it appears that Arab public opinion at home and abroad would not have allowed him to sign an agreement in which Syria would absorb hundreds of thousands of Palestinian refugees.

178 *The resettlement question*

Such a step would be interpreted in the Arab street as a betrayal, since it would have removed the (theoretical) possibility of realizing the principle of repatriation. Driven by deep apprehensions that public opinion would not take such an agreement lightly, on several occasions, Selo requested the UNRWA refrain for the time being from publicizing the regime's offer regarding the refugees.[50]

After hopes of realizing this colossal resettlement plan were dashed, the UNRWA tried, in the course of winter 1952–3, to take smaller and more modest projects forward in Syria,[51] but these projects met the same gloomy fate as the offer to absorb half a million refugees.[52]

Problems with the aid Damascus requested and fear of hostile public opinion served as a barrier to the realization of the UNRWA rehabilitation programs in Syria after the fall of al-Shishakli's regime in February 1954 as well. Furthermore, during this period, Syria was characterized by political instability and lacked a strong center of authority that could take decisive action on tough issues. Moreover, the Syrian political establishment, particularly after the September 1954 elections, stood firm in an ardent anti-western and anti-Israel stance and leaned towards the Communist bloc.[53]

The fate of the Palestinian refugees was of little interest to the largest of the Arab states, Egypt. Cairo could afford to exhibit such disinterest since the 200,000 refugees under its responsibility didn't reside in Egypt proper, but rather in the Gaza Strip, which was beyond Egypt's sovereign borders. Consequently, Cairo was not forced to grapple with the economic, social and political ramifications emanating from the presence of a large, poverty-stricken, and bitter refugee population within Egyptian society. Since 1948, Egypt had refused to annex the Strip and held it as a close territorial unit – from a fiscal and political standpoint. Its status was defined as "an area of southern Palestine" under Egyptian responsibility.[54]

Israel learned of the little interest Cairo showed in the refugee problem first hand, from secret talks Israeli representatives held with Egyptian representatives (mostly in New York and Paris). During the reign of King Faruq, while only a handful of meetings were held, they sufficed to clarify that the primary Egyptian condition for any political settlement with Israel was Jerusalem's willingness to relinquish all of the Negev or a large part of it, so territorial continuity could be established between Egypt and the Arab world to the East.[55] On the other hand, the Egyptians hardly mentioned the refugee problem. Israel surmised that the refugees' fate was certainly not a priority for Egypt.[56]

Political contact between the two countries became more frequent and businesslike after the Free Officers Revolution on 23 July 1952.[57] The military junta set two core objectives for itself: economic-social reforms and expulsion of the British presence from Sudan and the Suez Canal. In order to realize these objectives, Egypt needed massive aid – economic, military, and political – from the Americans. For this purpose, in secret talks Egyptian officials conducted with Israeli representatives, as well as with western diplomats and other mediators,[58] they presented (like the Syrians) a relatively moderate

The resettlement question 179

stand on all aspects of the Arab-Israeli conflict, which at the core demonstrated readiness to arrive at some kind of political settlement with the Jewish state.[59] In exchange, Egypt demanded that Israel relinquish an overland corridor in the Negev. After they took care to emphasize the territorial issue, the Egyptians gave lip service to the refugee problem. They admitted that the chances of realizing the principle of repatriation were very low. However, on several occasions, they proposed to settle some of the refugees in territory that Israel would relinquish. Other than this, from time to time, the issue of compensation for abandoned refugee property was raised by Cairo.[60]

The Egyptians' indifference to the fate of the Palestinian refugees was reflected in practice in the slow and drawn-out manner in which Cairo discussed resettlement projects with the UNRWA.[61] In mid 1950, Cairo hinted that it was willing to allow refugees from the Strip to settle in the Sinai Peninsula.[62] Yet this verbal readiness only ripened into an actual deed at the outset of 1951. In January of that year Egypt gave the UNRWA permission to investigate whether there was a source of water in El-Arish that could make settlement of 10,000 refugee families there feasible.[63] The survey did not produce any positive findings, but the UNRWA didn't give up. The agency put intense pressure on Cairo to cooperate on other programs to rehabilitate the refugees, in the framework of the Blandford Plan. The Egyptians tried to weasel out of doing so using all sorts of excuses, but under a steamroller of pressure from the UNRWA, the Egyptians were forced to abandon their negative position. On 30 June 1953 the UNRWA reached an agreement with the Egyptian government in which half a million dollars would be allotted to examine whether various refugee rehabilitation projects could be carried out inside the Gaza Strip and in Sinai. An additional sum of 29.5 million dollars was earmarked to finance projects that could be shown to be feasible. On 14 October 1953, the two sides signed an agreement to execute a project that was found to be suitable for rehabilitating refugees, in the framework of the Blandford Plan. The project called for settling between 50,000 and 70,000 refugees on a tract of land east of the Suez Canal that was supposed to receive water from the Nile.[64] In the summer of 1955, experts sponsored by the UNRWA and the Egyptian government completed economic, geographic, and topographic surveys for the initiative.[65] The findings were submitted to the Egyptian government at the end of 1956, but the military crisis in the region prevented further progress.[66]

In the small and arid Gaza Strip almost no rehabilitation projects were carried out, except for forestation of desert sectors and the gradual transfer of refugees to permanent housing.[67]

Already in the course of 1952, the UNRWA reported that programs for the rehabilitation of refugees in the Arab states were progressing "at a slow pace."[68] At the end of the year, the General Assembly was forced, on the recommendation of the agency, to increase the sum earmarked for refugee relief because rehabilitation plans were more or less at a standstill.[69] In October 1953 the British Foreign Office stated that progress on resettlement

180 *The resettlement question*

plans in the years 1951 to 1953 was "very disappointing" and that the time slot set for the Blandford Plan was unrealistic. The British believed that the primary reasons for the failure of the Plan were: (a) poor cooperation on the part of the Arab governments; (b) technical difficulties tied to resettlement of such a large number of refugees; (c) lack of economic development in the region.[70] The UNRWA's report to the United Nations General Assembly in the closing days of 1954 also cited these factors as responsible for the failure of the three-year plan.[71]

Thus, between 1 July 1951 and 30 June 1954, the UNRWA spent approximately seven million dollars (out of 200 million budgeted according to the Blandford Plan) to finance rehabilitation projects in the Arab states. This sum assisted only 10,000 refugees to extricate themselves from the relief rolls (while the refugee population was growing at a rate of 25,000 persons a year).[72]

The fly in the ointment: resettlement in proximity to the armistice lines

Israel followed with great interest the UNRWA's efforts to take the Blandford Plan into action. Israel, of course, wanted such endeavors to succeed since they ensured implementation of the resettlement principle.[73] Yet, at the same time, together with its support of the Blandford Plan, it was understood in Israel that projects in the program – for example, the Jordan Valley project of the Hashemite Kingdom, El-Arish in Egypt, and the rehabilitation of refugees in southern Syria – would mean hundreds of thousands of Palestinian refugees would be permanently situated along the armistice lines. In Israel there were apprehensions that this state of affairs would increase one of the most grave security problems that the Jewish state had been grappling with in the 1950s: infiltration.

The infiltration problem was inseparable from the refugee problem; the scope of infiltration grew and flourished among this population.[74] In an 11 March 1949 review by the head of the IDF's Operations Division, it was stated that the infiltration phenomenon would exist "as long as there are Palestinian refugees in the Arab states bordering Israel, or in the Arab part of the country [Palestine] that was not conquered by us."[75] Similar views were voiced by the commander of the Southern Command, Moshe Dayan, in a 19 November 1951 meeting of the Foreign Affairs and Defense Committee.[76] At the outset of 1953, in light of the deteriorating security situation along the Israeli-Jordanian border, the IDF's Intelligence Division wrote a document that examined Israel's security policy along its eastern border. Of all the factors impacting on the situation in this sector, the document cited the concentration of hundreds of thousands of refugees just across the border.[77]

The infiltration began within weeks of the establishment of the State of Israel in May 1948,[78] spread in the course of 1951, and reached its peak in the year leading up to the outbreak of the 1956 Sinai Campaign.[79] Its

The resettlement question 181

motivations were both political and non-political. In the first category were infiltrations designed to plant land mines and other explosive devices, to fire on Jewish transport and settlements, to kidnap Israeli soldiers and citizens, and to collect intelligence. In the second category were infiltrations by refugees who came to work their fields from before the 1948 war and to graze their herds, to retrieve abandoned property, to rob and to steal, to engage in smuggling activity, to visit relatives, to resettle in the country or to travel to surrounding countries through Israeli territory.[80] The "political" infiltration was only a small part of overall infiltration; most was motivated by economic factors and social forces.[81] The overwhelming majority of infiltrators were Palestinian refugees. There were, however, several cases of non-refugees who infiltrated. One such case was of Palestinian peasants who resided on the border between the West Bank and Israel; their lands (i.e. livelihoods) were suddenly, due to the vicissitudes of war, situated on the "other side" (the Israeli side) of the armistice line between Israel and Jordan.[82] A similar problem, but on a smaller scale, existed in border areas between the Gaza Strip and Israel as a result of the Armistice Agreement between Israel and Egypt, but there the problem was resolved through a 1950 exchange of territory.[83] Besides these, there were also Bedouin tribes that traversed the Negev back and forth on their way between Sinai and Jordan.[84]

Infiltration caused serious loss of life: 258 Israeli soldiers were killed in the years 1951 to 1956; and 284 civilians were murdered and approximately 500 wounded between 1949 and 1956.[85] It also harmed the economy; the direct damage between the years 1950 and 1956 was assessed to be in the vicinity of 10 million dollars.[86] Indirect economic damage was much more substantive, including large expenditures on security; loss of work days by residents in border areas due to security constraints in their settlements; loss of yields to theft and sabotage of agricultural and industrial equipment; damage resulting from abandonment of cultivated fields close to the border; and loss of customs and excise taxes by the government due to smuggling.[87]

The expense of infiltration included a psychological cost as well. The robberies, sabotage, and murders had a cumulative effect on the Israeli civilian population: this was registered in a strong sense of anxiety, panic, and distress among Israelis. Most vulnerable were new frontier settlements established along Israel's borders, since they found themselves in the fire line of hostile actions, particularly infiltration. The gravest side effect of deterioration in the sense of security of those on the periphery was abandonment of settlements – not just individual families, but sometimes the collapse of an entire community.[88] From the perspective of the country's leadership, such a state of affairs was intolerable since settlements in frontier areas were designed to achieve an important political objective, second to none: to demonstrate Israel's sovereignty along the armistice lines. Through settlement, Israel sought to fortify its demand that these lines would not be changed, as the Arab states and the international community demanded, but would remain the permanent borders of the country.[89]

182   *The resettlement question*

Infiltration, and particularly the political infiltration, was one of the core factors fueling escalation of the Arab-Israeli conflict. Israel publicly announced that the Arab states bordering it were responsible for the phenomenon of cross-border infiltration and its results, and therefore beginning in 1949 Israel responded with retaliatory actions against civilian targets and from 1954 against military targets in Arab-controlled territories.[90] Retaliatory actions not only deepened hostilities between Israel and its Arab neighbors; they also caused serious political damage to Israel in the international arena (for example, the IDF operation against the West Bank Arab village of Qybia in October 1953, which ended with scores of civilian casualties).[91] Israel's image was also harmed by transfer of Arabs from Israeli territory to the Arab states, as part of the combat against the infiltration phenomenon. An example of this was the case of the Azazme tribe, a Bedouin tribe which had gained notoriety for its hostile actions against the Jewish community even in Mandate times. In the course of 1950, the Azazme tribe was expelled to Egypt.[92] Another case was the evacuation of 2,500 Arabs from the township Majdal (Ashkelon), adjacent to the Gaza Strip.[93] This township had served as a transfer point, providing shelter and information for infiltrators from Gaza headed for Jaffa, Lod, and Ramle. Consequently, Majdal was subjected to military government, and eventually it was decided to transfer its residents to other places. In the course of the summer and fall of 1950, most of the residents were transferred to the Gaza Strip. Several dozen went to Jordan, and several hundred others were dispersed throughout Israel. The Egyptians, although aware of the transfer, having been informed via the Mixed Armistice Commission of the pending action, accused Israel of a forced evacuation. Israel claimed that most of the residents of the town had expressed willingness to join their kin in the Gaza Strip.[94]

In the domestic Israeli political arena, from 1953 the government's retaliation policy became a key issue in the ideological clash that already existed between Ben-Gurion and Sharett: the former, a champion of the hawkish activist school; the latter, a champion of a more dovish conciliatory approach to resolution of the Arab-Israeli conflict.[95]

Apprehensions that masses of refugees would settle in proximity to the borders were magnified by repeated threats from certain Arab circles to conduct a "refugee march" into Israeli territory[96] and repeated "promises" by Arab leaders to employ masses of refugees as auxiliary military forces against the Jewish state, when the time was ripe.[97]

In light of this state of affairs, it is not surprising that Israel viewed with great uneasiness the UNRWA's resettlement plans, which were supposed to be carried out in proximity to the armistice lines. At the end of January 1952, the first secretary at the Israeli embassy in Washington, Meir de Shalit, talked with State Department official Arthur Gardiner about implementation of the 6th General Assembly's resolutions regarding the refugees. In de Shalit's report to the Ministry of Foreign Affairs United States Division, he said that Gardiner related that the Jordanians and the Egyptians agreed to settle the refugees on

The resettlement question   183

their borders, and the Egyptians had earmarked the El-Arish area for this purpose.[98] Israel's representative in Turkey, Eliahu Sasson, wondered why de Shalit had not considered it fitting to clarify to the American diplomat on the spot that Israel had reservations regarding plans to resettle refugees in this area, so close to the Israeli border. He wrote to the Ministry of Foreign Affairs United States Division, "It seems to me, that we must fight with all our might any plan for settling refugees in Sinai," and expressed hopes that the embassy staff in Washington "are vigilant on this matter."[99] The division replied to Sasson and admitted that:

> Our situation is such, that all the practical proposals for resettlement of the refugees are not welcomed by us, since agreement to settlement of refugees by the Arab states has been forthcoming only by Egypt – in Sinai, and by Trans-Jordan – in Arab Eretz Yisrael (i.e. the West Bank) and in the Jordan Valley [that is, adjacent to the armistice lines]. Even if Syria will settle refugees, [...] [after all] it is thinking of the Israeli border, at least at the outset, although from an economic standpoint it would be better in the north of the country or in Iraq, of course.

Despite this complex state of affairs, the United States Division rejected Sasson's recommendation that Israel "declare war" on the UNRWA's policy and its resettlement plans. The division explained that the western powers and the United Nations would, in any case, grasp any opportunity to settle refugees, even if it be along Israel's borders. It also expressed doubts "whether any benefit could be derived for us appearing as opponents to a practical plan for resolution of the problem."[100]

De Shalit was surprised by the assertion presented at the outset of the United States Division's letter that it would be detrimental to Israel's interests if the refugees would be settled close to its borders. He requested to know whether the embassy in Washington ought to oppose the rehabilitation program in the Sinai desert. De Shalit told the division:

> I talked about this with the Ambassador and we don't know of any decision of ours [by the cabinet] to oppose settlement of the refugees in the El-Arish region [...] What is the legal background [basis] to our opposition? Can we oppose the settlement of Arab refugees in Arab territory?[101]

Pinhas Eliav, the second secretary at the Israeli embassy in Washington, had to grapple with that issue in a conversation he conducted with the assistant to the representative of the United States on the UNRWA's advisory commission, Donald Bergus. After Bergus asked whether Israel would oppose settlement of 150,000 refugees in the Jordan Valley, Eliav answered that, in principle, Jerusalem had no legal basis to oppose settlement programs in the territory of sovereign states, but certainly it could raise "justified arguments" if the UNRWA would decide to rehabilitate them on the border. He reminded Bergus of the Arabs'

184   *The resettlement question*

repeated demands to settle the refugees specifically on the borders, to prepare them in this manner for "the day of vengeance and payment [the day of reckoning]."[102]

Several officials in the Ministry of Foreign Affairs were in agreement with Sasson's position. One was the acting spokesman of the Ministry of Foreign Affairs, Michael Elizur. In a letter to Walter Eytan Elizur wrote that "the long term interests of the State [of Israel] is to do whatever we can in order to prevent over-crowding the areas adjacent to our borders, and particularly their settlement by refugees." It was clear to Elizur that Israel couldn't call the shots, but efforts in this direction had to be made. At the end of the telegram, he pointed out that there were others who shared his view among those involved in Arab affairs in the Research Division.[103] The legal adviser of the Ministry of Foreign Affairs, Shabtai Rosenne, wrote to Eytan in a similar spirit. He alerted Eytan to an item that had appeared in the Jerusalem Arabic-language newspaper *al-Defaa*, which reported that with the assistance of the UNRWA, establishment of dwelling units for Palestinian refugees in Jordanian villages on the border with Israel was planned. Rosenne wrote:

> In my opinion, we must oppose unequivocally this plan whose end [product] will be to plant enormous bitterness of spirit along the length of the border that in the future will amplify tensions along the length of the border unnecessarily.

Even if Arab governments are free to settle refugees "wherever they like," it's another thing for an international body [i.e. the UNRWA] to assist in carrying out "these irresponsible acts." "Plain sense demands", concluded Rosenne, "that the permanent settlement of Palestinian refugees will be carried out as much as possible far away from the borders, not the opposite."[104]

Eytan's deputy, Michael Comay, voiced a totally converse position. In his view, Israel did not need to intervene in the UNRWA's rehabilitation programs in Jordan or Egypt or to protest this matter. On the contrary, it must encourage any action designed to resettle the refugees in the Arab states.[105] For after all, a much greater peril would await Israel if the UNRWA's rehabilitation programs didn't succeed and the world decided to pull out (of dealing with) the problem:

> The very idea shocks me […] if these multitudes of people will be allowed to crowd together on our border, bitter and dying of hunger. Under such conditions […] the current [level of] infiltration is liable to be breached [explode] and increase a hundred fold, until it will be impossible to control it.[106]

In the end, Comay's position and that of the United States Division became the official Israeli position regarding the location issue of UNRWA resettlement programs. That is to say, Israel hoped the programs would be implemented as far away as possible from the armistice lines,[107] and from time to time even shared this hope with officials in the UNRWA and the State Department, but refrained from launching an actual diplomatic offensive to convince them to act accordingly. In the last analysis, Israel had no legal or political basis upon which it could base such a battle. Moreover, if it opposed programs designed in principle to resettle the Palestinian refugees in the Arab states – a solution it championed consistently – it would have appeared ludicrous. Sharett, now prime minister,[108] expressed the Israeli position well when he said:

> We are interested that a start will be made in settlement of the refugees. Of course there are grades between more desirable and less desirable things. Perhaps it would be desirable for us that refugees wouldn't exist at all, but they exist; it would have been desirable that they be settled far away, for instance in Argentina, that would be the most desirable solution. Such a thing isn't possible, at this time at any rate. It would have been desirable for us that if they would be settled in the Arab world [...] it would be desirable that they be settled in northern Iraq and northern Syria and not precisely on our borders. So the matter is, apparently, not so simple.[109]

Thus, Sharett defined the ideal location for resettlement of the refugees as "far away" – a sentiment shared by officials in the Ministry of Foreign Affairs and the prime minister's office.[110] They raised creative ideas for the transfer of Palestinian refugees to countries in North Africa and South America, first and foremost to Libya, and sometimes even sought to take them forward on a practical level. Such notions were not totally detached from reality. Already in 1950, British representatives in the Middle East had conducted widespread correspondence among themselves, and with the Foreign Office in London, regarding the rehabilitation of Palestinian refugees in these regions. Like the Israelis, they pinned their hopes primarily on Libya.[111] The UNRWA didn't remain mum either. On 23 November 1952, following deliberations and investigations, it signed an agreement with Tripoli that Libya would absorb about 1,200 Palestinian refugee families (approximately 6,000 persons).[112] Yet, almost two years later, in the summer of 1954, the UNRWA reported that it was still conducting talks with the Libyans regarding implementation of the agreement.[113] Until the end of the period under study, no actual progress was made on this concept. A proposal to settle refugees in Libya was raised in Israel already in May 1949. The head of the United States Division at the time, Teddy Kollek, and the head of the Middle East Division, Ezra Danin, established contact through a third party with British companies, primarily in oil production, who had business interests in the Arab world and proposed that they hire Palestinian refugees to work on projects in Libya, Iraq, and northern Syria. These entities, however, showed little interest in adopting such an initiative. Israeli leadership also refrained from embracing and supporting this concept. With no other option, the two were forced to relinquish the idea.[114]

186   *The resettlement question*

However, "the Libyan connection" was resuscitated a year later. At the end of March 1950, Mordecai Kidron wrote Walter Eytan that the possibility of settling Palestinian refugees in Italian Somalia should be examined. Likewise, he sought to bring to Eytan's attention the idea of transferring Palestinian refugees to Libya, in place of 18,000 Jews who had arrived in Israel from Libya since 1948. As for the 15,000 Jews still in Libya, he claimed that they were prevented from leaving the country due to the difficulty of taking their assets with them. Therefore, he suggested investigating whether there was a way to link liquidation of Jewish property and "compensation for Palestinian Arab settlers."[115] The prime minister's advisor on Arab affairs, Yehoshua Palmon, said that if Israel would be prepared to budget a set sum to settle the refugees, then "it would be possible to set aside a suitable sum proportional to the number of refugees who would want to settle in Somalia and in Libya." This sum could be given to the refugees by transferring the Jewish assets in these countries to the refugees. The owners of Jewish property would receive the equivalent of their assets "in cash or in real estate" in Israel.[116]

From the second half of 1951, as the Blandford Plan crystallized, again voices were heard in the Ministry of Foreign Affairs calling for examination of the idea of settling the refugees "far away." A ministry document from late July 1951 that dealt with Arab-Israeli relations recommended as the desired solution to the refugee problem: "(a) resettlement of the refugees as far away as possible from Israel's borders; (b) their dispersion in various countries. Emigration outside the Middle East [is] preferable."[117] In March 1952, Middle East Division official Moshe Sasson proposed an integrated plan to Foreign Minister Sharett: (a) propertied Arab citizens of Israel would emigrate to Libya and, in their place, Libyan-Jews would immigrate to Israel. There would be a reciprocal and egalitarian exchange of assets in the course of this population exchange; (b) the possibility of settling Palestinian refugees in Libya would be examined. "The propaganda and political payback [the political and public diplomacy reward] emanating from emigration of Arab [citizens] from Israel after they were allowed to live there [in a Jewish state], and the lesson for [Palestinian] refugees still seeking to return would be great," Sasson argued.[118] Israel's representative in Turkey, Eliyahu Sasson (who was Moshe Sasson's father), remarked in regard to his son's proposal: "to speak of the two [settlement of Palestinian refugees in Libya and emigration of Arab citizens from Israel to Libya] in one breath, and as one plan is, after all, tough, complicated, and perhaps beyond our powers and the powers of the United Nations." If one had to choose between the two, it would be preferable to focus on resettling the refugees, since this issue was causing Israel numerous difficulties.[119] The "familial" differences of opinion did not prevent Moshe and Eliyahu Sasson from continuing to examine in the weeks to come the possibility of resettling Palestinian refugees in Libya, parallel to efforts to save the assets of Libyan-Jews.[120]

The deliberations that the UNRWA conducted with the Libyans on the Palestinian refugee issue in the fall of 1952 were integrated into the Israel plans. In mid September, in a meeting between an official in the Ministry of Foreign Affairs' International Institutions Division, Alexander Dotan, and the UNRWA's designated representative to Libya, Max-Henry Huber, the latter reported that the agency and the Libyan government had reached an agreement, in principle, to settle refugees in Libya. His role, Huber related, was to examine the plans and to oversee their actualization. Dotan immediately replied that Israel was prepared to assist: (a) to provide background material on Libya; (b) to arrange a meeting between the UNRWA's representative and Israeli settlement experts; (c) to locate Arab candidates suitable to assist Huber in carrying out the UNRWA's work; (d) to provide political support in United Nations circles. Dotan promised the UNRWA representative to keep in close contact with him in writing during Huber's sojourn in Libya and offered if the need would arise "to conduct a secret exchange of letters."[121] Due to this commitment, the Ministry of Foreign Affairs Research Division prepared background reports on the parties, the government, and the press in Libya, together with biographies of three members of the government.[122] The UNRWA, however, refrained for political reasons from establishing contact with Dotan.

Although Libya didn't uphold its agreement with the UNRWA, and in the end didn't absorb refugee families as it had committed to do, Israeli officials continued to study the concept in years to come. Thus, in the course of 1954, the Ministry of Foreign Affairs decided to try and take forward a plan to settle Palestinian refugees in Libya on land that in the past had belonged to Italian settlers. The intention was to locate refugees, primarily in Jordan, whose assets were in the hands of Israel's state custodian for absentees' property, and to offer them tracts of land in Libya that would be purchased with compensation monies to which they were entitled. These refugees would then commit to employ Palestinian farmers, apart from Libyans. In the end, the plan failed after it was leaked to the press.[123]

At the end of 1952 and beginning of 1953, the Ministry of Foreign Affairs also examined the feasibility of settling refugees in Sudan, although on a much smaller scale.[124] Ideas for the transfer of refugees to South America (particularly Brazil) were also raised.[125] However not one of these ideas ripened into a program that could be executed. After all, such a complex international action was beyond the organizational abilities of such a small country as Israel to orchestrate, not to mention the fact that the main actors in such a move (the Palestinians and the Arab states) were deeply embroiled in conflict with Israel.

Eric Johnston's mission

In order to try to take refugee rehabilitation projects forward, in the course of 1952, the UNRWA turned to the Tennessee Valley Authority and requested that it prepare a research study that would examine the feasibility of developing the Jordon and the Yarmuk waters. The authority replied in the affirmative

188 *The resettlement question*

and assigned a Boston engineering company, under the management of Charles Main, for the mission. Main was asked to prepare an outline for a plan to utilize the waters of the two watercourses for irrigation and hydroelectric power production. This plan, the planners were told, should ignore the political boundaries. On 31 August 1953, the Tennessee Valley Authority submitted the findings of Main's study to the UNRWA and the American government.[126] The plan suggested: (a) to irrigate the Jordan Valley with water from the Jordan and its tributaries; (b) to use the Sea of Galilee as the chief reservoir for excess water flowing in from the Yarmuk and the Jordan; (c) to allocate the water pumped from the rivers according to the following allocation: 63.5 percent to Jordan, 32.5 percent to Israel, and 4 percent to Syria.[127]

The idea of the development of regional water resources jointly by Israel and its Arab neighbors received an enthusiastic reception in Washington. The administration thought it would be possible to realize several vital objectives through the plan: (a) to bolster local economies; (b) to resettle the refugees, primarily in the Jordan Valley, which was under the control of the Hashemite Kingdom; (c) to use the project as a vehicle to overcome the political impasse between Israel and its Arab neighbors.[128] Of the three objectives, the refugee issue won special attention.

The Americans didn't waste any time. On 7 October 1953, President Dwight Eisenhower appointed the chair of the American government's Advisory Board for International Development, Eric Johnston, as his personal envoy, with the rank of ambassador, to the Middle East. One of Johnston's primary objectives, according to Eisenhower's announcement of 16 October, was to discuss with Israel and its Arab neighbors joint development of water resources in the Jordan Valley. From the president's directive, it was evident that the United States hoped that investment in the water dimension would assist in particular with the rehabilitation of the refugees.[129]

Days prior to his departure for the Middle East, Secretary of State John Foster Dulles clarified in a letter to Johnston that he should try and obtain the agreement of Israel, Jordan, Syria, and Lebanon for a joint water project that would be based on Charles Main's suggestions. In order to tailor Main's plan to political needs, Johnston was requested to take into account the importance of settling as many refugees as possible in the short period of time, as well as the desire of the United States to assist in the economic development of Israel and the Arab states.[130] This was the first time that the United States sought to implement a large-scale economic initiative on its own, without the UNRWA, designed to rehabilitate Palestinian refugees.[131]

To take the regional water project forward, Johnston conducted four rounds of talks in Israel and the Arab states bordering Israel over a period of two years, from the winter of 1953 to the fall of 1955. During his first tour, the response of Arab leaders was hostile and negative. They clarified to the American envoy that they did not wish to participate in a project in which the Jewish state would participate, directly or indirectly.[132] The Israelis, on the

The resettlement question   189

other hand, did not entirely reject the plan, but asked for a number of substantive alterations: (a) inclusion of the waters of the Litani tributary in southern Lebanon in the project; (b) utilization of the waters of the Jordan River beyond the Jordan Valley region; (c) direct talks between Israel and the Arab states about the project. Israel also expressed its displeasure that it had been allocated a small portion of the water, relative to Jordan.[133] Johnston explained to the Israelis that it was important to warm the Jordanians to the program. Their participation, he said, would be beneficial to Israel since it would promote resolution of the refugee problem.[134]

At the outset of January 1954, the Arab leaders decided to establish a technical committee under the auspices of the Arab League that would produce an alternative option in the spirit of the Main plan. Two months later, in March 1954, the technical committee published its alternative plan, which called for: (a) rejection of the proposal that the Sea of Galilee serve as the chief reservoir; (b) allocation of water to Lebanon as well; (c) international supervision of water allocation. According to the Arab plan, Israel would receive only 20 percent of the water.[135]

In June of the same year, Israel also floated a plan of its own, which incorporated its standing demands that the Litani River be part of the project and that water could be used for projects beyond the Jordan Valley, while increasing Israel's water quota (by up to 50 percent of the water).[136]

Policymakers in Jerusalem were ambivalent about Johnston's plan. On one hand, they feared the involvement of international entities in Israel's water sources and agricultural plans;[137] on the other hand, they hoped a regional water project of such magnitude would succeed in breaking down the wall of hostility between Israel and its Arab neighbors.[138] Besides this, and no less important, they expected that the project would bring about implementation of the principle of resettlement. Prime Minister Moshe Sharett put great emphasis on this point when he sought to convince his colleagues in the country's leadership to support the regional water plan. He did so in a private conversation he conducted at the outset of June 1954 with several cabinet ministers,[139] and he reiterated this passionately in his remarks to the cabinet on 23 June;[140] in a meeting of Mapai's political committee on 27 June;[141] and in a meeting of the Foreign Affairs and Defense Committee that took place two days later.[142] Throughout the first half of 1955, Sharett continued to emphasize the tie between the resettlement issue and the regional water project.[143] According to his biographer, Sharett dove deeply into the study of these two topics – water and refugees – and in the end became "the chief expert" in the government on these issues.[144]

In his second round of talks in the region in the latter half of June 1954, Johnston succeeded in bringing the rival parties' positions closer together,[145] and even more so during his third round of talks at the outset of 1955.[146] Throughout this time, Johnston and officials in the Eisenhower administration endeavored to demonstrate to Israel why the water project was important to the resettlement of the Arab refugees.[147]

190 *The resettlement question*

After Johnston's fourth round of talks in the region, from the end of August until the beginning of September 1955, the Arab League's technical committee decided to approve Johnston's "united" water plan – a plan that accepted bits and pieces of alterations that the two rival sides demanded. However, the accelerated deterioration in relations between Israel and the Arab states that began at the latter half of 1954 (to be discussed in Chapter 10) made it impossible for political echelons in the Arab states to approve such a mammoth joint economic project between Israelis and Arabs. Such a move would constitute recognition of the Jewish state, a step that was out of the question under realities at the time. Moreover, Arab leaders were dissatisfied with the strategic advantages that Israel stood to gain from the regional water project, primarily in regard to irrigation of the Negev, making it suitable for Jewish settlement. In a meeting of Arab foreign ministers in mid October 1955, it was therefore decided to freeze the Johnston Plan.[148]

Nevertheless, opinions were not identical throughout the Arab camp. Jordan, unlike Lebanon and Syria, keenly wanted the Americans to succeed in taking a regional water project forward that could develop their agricultural sectors. Such a scheme could provide viable employment for hundreds of thousands of refugees that had settled in Jordan, as well as masses of destitute Jordanians. Yet the Hashemite regime didn't dare express its true position, which ran counter to that of the rest of the Arab states.[149]

Notes

1 UNPCC, A/1985, p. 10.
2 UNRWA, A/1905, pp. 9–10.
3 Rony E. Gabbay, *A Political Study of the Arab-Jewish Conflict – The Arab Refugee Problem (A Case Study)*, Geneve: Librairie E. Droz, 1959, pp. 396–9.
4 FRUS, 1951, V, pp. 892–6, Department of State Position Paper, 12 October 1951; FRUS, 1951, V, pp. 930–1, Memorandum of Conversation, 15 November 1951; FRUS, 1951, V, p. 941, The Secretary of State to the Department of State, 22 November 1951; DEPI, Vol. 6, Document 474, E. Herlitz to M. Sharett and W. Eytan, 8 November 1951; ISA, 7562/12 A, Foreign Affairs and Defense Committee Meeting, 31 December 1951, pp. 10–11.
5 DEPI, Vol. 7, Editorial Note (pp. 12–13).
6 DEPI, Vol. 7, Editorial Note (pp. 30–1).
7 DEPI, Vol. 7, Editorial Note (pp. 35–6).
8 ISA, MFA 339/8, A. Eban to P. Jessup, 20 January 1952.
9 DEPI, Vol. 7, Editorial Note (pp. 52–3).
10 George J. Tomeh (ed.), *United Nations Resolutions on Palestine and the Arab-Israeli Conflict, 1947–1974*, vol. 1, Washington, DC: Institute for Palestine Studies, 1975, p. 24.
11 Tomeh, *United Nations Resolutions*, pp. 24–5.
12 ISA, MFA 2404/11I, G. Rafael to the Foreign Minister, 27 January 1952.
13 ISA, Government Meeting, 27 January 1952, pp. 10–16. During a discussion of the political situation held on 4 February in the Knesset, Sharett reiterated that Resolution 512(6) was important from an Israeli perspective: "This is the first resolution dealing with the general scope of the problem that does not mention the return of the refugees, and in fact, it also does not mention

The resettlement question 191

the payment of compensation." *Knesset Minutes*, vol. 11, 4 February 1952, p. 1164.

14 Walter Eytan, *The First Ten Years: A Diplomatic History of Israel*, London: Weidenfeld and Nicolson, 1958, p. 119.

15 ISA, MFA 2445/1B, A. Biran to the Director-General of the Ministry of Foreign Affairs, 20 February 1952.

16 ISA, MFA 3061/7, Arabs' Responses to the Various Plans for Refugee Resettlement, 11 January 1952; ISA, MFA 3061/7, Subject: Palestinian Refugees Protest against the Resettlement Plans, 19 February 1952.

17 UNRWA, A/2470, p. 9.

18 UNRWA, A/2717, p. 9.

19 UNRWA, A/2717, pp. 9–10.

20 UNRWA, A/3686, p. 24.

21 UNRWA, A/2171, p. 9; UNRWA, A/2717, pp. 10–12; UNRWA, A/2978, p. 3; UNRWA, A/3212, pp. 4, 8; UNRWA, A/3686, pp. 24–6.

22 In conversations with UNRWA officials, the Jordanians claimed that their country could absorb all the refugees situated within Jordanian territory. ISA, MFA 2477/2A, Conversation with Mr. D. H. Bergus, Aide to the American Representative to the UNRWA Advisory Commission, 21 March 1952; ISA, MFA 4374/2, S. Divon to R. Shiloah, 16 November 1952.

23 UNRWA, A/2717, p. 4; Avi Plascov, *The Palestinian Refugees in Jordan, 1948–1957*, London: Frank Cass, 1981, pp. 62–5; Milton Viorst, *UNRWA and Peace in the Middle East*, Washington, DC: The Middle East Institute, 1989, p. 37.

24 ISA, MFA 339/8, The Refugee Problem Is Causing a Crisis in the Lebanese Government, 6 January 1952; ISA, MFA 2445/2, The Refugees in Lebanon, 19 November 1952; UKNA, FO 371/91433, E1011/1, Lebanon: Annual Review for 1950, 15 January 1951; FRUS, 1952–1954, IX, pp. 1210–12, Department of State Position Paper: Lebanon, 5 May 1953; UNRWA, A/2171, pp. 45–6; Reuven Erlich, *The Lebanon Tangle: The Policy of the Zionist Movement and the State of Israel towards Lebanon, 1918–1958*, Tel Aviv: Ma'arachot, 2000, p. 396 (Hebrew); Wade R. Goria, *Sovereignty and Leadership in Lebanon, 1943–1976*, London: Ithaca Press, 1985, p. 38; Simon Haddad, *The Palestinian Impasse in Lebanon: The Politics of Refugee Integration*, Brighton and Portland: Sussex Academic Press, 2003, pp. 22–4.

25 UNRWA, A/2171, p. 8; UNRWA, A/2717, p. 14; UNRWA, A/3686, p. 26.

26 ISA, MFA 2477/2A, Conversation with Mr. D. H. Bergus, Aide to the American Representative to the UNRWA Advisory Commission, 21 March 1952; ISA, MFA 2402/9, Problems Regarding the Economic Rehabilitation of the Arab Refugees from Palestine, undated, pp. 77–82; Laurie Brand, "Palestinians in Syria: The Politics of Integration," *The Middle East Journal* 42(4), 1988, p. 622.

27 UNRWA, A/2171, pp. 46–8; Brand, "Palestinians in Syria," pp. 622–3, 636.

28 Moshe Ma'oz, *Syria and Israel: From War to Peacemaking*, Oxford: Clarendon Press, 1995, p. 21; Aryeh Shalev, *The Israel-Syria Armistice Regime, 1949–1955*, Boulder, CO: Westview Press, 1993, pp. 15–16; Avi Shlaim, "Husni Za'im and the Plan to Resettle Palestinian Refugees in Syria," *Journal of Palestine Studies* 15(4), 1986, p. 69.

29 Ma'oz, *Syria and Israel*, p. 22; Itamar Rabinovich, *The Road Not Taken: Early Arab-Israeli Negotiations*, New York: Oxford University Press, 1991, pp. 85–7; Shlaim, "Husni Za'im," pp. 71–3.

30 Ma'oz, *Syria and Israel*, p. 20; Rabinovich, *The Road Not Taken*, pp. 69–71.

31 BGA, BGD, 16 April 1949.

32 Elad Ben-Dror, *The Mediator: Ralph Bunche and the Arab-Israeli Conflict,1947–1949*, Sede Boqer: The Ben-Gurion Research Institute, 2012, p. 269 (Hebrew).

33 Ben-Dror, *The Mediator*, p. 270.

192   The resettlement question

34 Rabinovich, *The Road Not Taken*, pp. 98–9; Shalev, *The Israel-Syria Armistice Regime*, pp. 34–5; Shlaim, "Husni Za'im," pp. 75–6; Shaul Zeitune, *Deterrence and Peace: Israel's Attempts to Arrive at a Settlement*, Tel Aviv: Tcherikover, 2000, p. 79 (Hebrew).

35 David W. Lesch, *Syria and the United States: Eisenhower's Cold War in the Middle East*, Boulder, CO: Westview Press, 1992, p. 19; Yaacov Shimoni and Evyatar Levine, *Political Dictionary of the Middle East in the Twentieth Century*, London: Weidenfeld and Nicolson, 1972, pp. 350–1.

36 Douglas Little, "Cold War and Covert Action: The United States and Syria, 1945–1958," *The Middle East Journal* 44(1), 1990, pp. 59–61; Ma'oz, *Syria and Israel*, p. 29; Shalev, *The Israel-Syria Armistice Regime*, pp. 93–4. The following American documents describe requests that al-Shishakli sent to American government representatives during the years 1951 to 1954, in which he sought economic and military assistance: FRUS, 1951, V, pp. 1090–1, The Secretary of State to the Legation in Syria, 14 December 1951; FRUS, 1952–1954, IX, pp. 1204–5, Department of State Position Paper: Syria, 5 May 1953.

37 FRUS, 1951, V, pp. 1090–1, The Secretary of State to the Legation in Syria, 14 December 1951; FRUS, 1952–1954, IX, pp. 1009–11, The Minister in Syria to the Department of State, 25 September 1952; FRUS, 1952–1954, IX, pp. 1204–7, Department of State Position Paper: Syria, 5 May 1953.

38 Little, "Cold War and Covert Action," pp. 60–1; Ma'oz, *Syria and Israel*, pp. 29–30; Shalev, *The Israel-Syria Armistice Regime*, p. 94.

39 UKNA, FO 371/91400, E1821/27, From Damascus to Foreign Office, 15 February 1951; UKNA, FO 371/91412, E1828/21, Summary Record of the 84 Meeting of the Director and the Advisory Commission, 9 March 1951; UKNA, FO 371/91412, E1828/26, Summary of the Decisions Taken at the Informal Meeting of the Advisory Commission and the Director with the Palestine Conciliation Commission, 4 May 1951; UKNA, FO 371/91402, E1821/82, From Beirut to Foreign Office, 9 June 1951.

40 FRUS, 1951, V, pp. 790–1, The Chargé in Lebanon to the Department of State, 23 July 1951; FRUS, 1951, V, pp. 829–31, The Chargé in Lebanon to the Department of State, 10 August 1951; UKNA, FO 371/91402, E1821/100, FO Minute, Waterlow, 15 August 1951; UKNA, FO 371/91413, E1828/50, Meeting of UNRWA Country Representatives, 18 and 20 August 1951.

41 UKNA, FO 371/98508, E1825/2, Evans to Knight, 6 February 1952; UKNA, FO 371/98508, E1825/3, Knight to Evans, 9 February 1952; UKNA, FO 371/98508, E1825/5, Montagu-Pollock to Evans, 18 February 1952.

42 UKNA, FO 371/98508, E1825/8, From Beirut to Foreign Office, 18 April 1952.

43 UKNA, FO 371/98520, E18216/5, Knight to Evans, 6 May 1952; UKNA, FO 371/98508, E1825/17, Rapp to Evans, 28 May 1952; ISA, MFA 2491/5, Stages of the Negotiations between the Director of UNRWA and the Syrian and Jordanian Governments on the Issue of Refugee Resettlement, 6 July 1952.

44 UKNA, FO 371/98508, E1825/8, From Foreign Office to Beirut, 19 April 1952.

45 FRUS, 1952–1954, IX, p. 928, The Secretary of State to Certain Diplomatic and Consular Offices, 8 May 1952.

46 FRUS, 1952–1954, IX, p. 261, Memorandum by Hoskins to Byroade, 25 July 1952.

47 UKNA, FO 371/98512, E1826/42, FO Minute, Knight, 28 May 1952; UKNA, FO 371/98254, E1056/41, FO Minute, Middle Eastern Secretariat, 6 June 1952; UKNA, FO 371/104477, E18213/3, FO Minute, Brief for the Secretary of State's Visit to the United States of America, 25 February 1953; FRUS, 1952–1954, IX, p. 910, The Chargé in Jordan to the Department of State, 3 April 1952; FRUS, 1952–1954, IX, p. 1058, Memorandum of Conversation, by the Officer in Charge of Lebanon-Syria-Iraq Affairs, 15 November 1952; UNRWA, A/2470, p. 4; ISA,

MFA 2477/2A, Conversation with Mr. D. H. Bergus, Aide to the American Representative to the UNRWA Advisory Commission, 21 March 1952; ISA, MFA 2406/17, G. Rafael to the Director-General of the Ministry of Foreign Affairs, 19 June 1952; Lesch, *Syria and the United* States, p. 20.

48 FRUS, 1952–1954, IX, p. 1059, Memorandum of Conversation, by the Officer in Charge of Lebanon-Syria-Iraq Affairs, 15 November 1952; UKNA, FO 371/98258, E1056/82, Conference of Her Majesty's Representatives in the Middle East, 20 June 1952; UKNA, FO 371/98258, E1056/84, Conference of Her Majesty's Representatives in the Middle East, 23 June 1952; ISA, MFA 2491/5, Stages of the Negotiations between the Director of UNRWA and the Syrian and Jordanian Governments on the Issue of Refugee Resettlement, 6 July 1952.

49 Lesch, *Syria and the United States*, pp. 20–3; Little, "Cold War and Covert Action," pp. 60–1; Bonnie F. Saunders, *The United States and Arab Nationalism: The Syrian Case, 1953–1960*, London: Praeger, 1996, pp. 13–14.

50 UKNA, FO 371/98508, E1825/8, From Beirut to Foreign Office, 18 April 1952; UKNA, FO 371/98511, E1826/16, Bowker to Frulonge, 19 April 1952; BGA, BGD, 26 May 1952; Ma'oz, *Syria and Israel*, pp. 31–2; Saunders, *The United States and Arab Nationalism*, pp. 11–12.

51 UNRWA, A/2470, p. 10.

52 UNRWA, A/3212, p. 26.

53 Lesch, *Syria and the United States*, pp. 53–61; Little, "Cold War and Covert Action," p. 63; Ma'oz, *Syria and Israel*, pp. 42–5; Saunders, *The United States and Arab Nationalism*, pp. 28–9.

54 Jacob Tovy, "Israeli Policy in the Gaza Strip and the Palestinian Refugees, November 1956–March 1957," *Jama'a* 7, 2001, p. 13 (Hebrew).

55 ISA, MFA 2454/2, Conversations and Contacts Regarding the Possibility of an Israel-Egypt Arrangement, 1949–1955, 18 January 1956, pp. 1–2; Rabinovich, *The Road Not Taken*, pp. 171–92; Moshe Sasson, *Talking Peace*, Or Yehuda: Ma'ariv, 2004, pp. 39–42 (Hebrew); Zeitune, *Deterrence and Peace*, p. 179.

56 DEPI, Vol. 5, Document 340, A. Biran to M. Sharett, 15 August 1950; DEPI, Vol. 6, Document 32, E. Sasson to M. Sasson, 24 January 1951.

57 Itamar Rabinovich, "Egypt and the Palestine Question before and after the July Revolution," *Zmanim* 32, 1989, p. 81 (Hebrew).

58 The phrase "various mediators" refers, primarily, to the mission of a Quaker envoy, Elmore Jackson, in the summer of 1955. See Elmore Jackson, *Middle East Mission*, New York: Norton and Company, 1983, pp. 28–38.

59 Muhammad Abd el-Wahab Sayed-Ahmed, *Nasser and American Foreign Policy, 1952–1956*, London: Laam, 1989, p. 103; Jon Alterman, "American Aid to Egypt in the 1950s: From Hope to Hostility," *The Middle East Journal* 52(1), 1998, pp. 51–2, 68–9; R. Hrair Dekmejian, *Egypt under Nasir: A Study in Political Dynamics*, Albany, NY: State University of New York Press, 1971, p. 44; Matthew F. Holland, *America and Egypt: From Roosevelt to Eisenhower*, London: Praeger, 1996, pp. 31–2, 44, 53–8; Michael B. Oren, *Origins of the Second Arab-Israel War: Egypt, Israel And the Great Powers, 1952–1956*, London: Frank Cass, 1992, pp. 98–103, 106; Howard M. Sachar, *Egypt and Israel*, New York: Richard Marek Publishers, 1981, pp. 79–80.

60 ISA, MFA 2454/2, Conversations and Contacts Regarding the Possibility of an Israel-Egypt Arrangement, 1949–1955, 18 January 1956, pp. 1–11, 30–3; ISA, MFA 2446/7B, Consultation Regarding Israel's Diplomatic Paths of Action in the Middle East, 25 August 1953; DEPI, Vol. 7, Document 455, E. Sasson to W. Eytan, 21 November 1952, and Note 1; DEPI, Vol. 7, Document 459, M. Sharett to A. Eban, 23 November 1952; DEPI, Vol. 7, Document 468, E. Elath to M. Sharett, 25 November 1952; DEPI, Vol. 8, Document 77, R. Shiloah to E. Sasson, 11 February 1953; DEPI, Vol. 8, Document 120, Political Consultation of the Prime

194 *The resettlement question*

Minister with the Heads of the Ministries of Foreign Affairs and Defence and of the Jewish Agency, 8 March 1953; DEPI, Vol. 9, Document 210, R. Shiloah to G. Rafael, 14 May 1954; DEPI, Vol. 9, Document 433, R. Shiloah to the Director-General of the Ministry of Foreign Affairs, 25 October 1954; FRUS, 1952–1954, IX, p. 1121, The Ambassador in Egypt to the Department of State, 7 February 1953; Natan Aridan, *Britain, Israel and Anglo-Jewry, 1949–1957*, London and New York: Routledge, 2004, p. 138; Ilan Asia, *The Core of the Conflict: The Struggle for the Negev, 1947–1956*, Jerusalem: Yad Izhak Ben-Zvi, 1994, p. 124 (Hebrew); Shimon Golan, *Hot Border, Cold War: The Formulation of Israel's Security Policy, 1949–1953*, Tel Aviv: Ma'arachot, 2000, p. 110 (Hebrew). Barry Rubin argued in his book that until the mid 1960s, Palestine was rarely a matter of major importance for Egyptian foreign policy: see Barry Rubin, *The Arab States and the Palestine Conflict*, Syracuse, NY: Syracuse University Press, 1981, p. 8.

61 In a secret report summing up the contacts between Israel and Egypt during the years 1949 to 1955, Gideon Rafael noted the following: "Egypt took a principled position on the refugees that was more convenient [for Israel], but in actuality, on this subject as well, it took no part in any general or partial measure designed to resolve the problem. Egypt, through the current time, has failed to smooth the way for the family reunification program, and has even sabotaged the program for releasing the blocked accounts, [it] did not resettle refugees on its territory and agreed only to having the UN carry out a study regarding the possibility of resettling refugees in the Sinai desert." ISA, MFA 2454/2, G. Rafael to the Foreign Minister, 19 January 1956.

62 UKNA, FO 371/82256, E18211/1, Evans to Knight, 24 May 1950; FRUS, 1950, V, p. 948, Ambassador John B. Blandford to the Secretary of State, 8 July 1950.

63 UNRWA, A/2171, p. 8; UNRWA, A/2717, p. 13; UKNA, FO 371/91429, E18222/2, Evans to Knight, 1 February 1951.

64 UNRWA, A/2717, p. 13.

65 UNRWA, A/3212, p. 25.

66 UNRWA, A/3686, p. 24.

67 UNRWA, A/2978, p. 3; Gabbay, *A Political Study*, p. 463.

68 UNRWA, A/2171, p. 7.

69 Tomeh, *United Nations Resolutions*, p. 26.

70 UKNA, FO 371/104479, E18219/37, FO Minute, 3 October 1953.

71 UNRWA, A/2717, p. 4.

72 UKNA, FO 371/104466, E1825/87, Palestine Refugees, 23 June 1953.

73 DEPI, Vol. 7, Document 25, Meeting: M. Sharett – M. Davis (Tel Aviv, 23 January 1952); ISA, MFA 339/7, UNRWA's Plans, 16 September 1951.

74 The Israel Army defined infiltration as follows: "Any penetration, other than in a legal fashion, into the territory of the State of Israel by an individual or group who are not visually identifiable from a distance as soldiers in the armies of Arab countries or in other armies." See Shimon Golan and Shaul Shay, "The Challenges of Infiltration and the Response to Them, 1949–1956," in Haggai Golan and Shaul Shay (eds), *When the Engines Roared: 50th Anniversary to the Sinai War*, Tel Aviv: Ma'arachot, 2006, p. 179 (Hebrew).

75 IDFA, 2539/50/14, Subject: The Infiltration, 11 March 1949.

76 ISA, 7562/11 A, Foreign Affairs and Defense Committee Meeting, 19 November 1951, p. 17.

77 IDFA, 540/55/99, Security Policy for the Border on the Jordan River, 10 February 1953.

78 Benny Morris, *Israel's Border Wars, 1949–1956: Arab Infiltration, Israeli Retaliation and the Countdown to the Suez War*, Tel Aviv: Am Oved, 1996, p. 45 (Hebrew).

The resettlement question 195

79 Morris, *Israel's Border Wars*, pp. 69–70; David Tal, "Israel's Retaliation Attacks: From Tactical to a Strategic Tool," in Motti Golani (ed.), *Black Arrow: Gaza Raid and Israeli Policy of Retaliation during the Fifties*, Tel Aviv: Ma'arachot, 1994, p. 68 (Hebrew).

80 IDFA, General Staff Meeting, 5 July 1949, pp. 14–16; IDFA, 108/52/34, Subject: The Infiltration, undated; Morris, *Israel's Border Wars*, pp. 50–61; David Tal, *Israel's Day-to-Day Security Conception: Its Origin and Development, 1949–1956*, Sede Boqer: The Ben-Gurion Research Institute, 1998, p. 23 (Hebrew).

81 Morris, *Israel's Border Wars*, pp. 65–7; Zaki Shalom, *Policy in the Shadow of Controversy: The Routine Security Policy of Israel, 1949–1956*, Tel Aviv: Ma'arachot, 1996, p. 12 (Hebrew); Tal, *Israel's Day-to-Day Security Conception*, p. 25.

82 Robert L. Jarman (ed.), *Political Diaries of the Arab World: Palestine and Jordan, 1948–1965*, vol. 10, Slough: Archive Editions, 2001, p. 533.

83 Morris, *Israel's Border Wars*, p. 18.

84 Tal, "Israel's Retaliation Attacks," p. 67.

85 Morris, *Israel's Border Wars*, pp. 69–70, 113–14.

86 Morris, *Israel's Border Wars*, pp. 115–16.

87 Morris, *Israel's Border Wars*, p. 117.

88 Morris, *Israel's Border Wars*, pp. 121–2; Shalom, *Policy in the Shadow of Controversy*, p. 29.

89 Amnon Kertin, "A Geographical Study of the Impact of Hostile Relations between Neighboring Countries on the Characteristics of Settlement in their Common Frontier Zones: The Case of Israel's Frontier Zones," PhD thesis, Tel Aviv University, 1995, pp. 223–4 (Hebrew); Morris, *Israel's Border Wars*, p. 123; Shalom, *Policy in the Shadow of Controversy*, p. 29.

90 Morris, *Israel's Border Wars*, pp. 199–211; Shalom, *Policy in the Shadow of Controversy*, p. 15.

91 DEPI, Vol. 8, Document 464, G. Rafael to M. Sharett, 23 October 1953; Morris, *Israel's Border Wars*, p. 211.

92 IDFA, 2539/50/14, Subject: Bedouin Tribes in the Negev, 15 November 1949; IDFA, 108/52/34, Survey of Hostile Bedouins in the Negev, undated; DEPI, Vol. 5, Document 394, W. Eytan to the Israel Delegation to the United Nations, 24 September 1950.

93 A comprehensive study of the events concerning the Palestinian town of Majdal between the years 1948 and 1950 can be found in Orna Cohen, "The Arabs of Majdal (Ashqelon): Changes of Their Situation between the War of 1948 and Their Evacuation from the State of Israel," MA thesis, The Hebrew University, 1999 (Hebrew).

94 IDFA, 2539/50/14, Subject: The Evacuation of Majdal, 21 November 1949; IDFA, 1338/79/714, On the Evacuation of the Arab Residents of Majdal-Gad, 22 October 1950; DEPI, Vol. 5, Document 394, W. Eytan to the Israel Delegation to the United Nations, 24 September 1950; Moshe Dayan, *Story of My Life*, Jerusalem: Steimatzky's Agency, 1976, pp. 122–3; Golan, *Hot Border, Cold War*, pp. 250–1; Benny Morris, *Correcting a Mistake: Jews and Arabs in Palestine, 1936–1956*, Tel Aviv: Am Oved, 2000, pp. 149–75 (Hebrew).

95 For an examination of the differences between David Ben-Gurion's and Moshe Sharett's views on the Arab-Israeli conflict, see: Daniel Ben-Horin, "The Crystallization of Two Orientations to the Arab-Israel Conflict: David Ben-Gurion and Moshe Sharett," PhD thesis, University of Haifa, 1991, pp. 119–63 (Hebrew); Uri Bialer, "Ben-Gurion and Sharett – Two Perceptions of the Arab-Israeli Conflict," in Benyamin Neuberger (ed.), *Diplomacy and Confrontation: Selected Issues in Israeli Foreign Relations, 1948–1978*, Tel Aviv: The Open University, 1984, pp. 189–206 (Hebrew); Yair Evron, "Foreign and Defence Policy: Structural and Personal Aspects, 1949–1956," *Zionism* 14, 1989, pp. 225–9 (Hebrew); Gabriel

196 *The resettlement question*

Sheffer, *Resolution vs. Management of the Middle East Conflict: A Reexamination of the Confrontation between Moshe Sharett and David Ben-Gurion*, Jerusalem: Magnes Press, 1980; Avi Shlaim, "Conflicting Approaches to Israeli Relations with the Arabs: Ben-Gurion and Sharett 1953–1956," *The Middle East Journal* 37 (2), 1983, pp. 180–201.

96 See, for example, DEPI, Vol. 11, Document 229, A. Eban to the Ministry of Foreign Affairs, 30 April 1956, Note 2.

97 ISA, MFA 3062/4, The Palestinian Refugees and the Arab Aggression against Israel, 26 November 1952; BGA, Ben-Gurion's Bureau – As Prime Minister, Container 110 (Israel-Arab Relations), On the Future of the Refugee Problem, 5 May 1953.

98 ISA, MFA 2491/5, M. de Shalit to the United States Division in the Ministry of Foreign Affairs, 22 January 1952.

99 ISA, MFA 2566/14, E. Sasson to the United States Division in the Ministry of Foreign Affairs, 3 March 1952.

100 ISA, MFA 2566/14, A. Yafeh to E. Sasson, 9 March 1952.

101 ISA, MFA 2491/5, M. de Shalit to the United States Division in the Ministry of Foreign Affairs, 25 March 1952.

102 ISA, MFA 2477/2A, Conversation with Mr. D. H. Bergus, Aide to the American Representative to the UNRWA Advisory Commission, 21 March 1952.

103 ISA, MFA 2603/4, M. Elizur to the Director-General, 3 November 1952.

104 ISA, MFA 2603/4, The Legal Adviser to the Director-General, 11 February 1953.

105 ISA, MFA 2603/4, M. Comay to the Director-General, 28 May 1953.

106 ISA, MFA 2477/2A, M. Comay to the Foreign Minister, 19 September 1952.

107 ISA, MFA 2445/1B, A. Biran to the Director-General, 20 February 1952; ISA, MFA 4374/2, S. Divon to R. Shiloah, 16 November 1952; ISA, MFA 2477/2A, Upon UNRWA's Submission of Its Report to the General Assembly Concerning the Arab Refugees, 30 October 1953.

108 Towards the end of January 1954, Sharett replaced Ben-Gurion as prime minister, but continued to head the Ministry of Foreign Affairs. Ben-Gurion returned to the premiership at the beginning of November 1955, and Sharett remained in place as the foreign minister.

109 ISA, 7564/4 A, Foreign Affairs and Defense Committee Meeting, 29 June 1954, p. 5; Sharett repeated this position in a speech he delivered to the Mapai Political Committee on 4 June 1955. See Yemima Rosenthal (ed.), *Moshe Sharett – The Second Prime Minister: Selected Documents (1894–1965)*, Jerusalem: Israel State Archives, 2007, p. 526 (Hebrew).

110 See for example the letter to Liff written in August of 1949 by an official at the Ministry of Foreign Affairs, in which the official called for an effort to be made to disperse the Arab refugees within Arab countries "as far away as possible from Israeli territory." Officials from the Ministry of Foreign Affairs and the prime minister's office had been making proposals of this type since the end of the 1948 war: ISA, GL17116/2, M. C. El-Hasid to Zalman Lifshitz, 9 August 1949.

111 The British archives include several files from the British Foreign Office containing many documents testifying to the substantial British interest in the resettlement of Palestinian refugees in North Africa (primarily in Libya, but also in Sudan) and in several countries in South America. The following are some of the documents dealing with this subject: UKNA, FO 371/82239, E1823/13, FO Minute, 6 April 1950; UKNA FO 371/82239, E1823/16, Amman Chancery to Middle East Secretariat, 24 April 1950; UKNA, FO 371/82239, E1823/18, The British Consular at Beirut to the British Residency at Benghazi and the British Secretariat at Tripoli, 16 May 1950; UKNA, FO 371/82239, E1823/19, Resettlement of Palestinian Arab Refugees, 16 May 1950; UKNA, FO 371/82239, E1823/19, From Benghazi to Foreign Office, 20 May 1950; UKNA, FO 371/82239, E1823/21, The British

Secretariat at Khartoum to African Department at Foreign Office, 28 May 1950; UKNA, FO 371/82240, E1823/24, B.M.E.O. to the British Secretariat at Tripoli, 21 June 1950; UKNA, FO 371/82240, E1823/26, B.M.E.O. to Keen, 27 June 1950.

112 UNRWA, A/2470, p. 11.

113 UNRWA, A/2717, p. 14.

114 Teddy Kollek, *For Jerusalem*, Jerusalem: Steimatzky's Agency, 1978, pp. 90–1.

115 ISA, MFA 2402/15, M. Kidron to the Director-General of the Ministry of Foreign Affairs, 24 March 1950.

116 ISA, MFA 2402/15, Yehoshua Palmon to the Director-General of the Ministry of Foreign Affairs, 17 April 1950.

117 BGA, Correspondences, Our Arab Policy – Presentation of Problems for Consultation, 24 July 1951.

118 ISA, MFA 2402/15, M. Sasson to the Foreign Minister, 13 March 1952.

119 ISA, MFA 2566/14, Eliahu Sasson to Moshe Sasson, 23 March 1952. The possibility of encouraging the emigration of Arabs from Israel interested a number of officials and entities during the first years of the state's existence. One of the more serious proposals was that of Yosef Weitz, who worked on a plan to have Arabs from the Gush Halav area move, voluntarily, to Argentina. The plan, which was never carried out, was code-named "Operation Yochanan." See Uzi Benziman and Atallah Mansour, *Subtenants: Israeli Arabs – Their Status and the Policy toward Them*, Jerusalem: Keter, 1992, pp. 58–9 (Hebrew). The formulation of the program appears to have been encouraged by Foreign Minister Sharett, with approval from Prime Minister Ben-Gurion: see Yossi Katz, "Yoseph Weitz and the Transfer of Arab Population," *Iyunim Bitkumat Israel* 8, 1998, pp. 351–2 (Hebrew). One theory is that the plan was dropped (at the beginning of 1953) after the Argentine authorities pulled out: see Ariel Leibovich, "The Palestinian Refugee Issue in Israeli Foreign Policy 1948–1967," PhD thesis, University of Haifa, 2012, p. 243 (Hebrew). The Central Council on Arab Affairs – which the government established on 9 March 1952 for the purpose of advising the government authorities with regard to the treatment of the Arab sector – determined at its sixth meeting on 3 July 1952 that it "saw a Need for studying and clarifying the possibility of having Arabs move out of Israel – an examination of the technical and objective possibilities, currency Issues, the chances of emigration, etc": ISA, GL 17111/24, The Central Council on Arab Affairs – Minutes of the Sixth Meeting, 3 July 1952. Israel was not the only country examining this issue. During the years 1951 to 1952, there were those at the British Foreign Office who had proposed that Israel should allocate a sum of money with which to transfer the Arabs still living within its territory to other countries, primarily Arab countries. In this way, they argued, Israel would have a homogeneous country: see Aridan, *Britain, Israel and Anglo-Jewry*, p. 129.

120 See, for example: ISA, MFA 2445/1, M. Sasson to M. Kidron, 31 March 1952; ISA, MFA 2566/14, M. Sasson to E. Sasson, 1 April 1952; ISA, MFA 2566/14, S. Toyil to E. Sasson, 3 April 1952; ISA, MFA 2566/14, M. Sasson to E. Sasson, 8 May 1952.

121 ISA, MFA 3062/4, UNRWA Considers Settling Refugees in Libya, 16 September 1952.

122 ISA, MFA 3062/4, Katriel Katz to the United Nations Division in the Ministry of Foreign Affairs, undated.

123 ISA, MFA 2402/7, M. Shtener to the Prime Minister, 15 May 1955; Ezra Danin, *Unconditional Zionist*, Jerusalem: Kidom, 1987, pp. 323–5 (Hebrew); Kollek, *For Jerusalem*, p. 120; Moshe Sharett, *Personal Diary*, vol. 4, Tel Aviv: Am Oved, 1978, p. 1009 (Hebrew); Sharett, *Personal Diary*, vol. 5, pp. 1334–5; Joseph Weitz,

198　*The resettlement question*

    My Diary and Letters to the Children, vol. 4, Ramat Gan: Massada, 1965, pp. 324–5, 329–30, 335 (Hebrew).
124　ISA, MFA 3062/4, A Letter from Abd al-Rahim Farrakhan to Rabbi Morris Kertzer, 15 August 1952; ISA, MFA 3062/4, R. Shiloah to G. Rafael, 21 December 1952; ISA, MFA 3062/4, Rabbi Morris Kertzer to Abd al- Rahim Farrakhan, undated; ISA, MFA 3062/4, G. Rafael to R. Shiloah, 2 January 1953; ISA, MFA 3062/4, G. Rafael to R. Shiloah, 9 January 1953.
125　ISA, MFA 328/12, P. Eliav to G. Avner, 5 December 1955; Sharett, *Personal Diary*, vol. 3, pp. 622, 630.
126　Miriam R. Lowi, *Water and Power: The Politics of a Scarce Resource in the Jordan River Basin*, Cambridge: Cambridge University Press, 1993, p. 83.
127　DEPI, Vol. 8, Document 452, A. Eban to M. Sharett, 20 October 1953, Note 2; Lowi, *Water and Power*, pp. 83–6; Aaron T. Wolf, *Hydropolitics along the Jordan River: Scarce Water and Its Impact on the Arab-Israeli Conflict*, Tokyo: United Nations University Press, 1995, p. 46.
128　ISA, Government Meeting, 4 April 1954, p. 20; Gabbay, *A Political Study*, pp. 467– 8.
129　Meron Medzini (ed.), *Israel's Foreign Relations: Selected Documents, 1947 –1974*, Jerusalem: Ministry for Foreign Affairs, 1976, pp. 482–3.
130　FRUS, 1952–1954, IX, pp. 1348–9, The Secretary of State to the Chairman of the Advisory Board for International Development, 13 October 1953.
131　Abd el-Wahab Sayed-Ahmed, *Nasser and American Foreign Policy*, p. 104.
132　Lowi, *Water and Power*, p. 88.
133　DEPI, Vol. 8, Document 478, United States Division to the Israel Embassies in Washington, London and Paris, 28 October 1953; Sharett, *Personal Diary*, vol. 1, pp. 88–9.
134　ISA, 7563/14 A, Foreign Affairs and Defense Committee Meeting, 3 November 1953, p. 9; Sharett, *Personal Diary*, vol. 1, p. 94.
135　Lowi, *Water and Power*, pp. 89, 209–10; Samir N. Saliba, *The Jordan River Dispute*, The Hague: Martinus Nijhoff, 1968, pp. 96–9.
136　Saliba, *The Jordan River Dispute*, pp. 99–101; David M. Wishart, "The Breakdown of the Johnston Negotiations over the Jordan Waters," *Middle Eastern Studies* 26(4), 1990, p. 538.
137　Lowi, *Water and Power*, p. 87.
138　Michael Brecher, *Decisions in Israel's Foreign Policy*, London: Oxford University Press, 1974, pp. 183–5.
139　Sharett, *Personal Diary*, vol. 2, pp. 535–6.
140　ISA, Government Meeting, 23 June 1954, p. 37.
141　ILPA, 2-26-1954-16, Political Committee Meeting, 27 June 1954, pp. 16–17.
142　ISA, 7564/4 A, Foreign Affairs and Defense Committee Meeting, 29 June 1954, pp. 5–6.
143　ILPA, 2-23-1955-65, Central Committee Meeting, 17 February 1955, pp. 3–4; ILPA, 2-26-1955-17, Political Committee Meeting, 4 June 1955, pp. 46–7.
144　Gabriel Sheffer, *Moshe Sharett: Biography of a Political Moderate*, Oxford: Clarendon Press, 1996, p. 691.
145　Lowi, *Water and Power*, pp. 92–3; Yoram Nimrod, *Anger Waters: The Controversy over the Jordan River*, Givat Haviva: Center for Arabic and Afro-Asian Studies, 1966, pp. 51–4 (Hebrew).
146　Lowi, *Water and Power*, pp. 93–8; Thomas Naff and Ruth C. Matson, *Water in the Middle East: Conflict or Cooperation?*, Boulder, CO: Westview Press, 1984, p. 41; Nimrod, *Anger Waters*, p. 55; Saliba, *The Jordan River Dispute*, pp. 103–4.
147　ISA, MFA 7226/14A, Thursday Afternoon Session, 27 January 1955; ISA, MFA 7226/14A, Ambassador Johnston's Statement to the Israeli Committee, 30 January 1955; Sharett, *Personal Diary*, vol. 3, p. 734.

148 Brecher, *Decisions in Israel's Foreign Policy*, p. 205; Lowi, *Water and Power*, pp. 100–2; Nimrod, *Anger Waters*, p. 64; Saliba, *The Jordan River Dispute*, pp. 104–6; Wolf, *Hydropolitics along the Jordan River*, p. 48.
149 ISA, MFA 39/24, M. Gazit to the Ambassador, 2 April 1954; Eyal Kafkafi, "Ben-Gurion, Sharett and the Johnston Plan," *Studies in Zionism* 13(2), 1992, p. 181; Lowi, *Water and Power*, p. 103; Nimrod, *Anger Waters*, p. 63.

9 Toughening Israel's position

Compensation policy since the winter of 1952

On 21 April 1952, the Conciliation Commission convened at the United Nation's headquarters in New York to discuss its path after passage of Resolution 512(6). The American State Department thought the commission needed to focus on the compensation issue, as well as blocked bank accounts. As for compensation, the Americans believed that the primary objective should be to broaden and detail the Refugees Office's summer 1951 report.[1] The Conciliation Commission adopted the Americans' view and in its first meeting stipulated that, from now on, its work would be devoted exclusively to these two economic issues. Accordingly, the commission decided to try and obtain reaffirmation of the Israeli delegation's declaration of 14 November 1951 that Israel was willing to pay compensation to Arab refugees. In addition, it sought to ascertain Israel's position regarding the way the value of Palestinian abandoned property should be determined. In another meeting of the commission, it was decided to direct the Refugees Office's expert in land affairs, John Berncastle, to go to the Middle East and conduct talks on the compensation issue.[2] Parallel to this, the American delegate on the commission, Ely Palmer, was sent to discuss the issue of the blocked bank accounts with the Israelis (to be discussed in Chapter 11).

Following Berncastle's talks in the latter half of 1952 with officials in Israel and the Arab states and representatives of the refugees, the Conciliation Commission concluded that a campaign should immediately be launched to identify and valuate in a precise and detailed manner the abandoned property of the Palestinian refugees (not a rough estimate like those presented in the summer of 1951 by the Refugees Office).[3] In keeping with this decision, towards the close of 1952, the commission established a special team at United Nations headquarters in New York that examined microfilms of land registration in Palestine to extract data regarding the ownership, location, description, and value of hundreds of thousands of plots of land. Due to illegible notations and many omissions in the microfilms, the team was forced to utilize other data, for example, British Mandatory Government tax records.[4]

Since Israel didn't have the economic ability at all to withstand the tremendous financial burden payment of compensation would entail, the work carried out by the Conciliation Commission to identify and valuate abandoned property did not herald an imminent solution to the compensation issue.

The British had correctly assessed this point and stated that the problem of compensation would reach a solution only if Israel received large-scale financial assistance from the international community, first and foremost from the United States.[5] Washington, however, was not yet willing to underwrite the compensation.[6] Although the administration was very aware of Israel's financial limitations,[7] it believed that Jerusalem needed to make every effort to pay the compensation by itself. The Americans hoped that the reparations agreement just signed between Israel and West Germany (in mid September 1952)[8] would assist Israel in bearing the burden of compensation.[9] In light of this, the administration continued to put pressure on Israel, albeit modest pressure, in an effort to take resolution of this issue forward.[10]

In its 19 October 1952 meeting, the Israeli cabinet addressed the compensation question in deliberations designed to discuss the upcoming opening of the 7th United Nations General Assembly. Foreign Minister Sharett reported that the Arabs were preparing, as every year, to complain to the General Assembly that Israel was refusing to repatriate the refugees and to pay compensation. The Conciliation Commission was examining the possibility of obtaining from Israel agreement to enter negotiations with it on payment of compensation. The Ministry of Foreign Affairs believed Israel should respond positively to this initiative since it "took the wind out of the sails of the [Arab] attack against us." Progress on the compensation question was also essential in light of the ministry's assessment that "during the next year, and it is possible that we will already encounter the first signs of this trend during the [current] Assembly, pressure will be put on us by the United States to seriously go into the business of payment of the compensation." This pressure, Sharett told the cabinet, was the derivative, among other things, of feelings in Washington that reparations from Germany enhanced Israel's economic abilities. Therefore, the foreign minister requested that the cabinet allow the Israeli delegation to the United Nations to reply in the affirmative to the Conciliation Commission's compensation initiative, when requested. Prime Minister Ben-Gurion categorically rejected the suggestion. He told the cabinet:

> I am doubtful if it is worthwhile for us to enter negotiations on compensation during the [7th General] Assembly. [...] The rationale of taking the wind out of their sails – isn't a reason; the sails aren't terrible, and the wind isn't terrible.

Ben-Gurion continued to argue that entering discussion of the compensation issue would force Israel to take upon itself "a large commitment," and this at a time when it was in terrible economic distress. "We don't need," he stated, "to start with a commitment for our part, we don't know how far we will [have] to go [...] [Only if] the time will be right for this – we will pay." Upon

202 *Toughening Israel's position*

hearing Ben-Gurion's remarks, Sharett sought to remind the prime minister of "the commitment on principle" to enter into negotiation on the compensation issue without any linkage to peace, which Israel had already given. He stressed that "what has been suggested here is not a new turning point, but rather the beginning of implementation," explaining "I'm talking about entering negotiation with [the Conciliation] Commission" that will deal first of all with calculation of "the value of the land and what is the part that we are prepared to pay." Israel, Sharett claimed, only stood to gain from expressing such readiness, since such a move would prevent anti-Israeli resolutions in the 7th General Assembly. Moreover, Washington "will advise us to do this, otherwise it will have to take a harsher line [against Israel]." Yet Sharett's clarifications failed to convince Ben-Gurion, and he rejected the foreign minister's warning in regard to the measures one could expect from the United States. The Americans, the prime minister explained, are busy with elections now. That is, they can't make time for the Middle East conflict, and therefore Israel does not need to take any action right now. "There will be a time when it will be easy to pay," he concluded, "there will be political circumstances [when] it will be worthwhile to pay."[11]

Not one cabinet member spoke up in favor of Sharett's proposal, and the cabinet meeting was adjourned. Ben-Gurion's approach was woven into Israel's official compensation policy (presented by Sharett to the Knesset on 4 November 1951) and made it much more rigid. According to the new policy, as it unfolded in coming weeks, Israel would agree, as it had indicated earlier, to enter negotiation with a United Nations institution to discuss the compensation issue, irrespective of a comprehensive peace settlement, but it would pay the sum that would be set only after the Arabs declared themselves willing to make an economic-political sacrifice on their part – abolishing the economic warfare, that is removal of the Egyptian maritime blockade and the Arab League's economic boycott. In the foreign minister's speech before the Knesset at the outset of November 1951, and in the remarks made by the Israeli delegation in Paris to the Conciliation Commission ten day later, Israel (as noted) had refrained from specifically hinging payment of compensation on abolition of the economic warfare. It was only clarified that such warfare would surely impact on the magnitude of the sum that Israel would pay.

Ben-Gurion's tougher stand on the compensation issue was the direct outcome of the fact that the Arab-Israeli conflict had gotten permanently stuck in a rut and, even far worse, was showing first signs of deterioration. A host of factors testified to this state of affairs. The repeated attempts of the Conciliation Commission to take political settlements between the rival sides forwards, at Lausanne, in Geneva, in Paris – comprehensive or even partial – had failed to produce any results. The secret peace talks that Israel conducted with Abdullah's Jordan also came to naught, as had political contacts between Israel and Egypt. On the other hand, the Arabs' struggle against Israel continued and even began to escalate: political infiltration increased, the economic boycott and maritime blockade deepened, and political rhetoric and Arab propaganda against Israel's very right to exist amplified. Among all these avenues employed against the Jewish state, the economic warfare was the most effective tool in the Arab arsenal. The cumulative damage to the Israeli economy was considerable, and the Arabs' determination to continue and even heighten it meant the damage would worsen even more. The economic damage was of such a magnitude that it threatened to surpass the sum total of damage to the Israeli economy caused by the 1948 war and the freezing of Jewish assets in Iraq. Thus, by coupling economic warfare to the compensation issue, Israel sought to achieve two objectives: first, to remove such a destructive weapon from the Arab arsenal, since after all Israel could hardly agree to take on the burden of paying compensation while the Arabs waged an economic war to weaken its economy; and second, to signal to the Arab states, to the western powers, and to the United Nations Israel's dissatisfaction with the direction the Arab-Israeli conflict was headed, and perhaps also to coax them to take action on the political plane to change the dim situation.

In a 19 November 1952 telegram to the director-general of the Ministry of Foreign Affairs, Walter Eytan, Abba Eban wrote that the assistant United States secretary of state for Near Eastern, South Asia and Africa Affairs, Henry Byroade, requested to meet with him to talk about the refugee problem, "principally on compensation." Eban was convinced that there was nothing new he could say to Byroade, and he could only underscore two things: first, that Israel confirmed its position on the compensation question, as declared to the Knesset; second, that payment would require the fiscal assistance of the United States, "and cannot in logic and morality be undertaken while Arabs reduce our financial capacity by blockade."[12] In the conversation the two conducted, Byroade requested to know whether Israel could open some sort of compensation fund where monies could be deposited, even before the final sum Israel would have to pay was set. Eban explained that Israel was willing to discuss the compensation issue, but before it would pay it wanted to see proof of the Arabs' desire for peace. Such a step would be removal of the Egyptian maritime blockade.[13]

In his speech before the 7th United Nations General Assembly Ad Hoc Political Committee, as it addressed the Palestine issue, Eban publicly declared Israel's new position regarding compensation. He asserted that one of the prime factors that impacted on Jerusalem's ability to pay was the boycott and blockade imposed by the Arabs. "Removal of these abnormal conditions," Eban clarified, "will impact directly on the level and the rate of progress on payment of compensation."[14]

The change in Israel's position on its compensation policy took place parallel to the change in administrations in Washington. In January 1953, Dwight Eisenhower entered the White House and appointed John Foster Dulles as his secretary of state. Israel viewed the new administration with apprehension. It was widely held that President Eisenhower and the Republican Party would be less committed historically and less sympathetic emotionally towards the Jewish state than the previous administration under President

204   *Toughening Israel's position*

Harry Truman and the Democrats. Moreover, the Republicans, unlike their political rivals, weren't dependent on the "Jewish vote" in America, which was overwhelming Democratic and therefore carried little weight among conservative Republicans.[15]

Indeed, the first declarations by senior officials in Washington were hardly good harbingers for Jerusalem. Civil servants in the new Eisenhower administration indicated their intentions to strengthen the United States' stature among the Arab states, in essence, to "repair" the damage to American-Arab relations caused by Truman's open support for Israel, which State Department officials viewed as the product of pressure from the Jewish lobby in America.[16]

At the outset of March 1953, a joint meeting was held including the prime minister, the foreign minister and senior officials in the Ministry of Foreign Affairs, the military establishment, and the Jewish Agency to discuss the influence of leadership changes in Washington and their possible ramifications for the United States' actions in the Middle East. The anxiety about what the future held in regard to the new administration did not prompt the Israeli leadership to cancel the tougher compensation policy it had recently adopted. Foreign Minister Sharett surmised that the Americans would pressure Israel to make progress on the compensation question, and therefore Israel would have to declare that it was willing "to sit down right now and finish the compensation issue in order to begin to pay." Having said that, actual payment hinged on two conditions: first, the Arab boycott and blockade. "One can't demand that we will pay the Arab world, when the Arab world has taken away our ability to pay. These two things have to go concurrently [go hand in hand]." The second condition was the appointed schedule of payments and the size of payments. "In our [economic] situation, the degree [sum] must be small and the period of payment very long."[17] Foreign Minister Sharett, it seems, had internalized the change that Prime Minister Ben-Gurion had made in compensation policy.

Jerusalem was careful to clarify to the new administration in Washington that it did not intend to retreat from its new rigid position on the compensation question. Thus, at the close of March, Sharett raised the idea before two American officials that Israel would establish a compensation fund where monies the Israeli government saved by removal of the blockade and abolishment of the economic boycott would be deposited. If this economic warfare did not cease, he warned, Israel would refrain from reserving monies for compensation, "not when [as long as] they [the Arabs] are causing us such losses."[18] When Henry Byroade asked Sharett in mid April about Israel's position on the refugee problem, the foreign minister reiterated Israel's familiar stand – that it categorically rejected repatriation. As for compensation, he again assured Byroade that Israel intended to pay it, but this hinged on ending the boycott and the blockade.[19]

Concern in Jerusalem that in revamping overall American policy, the new administration would adopt a stand on the refugee issue that would be very uncomfortable for Israel quickly turned out to be largely unfounded. The Eisenhower administration embraced the pro-Israel refugee policy that had crystallized during the Truman administration,[20] then further strengthened it until it was almost identical to the Israeli position and – most important – gave it an official and public American stamp of approval.

Already in the first months of his presidency, Eisenhower approved a National Security Council document on the Middle East that recommended solving the Palestinian refugee problem through "resettlement in neighboring Arab Countries," and only "to the extent feasible" by rehabilitation of some in areas "now controlled by Israel" or in countries beyond the region.[21] In an overview that Eban gave to the government at the end of August 1953, he stated that one could sense "an ongoing process of developments" in Washington's position vis-à-vis the refugee problem, to such an extent that "[one] could define the position [of the Americans] as unwillingly resigned to the idea of the necessity of absorbing the refugees in the Arab states." Although this process wasn't complete, since the Americans were still pressuring Israel to permit "partial return" of refugees, nevertheless, one could say that it had reached its peak from Israel's standpoint – "up to 90 percent complete." The Israeli ambassador clarified that Israel must remain on its guard and not let the remaining 10 percent of the refugee population that the Americans still felt needed to be repatriated "embitter our lives […] and […] cloud the atmosphere in our relations with the United States."[22]

An expression of the strong support that the powers that be in Washington gave to the principle of resettlement can be found in two separate reports on the refugee problem composed in the course of 1953 by the two houses of the United States Congress.

One was a research report on the topic carried out by a sub-committee of the Senate Foreign Relations Committee. The research included testimony by Dulles' under-secretary of state, Walter Bedell Smith, Gardiner, Blandford, and several experts on the subject. Dulles also spoke to the sub-committee about the refugee issue. In mid 1953, after several months of investigation, the findings were published. While the sub-committee didn't raise unequivocal recommendations on the solution of the refugee problem, it did state that it would not be possible to settle more than a few percent of the refugees in Israel, and the majority would need to be absorbed through UNRWA rehabilitation programs in the Arab states.[23]

A sub-committee of the Foreign Relations Committee of the House of Representatives also studied the matter. This sub-committee went on a five-week tour of the Middle East during which it met with leaders, visited refugee camps, and examined UNRWA projects. In its report, the House Committee stated that the mission was to transform the Palestinian refugees into citizens of the Arab states. It also said that the Arab states must be responsible for the rehabilitation programs and that incentives should be given to the Arabs so they would open their doors to the refugees and help them integrate into their

206 *Toughening Israel's position*

host societies. Israel's role, according to the report, was to pay compensation for the abandoned property of the refugees.[24]

Indeed, the new Republican administration, like its Democratic predecessor, continued to insist that Israel pay compensation or at least take practical steps in this direction, such as setting the amount or putting aside monies for this purpose.[25] While the Eisenhower administration understood that Israel would find it difficult to withstand this financial burden,[26] and that compensation would, in essence, only solve the problem of wealthy refugees that constituted only a small portion of the problem,[27] Washington could not accept the Israeli position on repatriation practically "as is," without demanding that Israel make at least some sort of gesture towards resolution of the problem. If it had released Israel from all responsibility, it would have undermined the United States' position among the masses throughout the Arab world, which was already shaky in any case.

In an attempt to observe first-hand the problems of the Arab world (and Israel), the new secretary of state, Dulles, embarked in May 1953 on a tour of the Middle East that included seven states: Egypt, Israel, Jordan, Syria, Lebanon, Iraq, and Saudi Arabia. For Israel, as well as several Arab states, it was the first visit by an American secretary of state.[28]

In his visit to Arab capitals, Dulles learned that the repatriation issue, which the Arab leaders had been publicly declaring was the heart of the refugee problem, in fact was not at the top of their agenda, and that was an understatement. The rulers in Cairo sought to focus primarily on the British presence in the Suez Canal Zone, supply of American armaments to Egypt, and the west's proposal to establish an anti-Communist regional defense pact. The Arab-Israeli conflict was raised briefly, in passing. In this context, the Egyptians reiterated their demand to create a land bridge through Israel that would connect Egypt to the Arab countries to the east.[29] The Palestinian refugee problem was "forgotten" altogether by them. The Jordanians, for their part, talked at length about the refugee problem, but refrained from clearly and precisely demanding implementation of the repatriation principle. Prime Minister Fawzi al-Mulqi suggested that Israel relinquish territory it held in order to solve the problem of masses of Palestinian "economic refugees." It is fairly certain that he was speaking of villages along the border between Israel and the West Bank, whose lands had been taken from them as a result of the armistice agreement.[30] In another talk the Jordanian leader praised the Yarmuk resettlement plan for the possibility it presented to liberate the refugees from their dire predicament.[31] The Syrian leader Adib al-Shishakli demanded in his meeting with Dulles implementation of United Nations resolutions regarding the Arab-Israeli conflict, including those that addressed the refugee problem. At the same time, he believed only a small number of refugees would actually want to return. All those left in the Arab states, stated al-Shishakli, would need outside assistance to be resettled.[32] Dulles, for his part, sensed that Syria, a large country with a sparse population, could absorb many of the refugees that were currently situated in other Arab countries. He

Toughening Israel's position   207

surmised that Syria could be a key to resolving the refugee problem. When the secretary of state floated this thesis with al-Shishakli, the Syrian leader's response was positive.[33] Similar to his colleague in Damascus, the president of Lebanon, Camille Sham'un, demanded Israel comply with the United Nations resolutions and requested that the refugees be allowed to return to their homes and lands or receive compensation.[34] In Dulles' visit to the UNRWA's headquarters in Beirut, the acting director of the UNRWA, Leslie Carver, surveyed the rehabilitation activities of the agency. In response to a question posed by Byroade (who had accompanied Dulles in his travels) about the wishes of the refugees to return to Israel, Carver replied that although many of the Palestinian refugees may request this, very few would choose to remain in Israel over time. They would need to compete with the Israeli Jews for the limited economic resources of the Jewish state, he explained.[35]

On the eve of Dulles' visit to Israel, Israel's leaders held consultations devoted to the question of compensation, among other things; repatriation, by contrast, wasn't raised for discussion. This clearly reflected the outlook that had been widespread among Israeli policymakers for some time: in practice, the subject wasn't even on the agenda.[36]

Dulles' visit to Israel lasted two days. In his talks with Sharett and Ben-Gurion, the two voiced Israel's standing position regarding solution of the refugee problem: resettlement in the Arab states and granting of compensation by Israel. Sharett saw to it to clarify to the secretary of state that Jerusalem agreed to pay "fair compensation," but it expected the international community would take into consideration Israel's economic situation.[37]

Upon his return to the United States, Dulles met with Eisenhower and shared with the president his impressions from his visit to the region. In regard to Israel, Dulles said that its economic situation was grave, and it had been hard hit by the Arab boycott.[38]

On 1 June, Dulles gave a report of his diplomatic tour of the Middle East in a radio broadcast to the nation, in which he set forth some of the pillars of United States policy in the region. In regard to the Palestinian refugees, the secretary of state said that they were living under harsh and degenerating conditions, left to rot away spiritually and physically. As for the solution, he said that "some of these refugees could be settled in the area presently controlled by Israel. Most, however, could more readily be integrated into the lives of the neighboring Arab countries."[39] Two days later, in the wake of the broadcast, Dulles said in a closed hearing before the Senate that "any realistic solution" to the refugee problem lay in development of water sources in the region, not only in the Jordan Valley but also the Tigris and Euphrates Basin, the objective being that there would be more fertile land there [in the Arab territories] on which the refugees could settle.[40]

In his publicly broadcasted policy statement to the nation, Dulles' expression of Washington's commitments to resettlement was groundbreaking. Such a clear and open declaration by an American official in support of resolving the

208   *Toughening Israel's position*

refugee problem based on the resettlement principle had never been voiced before, all the more so by such a senior official. The crux of Israel's position on this matter had won the public support of the strongest power in the world. The secretary of state's recommendation that a small number of refugees be allowed to return to Israel wasn't a surprise. Since the spring of 1949, the Americans had repeatedly demanded that Israel allow a limited number of refugees to return to their homes. Over the years, policymakers in Washington realized that for economic and political reason, the number of refugees that would return to Israel would be very small, in essence a token number relative to the magnitude of the problem.

Israel, however, was unwilling to absorb even a small number of Palestinian refugees, no matter how "symbolic," since it believed that such a move was totally detached from the problematic reality of relations between Israel and the Arab states now brewing in the Middle East (the catalyst behind Ben-Gurion's decision to toughen Israel's stand on the compensation question).[41] All the more so. Repatriation of Palestinian refugees would not promote peace since, after all, in the Arabs' bag was a host of other demands, as Israel had already discovered from various political interactions with the Arabs in the past.

The Israeli government discussed the secretary of state's speech in its 7 June cabinet meeting. Foreign Minister Sharett praised to the sky the secretary of state's public recommendation to rehabilitate most of the refugees in the Arab states: "Maybe this is the first time that America says in an official communiqué that most of the refugees could have been absorbed in neighboring countries." But the positive impression of this passage in the speech was pushed onto the sidelines in light of Dulles' recommendation that "some" of the refugees would return to "the area presently controlled by Israel." It wasn't clear to Sharett whether by this remark Dulles meant that Israel should simply repatriate refugees to its territory or it should relinquish territory that it had seized beyond the borders of the 1947 Partition Plan (in the course of the 1948 war), in order to settle Arab refugees there. Either way, Sharett believed that if the administration would follow this recommendation, it was likely to bring Israel into a "serious clash" with the United States. Prime Minister Ben-Gurion also saw a great danger in the phrase that recommended repatriation of some of the refugees. He was particularly concerned about the possibility that the Americans would want to settle this part of the refugees in the Galilee. In Ben-Gurion's mind, Israel had to make a major effort to settle Jews in this area in light of the political uncertainty hanging over the Galilee.[42]

The Israeli political arena received the American secretary of state's speech with overt hostility. The secretary's historic public declaration that the solution to the refugee problem lay, for the most part, in the resettlement principle was ignored almost entirely by the Knesset factions. The various parties preferred to underscore, through their newspapers,[43] the disappointing half-empty cup from Israel's perspective – the possibility that "some" of the refugees would return.

Davar believed that if Dulles' proposal that some of the refugees be returned to Israel were translated into American pressure, "the nation as a whole" would oppose it.[44] "There isn't any power in the world," the paper warned, "that can force Israel to absorb refugees against its will."[45] *Al Ha-Mishmar* claimed that the secretary of state's proposals, including repatriation of a small number of refugees, "were a continuation of the [anti-Zionist] British [Mandatory] policy in an American edition," that is, appeasement of the Arabs to promote western interests in the region at the Jews' expense.[46] *Ha-Boker* felt that the speech was "an American attempt to arouse a positive and sympathetic echo [response] in the Arab world."[47] *Ha-Modia* cited scornfully that "it seems Mr. Dulles thinks that he's found the magic remedy to the Arab states' sterile opposition to peace with Israel [...] – the settlement of a portion of the Arab refugees [within the State of Israel]."[48] *Ha-Tzofe* believed that Dulles, in his proposal regarding the refugees, "doesn't want to see the landmines for Israel hidden in the return of refugees." The State of Israel, the paper clarified, "won't commit suicide. Its gates will be closed to entrance of enemies."[49] *Herut*, the party organ of the right-wing opposition Herut Party, as could be expected, accused the Labor Movement–led government of responsibility for Dulles' "pro-Arab" speech. The paper's 3 June headline screamed: "With the Israeli statesmen's agreement! Dulles will work to strengthen the Arab League, for the return of the refugees, and internationalization of Jerusalem."[50] A couple of days later, the paper carried the remarks of one of the Herut Party's leaders at a meeting of party activists, in which the speaker said that Dulles' proposals regarding repatriation of refugees was entirely in keeping with the policy Sharett suggested during the Lausanne Conference of absorbing 100,000 Palestinian refugees.[51] Another edition of the paper published an article by the Movement's leader, Menachem Begin, stating that the American secretary of state's plan was "a clear anti-Israel plan," since after all it demanded, among other things, the return of "tens of thousands of [Palestinian] escapees – past murderers and future murderers."[52]

The non-party papers presented an equally negative outlook. In a 3 June column, *Ha'aretz*'s political correspondent labeled Secretary of State Dulles' remarks about the refugees "disappointing."[53] An editorial the next day held that several remarks in the speech, including those regarding the refugees, sought in essence to achieve one supreme objective: to ease deep Arab grievance and resentment towards the United States caused by the establishment of the State of Israel.[54] The editor-in-chief of *Ma'ariv* labeled the proposal on the refugee issue "unreasonable" and "unpractical."[55] The political correspondent of the *Jerusalem Post* believed that:

> if most of the refugees can be resettled in the Arab countries, then all of them can; and the call for the return of "some" to Israel is merely a vain hankering after one of these gestures or tokens of good will which Israel, mainly on American advice, has made so often – without the slightest result.[56]

210   *Toughening Israel's position*

Several American diplomats with whom Eban talked regarding the secretary of state's speech were of the opinion that the harsh responses resonating from Israel were an overreaction. Dulles' under secretary of state, Walter Bedell Smith, claimed emphatically that there was no reason for Israel to be alarmed, since no change to Israel's detriment had taken place, and American policy remained as it was.[57] The American ambassador in Tel Aviv, Monnett Davis, believed that Israel should view the passage that dealt with the refugees as fully an Israeli gain. "The operative sentence" in this passage was the one that spoke of the resettlement of most of the refugees in the Arab states. As for repatriation of a small number of them to Israel, the conditions under which the United States was likely to request Israel carry out such a move were far from near at hand, since there were no signs that Arab-Israeli relations were on the threshold of peace. Thus, the ambassador recommended that Israel refrain from quarreling with the administration over what was only an "academic point."[58] Byroade, for his part, clarified that the phrase "area presently controlled by Israel" got mixed into the text by mistake, and there were no latent meanings behind this phrase. As for the refugee issue, Dulles intended to say that "if" there were areas in Israel where it would be possible to settle refugees, it would be good for all. Yet Washington was not thinking of specific areas such as the Galilee or the Negev and didn't even want to specify a number of returnees.[59]

Following such clarifications by American diplomats, Sharett recommended in a 14 June cabinet meeting that, for the present, Israel not embark on any "open and official" quarrel with the Americans regarding the content of Dulles' speech. At the same time, the government should be on guard and take care "that there would be no misunderstanding by the United States government" in regard to Israel's red lines. For example, that Israel would not agree to the return of even a small number of refugees.[60]

However, the foreign minister understood that parallel to standing firm against the repatriation of any refugees, Israel must prepare for the possibility that it would be forced to make good on its commitment to take the compensation issue forward, since the new American government would find it extremely difficult to concede to Jerusalem on both issues at the same time.

Progress on the compensation question required preparation of comprehensive, updated, background material on this issue; the last time an official in-depth document had been prepared on the subject had been by the Liff Committee at the beginning of 1950, more than three years earlier. Therefore, on 21 June Sharett recommended to the government that a committee of experts be established that would delve into the issue and examine compensation from various perspectives: (a) estimation of the value of abandoned Arab property; (b) calculation of the sum that Israel was prepared to pay; (c) establishment of conditionals for payment; (d) outline of ways payment would be carried out. Sharett recommended that the newly appointed governor of the Bank of Israel, David Horowitz, head the committee.

"I want that we will clarify this internally for ourselves, so we will be ready with a particular position when the time will come," Sharett explained. Such

Toughening Israel's position 211

a time, he added, could come, as every year, at the upcoming General Assembly of the United Nations, which was liable to be tough from an Israeli perspective.[61] Sharett's proposal was accepted, and the government decided to establish a special committee to study the compensation question.

Establishment of the committee didn't in any way herald the abandonment of the tough stance that Ben-Gurion had outlined and that the government had adopted on the compensation question in the winter of 1952. This stance remained solidly in place. Thus, at a large gathering dedicated to "Israel's diplomatic paths of action in the Middle East," which took place on 24 and 25 August 1953 (attended by heads of the Ministry of Foreign Affairs and Israeli representatives in western capitals), Ambassador Eban stated unequivocally that Israel could not make concessions on the compensation issue without receiving something in return from the Arabs. Senior members of the Israeli diplomatic corps in Washington, Eban related, complained in their conversations with officials in the State Department that "the same Arabs who would have benefited from the compensation, are the ones who deprive us of the power to realize this demand through the blockade and suffocation. It's out of the question that they will choke us with one hand and get ours [our 'life breath'] with the other hand." Eban reported that Israeli diplomats in Washington had raised "suggestions for a partial settlement" such as realization of Israel's commitment on the compensation question, in exchange for cancellation of the blockade.[62] The summary adopted at the end of the gathering was in the spirit of Eban's sentiments: "No unilateral concessions [...] should be made, rather it should be demanded that every step taken by Israel to improve the situation, will be accompanied by a contribution by the Arab states."[63]

Two weeks later, on 7 September, the upper echelons of the Ministry of Foreign Affairs discussed the question of Israel's relations with the Arab states. The refugee question occupied most of the deliberations, including the compensation issue in particular. When the foreign minister took the floor, it became apparent that he had begun to question the validity of Israel's current compensation policy, that is, the position that pinned payment of compensation on cancellation of the Arabs' economic warfare. "If you ask me, at the base [the bottom line is]: What will be the payback for payment of compensation? I would answer: The payback is resolution of the refugee problem." Even if payment of compensation wouldn't solve the problem entirely, Sharett clarified, it would still be worthwhile for Israel since as long as Israel wasn't paying compensation, it would remain under political pressure to do so.[64]

The foreign minister was well aware that this approach was impossible for the public at large to swallow and lacked support in the halls of government. He therefore was careful not to give it a public airing or take action to promote this conciliatory position, but he continued to ponder it in the coming months, particularly in his own mind. On 19 October Sharett wrote in his diary that after he heard in the cabinet meeting Ben-Gurion's survey of the increase in the military power of the Arab states, he pondered the need to find

212 *Toughening Israel's position*

a solution to the conflict through non-military means, for example solving "the refugee problem by a daring and concrete proposal from our side for payment of compensation."[65] In April 1954, Sharett wrote in his diary: "The only two domains where it's in our hands to create new facts, and by this perhaps set in motion new processes in Israeli-Arab relations, are the situation of the Arab minority in Israel [...] and the matter of payment of compensation."[66] In the course of 1954[67] and at the beginning of 1955,[68] he even weighed diverting a small part of the reparations from West Germany towards payment of compensation. However, in the end such thoughts about the compensation issue were "safely" locked in Sharett's own head.

On 22 December 1953, the Horowitz Committee submitted its conclusions to Foreign Minister Sharett. In the opening, the report argued that the Palestinian refugee problem "is the key to Israel's relationship with the nations of the world and the Arab nations [...] an Archimedean point for our future in the political, security and economic domain as one"; its resolution, therefore, was "the necessity of the hour [the order of the day]." Not surprisingly, the Horowitz Committee rejected the principle of repatriation: if a large number of refugees were to be repatriated under the prevailing territorial, demographic, topographic, economic, and security conditions of the State of Israel, the fate of the Jewish state would be sealed – extinction. On the other hand, from an ethnic and economic standpoint, the refugee population could easily be absorbed in the Arab states. Israel's sole contribution to resolution of the problem would be payment of compensation. Yet Israel must demand that the money be attached to resettlement plans, "otherwise, the means [resources] would be wasted without having the desired effect." The authors of the report assessed the cost of rehabilitation of the refugees (whose numbers were estimated to be 700,000 souls) would be in the vicinity of 300 million dollars. However, Israel did not have to give the entire sum. At the most, for a number of reasons, Israel should give a third – that is 100 million dollars: first of all, because the Arab states were responsible for the creation of the problem; second, because Israel suffered heavy economic damage due to the Arabs' aggression in 1948; third, because it was a world consensus that no nation should be imposed with payments of compensation beyond its ability to pay. "The State of Israel can obtain this sum only one way: by using the last payments of reparations," said the report. The committee rejected personal compensation, arguing that in such a case Israel would have to pay compensation "in amounts that it is unable to bear," and because most of the refugees didn't have assets at all. Nevertheless, the committee suggested considering paying compensation to several wealthy refugee families "to buy their sympathy for the resettlement principle," particularly in light of their ability to impose "great influence" on masses of refugees.[69]

The Horowitz Committee ardently supported the actualization of Israel's commitment to pay compensation and therefore overtly refrained from suggesting that Israel's leaders hinge payment on abolition of the Arab economic warfare. But Israeli leadership was categorically unwilling to relinquish the economic warfare "card," certainly not against the backdrop of escalation of the conflict between Israel and the Arabs that began in the latter half of 1954.[70]

During the years 1954 to 1956 the compensation issue was sidelined. Jerusalem was occupied with bigger and more burning political-security matters. The only ones who still addressed compensation (and then, only due to their positions) were a handful of officials in the Ministry of Foreign Affairs. Their superior, Sharett, and afterwards Golda Meir, showed interest in this issue from time to time. Their remarks on the compensation question during this period clarified that Israel had no intention of swaying from the position it had adopted in late 1952. At the end of November 1954, Ministry of Foreign Affairs official Michael Comay declared before the 9th General Assembly's Ad Hoc Political Committee that the Israeli government was still willing to pay compensation for abandoned Arab lands, but had difficulty acting on this commitment, due to two factors: first, lack of financial resources; and second, Arab economic warfare. The magnitude of economic damage to Israel from six years of economic warfare, Comay claimed, was comparable to the value of abandoned Arab land set by the Refugees Office. The economic boycott and the maritime blockade were detrimental to Palestinian refugees since they blocked Israel's ability to pay compensation. The Arab governments, charged Comay, "have to choose what is more important: to continue the anti-Israel battle or transformation of compensation into a feasible matter."[71] Similar sentiments were voiced by Eban in reply to a congressman who questioned the Israeli ambassador about the refugee problem.[72]

In a discussion in Mapai's National Council on 21 August 1954, Sharett reiterated Israel's commitment to pay compensation, provided Arab economic warfare were abolished.[73] In political consultations in the government on 10 October, Minister of Finance Levi Eshkol asked if it was not sensible for Israel to declare that when the time came to pay compensation, Israel would need assistance. Sharett replied in short that this would be done only "if we decide to make progress."[74] Such progress, he stated on another occasion (a meeting of Israeli ambassadors in May 1955), still hinged on the same parameters set two and a half years earlier: "If they [the Americans] are prepared to bring the Egyptians around to abolish the blockade in the Suez and bring all the Arab countries around to stop the aggressive boycott."[75]

Israel's policy on the compensation issue led to an unavoidable clash with the Conciliation Commission. Between 1953 and 1954, the commission had dealt with identifying the abandoned property of Palestinians and its valuation; parallel to this, it requested to ascertain what Israel intended to do about payment of compensation. On 9 October 1953, Eban announced to the Conciliation Commission that the government of Israel was busy preparing to implement its declared policy that offered compensation for abandoned land in Israel, and the minute the investigation was completed, the government would be able to announce its position on the matter. Eban was referring to the work of the Horowitz Committee. In the first half of 1954, the

214   *Toughening Israel's position*

Conciliation Commission turned to Israel again, to determine if there was anything new to report on the compensation issue. The head of the Division for International Organizations in the Ministry of Foreign Affairs, Hanan Cidor, announced on 1 August that Israel would submit the findings of its investigation on this matter "at the first suitable opportunity."[76]

In June 1955, the commission conducted an evaluation of the situation regarding identification of abandoned Arab property. The conclusion was that if things continued at the present pace, it would take 15 years to complete this task, and therefore it was decided to speed up the process. British land affairs expert John Berncastle was requested to go to Jerusalem to mobilize a team that would focus on identification of abandoned Arab property and its valuation, parallel to the work of another team in New York. All hoped that the two teams, by working hard, could finish this project by mid 1957.[77]

At the outset of 1956, the Conciliation Commission was very satisfied with the tempo of the teams' work and therefore again decided to query Israel on the issue of payment of compensation. On 14 February the commission addressed a letter to Cidor, reminding him of Israel's promise to inform the commission of the government's intentions regarding the compensation issue. In light of the good progress being made in identifying the abandoned Arab property and its valuation, the commission needed to know as soon as possible what were Israel's findings on the matter.[78] Following consultation with Sharett, Cidor penned a reply to the commission[79] in which he stated that it would not be possible to consider the compensation issue for abandoned Arab lands while ignoring the relations between Israel and the Arab states as a whole. Since Israel's response to the commission in 1953 to 1954, explained Cidor, "the Arab governments have intensified their economic warfare against Israel" and at every opportunity have sought to weaken its economic situation. As Israeli spokespersons had already clarified, the Arab states could not expect to impose a blockade and economic boycott on Israel, meaning a noose around Israel's neck, and at the same time expect Israel would bear a heavy economic burden (for the Palestinian refugees). The Israeli government felt it would be futile for Israel to offer a compensation payment plan under prevailing conditions. As long as conditions in the region didn't allow it, there was no sense in even beginning to investigate details tied to the compensation question.[80]

The commission, as could be expected, expressed before the Israeli government its disappointment with the Israeli reply, which it branded a "patent retreat" from Israel's previous position on the compensation issue (as presented in November 1951). The commission expressed its hope that the government would reconsider its position.[81] However, a change in the Israeli position did not materialize. Israel's official position by the end of the period under study – the toughened stand outlined by Ben-Gurion in the winter of 1952 – remained firm. Thus, in an October 1956 briefing by the Ministry of Foreign Affairs to the Israeli delegation to the 11th United Nations General Assembly (whose content was approved by the government), it was stated that in regard to the compensation issue, the delegation should hold firm on the following line: "(a) stipulating abolition of the boycott; (b) payment as a vehicle for settling the refugee problem."[82]

Notes

1 FRUS, 1952–1954, IX, pp. 916–17, The Secretary of State to the United States Representative on the Palestine Conciliation Commission, 19 April 1952.
2 UNPCC, A/2121, p. 4.
3 UNPCC, A/2216, p. 6.
4 UNPCC, A/2629, p. 3; Michael R. Fischbach, "The United Nations and Palestinian Refugee Property Compensation," *Journal of Palestine Studies* 31(2), 2002, pp. 40–3.
5 UKNA, FO 371/91410, E1826/44, FO Minute, Oliver, 11 December 1951; UKNA, FO 371/98518, E18210/1, FO Minute, Oliver, 21 December 1951; UKNA, FO 371/98258, E1056/83, Conference of Her Majesty's Representatives in the Middle East, 23 June 1952; UKNA, FO 371/104477, E18213/3, FO Minute, 25 February 1953.
6 When, towards the end of the Paris Conference, Foreign Minister Sharett raised the issue of compensation to the refugees, Washington refused, according to Sharett, "to encourage us to carry it out without delay." The reason for this, he believed, was that "they [the Americans] are not enthusiastic about taking on the burden of additional financial commitments to us": ISA, MFA 2447/III, In Anticipation of the General Assembly Discussion of the Palestine Problem, 2 January 1952.
7 FRUS, 1952–1954, IX, p. 1026, Department of State Position Paper, 4 October 1952.
8 An agreement had been signed on 10 September 1952 between Israel and West Germany, in which Bonn agreed to provide Jerusalem with 3 billion marks (approximately 740 million dollars) in goods and services, over the course of 12 to 14 years. These goods and services were intended to serve as compensation for the crimes committed by the Nazi regime against the Jewish people. For an in-depth examination of the subject, see Yeshayahu A. Jelinek, *Deutschland und Israel, 1945–1965: Ein Neurotisches Verhaltnis*, Munchen: R. Oldenbourg Verlag, 2004, pp. 39–216.
9 FRUS, 1952–1954, IX, pp. 1065–7, The Acting Secretary of State to the Embassy in Israel, 18 November 1952.
10 DEPI, Vol. 7, Document 163, T. Kollek to D. Ben-Gurion, 21 May 1952; DEPI, Vol. 7, Document 366, Meeting: A. Eban – D. Acheson and H. Byroade (Washington, 22 September 1952).
11 ISA, Government Meeting, 19 October 1952, pp. 19–27.
12 DEPI, Vol. 7, Document 448, A. Eban to W. Eytan, 19 November 1952.
13 ISA, MFA 2451/13A, A. Eban to M. Sharett, 21 November 1952.
14 ISA, MFA 2446/6, Statement on the Near East by Ambassador Abba Eban in the Ad Hoc Political Committee of the United Nations, 1 December 1952.
15 ISA, MFA 7226/1A, M. de Shalit to the United States Division in the Ministry of Foreign Affairs, 14 November 1952; ISA, 7563/9 A, Foreign Affairs and Defense Committee Meeting, 17 March 1953, pp. 8–9; ILPA, 2-26-1953-12, Political Committee Meeting, 28 March 1953, pp. 1–2.
16 DEPI, Vol. 8, Introduction, p. XIII; Isaac Alteras, *Eisenhower and Israel: U.S.-Israeli Relations, 1953–1960*, Gainesville, FL: University Press of Florida, 1993, p. 21; Abba Eban, *Personal Witness: Israel through My Eyes*, New York: G.P. Putnam's Sons, 1992, p. 233; Herbert Druks, *The Uncertain Friendship: The U.S. and Israel from Roosevelt to Kennedy*, Westport, CT: Greenwood Press, 2001, p. 153.

216   *Toughening Israel's position*

17 DEPI, Vol. 8, Document 120, Political Consultation of the Prime Minister with the Heads of the Ministries of Foreign Affairs and Defence and of the Jewish Agency, 8 March 1953.

18 ILPA, 2-26-1953-12, Political Committee Meeting, 28 March 1953, pp. 2–5.

19 DEPI, Vol. 8, Document 172, M. Sharett to D. Ben-Gurion, 17 April 1953.

20 During the last months of Truman's presidency, some senior officials indicated that his Democratic administration would be willing to adopt Israel's position on the repatriation of the refugees in a more sweeping fashion than had been anticipated. See: FRUS, 1952–1954, IX, pp. 1074–5, Minutes of the Fifteenth Meeting of the United States Delegation to the Seventh Regular Session of the United Nations General Assembly, 28 November 1952; DEPI, Vol. 7, Document 415, A. Eban to W. Eytan, 31 October 1952; ISA, MFA 2475/1, Address by the Honorable Henry A. Byroade, 4 December 1952.

21 Deborah J. Gerner, "Missed Opportunities and Roads Not Taken: The Eisenhower Administration and the Palestinians," *Arab Studies Quarterly* 12(1–2), 1990, pp. 74–5.

22 ISA, Government Meeting, 30 August 1953, p. 6.

23 ISA, MFA 3062/4, Report of the Subcommittee on the Near East and Africa, Foreign Relations Committee on the Problem of Arab Refugees from Palestine, 24 July 1953.

24 United States Congress – Committee of Foreign Affairs, *The Arab Refugees and Other Problems in the Near East*, Washington, DC: U.S. Government, 1954.

25 UKNA, FO 371/104477, E18213/1, Baker to Crosthwaite, 27 February 1953; UKNA, FO 371/104463, E1825/26, Knight to Richmond, 27 February 1953; ISA, MFA 360/18, M. de Shalit to the United States Division in the Ministry of Foreign Affairs, 19 March 1953.

26 FRUS, 1952–1954, IX, pp. 1215–17, Department of State Position Paper, 7 May 1953.

27 UKNA, FO 371/104465, E1825/72, Arab Refugees: Note of Meeting Held at the Foreign Office on Monday, 27 April 1953.

28 ISA, 7563/11 A, Foreign Affairs and Defense Committee Meeting, 19 May 1953, p. 2; DEPI, Vol. 8, Editorial Note (p. 357); Alteras, *Eisenhower and Israel*, p. 57.

29 FRUS, 1952–1954, IX, pp. 8–18, Memorandum of Conversation, 11 May 1953; FRUS, 1952–1954, IX, pp. 19–25, Memorandum of Conversation, 12 May 1953; Muhammad Abd el-Wahab Sayed-Ahmed, *Nasser and American Foreign Policy, 1952–1956*, London: Laam, 1989, p. 82; Alteras, *Eisenhower and Israel*, pp. 57–9; See also ISA, 7563/11 A, Foreign Affairs and Defense Committee Meeting, 19 May 1953, p. 3.

30 FRUS, 1952–1954, IX, p. 42, Memorandum of Conversation, 15 May 1953.

31 FRUS, 1952–1954, IX, p. 44, Memorandum of Conversation, 15 May 1953.

32 FRUS, 1952–1954, IX, p. 59, Memorandum of Conversation, 16 May 1953.

33 James T. Donohue, "Before Suez: John Foster Dulles and the Arab-Israeli Conflict, 1940–1954," PhD thesis, University Microfilms, 1989, p. 229.

34 FRUS, 1952–1954, IX, p. 66, Memorandum of Conversation, 16 May 1953.

35 FRUS, 1952–1954, IX, pp. 79–80, Memorandum of Conversation, 17 May 1953.

36 ISA, MFA 2414/29, Discussion in Anticipation of the Visit of the United States Secretary of State, 4 May 1953.

37 DEPI, Vol. 8, Document 207, Meeting: M. Sharett and Senior Officials of the Ministry of Foreign Affairs – J.F. Dulles and the U.S. Delegation (Tel Aviv, 13 May 1953); DEPI, Vol. 8, Document 211, Meeting: D. Ben-Gurion and M. Sharett – J.F. Dulles and the U.S. Delegation (Jerusalem, 14 May 1953).

38 FRUS, 1952–1954, IX, p. 381, Memorandum of Conversation, 1 June 1953.

39 J. C. Hurewitz (ed.), *Diplomacy in the Near and Middle East: A Documentary Record, 1914–1956*, New York: Octagon Books, 1972, pp. 337–42.

Toughening Israel's position 217

40 Douglas Little, *American Orientalism: The United States and the Middle East since 1945*, Chapel Hill, NC: The University of North Carolina Press, 2002, p. 273.

41 ISA, MFA 2446/7B, Consultation Regarding Israel's Diplomatic Paths of Action in the Middle East, 25 August 1953; ISA, MFA 2384/14A, G. Rafael to the Director-General of the Ministry of Foreign Affairs, undated; Mordechai Bar-On, "Status Quo Before – or After? Commentary Notes on Israel's Defense Policy 1949–1958," *Iyunim Bitkumat Israel* 5, 1995, pp. 88–9 (Hebrew); David Tal, *Israel's Day-to-Day Security Conception: Its Origin and Development, 1949–1956*, Sede Boqer: The Ben-Gurion Research Institute, 1998, p. 137 (Hebrew).

42 ISA, Government Meeting, 7 June 1953, pp. 5–28.

43 The secretary of state's speech was not discussed in the Knesset plenum. The Foreign Affairs and Defense Committee heard Foreign Minister Sharett's report on the speech and on its consequences, but did not discuss it afterward: see ISA, 7563/11 A, Foreign Affairs and Defense Committee Meeting, 5 June 1953. Within the government, only the prime minister and the foreign minister spoke on the matter. The party forums also failed to discuss the speech, and the political system only referred to it in the parties' various newspapers.

44 *Davar*, 3 June 1953.

45 *Davar*, 5 June 1953.

46 *Al Ha-Mishmar*, 3 June 1953.

47 *Ha-Boker*, 3 June 1953.

48 *Ha-Modia*, 3 June 1953.

49 *Ha-Tzofe*, 3 June 1953.

50 *Herut*, 3 June 1953.

51 *Herut*, 7 June 1953.

52 *Herut*, 5 June 1953.

53 *Ha'aretz*, 3 June 1953.

54 *Ha'aretz*, 4 June 1953.

55 *Ma'ariv*, 2 June 1953.

56 *The Jerusalem Post*, 3 June 1953.

57 ISA, Government Meeting, 14 June 1953, p. 8.

58 DEPI, Vol. 8, Document 253, A. Eban to the United States Division, 8 June 1953.

59 FRUS, 1952–1954, IX, pp. 1233–6, Memorandum of Conversation, 9 June 1953.

60 ISA, Government Meeting, 14 June 1953, pp. 7–13.

61 ISA, Government Meeting, 21 June 1953, pp. 4–7.

62 ISA, MFA 2446/7B, Consultation Regarding Israel's Diplomatic Paths of Action in the Middle East, 25 August 1953.

63 ISA, MFA 2384/14A, G. Rafael to the Director-General of the Ministry of Foreign Affairs, undated.

64 ISA, MFA 2384/14A, Consultation on the Subject of Relations with the Arab Countries, 7 September 1953.

65 Moshe Sharett, *Personal Diary*, vol. 1, Tel Aviv: Am Oved, 1978, pp. 54–5 (Hebrew).

66 Sharett, *Personal Diary*, Vol. 2, pp. 452, 455.

67 Sharett, *Personal Diary*, Vol. 3, pp. 729, 790

68 Sharett, *Personal Diary*, Vol. 4, p. 933.

69 ISA, MFA 2445/2B, D. Horowitz to M. Sharett, 22 December 1953.

70 Benny Morris, *Israel's Border Wars, 1949–1956: Arab Infiltration, Israeli Retaliation and the Countdown to the Suez War*, Tel Aviv: Am Oved, 1996, pp. 292, 346–52 (Hebrew); Tal, *Israel's Day-to-Day Security Conception*, pp. 137, 162–236.

71 ISA, MFA 3743/12, The Delegation in New York to the Ministry of Foreign Affairs in Jerusalem, 28 November 1954.

218 *Toughening Israel's position*

72 ISA, MFA 2491/6, A., Eban to W. Poge, 10 January 1955.
73 ILPA, 2-22-1954-90, Council Meeting, 21 August 1954, pp. 76–7.
74 ISA, Government Meeting, 10 October 1954, pp. 10–11.
75 ISA, MFA 2446/8, The Prime Minister's Remarks at the Conference of Ambassadors, 28 May 1955.
76 UNPCC, A/2897, p. 2.
77 UNPCC, A/3199, p. 2.
78 ISA, MFA 1989/10, A. Ladas to H. Cidor, 14 February 1956.
79 ISA, MFA 2014/7, H. Cidor to the Foreign Minister, 4 March 1956.
80 ISA, MFA 1989/10, H. Cidor to A. Ladas, 11 March 1956.
81 UNPCC, A/3199, p. 3.
82 ISA, MFA 2404/14B, Briefing for Israel's Delegation to the 11th Session of the United Nations Assembly, 25 October 1956.

10 The Alpha Plan

From mid 1954, relations between Israel and Egypt deteriorated dramatically, fueled by a number of events: a Jewish sabotage ring operating in Cairo and Alexandria in the summer of 1954 on behalf of Israel was caught and two of its members were executed;[1] at the end of 1954, the Israeli vessel *Bat Galim* was stopped and seized by Egypt after trying to enter the Suez Canal;[2] political and non-political infiltration from the Gaza Strip increased;[3] and Egyptian soldiers began to fire on Israeli patrols along the border.[4] Besides these events, Egypt continued, like the rest of the Arab League's members, to carry out a relentless cold war against Israel: economic warfare intensified and slanderous hate propaganda in the diplomatic arena against Israel's very existence deepened and amplified.

In late October 1954, the British assistant under secretary of state, Evelyn Shuckburgh, embarked on a comprehensive tour of the Middle East to assess the explosive situation. The British diplomat met with Arab and Israeli leaders and conducted consultations with on-site British representatives.[5]

Shuckburgh's visit set in motion a British initiative designed to achieve a political settlement between Israel and its neighbors, particularly between Israel and Egypt.[6] London sought to rehabilitate its standing (and that of the west as a whole) in the region, and in Egypt in particular, by brokering a settlement between Israel and the Arabs. Rehabilitation of relations with the Arab states was imperative for the western powers in light of the growing Soviet threat in the Middle East.[7]

A week after Shuckburgh embarked on his tour, London asked its ambassador to the United States to suggest to the American secretary of state that the two countries launch a joint political initiative to solve the Middle East conflict. The ambassador was instructed to ask Dulles whether he was willing to send one of the State Department's experts in Middle East affairs to London to work with Shuckburgh "on the primary elements" for resolutions of the conflict between Israel and the Arabs.[8]

Dulles received the British initiative with open arms and was prepared to join it.[9] At the same time, and unconnected with the British move, the State Department had been engaged in a reassessment of all the problems dividing Israel and its neighbors, in order to revamp American policy accordingly.[10]

220   The Alpha Plan

On 17 November, Washington accepted the British invitation and suggested the two countries hold joint discussions from mid January 1955, after the State Department concluded its reassessment. The British were told that the chief American representative in talks with Shuckburgh would be Francis Russell, an adviser at the American embassy in Tel Aviv.[11] Several days later, the State Department asked its representatives in the Middle East to share their opinions regarding the chances of achieving a political settlement between Israel and its Arab neighbors.[12] The replies, which arrived by the outset of January 1955, were pessimistic: the gaps between the sides were too great in a number of areas.[13] The Palestinian refugee issue, however, was not one of them. American diplomats reported that implementation of the repatriation principle as a proviso to a settlement with Israel was not a top priority of the Arabs. The American ambassador in Cairo spoke at length about the Egyptian demand for a land bridge to Jordan and only after that wrote briefly that Cairo would also like "to get rid of the Gaza Strip and its refugees."[14] In the telegram from the American ambassador to Syria, the refugee issue wasn't mentioned at all.[15] America's representative in Jordan related that while the Jordanians demanded that Israel recognize the repatriation principle, they understood that only a few refugees would return to Israel and remain there. By contrast, Amman stood firm that a solution to the compensation issue must be found.[16]

A political settlement between Israel and its neighbors was discussed at length in a meeting of American representatives in the Middle East, held in Damascus in mid December 1954. Regarding the Palestinian refugee problem, all agreed that the key to its resolution lay in implementation, almost totally, of the resettlement principle.[17] This outlook was the dominant perception in Washington, both in the White House and in the State Department. As evidenced in the previous chapter, in the course of 1953 various American elements had expressed their support of this outlook in all kinds of forums, and in the course of 1954–5, members of the administration continued to argue that resettlement was, in practice, the only path. This was the message Russell conveyed in a conversation with Ministry of Foreign Affairs official Gideon Rafael. Israel's contribution to solving the refugee problem, said Russell, boiled down to giving compensation and absorbing 40,000 to 70,000 refugees only (out of 900,000 on UNRWA welfare rolls).[18] The same message was relayed by State Department official Arthur Gardiner in his 7 May 1954 testimony before the House of Representatives' Foreign Relations Committee. The State Department's demands from Israel on the refugee question, he said, boiled down to payment of compensation, unfreezing blocked bank accounts, and "studying" the "possibility" of repatriating refugees.[19] Several months later, during discussion of the UNRWA's annual report, the American representative on the United Nations Ad Hoc Political Committee stated that his delegation was convinced that, in the end, the Palestinian refugee problem would be solved when the Arab states would see the refugees as "permanent members of the community." Israel, he added, would need to provide one out

The Alpha Plan 221

of two of their rights: either repatriation or compensation.[20] Of course, Israel's ambassador, Eban, was quick to praise the declaration.[21] Eban's colleague in the embassy, the minister Reuven Shiloah, wrote to the director of the United States Division in the Ministry of Foreign Affairs, Yaacov Herzog, that "in the various conversations in London and in New York, we heard the faintest of hints about borders and about symbolic repatriation of refugees."[22]

With Shuckburgh's return to London in mid December 1954, he presented a detailed report to his superiors on the Arab-Israeli conflict, in which, among other things, ideas for resolving the various issues were raised. On the territorial issue, certain border adjustments were suggested, mostly on behalf of Jordan, as well as granting an overland corridor through the Negev, south of Beersheva, for Egypt and Jordan.

As for the refugee problem, Shuckburgh said in the memorandum that Israel would not agree to the principle of repatriation, although it might be willing to accept a certain number of refugees in its territory by expanding the family reunification program. In regard to compensation, Israel would need a loan in order to withstand this financial burden, but it would not agree to pay as long as the Arabs continued their economic boycott and maritime blockade. These actions were injurious to Israel's economy and were likely to have even harsher ramifications in the future. He therefore proposed that steps be taken to remove the economic warfare in the framework of a comprehensive political settlement. The Arab states' contribution to resolving the refugee problem would be curtailment of the limitations they had imposed on the refugees' freedom of movement throughout the Arab world and their right to work in Arab countries. Shuckburgh surmised that it would be advisable to attract the refugees primarily to Syria and Iraq.[23]

Israel was able to learn about the report in real time.[24] Already on 17 December, Eban reported to Prime Minister Sharett that "from a highly-placed official I heard today, confidentially: [...] the Shuckburgh report had arrived at the [American] State Department." Eban related that Shuckburgh recommended that Israel relinquish territory "within which a small number of refugees would be settled."[25] Although Israel did not know the scope of the territorial and demographic concession demanded, it was quick to reject the British proposals. In a meeting with the American under secretary of state, Herbert Hoover, Eban stated, referring indirectly to the Shuckburgh report, that if the western powers "will go for [a peace plan in the Middle East] along the well-trodden path of proposals for repatriation of refugees or concession of territory [by Israel]," the attempt will not succeed; in fact, just the opposite, "[it] would cause clashes and bitterness." Israel's contribution to a peace settlement, Eban underscored, would be payment of compensation, provided the Arab economic boycott would be abolished.[26] The Israeli ambassador pointed out to Hoover similar things that Comay had said to the United Nations General Assembly's Ad Hoc Political Committee regarding the Palestinian refugee question.[27]

222   The Alpha Plan

Israel's attempt to nip the British under secretary of state's ideas in the bud failed, and they served as fertile soil upon which the Alpha Plan sprouted. Approximately a week before deliberations over it began, the State Department in Washington prepared a memorandum that dealt with resolution of the Middle East conflict. Many of the proposals in that document were in line with the Shuckburgh report. Thus, for example, on the refugee issue: in the American document as well, the refugees were supposed to be resettled in the Arab states; by contrast, the repatriation principle wasn't mentioned at all. As for compensation, the American working paper stated, as did the British report, that Israel would be able to pay the money only with international assistance – some of which the United States would provide, and some of which would come from Britain and France. Further on in the document, it was suggested that it be explained to the Israeli government that the United States' proposals for resolving the Middle East conflict, including the refugee problem, were similar in many ways to the ideas that Israel itself had raised in the past.[28]

On 21 January 1955, the first round of talks between the two partners in the British-American peace initiative were held in Washington.[29] The talks were conducted behind closed doors, for the most part out of fear that if the contents of the deliberations would leak out, it would doom the plan to failure and complicate relations with the Arabs.[30] After many deliberations that took place alternately in Washington and London, and after a huge body of working papers was produced, finally, on 10 March 1955 a document emerged in final form that was code-named "Alpha."[31]

The Alpha document dealt with every point of controversy between the rival parties in the Middle East: territory, refugees, Jerusalem, Arab economic warfare, and communications and transportation agreements. In regard to territory, the document proposed border adjustments between Israel and Jordan so that West Bank Palestinian peasants whose lands had been taken from them (by Israel) as a result of the Armistice Agreement ("economic refugees") would receive a portion of their land back. It was also suggested that Israel relinquish territory in the southern Negev on behalf of Egypt and Jordan. These swatches consisted of two small triangular sections where the base of one triangle ran along the Israeli-Jordanian border and the other along the Israeli-Egyptian border; the apexes of both triangles intersected at the same point, on the road leading to Eilat. Thus, the overland corridor that Egypt had demanded for some time could be created.

The topic that occupied most of the Alpha document was the Palestinian refugee problem. The architects of Alpha felt that in order for their proposals for resolution of the problem to be acceptable to the Arabs, repatriation (as well as compensation) needed to be included. Nevertheless, they refused to *found* the solution on repatriation: in fact, they judged that apparently only a small number of refugees wanted to return, and "in general it would not be desirable to increase too greatly Israel's Arab population." According to this approach, the Alpha Plan proposed that Israel repatriate a token number of refugees – "up to 75,000," 15,000 per year over 5 years. Priority would be given to refugees situated in the Gaza Strip. The UNRWA would underwrite part of the cost of their settlement. The final rehabilitation of the refugee population as a whole hinged on regional economic development, implementation of the UNRWA's programs, and lifting of restrictions on the refugees' freedom of movement. According to the Alpha Plan, it would be possible to settle 200,000 refugees in Jordan (the Jordan Valley projects), 80,000 in Syria, 70,000 in Egypt (the Sinai Peninsula), 60,000 in Iraq, 40,000 in Lebanon, and 50,000 in Israel (the document explained that "it is very doubtful that the full 75,000 would want to return").

As for compensation, the document stated that the parties had considerable compensation demands. Israel's demands for compensation were: war damages and the frozen assets of Jews from the Arab countries and Jewish property in Palestine that had fallen to the Jordanian Legion in the 1948 war. The Arab demands for compensation were: abandoned unmovable assets and abandoned moveable assets and lost income from the use of immovable property since 1948. The composers of the Alpha Plan believed they could arrive at an agreement with Israel regarding the sum of compensation that should be taken into account, including all claims and counterclaims. This sum should be 100 million pounds sterling. The authors thought it would be preferable that Israel pay as large a part of the lump sum of compensation as possible. First of all, there was the need to prove to the Arab states that Israel was actively participating in resolution of the refugee problem; second, this would reduce the financial burden that would fall on the British and the Americans. At the same time, it was clear to the western diplomats that "unassisted she [Israel] is unable to finance such a large sum." Consequently, it was proposed that the sum of compensation would be paid over a ten-year period: 30 percent would be paid by Israel and world Jewry, and 70 percent would be underwritten by the international community – first and foremost the western powers, through loans to Israel. Payment was conditional on the Arabs abolishing the maritime blockade in the Suez Canal; lifting the secondary boycott;[32] and closing the national boycott offices.[33]

Thus, after examining the Alpha proposals for resolution of the Palestinian refugee problem, it became evident that the United States, like the United Kingdom before it, adopted the principle of resettlement as the only way to solve this problem. According to the Plan, Israel was supposed to absorb 75,000 refugees at the most, out of a population that numbered 906,000 souls.[34] That is, according to the western powers, only about 8 percent of the refugees were, at most, slated to return. The number of returnees proposed was low, both in absolute numbers and in relative terms, in comparison to "the 100,000 Proposal" that Israel had floated six years earlier, and which the Truman administration had rejected as not going far enough. As for compensation, the Plan's architects chose to set a sum that was minute compared to the Arab League's estimate (approximately two billion pounds sterling).[35]

224 *The Alpha Plan*

Furthermore, for the first time, there were signs that America was prepared to assist Israel in payment of compensation.

For Washington and London, the next step was to inform the rival sides about the Plan, in the hopes that it would move them towards discussion of a comprehensive political settlement. At the opening of the Alpha document, it was stipulated that representatives of the powers would approach Egypt's rulers first, and only afterwards approach Israel.[36] The authors believed the document should not be presented to Israel and its Arab neighbors in full; rather, attempts should be made to raise the main points in the course of discussion – not all at once. The document said that if the sides would not demonstrate readiness to make progress, it would be appropriate to consider carefully whether it would be wise to go public with the Alpha Plan's concepts.

In practice, the two powers encountered serious difficulties in making progress on the road they had mapped out, due to the tense atmosphere in the region in the spring of 1955,[37] marked by a number of events:

1 Border incidents and murderous political infiltrations from the Gaza Strip into Israel continued unabated. Such incursions led to harsh retaliatory actions by Israel, which reached a peak in a 28 February retaliatory operation that targeted the Egyptian army in Gaza.[38] This action spurred the Egyptians to embark on terrorist operations by *feda'iyin* against Israeli targets.[39]
2 Signing of a political-military pact between Iraq and Turkey on 24 February ("the Baghdad Pact") generated anxiety both in Egypt and Israel. The Egyptians feared this turn of events would undermine Egypt's status in the Arab world, fears that augmented as Iraqi-Turkish cooperation increased and others (Britain, Pakistan, and Iran) joined the pact. Israel was apprehensive that as a result of the pact, its avowed enemy Iraq would be armed with advanced western weaponry.[40]
3 The participation of Egyptian leader Gamal Abd al-Nasser in the Afro-Asian Conference of unaligned nations in Bandung in April 1955 limited Egypt's freedom of action. Following his meetings with leaders of the Third World at the conference and the enthusiasm with which he was received, the Egyptian leader was confident of his ability to advance Egypt's position in the Arab world and in the Afro-Asian sphere of unaligned nations. Yet moving closer to Israel and the west at this time would only have smashed such plans.[41]

Despite the tense mood, American and British representatives decided to try and raise the Alpha document's ideas in talks with Egypt's rulers and afterwards in talks with Israeli leaders. Already during his visit to Cairo at the end of February 1955, British Foreign Secretary Anthony Eden had raised with Nasser the possibility of an Arab-Israeli political settlement.[42] A month later, the newly appointed American ambassador in Cairo, Henry Byroade, met with the Egyptian foreign minister, Mahmud Fawzi. The Egyptian statesman reiterated Egypt's unyielding demands for a land bridge between Egypt and the Arab world to the east, but continued to hold firm with Egypt's moderate stance vis-à-vis the refugees. Fawzi said that Egypt's position on the refugee issue was more realistic than the position of many other Arab states; Egypt understood that the Palestinian refugees couldn't return to Israel and that compensation would be measured. Moreover, Egypt even understood that it was not feasible for the entire sum to come out of Israel's pocket, even if Cairo would prefer this.[43] In another meeting between the two several days later, Fawzi asked Byroade how he felt about the contents of their previous conversation. In response, the American ambassador presented the ideas contained in the Alpha document in general terms, without referring to it explicitly by name. He reported back to Washington that Fawzi agreed to the proposals.[44] The next day Byroade met with Nasser and offered him, also in general terms, the concepts for a settlement. Nasser expressed less willingness than his foreign minister to embrace the proposals, although he did not reject them out of hand.[45]

Towards the middle of April, Israel was officially informed of the existence of a western diplomatic initiative. At the time, the Israelis had hoped for a defense treaty with Washington, and ideas for a political settlement with the Arab neighbors were viewed with lesser interest. Israel felt isolated and more vulnerable than ever before. Behind this feeling were the sale of American weaponry to Iraq (in April 1954); the Anglo-Egyptian agreement (in October 1954) for evacuation of the huge British military bases in the Suez Canal Zone, which had served as a kind of buffer between Egypt and Israel; and the pacts crystallizing around Baghdad and Ankara (in the spring of 1955).[46] Israel's sense of vulnerability led its leaders to reconsider an idea that had been rejected by them in the past – official and public American guarantees for Israel's security. Jerusalem had already sought to obtain a defense treaty with Washington as early as September 1954. Such endeavors continued in 1955 and increased in the winter of the same year due to the Egyptian-Czech arms deal.[47]

On 13 April, Israel's ambassador to London, Eliahu Elath, met with Shuckburgh. In their talk, Shuckburgh presented some of the ideas that appeared in the Alpha Plan. Israel, the British diplomat hinted/warned, would have to sacrifice something in order to achieve peace with its neighbors.[48] On the very same day, Eban met with Dulles in Washington to raise Israel's requests for a defense treaty between the two countries and supply of American armaments. The secretary of state replied that it would only be possible to address these requests after the political points of controversy between Israel and its Arab neighbors, some or all of them, were resolved. He reported to Eban that Washington was considering a political initiative for a comprehensive settlement between the sides.[49] Following his exchange with Dulles, Eban was quick to clarify to the Americans that Israel would not agree to compromise on two issues: relinquishment of territory and repatriation of

226 *The Alpha Plan*

refugees.[50] Sharett wrote in a similar vein to Dulles on 4 May,[51] and Ambassador Eliahu Elath transmitted the same message to Shuckburgh at the outset of June.[52]

Having shared with Egypt and Israel their intentions to set in motion a political initiative and its foundations, the Americans sought a suitable time to discuss fully the proposals in the Alpha document. However, the tense situation in the region, as noted, did not make this objective an easy task. From the Americans' standpoint, time was short. The year 1956 was a presidential election year, and it was plain that the closer this came, the less Washington would be focused on foreign policy issues. In addition, the ability of the administration to bargain with the Jewish state in an election year would be reduced in some degree by the desire to take into account the "Jewish vote" (although the Republications were hardly dependent on the support of the American-Jewish community for Eisenhower's reelection to a second term). Furthermore, time was a serious issue due to the Soviet Union's increasing involvement in the region, particularly in Egypt, which only underscored the need to arrive quickly at a political settlement between Israel and Egypt whose advantages to the latter would be sufficiently attractive to tie Egypt to the west. Due to such considerations, and in light of the fact that contacts in the spring of 1955 between the western powers and Israeli and Egyptian representatives had not lead anywhere, the secretary of state decided to go public with some of the ideas contained in the Alpha Plan.[53] He hoped such a move would impel Israel and its Arab neighbors to discuss fully the proposals that appeared in the plan.

On 26 August 1955, after a series of consultations and coordination with the British,[54] Dulles delivered a speech before the American Council for Foreign Relations in which he described partially, and in general terms, the proposals in the Alpha document. The secretary of state cited three problems that interfered with relations between Israel and the Arab states: mutual fears, borders, and refugees. In regard to fears, Dulles said that President Eisenhower would recommend, after solutions to the rest of the problems were reached, that both of the rival sides would be granted security guarantees to prevent war and any attempt to unilaterally change borders by force. As for the borders, Dulles refrained from mentioning the idea of the "triangles" in the Negev, and sufficed with saying something vague about an arid piece of land in the region of "sentimental significance." He expressed his confidence in the possibility of reaching a compromise on the territorial issue, even if the parties had conflicting demands. As for the refugee problem, the secretary said that a solution must be found to end the distress of 900,000 refugees through resettlement "and – to such an extent as may be feasible – repatriation." To achieve this goal, more cultivatable land that could be given to refugees had to be created so they could make a living and establish homes there. Dulles also stated that Israel must pay compensation, but he was quick to stress that since Israel could not do so without assistance, an international loan might be possible for this purpose. The secretary of state claimed that

President Eisenhower would recommend that the United States loan a significant portion of the sum. Likewise, the president would recommend that America contribute money to develop water sources in the region and to implement projects for irrigation, "which would, directly or indirectly, facilitate the resettlement of the refugees."[55]

In this statement, the United States took the last decisive step on the long road towards the Israeli position on the Palestinian refugee question, and even gave this position official approval publicly. The repatriation principle was no longer presented as an essential, albeit secondary, element in resolving the refugee problem (as it had been presented in the secretary of state's June 1953 address to the nation); rather it was solely an option (whose implementation hinged on a host of factors).[56]

The day after Dulles' speech, the British government announced its unequivocal support for the key points he had made. It also declared its willingness to be a partner with the United States in extending security guarantees to the parties and granting monetary assistance to solve the refugee problem and take regional rehabilitation programs to fruition.[57]

Response to the speech in Egypt (and additional Arab states) was furious.[58] Yet it was not Dulles' words about the Palestinian refugees that generated their anger, rather it was the fact that Dulles had refrained from specifically promising Egypt a significant hunk of the Negev.[59]

Israel on the other hand feared that Dulles' remarks about a piece of arid land of "sentimental significance" were designed to deliver Egyptian demands for sovereignty over the Negev, as a whole or in part.[60] On the other hand, the part of the secretary of state's speech that addressed the refugee issue was met with a tremendous sense of satisfaction.

In a telegram to Prime Minister Sharett, Shiloah proposed that the Israeli response to the speech be measured and express Israel's willingness to examine it in detail. In his opinion, there were a number of positive tidings from Jerusalem's standpoint.[61]

The government deliberated Dulles' speech at length in its 28 August cabinet meeting. Sharett pointed out with undisguised pleasure the "progress [in Washington's stand], in support of [re]settlement outside Israel, while blurring the repatriation issue." He also expressed his great content with American willingness to help Israel shoulder the compensation burden. Yet American willingness to promote resolution of the compensation issue did not prompt Sharett to suggest to his ministers that they moderate Israel's compensation policy. He again reiterated the position adopted in the winter of 1952:

> If to pay compensation purposelessly, that means the flow of hard currency to the coffers of the Arab states. Should [we be] paying them while they carry out a boycott and blockade on us, when they cause us economic damages?

In contrast to Dulles' comments on the refugee issue, the secretary of state's comments on the territorial issue were the subject of harsh criticism by

228 *The Alpha Plan*

Sharett. In his view, Dulles had ignored the fact that there were already agreed-upon armistice lines, and his remarks created the illusion that the two sides had territorial demands, when only the Arabs were demanding territory, primarily in the Negev. Besides this, the prime minister expressed his disappointment with the linkage that the secretary of state had made between granting security guarantees and resolving the other problems. In discussion that followed the prime minister's remarks, the ministers agreed that the most positive part of the speech from Israel's perspective was the part that addressed the refugee problem.[62]

On the whole, the Israeli press welcomed Dulles' attitude towards the refugee problem. *Davar* surmised that for Dulles (i.e. for Washington):

> it was [now] clear that the solution to the Arab refugee problem lay in their settlement outside Israel, and that return of refugees to Israel was feasible by such a tiny extent that it couldn't make any significant contribution to resolution of the problem.

As for compensation, *Davar* said that Israel had "very well founded" counterclaims referring to war damages, economic warfare damages, and assets of Jews from Arab countries.[63] *Ha-Tzofe* felt that the United States' agreement "to help actively in resolution of the Arab refugee problem [through their resettlement] and guarantee of Israel's borders" constituted "a substantial political contribution and a serious stimulus for [peace]."[64] *Ha-Modia* stated that one could not deny "the positive facets" of the Dulles plan, "that it is, in practice, a very meaningful political innovation, particularly on the question of settlement of the Arab refugees in the Arab countries."[65] The party organ of the Progressive Party, *Zmanim*, concluded that "Mr. Dulles took a realistic approach in his remarks on return of a certain number of refugees to Israel, only if this is possible."[66] The political correspondent of *Lamerhav*, the party organ of the Ahduth Ha-Avodah party, noted with satisfaction that "it appears that the official position of the government of Israel that the refugees should be settled in the Arab states, with the assistance of loans and international funds, has fundamentally been accepted."[67] The ultra-Orthodox organ, *Shaarim*, focused at length on the hostile response to the American political plan, which in *Shaarim*'s view could be heard in the Arab camp. The paper said that if the Arabs respond negatively after Dulles expressed willingness "to give them huge sums of money to [re]settle the refugees," to carry out changes in the borders, and to reopen discussion of Jerusalem, this is a sign they are not interested in peace.[68] Exceptions to the rule in responses to Dulles' speech were registered in the mouthpieces of both extremes of the political spectrum: *Herut* on the right,[69] and the Communist Party's *Kol Ha-Am* on the left.[70] They both saw no positive tidings at all from Washington.

The independent newspapers devoted much space to the compensation issue. *Ha'aretz* viewed the idea of granting Israel international loans so it could bear the brunt of compensation "a productive idea." At the same time, the paper sought to underscore that there was also the problem of Jewish property frozen in Iraq.[71] The *Jerusalem Post* took the same stand.[72] *Ma'ariv* pondered why Israel must pay compensation to the Arabs at all, in light of the fact that they had launched a war against Israel in 1948 and had been waging economic warfare against it for the past seven years.[73] Comments in a similar spirit were published in *Yedioth Ahronoth*.[74]

On 29 August, a day after the cabinet discussed Dulles' speech, Sharett sent a telegram to Eban with instructions on how to respond in the American arena. The speech, Sharett said, "marks a great improvement that has occurred in the mood in the State Department towards us compared to the previous one [Dulles speech] in June 1953," especially in regards to the refugee matter. "Repatriation," explained the prime minister, "has been pushed onto the sidelines and in practice [re]settlement appears as the only solution." This and more: the Americans are adopting for the first time and officially the idea of a loan for compensation. However, some questions still remain unanswered in regards to this issue: (a) To whom would Israel pay? (b) Would the money be devoted to rehabilitation programs? (c) How would it be possible to pay, at a time when the Arabs' economic warfare continues? Sharett directed Eban to begin to discuss the compensation issue with the Americans, in order to clarify these questions. Likewise, he requested that Eban raise the issue of borders.[75]

In accordance with this directive, Eban and Shiloah met on 6 September with the assistant United States secretary of state for Near Eastern, South Asian and African affairs, George Allen. The two told Allen that Israel was impressed with the willingness of the United States to extend a loan so that the Jewish state could pay compensation, but it was important to ensure that the compensation would be used to resettle the refugees. Besides this, the Israeli diplomats warned that the issue of the Arab boycott and the maritime blockade still stood in the way of payment of compensation.[76]

Two days after that meeting, Sharett met in Tel Aviv with the American ambassador, Edward Lawson, also to discuss Dulles' speech. In the prime minister's opinion "two important axioms" had been set forth on the refugee issue: (a) "without pinning down the Secretary, the meaning of his remarks in practice is that [re]settlement, and not repatriation, is the practical solution"; (b) Israel's demand for an outside loan that would help it withstand payment of compensation had been publicly approved for the first time "by the United States on the President's authority." Sharett, however, felt that the secretary of state's remarks on compensation left several questions unsolved that required clarification: (a) Would the monies be earmarked for individuals or for a fund that would engage in settlement of the refugees? (b) Would Israel be forced to pay before the boycott and the blockade were lifted? (c) "What about Iraqi Jewish property?" Israel, Sharett clarified to his guest, had always declared that it would subtract from the compensation the value of the frozen property of Jews who immigrated to Israel from Iraq.[77]

On 9 September, the Prime Minister's Office released a special press release in response to Dulles' speech. As well as articulating disappointment with the

230 *The Alpha Plan*

secretary of state's remarks regarding the territorial issue, the press release expressed deep appreciation of Dulles' "realistic" and "refreshing" approach to the refugee problem. The announcement also hinted that the compensation settlement was liable to encounter difficulties due to several factors: the Arabs' economic warfare; freezing the property of Jews from Arab counties, and particularly Iraqi Jews; and the uncertainty that existed regarding the destination of compensation monies.[78] Sharett reiterated this position in a speech before the Knesset in mid October.[79]

A plethora of remarks by Prime Minister Sharett on the compensation issue testified that Sharett was in no hurry to resolve the issue, even now after the Americans had committed to assist in funding compensation and the possibility of payment could become a reality. There were two reasons for this. First of all, in practice Israel no longer had to adhere to the summer 1950 "exchange transaction" that the Conciliation Commission, the western powers, and several Arab states (particularly Jordan) had offered Israel: payment of compensation in return for resettlement of the refugees. The second part of this transaction – resettlement – had been "set in stone" in the international arena as the only solution to the refugee problem; Dulles' address was the most significant and telling evidence of this, all without Israel paying its part of the bargain. Thus, Jerusalem had no real incentive to pay compensation now, of all times. Second, from Israel's domestic standpoint, the ongoing economic pressure that the Arab states imposed on the Jewish state and escalation of security tensions of late made it impossible for Sharett to take a conciliatory stand toward the Arabs on the compensation issue. The prime minister, therefore, raised a variety of "questions" (in essence: demands) in regards to the compensation issue, leaving the impression that Sharett now sought to distance himself from any possibility of resolving this matter. The rigid position adopted by the prime minister on the compensation issue enjoyed the support of most of his ministers and, perhaps even more important, the support of the Israeli public, as reflected in the press.

Dulles' dramatic speech was never put to the test in the diplomatic arena. Security tensions, brewing just below the surface for quite a time, reached a boiling point, making it impossible to open full discussion (between Israel and its neighbours) of the elements raised in the Alpha document, as presented by Dulles in his speech.

On 27 September Nasser announced proudly that his country had signed a huge arms deal with (the Soviet satellite state) Czechoslovakia.[80] Egypt's dramatic move closer to the Soviet bloc[81] was met with dismay and rage by the western powers, but this didn't stop them from continuing to court Nasser all the more avidly.[82] They still hoped it would be possible, to one extent or another, to bring Egypt into the western defense treaty they had been nurturing since the beginning of the 1950s. With this objective in mind, they sought to take an Israeli-Egyptian settlement forward that would be based on the Alpha concepts and could satisfy Nasser.[83] The west rested this line of action, among other things, on the fact that even now, in the fall-winter of 1955, Cairo had not totally rejected some sort of settlement with the Jewish state.[84]

The Alpha Plan 231

Yet, as one scholar of the period remarked, Egyptian "moderation" was for the sake of appearances only. Before the Czech arms deal was executed, Nasser was interested in receiving military and economic aid from the United States and abolishing the Baghdad Pact and therefore was willing to show signs of flexibility in some points of the conflict that stood between Egypt and Israel.[85] Such deception continued after the arms deal was made public, in order to quell the western powers' fury.[86]

On 9 November 1955, British Prime Minister Anthony Eden gave a policy speech at London's Guildhall in which he discussed (among other things) the situation in the Middle East. In a last-ditch effort to put the peace initiative, as well as Nasser, back on track, Eden allowed himself to expose the principles that served as a foundation for the Alpha Plan far more than his colleague Dulles had. On the territory issue, he suggested that the sides reach a compromise between the Arab demands to return to the 1947 (Partition Plan) borders and Israel's stand that sanctified the cease-fire lines delineated by the 1949 armistice as borders. Eden said that the western powers would be willing to guarantee the borders agreed upon by the sides. As for the refugee problem, Eden promised that Britain and other powers would give "significant assistance," among other things financial aid, to resolve the problem.[87]

As could be expected, Eden's proposal in the territorial realm succeeded in squeezing positive responses from the Arab states, especially from Nasser's Egypt. No complaints were heard from the Arabs that Eden refrained from mentioning the repatriation principle.[88] In Israel, on the other hand, the speech in the Guildhall evoked great anger.[89] Prime Minister Ben-Gurion (who had retaken the reins of government on 3 November 1955) asserted in the Knesset that Eden's territorial proposal "lacked any legal, ethical or logical basis," and it "was likely to encourage and intensify the Arab countries' hostility [toward Israel] and reduce the chances for peace in the Middle East."[90] In a conversation between Foreign Minister Sharett and Secretary of State Dulles on 21 November, Sharett categorically rejected any thoughts that Israel would relinquish territory. He nevertheless responded in the affirmative to Dulles' request to answer him in writing whether Israel was willing to show flexibility on the other points in dispute between the Jewish state and the Arab states.[91]

As a result, the Israeli embassy in Washington composed a document that set forth the principles for an Arab-Israeli settlement; the draft was sent late in the month to Jerusalem for the perusal of the director-general of the Ministry of Foreign Affairs, Walter Eytan. According to the document, Israel would agree to discuss border adjustments with its neighbors, provided its own territorial contiguity would be preserved and there would be no demand that Israel relinquish territory of importance; Israel would agree to pay compensation to the refugees according to the terms it had already set forth in the past.[92]

In a telegram to Eban, Prime Minister Ben-Gurion asked to enter a number of amendments to the proposed draft. In regard to compensation, he sought to add the following condition: the Arabs would pay compensation to

232 The Alpha Plan

Jewish refugees from the 1948 war.[93] Here also, Ben-Gurion, like Sharett, was unwilling to pave the way for the Americans to resolve the compensation issue, particularly in light of the ongoing deterioration between Israel and the Arab states.

On 6 December, the embassy in Washington submitted to the State Department the memorandum containing Israel's proposals for settlement of the conflict between it and its neighbors. The paper included the changes that Ben-Gurion sought to enter. An hour after the memorandum was delivered, Sharett, accompanied by Eban and Shiloah, met with Dulles, Russell, and Allen to explain the Israeli proposals. In a discussion conducted later between Shiloah and Russell, the American official claimed that the Arabs were ready to agree to a political settlement that would be acceptable to Israel on all the subjects on the agenda, except the problem of the Negev. The Arab states were even reconciled to the fact that the refugees would not be repatriated, Russell stated, and what was now needed was to work diligently to find a formula that would preserve the Arabs' honor.[94] The Israeli peace initiative, however, didn't carry any real concessions, certainly no relinquishment of territory, and therefore it couldn't take the Alpha Plan forward.

On 8 December, in a last attempt to salvage the Alpha Plan, Russell shared with Shiloah all the details of the Plan as it had been formulated back on 10 March.[95] For Shiloah "this was a very frustrating moment." He expected to receive security guarantees from Washington, not demands for territorial or demographic concessions (regardless of how minor they might have been).[96]

A few days later, Sharett sent to Dulles Israel's response to the various proposals in the Alpha Plan. The foreign minister took issue with the two central elements that appeared in the plan: first, the idea of creating overland continuity between Egypt and Jordan through the Negev was rejected by Sharett hands down; secondly, as for the settlement of 75,000 refugees in Israel, he argued that in the best interests of both the Arab states and the Palestinian refugees and for the security of the region, the solution demanded resettlement in the Arab states. Israel, explained Sharett, had already contributed to resolution of the problem in several senses: (a) it had agreed to pay compensation; (b) it had accepted the Johnston Plan that allocated a large portion of the waters of the Jordan and its tributaries to the Arab states, by this enabling the settlement of refugees; (c) it had expressed willingness to unfreeze blocked bank accounts; (d) it had accepted the family reunification plan; (e) it had expressed willingness to assist Jordan in the economic-transportation realm (for example, with port rights in Haifa), thus easing Jordan's ability to absorb the refugees in its territory. The foreign minister asserted that Israel would not be able, in addition to all these burdens, also to absorb within it tens of thousands of refugees. Its economic and security straits would not allow this. Furthermore, if the refugees knew that there was even a tiny chance of returning to the homeland, their opposition to participating in any resettlement program would intensify.[97] To make this position via-à-vis the Alpha

Plan crystal clear, Sharett declared in a political debate in the Knesset at the outset of January 1956 that "Israel cannot under any circumstances [...] relinquish territory [...] nor to repatriate and settle refugees within it."[98]

At the same time, the foreign minister knew that Washington had adopted, in practice, many of Jerusalem's positions, particularly its position on the Palestinian refugee question. Alpha was, in the last analysis, solid proof of this. In deliberations in Mapai's Political Committee at the end of December 1955, Sharett said in this context:

> In light of my experience with the American Secretary of State [...] I can say that the gap between us [on the refugee question] has narrowed over the years, that is to say, America now demands from us a lot less than what it would have demanded, than what it demanded in practice at certain stages [junctures] in the past.[99]

At the same time that officials in the American State Department and their colleagues in the British Foreign Office were attempting to move the Alpha Plan forward (without much success), among officials at the Central Intelligence Agency (CIA) operating in the Middle East, a premise crystallized that a secret channel for talks between Israel and Egypt was needed. Those officials were greatly concerned that Egypt was rapidly slipping into the orbit of Soviet influence and that relations between Cairo and Jerusalem were deteriorating. These two factors prompted the CIA to recommend that President Eisenhower send a personal presidential envoy to Cairo and Jerusalem to open a secret dialogue between the leaders of the two countries.[100] The president accepted this proposal, and at the outset of 1956 he decided to send his personal friend Robert Anderson (Eisenhower's former secretary of the Navy and deputy secretary of Defense) on this mission.[101]

Before his departure for the region, Anderson met with the president and the secretary of state to discuss the situation in the Middle East. In regard to the refugees, it was agreed that action must be taken to resettle them, "including perhaps [absorption] of 50,000 in Israel." Anderson suggested the Sinai Peninsula as a possible place to resettle the refugees, as well as Iraq and Iran.[102]

Anderson's secret mission, which was given the code name "Gamma," was divided into two brief periods: one in the second half of January 1956, and the other during the first week of March. In talks with the heads of the two states, the American envoy presented the same principles for a settlement that had already been set forth in the Alpha document, particularly everything regarding the overland corridor through the Negev and the refugee problem.

The president's special envoy first met with Nasser on 17 January 1956. In their discussion, it became clear that the question of leadership of the Arab world worried Nasser much more than the conflict with Israel. He even refrained from talking in this first discussion about the territorial issue and

234 *The Alpha Plan*

refugees in detail.[103] Only in their second talk, two days later, was Nasser prepared to clarify these matters. In regard to the territorial question, he presented the consistent Egyptian position: demand for an overland corridor through the Negev that would link Egypt with the rest of the Arab world. As for the refugees, he stressed that no one in the Arab world could talk in their name; they needed to take the decisions regarding their fate. At the same time, in Nasser's opinion, no solution of the matter would be achieved unless Israel expressed willingness to accept the principle of repatriation. When Anderson remarked that such a move would flood Israel with masses of people, Nasser replied that in his opinion only a small percentage of the refugees would want to repatriate. In any case, he said, Israel must let the refugees choose between repatriation and compensation.[104] In their third meeting on 21 January, Nasser reiterated his position on the territorial issue and the refugees. He further clarified that direct meetings between Egyptian and Israeli representatives were out of the question; moreover, it would take time before a political agreement could be signed with Israel, since first there was the need to prepare public opinion in the Arab world for such a move.[105]

After he was updated about the talks in Cairo, Dulles wrote to Anderson that in regard to the refugee problem Nasser's position wasn't far from what was developed in the Alpha Plan. That is, Nasser, between the lines, was ready to embrace the resettlement principle.[106]

On 23 January, Anderson arrived for a round of talks in Israel.[107] In a meeting he held with the foreign minister, Sharett said that in his estimation the refugee problem was more resolvable than the Negev business. Anderson agreed with this diagnosis. Sharett suggested that Israel raise the number of refugees that would be allowed to return in the framework of the family reunification program, allowing Egypt to argue that it had obtained agreement for the repatriation of a certain number of refugees. Anderson replied that Nasser was not really worried about the number of refugees that would return, but demanded that they be allowed to choose between repatriation and compensation. Sharett clarified that acceptance of this demand would threaten the existence of Israel.[108] Ben-Gurion expressed a similar fear to the American envoy.[109] In addition, the two Israeli leaders clarified that they stood firm behind the need to conduct direct talks between Israel and Egypt to enhance the chances of achieving a political breakthrough.[110]

On 27 January, Anderson sent Dulles a summary report of his impressions from meetings in the region, particularly in Egypt. The main thing that bothered Nasser, said the report, was his political status in Egypt and realization of his national aspirations for Egypt in the Arab world. As for the conflict with Israel, Nasser was worried first and foremost about the Negev corridor issue and only "to a certain extent" with the refugees' freedom of some sort to choose between repatriation and compensation.[111] Mohamed Heikal, Nasser's friend and confidant at the time, verifies this analysis regarding the priorities of Egypt's ruler. Haikal wrote regarding the talks with Anderson:

Anderson traveled several times between Cairo and Tel Aviv. There were many problems [between Egypt and Israel] and many plans for overcoming them, but one of the biggest stumbling blocks – and it remains a valid argument today [as well] – was that there is no direct land transportation route between Egypt and the rest of the Arab world to the east.[112]

At the end of January, Anderson returned and met with Nasser to update him about his talks with the Israelis. The Egyptian ruler refused to reelaborate the issues that separated the two countries, and he again rejected the idea of direct talks with the Israelis.[113] Anderson related Nasser's position to Israel's leaders in a 31 January meeting. The American diplomat felt that the only ray of light in his talks was the refugee issue. From his meetings with the rival sides, Anderson concluded that both showed flexibility and hope with regard to that issue.[114] However, the Palestinian refugee problem was not the only issue at stake; between Cairo and Jerusalem there were other subjects of dispute about which the sides showed no conciliatory spirit whatsoever.

Thus, the American envoy's meetings with Nasser in early March ended like the previous ones, without any results. On 9 March, Anderson updated Ben-Gurion and Sharett with details of his meetings and immediately left the region.[115]

In a telegram to Dulles, Anderson claimed that Nasser feared that if he would try and take a political process between Israel and its neighbors forward, he would lose status in the Arab world.[116] A number of scholars claim that Nasser agreed to parley with Anderson not because he intended to reach a settlement with Egypt's neighbor to the east, but rather because he hoped that by stringing Anderson along, he could quell the bad feelings his arms deal with the Czechs had generated in Washington and gain time to absorb the new weaponry.[117]

A decade after his mission to the Middle East, Anderson talked about this historical episode with two Israeli diplomats. The American envoy stated that Ben-Gurion was prepared to pay compensation and to continue with limited family reunification to solve the refugee problem, but Egypt, like some other Arab states, was happy with keeping the problem alive and exploiting the existence of the refugee camps for propaganda purposes.[118]

It appears that the Alpha Plan, and its "heir" the Gamma Plan, both failed to achieve their objectives for several reasons:

1 At the time they were launched, Nasser had already established Egypt's senior position (and his status personally) in the Arab world, in the Muslim world, and among the non-aligned nations. He could not afford to join a western political initiative that championed conciliation with the Jewish state.
2 At a time when Israel's relations with the Arab states were deteriorating, the chance that Israel would take upon itself territorial and demographic

236 *The Alpha Plan*

concessions, even if they were smaller than those demanded in the past, was exceedingly thin.

3 The ability of the administration in Washington to be seriously involved politically in the Middle East at this particular point in time – 1955–6 – was very limited due to pending elections in America.

4 Washington didn't view itself as committed to the Alpha Plan to the same extent that London (which had initiated it) did, and the administration wasn't as enthusiastic about it. Thus, the Americans often demonstrated a lack of determination in nurturing progress in this direction.[119]

Notes

1 Benny Morris, *Israel's Border Wars, 1949–1956: Arab Infiltration, Israeli Retaliation and the Countdown to the Suez War*, Tel Aviv: Am Oved, 1996, pp. 346–9 (Hebrew).

2 David Tal, *Israel's Day-to-Day Security Conception: Its Origin and Development, 1949–1956*, Sede Boqer: The Ben-Gurion Research Institute, 1998, pp. 176–7 (Hebrew).

3 Ehud Ya'ari, *Egypt and the Fedayeen, 1953–1960*, Givat Haviva: Center for Arabic and Afro-Asian Studies, 1975, pp. 12–13 (Hebrew).

4 Tal, *Israel's Day-to-Day Security Conception*, pp. 238–9.

5 UKNA, FO 371/110783, V1056/7, Visit of Shuckburgh to Middle East, 28 October 1954.

6 Already in April of 1954, approximately six months before Shuckburgh's mission, British Foreign Secretary Anthony Eden had contemplated the idea of a joint British-American political initiative, the purpose of which would be the resolution of the Arab-Israeli conflict. See Scott Lucas and Ray Takeyh, "Alliance and Balance: The Anglo-American Relationship and Egyptian Nationalism, 1950–1957," *Diplomacy and Statecraft* 7(3), 1996, p. 641.

7 Nigel John Ashton, *Eisenhower, Macmillan and the Problem of Nasser: Anglo-American Relations and Arab Nationalism, 1955–1959*, London: Macmillan, 1996, p. 57; Mordechai Bar-On, *The Gates of Gaza: Israel's Road to Suez and Back, 1955–1957*, New York: St. Martin's Press, 1994, p. 84; John C. Campbell, *Defense of the Middle East: Problems of American Policy*, New York: Harper and Brothers, 1960, pp. 67–8; Michael B. Oren, *Origins of the Second Arab-Israel War: Egypt, Israel and the Great Powers, 1952–1956*, London: Frank Cass, 1992, pp. 111–13, Shimon Shamir, "The Collapse of Project Alpha," in Roger Louis and Roger Owen (eds), *Suez 1956: The Crisis and Its Consequences*, Oxford: Clarendon Press, 1991, p. 81.

8 UKNA, FO 371/111095, V1079/1, From Foreign Office to Washington, 4 November 1954.

9 UKNA, FO 371/111095, V1079/2, From Washington to Foreign Office, 5 November 1954.

10 UKNA, FO 371/111095, V1079/3, Beeley to Falla, 8 November 1954.

11 UKNA, FO 371/111095, V1079/4, Beeley to Falla, 17 November 1954.

12 FRUS, 1952–1954, IX, pp. 1695–1700, The Secretary of State to Certain Diplomatic and Consular Offices, 22 November 1954.

13 Neil Caplan, *Futile Diplomacy: Operation Alpha and the Failure of Anglo-American Coercive Diplomacy in the Arab-Israeli Conflict, 1954–1956*, London: Frank Cass, 1997, p. 82.

14 FRUS, 1952–1954, IX, pp. 1715–17, The Ambassador in Egypt to the Department of State, 11 December 1954.

The Alpha Plan   237

15 FRUS, 1952–1954, IX, p. 1718, The Ambassador in Syria to the Department of State, 13 December 1954.
16 FRUS, 1952–1954, IX, p. 1734, The Ambassador in Jordan to the Department of State, 23 December 1954.
17 UKNA, FO 371/110775, E10345/11, From Damascus to Foreign Office, 20 December 1954.
18 DEPI, Vol. 9, Document 178, G. Rafael to A. Eban, 20 April 1954.
19 DEPI, Vol. 9, Document 253, R. Shiloah to the United States Division, 17 June 1954, Note 1.
20 DEPI, Vol. 9, Document 507, A. Eban to the United States Division, 30 November 1954, Note 2.
21 DEPI, Vol. 9, Document 507, A. Eban to the United States Division, 30 November 1954.
22 DEPI, Vol. 9, Document 538, R. Shiloah to J. Herzog, 13 December 1954.
23 UKNA, FO 371/111095, V1079/10G, Notes on Arab-Israel Dispute, 21 December 1954.
24 As early as the end of November 1954, Israel's assessment was that the United States and Britain were putting together a peace plan that would commit Israel to territorial and demographic concessions: ISA, MFA 2451/13A, G. Rafael to the Israel Delegation in New York, 30 November 1954.
25 DEPI, Vol. 9, Document 549, A. Eban to M. Sharett and J. Herzog, 17 December 1954.
26 DEPI, Vol. 9, Document 550, A. Eban to M. Sharett, 17 December 1954.
27 Comay reiterated Israel's willingness to begin discussions about compensation with any appropriate UN institution, but noted that there were two main difficulties needed to be overcome: financing and the Arab countries' economic boycott of Israel – a boycott that had generated economic losses for Israel during the first six years of its existence which were no less than the value of the abandoned Arab property. See DEPI, Vol. 9, Document 488, A. Eban to M. Sharett, 19 November 1954, Note 3.
28 FRUS, 1955–1957: 1955, XIV, pp. 9–19, Memorandum Prepared in the Bureau of Near Eastern, South Asian and African Affairs, 14 January 1955.
29 Caplan, *Operation Alpha*, p. 90.
30 UKNA, FO 371/111095, V1079/9G, From Paris to Foreign Office, 17 December 1954; Caplan, *Operation Alpha*, p. 89.
31 A number of researches dealt with the "Alpha Plan." See, for example: Caplan, *Operation Alpha*; Oren, *Origins of the Second Arab-Israel War*; Shamir, "The Collapse of Project Alpha."
32 Boycott of firms in non-Arab countries that did business with Israel.
33 FRUS, 1955–1957: 1955, XIV, pp 98–107, Points of Agreement in London Discussions of Arab-Israel Settlement, 10 March 1955.
34 UNRWA, A/3686, p. 12.
35 ISA, MFA 3062/4, The Arab League and the Palestinian Refugees, 27 October 1952.
36 Britain and the United States had decided that Egypt would be the first Arab country they would approach concerning "Alpha" for several reasons: its influence, as the most important Arab country, on the other Arab countries; its alleged willingness to reach a political arrangement with Israel; the fact that it was the first of the Arab countries to sign an armistice agreement with Israel; and its close relations with the western powers, especially in light of the agreement regarding the British evacuation of the Suez Canal. See: Peter L. Hahn, *The United States, Great Britain and Egypt, 1945–1956: Strategy and Diplomacy in the Early Cold War*, Chapel Hill, NC: The University of North Carolina Press, 1991, p. 189. The two powers agreed between themselves that there was no reason to pressure Israel

238 *The Alpha Plan*

with respect to the political issue until it was established that Egypt was willing to accept "Alpha": see: Zaki Shalom, "From the PRO," *Iyunim Bitkumat Israel* 3, 1993, pp. 585–6 (Hebrew).

37 Caplan, *Operation Alpha*, pp. 106, 124; Evelyn Shuckburgh, *Descent to Suez: Diaries, 1951–1956*, London: Weidenfeld and Nicolson, 1986, p. 252.

38 On 28 February 1955, an IDF paratrooper force entered an Egyptian army camp at the Gaza city railroad station, destroyed buildings, and attacked the soldiers at the site. Eight paratroopers were killed, as well as 38 Egyptians. See Tal, *Israel's Day-to-Day Security Conception*, p. 181.

39 ISA, MFA 2402/14, Damages Caused by Infiltrators within Israel's Borders, undated; Morris, *Israel's Border Wars,* pp. 361–73; Ya'ari, *Egypt and the Fedayeen*, p. 19.

40 Geoffrey Aronson, *From Sideshow to Center Stage: U.S. Policy toward Egypt, 1946–1956*, Boulder, CO: Lynne Rienner Publishers, 1986, pp. 108–9; Ashton, *Eisenhower, Macmillan and the Problem of Nasser*, p. 50; Campbell, *Defense of the Middle East*, p. 54; Moshe Shemesh, "The Kadesh Operation and the Suez Campaign: The Middle Eastern Political Background, 1949–1956," *Iyunim Bitkumat Israel* 4, 1994, pp. 70–1 (Hebrew).

41 Bar-On, *The Gates of Gaza*, pp. 89–90; Caplan, *Operation Alpha*, p. 124; Ali E. Hillal Dessouki, "Nasser and the Struggle for Independence," in Roger Louis and Roger Owen (eds), *Suez 1956: The Crisis and Its Consequences*, Oxford: Clarendon Press, 1991, p. 33; Shemesh, "The Kadesh Operation," p. 72.

42 Hahn, *The United States*, p. 189.

43 FRUS, 1955–1957: 1955, XIV, pp 122–5, Memorandum of a Conversation, 26 March 1955.

44 FRUS, 1955–1957: 1955, XIV, pp. 129–33, Telegram from the Embassy in Egypt to the Department of State, 3 April 1955.

45 FRUS, 1955–1957: 1955, XIV, p. 141, Telegram from the Embassy in Egypt to the Department of State, 5 April 1955; Shuckburgh, *Descent to Suez*, p. 254.

46 ISA, Government Meeting, 28 April 1955, p. 10; Ashton, *Eisenhower, Macmillan and the Problem of Nasser*, p. 50; Meir Avidan, *Main Aspects of Israel-United States Relations during the 1950s*, Jerusalem: The Hebrew University, 1982, p. 27 (Hebrew); Caplan, *Operation Alpha*, p. 112; Steven Z. Freiberger, *Dawn over Suez: The Rise of American Power in the Middle East, 1953–1957*, Chicago: Ivan R. Dee, 1992, pp. 78, 92.

47 Caplan, *Operation Alpha*, p. 115; Zach Levey, *Israel and the Western Powers, 1952–1960*, Chapel Hill, NC: The University of North Carolina Press, 1997, pp. 7–34.

48 Eliahu Elath, *Through the Mist of Time: Reminiscences*, Jerusalem: Yad Izhak Ben-Zvi, 1989, pp. 67–8 (Hebrew).

49 ISA, MFA 2460/10, M. Erell to the United States Division in the Ministry of Foreign Affairs, 19 April 1955.

50 ISA, MFA 2460/10, M. Erell to the United States Division in the Ministry of Foreign Affairs, 19 April 1955.

51 FRUS, 1955–1957: 1955, XIV, pp. 170–4, Telegram from the Embassy in Israel to the Department of State, 5 May 1955.

52 ISA, MFA 325/16, E. Elath to M. Sharett, 2 June 1955.

53 Bar-On, *The Gates of Gaza*, pp. 90–1; Caplan, *Operation Alpha*, pp. 126, 129.

54 Caplan, *Operation Alpha*, pp. 131–8.

55 J. C. Hurewitz (ed.), *Diplomacy in the Near and Middle East: A Documentary Record, 1914–1956*, New York: Octagon Books, 1972, pp. 395–8.

56 Several weeks after his speech to the American Council for Foreign Relations, Dulles spoke to the political, security, and legal elites of the United States and reiterated the administration's position, which firmly established that the solution

to the Palestinian refugee problem would be based on the principle of resettlement. The secretary explained that in light of the fact that "the State of Israel was already packed-jammed with people, the demand of the Arabs for the resettlement of the refugees in Israel was altogether impossible to accept." The United States therefore proposed, Dulles stated, that it would invest funds in irrigating lands in Arab countries and have the refugees resettled in those areas: FRUS, 1955–1957: 1955, XIV, pp. 623–4, Memorandum of Discussion at the 262d Meeting of the National Security Council, 20 October 1955.

57 Bar-On, *The Gates of Gaza*, p. 92.

58 Muhammad Abd el-Wahab Sayed-Ahmed, *Nasser and American Foreign Policy, 1952–1956*, London: Laam, 1989, p. 114; Bar-On, *The Gates of Gaza*, p. 92; Caplan, *Operation Alpha*, pp. 141–2, 145–6; Herold Macmillan, *Tides of Fortune, 1945–1955*, London: Macmillan, 1969, p. 638.

59 The Egyptian response did not surprise the British. Some three weeks after Dulles' speech, they told the Americans that the Egyptian price for an arrangement with Israel would be a territorial concession in the Negev. This is "the crux of the matter," they asserted. Natan Aridan, *Britain, Israel and Anglo-Jewry, 1949–1957*, London and New York: Routledge, 2004, p. 144.

60 Abba Eban wrote about this in his memoirs: "Nothing could have irritated Israelis more than the reference to the Negev as having 'only' sentimental significance." Abba Eban, *Personal Witness: Israel through My Eyes*, New York: G.P. Putnam's Sons, 1992, p. 245.

61 ISA, MFA 2455/4, R. Shiloah to the Prime Minister, 27 August 1955.

62 ISA, Government Meeting, 28 August 1955, pp. 2–21.

63 *Davar*, 28 August 1955.

64 *Ha-Tzofe*, 28 August 1955.

65 *Ha-Modia*, 30 August 1955.

66 *Zmanim*, 28 August 1955.

67 *Lamerhav*, 28 August 1955.

68 *Shaarim*, 29 August 1955.

69 *Herut*, 28 August 1955.

70 *Kol Ha-Am*, 28 August 1955.

71 *Ha'aretz*, 28 August 1955.

72 *The Jerusalem Post*, 28 August 1955.

73 *Ma'ariv*, 28 August 1955.

74 *Yedioth Ahronoth*, 28 August 1955.

75 ISA, MFA 2403/14, M. Sharett to the Embassy in Washington, 29 August 1955.

76 FRUS, 1955–1957: 1955, XIV, pp. 451–3, Memorandum of a Conversation, 6 September 1955.

77 ISA, MFA 2474/4, Jerusalem to the Israel Embassy in Washington, 9 September 1955.

78 ISA, MFA 2446/3, Statement to the Press, 9 September 1955.

79 *Knesset Minutes*, vol. 19, 18 October 1955, p. 85.

80 Bar-On, *The Gates of Gaza*, p. 1.

81 Egypt's military ties with the Soviet Union first developed at the beginning of 1954. At the same time, its commercial relationships with the Communist bloc countries intensified. See Rami Ginat, *The Soviet Union and Egypt, 1945–1955*, London: Frank Cass, 1993, pp. 205–28, 230–8; S. Sinaisky, "USSR-Egypt Military Cooperation," *International Affairs: Russian Journal of World Politics, Diplomacy and International Relations* 59(2), 2013, pp. 150–3.

82 Abraham Ben-Zvi, *Decade of Transition: Eisenhower, Kennedy and the Origins of the American-Israeli Alliance*, New York: Columbia University Press, 1998, pp. 33–4; Ginat, *The Soviet Union and Egypt*, p. 220; Scott Lucas, *Divided We Stand: Britain, the U.S. and the Suez Crisis*, London: Sceptre, 1991, pp. 69, 77.

240   *The Alpha Plan*

83 Caplan, *Operation Alpha*, pp. 165–6.
84 FRUS, 1955–1957: 1955, XIV, p. 264, Memorandum of a Conversation, 24 June 1955; FRUS, 1955–1957: 1955, XIV, pp. 781–2, Telegram from the Embassy in Egypt to the Department of State, 17 November 1955; ISA, MFA 3772/50, G. Rafael to M. Sharett, 8 October 1955; Elmore Jackson, *Middle East Mission*, New York: Norton and Company, 1983, p. 28; Moshe Sharett, *Personal Diary*, vol. 4, Tel Aviv: Am Oved, 1978, p. 1200 (Hebrew).
85 Oren, *Origins of the Second Arab-Israel War*, p. 121.
86 Matthew F. Holland, *America and Egypt: From Roosevelt to Eisenhower*, London: Praeger, 1996, p. 73; Saadia Touval, *The Peace Brokers: Mediators in the Arab-Israeli Conflict, 1949–1979*, Princeton, NJ: Princeton University Press, 1982, p. 123.
87 Hurewitz (ed.), *Diplomacy in the Near and Middle East*, pp. 413–15.
88 Abd el-Wahab Sayed-Ahmed, *Nasser and American Foreign Policy*, p. 115; Lucas, *Divided We Stand*, p. 77; Shuckburgh, *Descent to Suez*, p. 301.
89 Elath, *Through the Mist of Time*, p. 72; Eban, *Personal Witness*, p. 245.
90 *Knesset Minutes*, vol. 19, 15 November 1955, p. 325.
91 FRUS, 1955–1957: 1955, XIV, pp. 793–6, Memorandum of Conversation, 21 November 1955.
92 ISA, MFA 2455/4, A. Eban to W. Eytan, 28 November 1955.
93 ISA, MFA 2455/4, D. Ben-Gurion to A. Eban, 28 November 1955.
94 ISA, MFA 2455/4, The Embassy in Washington to the Ministry in Jerusalem, 8 December 1955.
95 ISA, MFA 2455/8I, R. Shiloah to the Foreign Minister, 12 December 1955.
96 Haggai Eshed, *One Man "Mossad": Reuven Shiloah – Father of Israeli Intelligence*, Tel Aviv: Edanim, 1988, pp. 204–6 (Hebrew).
97 ISA, MFA 2455/4, M. Sharett to the American Secretary of State, 12 December 1955.
98 *Knesset Minutes*, vol. 19, 2 January 1956, p. 680.
99 ILPA, 2-26-1955-18, Political Committee Meeting, 27 December 1955, p. 4.
100 Caplan, *Operation Alpha*, p. 200; Holland, *America and Egypt*, p. 69; Shemesh, "The Kadesh Operation," p. 74.
101 Bar-On, *The Gates of Gaza*, p. 124.
102 FRUS, 1955–1957: 1 January–26 July 1956, XV, pp. 20–2, Memorandum of Conversation, 11 January 1956.
103 FRUS, 1955–1957: 1 January–26 July 1956, XV, pp. 28–36, Message from Robert B. Anderson to the Department of State, 19 January 1956.
104 FRUS, 1955–1957: 1 January–26 July 1956, XV, pp. 43–4, Message from Robert B. Anderson to the Department of State, 21 January 1956.
105 FRUS, 1955–1957: 1 January–26 July 1956, XV, pp. 47–50, Message from Robert B. Anderson to the Department of State, 22 January 1956.
106 FRUS, 1955–1957: 1 January–26 July 1956, XV, p. 50, Message from the Secretary of State to Robert B. Anderson, 23 January 1956.
107 For a description of Anderson's talks in Israel from an Israeli primary source, see: David Ben-Gurion, *Negotiations with Nasser*, Jerusalem: Israel Information Center, 1970; Gideon Rafael, *Destination Peace: Three Decades of Israeli Foreign Policy – A Personal Memoir*, London: Weidenfeld and Nicolson, 1981, pp. 48–52.
108 FRUS, 1955–1957: 1 January–26 July 1956, XV, pp. 58–9, Message from Robert B. Anderson to the Department of State, 24 January 1956; DEPI, Vol. 11, Document 54, M. Sharett to A. Eban, 26 January 1956.
109 FRUS, 1955–1957: 1 January–26 July 1956, XV, pp. 63–4, Message from Robert B. Anderson to the Department of State, 24 January 1956.
110 Ben-Gurion, *Negotiations with Nasser*, pp. 11, 19–20, 24–6.
111 FRUS, 1955–1957: 1 January–26 July 1956, XV, pp. 80–1, Message from Robert B. Anderson to the Department of State, 27 January 1956.

The Alpha Plan 241

112 Mohamed Hassanein Heikal, *The Cairo Documents: The Inside Story of Nasser and His Relationship with World Leaders, Rebels and Statesman*, Garden City, NY: Doubleday and Company, 1973, p. 56.

113 FRUS, 1955–1957: 1 January–26 July 1956, XV, pp. 86–8, Message from Robert B. Anderson to the Department of State, 28 January 1956; FRUS, 1955–1957: 1 January–26 July 1956, XV, pp. 88–91, Message from Robert B. Anderson to the Department of State, 28 January 1956; Ben-Gurion, *Negotiations with Nasser*, pp. 28–9.

114 FRUS, 1955–1957: 1 January–26 July 1956, XV, p. 122, Message from Robert B. Anderson to the Department of State, 1 February 1956; DEPI, Vol. 11, Document 76, J. Herzog to A. Eban, 7 February 1956.

115 DEPI, Vol. 11, Document 144, J. Herzog to A. Eban and R. Shiloah, 12–13 March 1956; Ben-Gurion, *Negotiations with Nasser*, pp. 45–8.

116 FRUS, 1955–1957: 1 January–26 July 1956, XV, p. 311, Message from Robert B. Anderson to the Department of State, 6 March 1956.

117 Michael Bar-Zohar, *Ben-Gurion: A Political Biography*, Tel Aviv: Am Oved, 1977, p. 1167 (Hebrew); Ofer Mazar, *In the Shadow of the Sphinx: Gamal Abdel Nasser and the Making of the Special U.S.-Israel Relations*, Tel Aviv: Ministry of Defence, 2002, pp. 24–5 (Hebrew). According to Yaacov Bar Siman Tov, the Israeli leadership itself suspected that Nasser was receptive to Anderson's mission only because he wanted to gain time: see Yaacov Bar Siman Tov, "Ben Gurion and Sharett: Conflict Management and Great-Power Constraints in Israeli Foreign Policy," *Middle Eastern Studies* 24(3), 1988, p. 347.

118 Zaki Shalom, "Gideon Raphael's Summary and Lesson From the Negotiations with Egypt, 1949–1955," *Iyunim Bitkumat Israel* 10, 2000, pp. 758–9 (Hebrew).

119 Freiberger, *Dawn over Suez*, p. 146; Shamir, "The Collapse of Project Alpha," pp. 85–8.

11 Three secondary aspects of the refugee problem where progress has been achieved

As covered in previous chapters, the main settlement aspects of the Palestinian refugee problem (repatriation or resettlement) and the main monetary aspect (compensation for abandoned property) remained unresolved throughout the period covered in the research at hand (1948–56). However, official under-standings were reached between Israel, the United Nations, and the Arab states on three secondary aspects of the refugee problem, bringing about a solution, at one level or another. In this chapter, these three aspects are examined in depth.

Blocked bank accounts

In their hasty departure from their homes, a small portion of the refugees left behind active bank accounts which included cash (and in some cases also stocks and bonds), as well as scores of safety-deposit boxes with valuables. The number of bank accounts was 6,047, and the total worth was estimated to be slightly over three million British pounds sterling (based on an exchange rate of one Israeli pound to one British pound sterling). Approximately 55 percent of all the Arab bank accounts – 3,343 accounts – held modest deposits of less than one hundred pounds per account. The value of 2,021 accounts ranged between one hundred and one thousand pounds per account, and 683 accounts held deposits of over one thousand pounds per account. Two British banks held 95 percent of the accounts: Barclays Bank held about 4,000 accounts, with a sum total value of 1.9 million pounds, and the Ottoman Bank held about 1,700 accounts, with a sum total value of 800,000 pounds. Several hundred additional bank accounts had been entrusted to a dozen other banks and commercial institutions.[1]

As already noted in Chapter 1, on 12 December 1948, Israel adopted Emergency Regulations Relating to Absentees' Property. These regulations, among other things, prevented Palestinian refugees from withdrawing capital assets they had left behind in the banks.

The issue of blocked bank accounts was first raised on the political agenda on 11 April 1949. The Conciliation Commission asked the Israeli government to declare that it had no intention of seizing these accounts and when peace

Three secondary aspects of the refugee problem 243

came they would be turned over to their legal owners.[2] Israel replied on 6 May that it indeed intended to do so.[3] The Conciliation Commission was satisfied with the answer,[4] but the Arabs were less pleased, and their representatives at the Lausanne Conference demanded that Israel unfreeze all the blocked bank accounts forthwith (that is, even before peace was achieved).[5] In late June, Israel announced that it was prepared to do so, provided Jewish accounts seized by the Arab states would also be freed. After a number of consultations between the Conciliation Commission and the Israeli and Arab delegations, it was agreed that a joint committee of experts would be established to address the blocked bank accounts issue, in which there would be an Israeli representative, an Arab representative, and a representative of the Conciliation Commission, who would serve as chair of the committee. The committee was charged with examining ways of achieving reciprocal release of frozen Arab and Jewish accounts in the countries of the region and presenting recommendations for a solution.[6] After a brief examination of the issue, it became evident that it was impossible to begin reciprocal and equal release of accounts, since out of all the Arab states, only Syria had blocked the accounts of Jews who immigrated to Israel, and the sum – several hundred British pounds sterling – was insignificant compared to the Arab blocked bank accounts.[7]

This initial failure didn't discourage the Conciliation Commission. Instead, it began to pressure Israel alone to release the Arab accounts it had blocked.[8] Israel decided to consent to the demand and on 15 February 1950, the rival sides reached a new agreement regarding the procedure: (a) the Arab states would pay Palestinian refugees with blocked accounts in their territories an advance of up to 100 British pounds sterling, in local currency; (b) an international financial institution would be established. It would receive from the government of Israel sums in negotiable currency equal to the sums that would be paid by the Arab states (to the refugees), after which the money would be transferred to these countries.[9] This arrangement, however, was not carried through. Besides technical difficulties placed in its path,[10] there were also political obstacles. The Arab states defiantly demanded that the payment on account be forwarded to them forthwith, while Israel reiterated that the money would be forthcoming only upon formulation of a comprehensive peace settlement.[11]

The chances of reaching a breakthrough on blocked bank accounts incurred a major blow following the Iraqi decision in March 1951 to freeze all the assets of Iraqi Jews who registered to emigrate, including their bank accounts. Israel quickly established a linkage between abandoned Arab property in its hands and the Iraqi Jews' assets.[12] This step made it all the more difficult for the Conciliation Commission to solve the problem of blocked bank accounts, since now a radical Arab state that had no intention of arriving at any settlement with the Jewish state – political or economic – had been added to the equation. Besides this, following the aggressive and brutal move by rulers in Baghdad, public opinion in Israel was even more adamant that Israel should make no concessions to the Arabs.[13]

244 *Three secondary aspects of the refugee problem*

At the Paris Conference in the fall of 1951, the Conciliation Commission proposed that Israel and the Arabs (that is, Syria) begin reciprocal release of blocked deposits. The Arab delegations declared their willingness to accept the proposal.[14] Israel agreed, provided that the proposed arrangement would also include the accounts of Iraqi Jews who had come to Israel (the Iraqi government was not a participant in the Paris talks).[15] The failure of the conference as a whole prevented further deliberation of the issue.

A short time after the 6th General Assembly convened, the United States began to show interest in the blocked bank accounts issue and pressed Israel to take steps to release them. As a result, Foreign Minister Sharett stated in an internal ministry memorandum that "on the question of the [Arab] deposits we will have to act with a certain [degree] of flexibility."[16] But this understanding did not prompt him to take any concrete steps. Washington continued its pressure and it demanded that the Israeli ambassador, Eban, tell the administration whether any sort of developments were afoot in Israel on this matter. Eban referred the question to the foreign minister,[17] and Sharett argued that it would be difficult for him to defend such a unilateral concession (to the Arabs) in government and among the public.[18]

The Americans did not give up. They "advised" the Conciliation Commission to focus on the Palestinian blocked bank accounts issue (as well as on compensation).

The commission, as expected, adopted this advice. In its meeting in the second half of April 1952, it decided to renew deliberations with Israel on the bank accounts issue.[19] For that purpose, the American representative on the commission, Ely Palmer, was authorized to approach the Israel representative in the United Nations and request that his government release all the Arab blocked bank accounts in Israel unconditionally.[20] On 5 May, Palmer met with Eban and presented the request to him.[21] In his reports to the Ministry of Foreign Affairs, Eban surmised that the party directing this move behind the scene was Washington, and if Israel would decline the Conciliation Commission's request, the Americans were liable to reduce economic aid to Israel. He therefore recommended that the government declare its agreement to begin discussion with the United Nations on the bank accounts problem and express readiness to unfreeze forthwith one million pounds. Eban rejected thoughts of creating a linkage between unfreezing the Arab bank accounts and unfreezing Jewish assets blocked by Iraq. It would be enough, he explained, that Israel simply approach the American government and request it assist in resolving the complex problem of Iraqi bank accounts.[22]

This development put the Arab bank accounts issue on the agenda of the government's 11 May cabinet meeting. Foreign Minister Sharett reported to the cabinet that the Americans were again pushing Israel to make progress on the issue. The foreign minister clarified:

They view it [unfreezing the Arab accounts] as the minimum of minimums; not border adjustments, not repatriation of refugees, but rather return of

Three secondary aspects of the refugee problem   245

a portion of the frozen accounts. They believe that we are surely not justified [in this matter] even less [justified] than in any other matter.

Sharett hinted to his colleagues that Israel could not leave the Americans empty-handed in this minor issue, since Washington had assisted Israel considerably, both economically and politically. He reported Eban's proposal to begin deliberations with the United Nations on the bank accounts issue and express willingness to begin with the transfer of one million pounds. At the same time, the foreign minister said, "We'll demand [...] from the United States to help us gain something from Iraq." Prime Minister Ben-Gurion announced that he supported Ambassador Eban's proposal with all his heart. In light of the unanimity between the two leaders, the government agreed unanimously "to give the Foreign Minister authority to decide and to commit in the name of the government in the matter of releasing [Arab] deposits that had been frozen in the banks [in Israel]."[23]

The next day, Sharett updated Eban regarding the government's decision and requested that Eban underscore to the Americans that, at this stage, the government of Israel could not offer more than one million pounds. Besides this, the foreign minister drew his attention to two prime limitations tied to this matter: first, Israel had a shortage of foreign currency; second, the public in Israel would find it difficult to understand such a gesture by the government if it did not see a similar step in this direction by the Iraqis regarding frozen Jewish assets in Iraq.[24]

On 15 May Eban met with Under Secretary of State for United Nations Affairs John Hickerson to update him on the government's decision. Eban said that, due to economic straits, Israel could not release all the blocked bank accounts at once, and therefore the process would take a long time and would hinge on Israel's foreign currency reserves. The sum that would be discussed would be one million pounds. Eban stressed that Israel did not seek to establish an official linkage between the frozen deposits of Iraqi Jews and the accounts of Palestinian refugees, but it saw a moral linkage between the two, and therefore it hoped that Washington would take steps to bring about unfreezing of the Iraqi Jews' accounts.[25] According to Hickerson's proposal, Eban had submitted a memorandum to the State Department on 2 June officially affirming the Israeli government's readiness to release some of the Arab blocked bank accounts.[26] Three weeks later, on 26 June, a memorandum to this effect was submitted to the Conciliation Commission.[27]

In the wake of this announcement, in mid July the Conciliation Commission began to discuss with Israel the freeing of the accounts. Over the next months, representatives of Barclays Bank and the Ottoman Bank joined the talks. In late November, procedures for releasing the accounts were finalized:

1   The UNRWA and the media in the Arab world would notify the Palestinian refugees of the campaign to release their blocked bank accounts in Israel.

246   *Three secondary aspects of the refugee problem*

2   Refugees with accounts who would be interested in unfreezing their deposits would fill out a claim form (in four copies) at one of the branches of Barclays Bank or the Ottoman Bank in Egypt, Jordan, Iraq, Syria, and Lebanon or would do the same at local UNRWA offices.

3   A central supervisory office would be established in Jewish Jerusalem by Barclays Bank and the Ottoman Bank. The refugees' requests would be transferred to this office through the auspices of the United Nations or by mail via Cyprus. One copy would remain in the supervisory office, and the other copies would be sent to the bank branch in Israel where the money had been deposited.

4   The bank branch would verify the claim, would reserve one copy for its own files, and return the two remaining copies to the central supervisory office in Jewish Jerusalem. The supervisory office would send the verified form to Israel's state custodian for absentees' property.

5   The custodian would compare the form against his lists and, if the details were correct, would send a permit to pay to the bank branch. The custodian's permit would oblige Israel's supervisor of foreign currency to unfreeze the sum in foreign currency.

6   The bank branch that received the permit would update the central supervisory office in Jerusalem and at the same time would prepare the sum approved for payment.

7   The central supervisory office would transfer the money to the account owner.

8   Israel's custodian would update the two British banks when the sum total of monies transferred approached the one million pounds sterling mark.[28]

On 4 December 1952, the government of Israel published a special communiqué regarding release of blocked Arab bank accounts in Israel. In the announcement, the terms of the agreement arrived at by Israel, the Conciliation Commission, and the two British banks were outlined briefly. It was also clarified that payment to each account holder whose claim had been approved would be up to 50 pounds sterling a month. The campaign would begin on 1 March 1953 (claim forms were available on that day) and would close on 31 May of the same year.[29]

Yet already at the outset the campaign encountered a crisis. Several refugee leaders, primarily in Jordan, voiced their opposition to the campaign – a position that garnered support among various circles and personages in the Hashemite Kingdom and beyond. Opposition was based on three prime points of objection: (a) Israel had deducted 10 percent of every Arab blocked bank account; (b) Israel would be seizing all sums beyond a ceiling of 500 pounds sterling per account; (c) signing on the claim form constituted recognition of Israel and its right to set terms regarding release of Arab abandoned assets.[30] In response, Israel claimed that 10 percent had been deducted in the past from all (Israeli) bank accounts, not just the deposits of refugees. It claimed that the deduction would be returned to every Arab bank account

Three secondary aspects of the refugee problem 247

that the custodian approved to be unfrozen. Israel clarified that sums over and above the 500 pound sterling ceiling had indeed been transferred to the custodian, but this act did not in any way mean they would not be released if the campaign for releasing blocked accounts continued. As for the refugee leaders' claim regarding the "recognition of Israel" implied by signing the claim form, Israel branded it "petty" and rejected it out of hand.[31] These explanations, however, fell on deaf ears. Refugee leaders continued to protest the campaign, and on 5 April 1953 Jordan's Council of Ministers was forced to instruct all the branches of Barclays Bank and the Ottoman Bank and all UNRWA offices to cease distribution of claim forms. The council also requested that refugees who had already received forms not submit them.[32]

In the face of such steps taken in Jordan to torpedo the campaign, Gideon Rafael registered his government's protest with the Conciliation Commission. In a conversation with the United States' representative on the commission, James Barco, Rafael hinted that Israel would need to reconsider the entire issue of releasing accounts.[33]

On 12 April, the Conciliation Commission published an announcement that the Israeli government had promised the commission that it did not intend to deduct 10 percent from unfrozen accounts and that transfer to the custodian of sums over and above the 500 pound sterling ceiling was a technical matter only that had no effect on the rights of account holders.[34] At the same time, the commission decided to send a special envoy to the region to try and overcome the crisis. After several weeks of deliberations with the Israeli and Jordanian governments and with the relevant banks, a satisfactory compromise was arrived at, and subsequently on 3 June the Jordanian Council of Ministers allowed refugees to again submit claims for their blocked accounts.[35] According to the compromise, the Conciliation Commission would append a special explanation to the original claim form that would clarify conditions for release of accounts; the Israeli government would commit not to seize sums over the 500 pounds sterling ceiling per account; and Israel would promise to return the 10 percent that had been deducted to every Arab account that was unfrozen. Besides this, several minor alterations would be made in the wording of the form to make it clearer and more understandable to claimants. Lastly, it was agreed that the cut-off date for receipt of claim forms would be 31 July 1953.[36]

By the end of May 1953, 933 forms for release of blocked bank accounts were received, of which 600 were approved. As a result of the compromise, the number of claims registered grew considerably. By 31 August (the new cut-off date for submission of claim forms) more than 3,200 forms had been received and about 1,600 were approved. The rise was not only due to Jordan's agreement to rejoin the campaign; it also reflected the willingness of refugees in Syria, Lebanon, and Egypt to submit requests. Although their own host governments hadn't joined the Jordanian protest, Amman's action had discouraged many refugees in these countries from joining the campaign.[37]

248   *Three secondary aspects of the refugee problem*

The first release campaign, which began in the spring of 1953, was consummated in the fall of 1954. After all the claim forms were processed, the number of blocked bank accounts approved for release stood at 2,761. The sum total of deposits unfrozen during that period was 742,145 pounds sterling (out of one million pounds sterling budgeted for the campaign).[38]

The issue of blocked bank accounts remained on the agenda even after the first release campaign came to a close. Already at the outset of 1953, the Conciliation Commission requested that Israel tell the commission what its plans were for release of "the second quota" of deposits.[39] Israel argued that it should not be asked to carry out an additional release campaign while Jewish assets in the Arab countries remained frozen and while the Arabs continued and even amplified their economic warfare against the Jewish state.[40] Israel's resolute stand,[41] as well as the crisis that accompanied the first campaign at the start, curbed subsequent attempts by the commission to continue to discuss this issue at this stage.

Nevertheless, the issue was raised again at the outset of 1954. Barclays Bank and the Ottoman Bank, and in their wake the government in London as well, began to show great interest in continuing the unfreezing of the monies. The British interest can be traced to the wave of legal actions filed by Palestinian refugees in Jordanian courts, particularly from mid 1953. Such refugees, who were unable or unwilling to wait for the gradual and limited release of their blocked accounts by Israel, demanded that the two British banks deposit in their Jordanian bank accounts immediately the equivalent of the full sum held by Israel. In many cases, Jordanian courts ruled in favor of the Palestinian plaintiffs. The two British banks feared that, besides the monetary damage incurred, if such suits were to continue their standing in the Arab states was liable to be undermined.[42] Against this backdrop, on 31 December 1953 the British government asked the Israeli government to continue to unfreeze blocked Arab bank accounts even after the close of the first campaign.[43] Israel clarified to the British that there was no point in discussing further releases when in the first stage only 700,000 pounds sterling had been unfrozen and paid, out of the ceiling of one million pounds sterling. Besides this, Israel argued that the Arabs had been apathetic towards the Israeli gesture and had demonstrated little willingness to collaborate. Moreover, they had increased their economic warfare against Israel and refused to release Jewish assets frozen in their countries. Under such circumstances, the government of Israel considered itself entitled to reject proposals that Israel launch another unilateral release campaign on behalf of the Arabs.[44]

Nevertheless, following a proposal floated by Barclays Bank in mid January 1954, Israel reconsidered its decision. Barclays Bank expressed its willingness to extend a loan to Israel for the sum total of all blocked deposits still in Israeli hands. In a consultation that took place on 31 January between Prime Minister Sharett and Minister of Finance Levi Eshkol, the latter said that Israel had much to gain from continuing to release the accounts, if the British bank would agree to give Israel a loan double the estimated value of blocked

Three secondary aspects of the refugee problem   249

bank accounts remaining in the hands of the state custodian for absentees' property.[45] The next day a meeting was held at the Ministry of Foreign Affairs in which Sharett took part, where it was decided to authorize Eshkol and his ministry "to try his luck with Barclays Bank."[46] Such a move, Israel surmised, would enable the country to preserve sound relations with an important financial institution such as Barclays Bank, while gaining economic benefits for Israel. Moreover, liquidation of the blocked bank accounts affair could improve Israel's political position in discussion of the refugee problem when the next General Assembly convened.[47]

Deliberations between Israel and Barclays Bank regarding the sum and the terms of the loan were drawn out, long, and exhausting, lasting months, and only at the outset of August did a breakthrough begin to emerge.[48] Six weeks later, on 26 September, Gideon Rafael, acting on behalf of the Israeli government, and R. Smith, the director-general of Barclays Bank, signed the agreement that set forth procedures for the release of the remaining blocked bank accounts and the amounts and the terms of the loan that Barclays Bank would extend to the government of Israel. The agreement stated that:

1 The government of Israel would release all Arab blocked bank accounts remaining in its hands, as well as the contents of refugees' safety-deposit boxes. Release procedures would be identical to those employed in the first campaign.
2 Barclays Bank would extend a loan of five million pounds sterling to Israel, divided as follows: (a) three million pounds sterling would be given as a loan for a period of ten years at 4 percent interest. This sum would serve to finance unfreezing blocked accounts; (b) one million pounds sterling would be given as a loan for a period of seven years at 4 percent interest. This sum could be used by Israel as it deemed fit; (c) one million pounds sterling would be given as a loan for a period of three years at 4 percent interest. This sum would be transferred to Israel's Electric Company.[49]

Following the agreement, on 16 November 1954, Israel published an announcement to the effect that it was beginning to release all blocked Arab bank accounts left in its hands and the contents of safety-deposit boxes.[50]

By 31 August 1956, the sum total of unfrozen accounts (stages one and two) stood at 2,633,175 pounds sterling – 87 percent of all blocked bank accounts. These monies were assets deposited only in branches of Barclays Bank and the Ottoman Bank. An additional sum of 300,000 pounds sterling (in some 350 blocked accounts), deposited in twelve banks and other commercial institutions, was not unfrozen at this time.[51]

In addition to the blocked accounts, securities valued at 70,000 pounds sterling were also released. Furthermore, 100 out of 142 safety-deposit boxes were opened at the owners' request, and their contents, totaling 130,000 pounds sterling, were transferred to their legal owners through the auspices of

250 *Three secondary aspects of the refugee problem*

the United Nations.[52] It is estimated that between 20,000 to 30,000 refugees were supposed to benefit from release of these deposits.[53]

Unfreezing of approximately 2.8 million pounds sterling in bank accounts, securities, and safety-deposit boxes made no impression on the Arab states or masses of Palestinian refugees. In their eyes, Israel had no legal, political, or moral right to hold these monies and it was required in any case to unfreeze them.[54] Moreover, the move Israel had made only touched a minor portion of the refugee population, and the overwhelming majority wasn't affected by it at all. A memorandum by the British embassy in Amman noted that in the Hashemite Kingdom, where the majority of the beneficiaries of the released bank accounts resided, there was no sense of gratitude towards Israel for the actions it had taken.[55]

Family reunification

In the second half of March 1949, Foreign Minister Sharett arrived in Washington for talks with heads of the administration about various issues of the Arab-Israeli conflict. Upon his arrival in the capital, the foreign minister asked the director-general of the Ministry of Foreign Affairs, Walter Eytan, to inquire as to Ben-Gurion's position regarding two aspects of the refugee problem: compensation and the reunion of broken Arab families.[56] Sharett surmised that he would face pressure from the Americans on the refugee issue, and he hoped to fend off pressure with several Israeli gestures. On 18 March, Eytan sent a telegram to Sharett containing the prime minister's position, saying Ben-Gurion "endorses [in] principle payment [of] compensation [...] says [:] do not mention reunion [of Arab] families unless question asked [about that]."[57] Sharett indeed refrained from mentioning this matter and as expected incurred heavy criticism from the Americans. They claimed that Israel wasn't willing to make progress on any aspect of the refugee problem, particularly on the repatriation question.[58] Members of the administration clarified to Sharett, and other Israeli diplomats, that the United States expected Israel to repatriate 200,000 to 250,000 refugees.[59] The Conciliation Commission for its part let Ben-Gurion know that the refugee problem – including the repatriation question – would stand at the center of the pending Lausanne conference.[60] After weighing the situation, the prime minister understood that it would be preferable to concede on the family reunification issue in order to win some sort of breather from the pressure placed on Israel on the repatriation question. Thus, several days prior to the opening of talks at Lausanne, Ben-Gurion updated the American representative on the Conciliation Commission, Mark Ethridge, that Israel would allow reunification of Arab families.[61]

The prime minister's agreement to embark on a reunification venture gave the official seal of approval to action that had been taking place up to this point in a limited and random manner. Issuance of entry permits for family reunification had been going on since the summer of 1948 by various bodies: government ministries, the military government,[62] and, at times, at the

Three secondary aspects of the refugee problem 251

discretion of individuals. This took place even though Israel's official and declared position was that refugees should not be permitted to return. Non-Israeli bodies also assisted in family reunification. Thus, for example, between the years 1948 and 1949 the Red Cross returned no small number of refugees, without Israel's permission and in defiance of its sovereignty.[63] The unofficial repatriation was particularly marked from Sinai (of Bedouin into the northern Negev) and from Lebanon (for the most part Christian Arabs).[64]

Foreign Minister Sharett and his people in the Ministry of Foreign Affairs claimed that throughout 1948–9 Israel had turned a blind eye to this movement of people on humanitarian grounds.[65] There is no question that there were army officers and civil servants in the Israeli establishment who were motivated by humanitarian concerns; others were pleased with the repatriation of Christian families that would increase the weight of Christians among the Arab minority; and there were those who sought to reward such Christian Arabs for their positive attitude towards the Zionist venture. The return of a person's relatives was, at times, also a "kickback" or reward that the military government handed out to collaborators – a practice that began in late 1948 and continued after the period under study, as well.[66]

Ben-Gurion's willingness to reunite Palestinian families was not lacking in provisos. On 5 May, Eytan told the Conciliation Commission that Israel agreed "to weigh positively" uniting refugee families torn asunder by the war, under two conditions: (a) their actual return would take place in the framework of a final peace settlement; (b) only first-degree kin would be permitted to return. The first proviso, however, didn't hold up for long; ongoing American pressure on the repatriation issue did its work. On 11 May the State Department made it clear to Israel that it expected that reunification of families would begin forthwith,[67] and on 29 May American pressure peaked: President Truman sent Prime Minister Ben-Gurion a sharp message demanding that Israel embark forthwith on repatriation of refugees and border alterations.[68] The Arab delegations to Lausanne only added to the steamroller of pressures put on Israel when on 18 May they demanded that the Conciliation Commission embark immediately on family reunification.[69]

The reply that Sharett transmitted on 8 June to the American president, on Ben-Gurion's behalf, stated that Israel was prepared to reunite Arab families who had become separated due to the 1948 war. Israel refrained from hinging implementation of such an action on achievement of a comprehensive peace settlement.[70] In the government's 14 June cabinet meeting, Sharett told his colleagues that Israel would permit Arab families to return their refugee kin to Israel, although "we will be very strict in choosing the people." The foreign minister made it clear that this referred to the return of women and small children.[71] Statements in a similar vein were made public in a speech Sharett delivered to the Knesset the next day.[72] In both instances, Sharett refrained from linking implementation of the campaign to achieving a peace settlement.

If Israeli policymakers still harbored qualms about the wisdom of this move – uncoupling family reunification from arrival at a comprehensive peace

252 *Three secondary aspects of the refugee problem*

agreement – cables from Israel's representative to the United Nations, Abba Eban, made the unavoidability of such a course clear. Israel is liable to face a serious political rupture with Washington if it does not permit the repatriation of family members, even before peace comes, he warned.[73] Two days later, Eban cautioned Eytan that Israel could not improve its position at Lausanne as long as it failed to carry out some of the gestures it had committed to make. If, for example, a campaign for family reunification were launched irrespective of a comprehensive settlement, it would impact greatly on Israel's position and generate better understanding of Israel's unyielding position on the core issue at stake (mass repatriation).[74]

The government's willingness to allow reunification of Arab families did not spark protests in the domestic political arena. Most parties were vehemently opposed to the repatriation principle, and from this perspective, they understood that there was no choice but to make a token Israeli gesture on the refugee issue in order to alleviate the pressure being placed on Israel regarding repatriation. Moreover, token repatriation (i.e. a trifling number) was not viewed as something that jeopardized the Jewish state's internal security, political and social identity, or economic situation. The prevailing mood on this matter can be seen in the responses of the party papers. Most supported the move. *Davar* praised the government's initiative on family reunification, saying it did not upset Israel's fundamental position of rejecting the repatriation principle.[75] *Ha-Boker* argued that internal security would increase as a result of the reunification of divided families, since it would solve the distress of many Arab families in Israel, who would, subsequently, be more loyal to the state.[76] *Ha-Tzofe* backed such an initiative, but demanded that the framework of repatriates not be expanded to include adult Arab men, so as not to undermine Israel's security.[77] In its editorial, the non-partisan paper *Ha'aretz* crowned the government's initiative "a humane step."[78] The only political entity that opposed the initiative was the right-wing Herut party. The party's paper, *Herut*, was unimpressed by the fact that the returnees would be women and children; it warned that such children "would reach draft age within a few short years."[79]

On 27 June, Eytan met with the chief secretary of the Conciliation Commission, de-Azcarate, and informed him that Israel had begun to make administrative arrangements to execute the reunification campaign. Success of the move, Eytan added, hinged on the willingness of the Arab states to cooperate in such an endeavor.[80] Four days later, Israel informed the governments of Egypt, Jordan, and Lebanon, through the Mixed Armistice Committees (an armistice had yet to be signed with Syria), about its intention to embark on a family reunification campaign. The Arab governments were told that the campaign related to the repatriation of spouses of Arab breadwinners and their small children. Israel proposed that checkpoints be established on the borders through which returning refugees would enter.[81]

By 7 July, the Ministry of Foreign Affairs formulated a procedure for family reunification, whose main points were as follows: (1) Arab family

Three secondary aspects of the refugee problem 253

heads residing legally in Israel could submit requests to admit to Israel family members situated beyond the borders of the state. Entrance would be permitted for: (a) spouses; (b) male offspring up to the age of 15; (c) unmarried daughters. (2) Heads of families would submit their requests to the district commissioner's offices in Haifa, Jerusalem, Jaffa, and Ramle. If the head of the family resided in an area under military government, he would submit the request to the local military governor's offices. (3) The request form would be printed in Hebrew and Arabic, setting forth the details of the head of the family and the particulars of the family members he sought to bring into the country. The head of the family would declare that the details were correct, accompanied by signed affidavits of two witnesses testifying to the truthfulness of the information. The forms would be reviewed by the security service. Following this review, the forms would be transferred to the Ministry of Immigration, where an interministerial committee would review the requests. Notification of approval or rejection would be sent by the Ministry of Immigration to the district commissioner's offices or to the local military governor's offices, to be delivered to the head of the family. The later could appeal negative decision.[82]

A short time later, it was set forth, with the agreement of the Arab states, that family reunification requests that had been approved by Israel would be transferred to the Arab authorities through the Mixed Armistice Commissions, and the authorities in the Arab states would try to locate the relatives among Palestinian refugee concentrations in their respective countries. The returnees would enter Israel through special checkpoints along the borders: Rosh Haniqra on the Lebanese border, the Mandelbaum Gate in Jerusalem, and a checkpoint on the border with the Gaza Strip. With their entrance into Israel, returnees would be accompanied by representatives of the Ministry of Immigration, who would register them in the Population Registry and issue them Israeli identity cards.[83] Reunification requests could be submitted between 1 August 1949 and 31 March 1950 (in the end, the cut-off date was extended to 30 April 1950).[84]

According to a draft declaration formulated on 5 August 1949, returning refugees were required to declare that they were peace-loving, and in exchange for the Israeli government's willingness to accept them as citizens in its territory, they asserted that they sought the wellbeing of the state and promised to obey its (Israel's) laws and the directives of the government. They also committed themselves "to fight the enemies of the state and [be prepared] to give my life for it" and proclaimed that they would defer any claims to their abandoned property until the government considered it fitting to examine this problem.[85]

Israel did not set an official quota or publish one regarding the number of refugees it was prepared to allow entrance under the family reunification campaign. There appear to be two reasons for this: first, the authorities didn't know how many people were involved, since no census on this subject had been taken among the 165,000 Arabs in the country; second, Israel sought to

254 *Three secondary aspects of the refugee problem*

conceal the fact that the family repatriation campaign was not designed to allow repatriation on the scale demanded by the Americans or the United Nations. Rather, it would be a symbolic return.

The first secretary at the Israeli embassy in Washington, Uriel Heyd, held that the refusal of the government to give "an actual figure" of the number of returnees undermined the chances of improving Israel's image of rigidity in the United States.[86]

As the campaign took shape, various estimates were heard regarding the expected number of returnees. As noted in Chapter 2, in the government's 5 July 1949 cabinet meeting, Sharett clarified that "the 100,000 Proposal" included some ten thousand refugees who would return under family reunification.[87] In a conversation at the end of June with a senior official in the British Foreign Office, the first secretary at the Israeli legation in London, Mordecai Kidron, estimated that "many thousands" could be expected to return.[88] Esther Herlitz, the acting director of the United States Division in the Ministry of Foreign Affairs, estimated during a conversation she conducted with representatives in the American embassy in Tel Aviv on 6 July that less than 25,000 refugees would return to Israel.[89] An internal report of the Ministry of Foreign Affairs, apparently from late 1955, claimed that at the outset the government assumed that the family reunification campaign would permit the entrance of only some 4,000 refugees.[90]

Either way, these numbers were relatively high compared to the number of refugees between May 1948 and August 1949 that the State of Israel had permitted to return and reunite with kin who had remained in Israel (in what was termed "special cases") – one thousand only.[91]

Implementation of the family reunification campaign was delayed by several months. Arab delegations to Lausanne claimed that Israel must broaden the framework of the campaign so as to include other family members (brothers and sisters, aunts and uncles, cousins).[92] This demand was an expression of the traditional Arab perception regarding the concept of "family." In Arab society the family unit was much larger than the nuclear family recognized by Israeli-Jewish society and the west; it included a pair of parents, their married sons (and their wives and children), as well as their unmarried sons and daughters. Sometimes, a father's "household" included tens and even hundreds of souls. The extended family was particularly suited to village life since lives were lived for the most part within the confines of the village framework, where all members of the family contributed to agriculture and other manual labor. Thrust beyond the village framework, lacking a large group of relatives upon whom one could depend economically and socially, the individual refugee was isolated, helpless, and subject to the vicissitudes of others.[93] It is clear that decision-makers in Israel (certainly in the Ministry of Minorities, in the bureau of the advisor on Arab affairs, and among staff in the military government) were familiar with the Arab family structure. However, it seems that they preferred to ignore it in order to prevent a flood of returnees and because they opposed the return of adult males, who constituted potential combatants.[94]

Three secondary aspects of the refugee problem 255

Israel categorically rejected the Arab demand to broaden the scope of the campaign. Sharett clarified to the Israeli delegation at Lausanne that under no circumstances should discussion of the family reunification question be opened, "not with the Commission and not with the Arab delegations." He asked the delegation to explain that the reunification offer was based on "humanitarian grounds" and that it was not part of the negotiations taking place at Lausanne. Sharett wrote:

> If the Arab states refuse to cooperate because they feel the government of Israel must return other categories of kin in the framework of this program, the responsibility will be laid upon them for the non-return of those categories that the government of Israel is prepared to accept.

In his opinion, the refusal of the Arabs to cooperate should be publicized and denounced.[95]

The Conciliation Commission proposed to the Israeli delegation a formula that it felt could satisfy both sides: all the refugees who before the outbreak of hostilities in Palestine had been economically dependent on the head of the family were entitled to family reunification, except those who had actively participated in the war. The delegation's representative, Eliahu Sasson, promised to pass the proposed formula on to his government. Sharett, however, viewed this proposal as an attempt by the commission to increase the number of refugees who would be returned and therefore rejected it.[96]

At the outset of October, a representative of the Conciliation Commission met with representatives of the Ministry of Foreign Affairs in Tel Aviv to clarify why the family reunification campaign had not yet been launched, four months after Israel approved it. His hosts explained that Israel had already made all the preparations to accept family members situated in the Arab states, and the relevant parties had a list of persons whose entrance had been approved. The commission representative was told that "the delay in implementation" was not Israel's fault, "rather it was the fault of the Arab governments that to date hadn't show any willingness to establish the necessary machinery for returning these refugees."[97] Such foot-dragging by the Arab states was prompted by their anger at Israel for not broadening the framework of the campaign.

In the closing days of 1949, after the Arab states failed in their attempts to change Israel's position or convince the Conciliation Commission that their claims were justified, Lebanon began to cooperate with the reunification campaign. On 22 November, Israeli radio reported that "the arrangements for the return of Arab families from the Lebanon are being put in place" and that "[Arab] residents [of Israel] whose request to return family members were approved, are receiving notification of such from the Ministry of Immigration."[98] Three weeks later, towards mid December, the first group of 72 Arab refugees arrived in Israel through the Rosh Haniqra checkpoint.[99] Lebanon, which according to its consistent policy held that the Palestinian refugees must be

256 *Three secondary aspects of the refugee problem*

removed from its territory, cooperated with Israel in the family reunification campaign throughout the period under study.[100] Days later, Jordan also joined the campaign. On 22 December, 51 Palestinian refugees crossed into Israel through the Mandelbaum Gate in Jerusalem.[101] Among the Egyptians, things progressed at a snail's pace; the first group of refugees from the Gaza Strip entered Israel only on 14 February 1950,[102] and a short time later, Cairo pulled out of the business and refused to locate refugees in its territory.[103] Syria refused to take any part in the campaign, and approximately 300 requests received by the outset of 1952 from Israeli Arabs requesting transfer to Israel of their relatives residing in Syria remained unanswered.[104] There is no documentation in the archives as to why these two Arab countries refused to cooperate in this endeavor. It is possible that they did not feel there was any urgency to make progress for a solution to the problem, since the presence of the refugees did not place any economic, political, or social burden on them as was the case in Lebanon and Jordan. Furthermore, at the time (December 1949) Syria was in the midst of a military coup that brought to power Colonel Adib al-Shishakli, and the military junta, it seems, was hardly concerned with this issue during such tumultuous times.

By the 30 April 1950 cut-off date for the campaign, it became evident that Israel's Arab citizens had submitted requests for the repatriation of 3,200 relatives. The Ministry of Immigration approved the entrance to Israel of 3,113 persons according to the following distribution: 1,412 from Lebanon, 1,021 from the Kingdom of Jordan, and 680 from Egypt. Out of this number 1,960 refugees actually crossed over into Israel: 1,070 from Lebanon, 670 from the Kingdom of Jordan, and 220 from Egypt (the overwhelming percentage of them from the Gaza Strip). It appears that Israeli Arabs did not take full advantage of the option to bring their family members back to Israel. The prime minister's advisor on Arab affairs, Yehoshua Palmon, believes one of the prime reasons for this behavior was that "many of the [Israeli] Arab residents had not yet weighed then whether to concentrate their family in Israel or wait to see what tomorrow would bring."[105]

The Israeli Arabs were given the opportunity to bring their dear ones to Israel even after the 30 April. As a humanitarian gesture, the Israeli government agreed to review requests that were received after the official cut-off date, and thus between May 1950 and September 1952, another 1,358 refugees entered Israel under the auspices of the family reunification campaign.[106] All told, from December 1949 to September 1952, more than 3,300 Palestinian Arab refugees arrived in Israel.

In the spring-summer of 1950, Israel agreed to allow another two categories of refugees to return. In late April, Palmon announced the foreign minister's decision to allow refugees who were not of Arab extraction (Armenians, Greeks, Baha'is) to enter the country if there was no security consideration that would prevent this; at the same time a number of persons from Nazareth whose sons were students studying primarily in Beirut asked permission for their sons to enter the country. In June, the advisor for Arab affairs announced that the authorities had agreed to permit the return of students who had left the country before 29 November 1947 (the beginning of the Arab-Israeli War) and whose families resided in Israel. Here as well, permission hinged on a security check.[107] Besides these categories, over time mixed couples (for the most part Jewish women married to Arab men) were allowed to return. There were only several dozen such cases.[108] At the end of February 1952, the government decided to make a one-time gesture, allowing 150 Arab men to enter the country whose wives and fiancées were left on their own in Israel.[109]

Such gestures under the family reunification program made little impression on the Arab side. In the summer of 1952, Jordan threatened to cease its participation in the campaign, claiming that Israel was not expanding in any substantive manner the categories of refugees permitted to return;[110] but in the end the Jordanians didn't carry through with their threats.

The Palestinian Arab public in the State of Israel was also dissatisfied with the demographic limitations placed by authorities on the family reunification campaign, and from 1951 (that is, after the official cut-off date of the campaign), Arab Knesset members raised demands to continue officially family reunification and expand its framework. They raised parliamentary queries from the floor addressed to the Ministry of Interior regarding Arab citizens who encountered difficulties bringing their kin to Israel under the campaign.[111]

The pressure of the Arab community in Israel, which won the support of left-wing elements, and the need to continue to present an Israeli contribution to solving the refugee problem, even in a token fashion, against the backdrop of the repatriation issue being sidelined, led the government to renew the family reunification campaign. On 15 September 1952, the campaign was officially renewed. The cut-off date was set at 31 March 1953, but it was extend until 30 June. At this point Israel added more refugee categories permitted to enter Israel: (a) fiancées of Israeli-Arab men; (b) male offspring who prior to 1 June 1952 were less than 17 years of age; (c) a limited number of Arab students over age 17, studying abroad.[112]

Due to the lack of interest that Damascus and Cairo had demonstrated in the first stage of the campaign, the Interior Ministry turned to Lieutenant Colonel Haim Gaon, the IDF officer in charge of the Mixed Armistice Commissions, requesting he "query the chairs of the Syrian and Egyptian delegations whether today they were willing to cooperate with us in the framework of family reunification."[113] The answers were negative. The two countries decided not to take part in this campaign as well. Jordan was inclined to follow Syria and Egypt, and from 1954 forward, it almost didn't participate in the family reunification scheme. Refugees only continued to arrive from Lebanon, although the frequency dropped and the numbers waned.

Theoretically, the second stage of the family reunification campaign was supposed to end towards the end of June 1953, but in practice continued longer, without any set limit. According to a May 1955 directive from the

258   *Three secondary aspects of the refugee problem*

Ministry of Interior, two additional categories were added: (a) parents above the age of 60; (b) husbands who were defined as "chronic infiltrators" whose wives and children legally resided in Israel.

In January 1955, Prime Minister Sharett announced that the policy of family reunification would continue and that further easing of demographic restrictions would take place "in keeping with [prevailing] circumstances."[114]

All in all, from the beginning of the family reunification campaign in late 1949 up until the outset of 1956, Israel issued approximately 5,200 entrance permits for refugees. Approximately 40 percent of the permits – 2,045 – were given to Lebanon (which had absorbed only 10 percent of the Palestinian refugee population), while 1,478 permits were given to Jordan – a negligible number compared with the size of the refugee population in the kingdom. Close to 85 percent of the permits (4,313) were issued in the first two years of the campaign, between December 1949 and December 1951. About 1,500 permits out of all those issued were given to non-Arabs: Armenians, Greeks, Baha'is, Druze, and Circassians. All in all, 4,300 refugees used their right to enter Israel, during the period under study.[115]

Internal refugees

Out of the 156,000 Palestinian Arabs that remained in Israel at the close of the 1948 war, approximately 28,000 were defined as "internal refugees."[116] The term designated primarily citizens who could not go back to the places where they had resided prior to the outbreak of hostilities and were forced to resettle elsewhere in the State of Israel. Over time, they came to be called "Present-Absentees." The expression characterized the anomaly of their circumstances: "Absentees" in terms of their property, "Present" from the standpoint of state machinery. The Arabs vehemently opposed the definition "Absentees," since they resided in the country. They viewed this as a form of discrimination, repression, and a quasi-legal attempt by the government to sanitize its seizing of their lands.[117]

Internal refugees were comprised of four sub-groupings:

1 Arabs who when their places of residence were overrun by the IDF had fled elsewhere – to areas under enemy control that afterwards became part of the State of Israel;
2 Arabs residing in the "Triangle" that was annexed to Israel as a result of the Rhodes Agreements. These individuals became Absentees in regard to their lands, which from the beginning were in the hands of the state;
3 Arabs who returned to the country after the war, whether with permission (for example, under the family reunification campaign) or without permission (infiltrators who were allowed to stay);
4 Arab citizens who were evacuated by force from their settlements during the war or in the immediate aftermath due to security needs or for development and Jewish settlement purposes.[118]

Three secondary aspects of the refugee problem 259

Ninety percent of the internal refugees were originally from the north,[119] most from villages in the Galilee.[120] Part came from areas along the coast of the cities of Haifa and Acre.[121] Approximately 90 percent of the internal refugees in Israel were Muslims, the remainder Christians.[122] Most of the refugees were absorbed in Arab settlements that remained standing after the war, almost all of them in the Galilee region. Some 3,000 to 6,000 persons settled in Nazareth.[123] About a thousand persons each settled in Acre and Tamra; 800 in Majd al-Kurum; 600 in al-Reine; and several hundred were absorbed by other villages in the Galilee.[124] Refugees also found their way to Arab settlements in the "Triangle" and in Wadi Ara.[125] According to a June 1952 Ministry of Foreign Affairs report, at the same time, internal refugees were absorbed in some 67 points of settlement, the overwhelming majority in Arab settlements, a few in mixed cities (Jewish-Arab).[126] A very small number of refugees were settled by the authorities in abandoned Arab villages, particularly in the Galilee.[127] Several hundred refugees established new unauthorized Arab settlements, particularly in the north of the country. Over time, such places came to be designated "unrecognized settlements."[128]

Already in the course of the 1948 war the internal refugees issue was on the agenda, albeit still not with its full weight. Behor Shitreet, who shortly would be appointed Minister of Minorities in the provisional government, told his colleagues in the leadership that an orderly machinery needed to be established that would deal with the Arab population remaining in the Jewish state, including the internal refugees. A memorandum to this effect was submitted by Shitreet to Ben-Gurion on 10 May 1948. Yet dire wartime conditions made it impossible for the country's leaders to take the time to address the issue.[129] They were able to give attention to the question only in November 1948 after battles in the north subsided and after they became aware that the situation in many of the Arab settlements within the country was deplorable. The government, consequently, decided to establish a special committee that would handle decisions and supervise the transfer of internal refugees from one place to another, according to various needs. The committee was comprised of Minister Shitreet, the director-general of the Ministry of Minorities, and representatives from the Ministries of Defense, Interior, Labor, and Agriculture. The committee gathered data on Arab refugees concentrations in the country and examined ways to resettle them. Most of their efforts focused on returning to Haifa refugees from the port city that had fled and taken shelter in Nazareth.[130]

On 11 September 1949, Foreign Minister Sharett ordered the establishment of a committee of experts to examine the internal refugees question. He gave the mission to three individuals: Jewish National Fund official Yosef Weitz, Ministry of Foreign Affairs Middle East Division official Ezra Danin, and advisor to the Government of Israel on Land Issues Zalman Liff.[131] This committee, which dealt with policy formulation, amalgamated at the end of 1949 with another committee that operated under the auspices of the Ministry of Agriculture and focused on finding practical solutions (settlement and

260 *Three secondary aspects of the refugee problem*

employment) to the problem. The two bodies became the Refugee Rehabilitation Authority.[132] In its four years of existence, the authority was responsible for formulation of policy on internal refugees and to a certain extent for execution of that policy. Over time it focused on finding places to settle the refugees, but its achievements on this score were meager. Throughout its period of operation, the authority was able to rehabilitate a small percentage of the internal refugees: some 1,500 persons.[133] There were two reasons for this. First of all, the authority lacked executive authority to implement policy and suffered from lack of interest on the part of the cabinet.[134] Second, the refugees themselves refused to accept the alternative living places they were offered[135] and repeatedly demanded that they "be allowed to return to their former places of residence."[136] The government, however, refused on security grounds and settlement considerations (detailed below) and turned down such demands.

Until the establishment of the UNRWA on 1 May 1950, several international charity organizations operated in Israel allocating food and clothing to internal refugees.[137] Several months after the UNRWA began its work in Israel, the government approached the agency and proposed that the state gradually assume responsibility for the refugees' welfare.[138] To a large extent, this proposal was raised due to the government policy that sought to prevent, as much as possible, creation of a separate framework for the internal refugees, in contrast to the rest of the Arab population. The leadership was not interested in creating a situation where there was a constant reminder of the Arab refugee problem within Israel's borders, due to the close linkage that existed between this issue and the question of land ownership and the return to the abandoned villages. Therefore, the population census made no distinction between an Arab refugee and an Arab permanent resident, and authorities were unwilling to recognize independent (self-organized) refugee organizations or to carry on a dialogue with them.[139]

Israel's proposal that the state gradually take over welfare functions was acceptable to the UNRWA. In an 8 December 1950 meeting with representatives of Israel, the agency presented a plan to close down its operations in Israel. The agency would continue to provide aid to the internal refugees until 1 April 1951. After that date, UNRWA aid would stop entirely. During this period, hard welfare cases among the refugees would be transferred gradually to Israeli authorities. The UNRWA would give Israel two dollars a month for every such refugee. Israel would be given a one-time lump sum from one to one and a half million dollars by the UNRWA earmarked for "integration of the [internal] refugees in the Israeli economy." The money would be used for housing construction and employment projects.[140] The UNRWA's plan, however, was never realized and remained on paper. Several weeks after it was raised, the agency came to the conclusion that fiscal difficulties would not enable the agency to withstand the financial commitments it had just proposed to Israel.[141]

In the fall of 1951, transfer of responsibility for internal refugees to Israel authorities was again raised. In a meeting with Foreign Minister Sharett at

Three secondary aspects of the refugee problem 261

the outset of September, Blandford hinted that Israel should agree that the foreign aid to the internal refugees be stopped since they were considered regular citizens. The State of Israel, he argued, could not discriminate between them and the rest of its subjects. The director of the UNRWA clarified to Sharett that the agency's proposal at the close of the previous year was no longer on the agenda. In response, Sharett promised that the matter would be brought up for discussion among policymakers in Israel.[142]

Although the new UNRWA proposal carried no monetary benefit, Israel couldn't reject it. First of all, Israel was still interested in abolishing the sub-sector of Arab refugees. Second, shelving the repatriation concept and establishing the principle of resettlement, as expressed in the 6th General Assembly, behooved Israel to contribute, no matter how modestly, to resolution of the refugee problem (as it had done in regard to family reunification and blocked bank accounts), so as not to leave the impression that the Arab states were alone carrying the entire burden.[143] Such an impression was liable to lead Arab leaders to refuse to cooperate with the three-year Blandford Plan, on the agenda at the time.[144]

In London, and in Washington as well, there were worries about the fate of the three-year Blandford Plan, if an Israeli gesture on the refugee issue were not forthcoming. In a discussion that the British foreign secretary, Eden, conducted with his Israeli counterpart, Sharett, in late November 1951, Eden asked whether Israel couldn't "at least" take upon itself responsibility for handling its internal refugees.[145] At the same time, American officials clarified to their Israeli interlocutor that the United States expected gestures from Israel on two aspects of the refugee problem: to take care of internal refugees and to release blocked bank accounts.[146]

In addition, Washington was concerned about the cost of the UNRWA's operations. The Americans, who were the primary underwriters of the agency's operations, were interested in reduction, small as it might be, in the agency's expenditures.[147]

Due to this state of affairs, Minister of Finance Eliezer Kaplan announced that he would not oppose abolition of UNRWA support for the internal refugee population if Sharett would propose this.[148] Ben-Gurion also supported this idea, arguing that the internal refugees were Israeli residents and therefore "the state needs to take care of their livelihood, and not the United Nations."[149] Yet, despite this firm approach, Israel was in no hurry to update the United States and the United Nations about its position, and its representatives in Washington sufficed with merely dispersing hints among American officials about the willingness of the Israeli government to tend to the needs of the refugee population within its domain.[150]

In mid April 1952, Ministry of Foreign Affairs official Michael Comay proposed to Sharett that he declare officially and clearly Israel's readiness to care for the internal refugees. In Comay's estimation, the UNRWA and the State Department should be informed right away "that we agree in principle to exempt UNRWA from all additional responsibility for these refugees, and

262 *Three secondary aspects of the refugee problem*

that we are prepared to accept them within four months, by the end of August." Such a move was desirable, said Comay, for several reasons: (a) this would be an answer to the American pressure over the issue of transferring the UNRWA's operations in Israel to the state authorities; (b) the move would be consummated before the 7th United Nations General Assembly convened – that is, Israel would arrive at this important international gathering with a gesture in the bag regarding the Palestinian refugee issue; (c) the plan was in keeping with the UNRWA's pressed financial straits (which according to an agency representative had a budget for Israel that could only last until September 1952).[151]

Comay's proposal was accepted, and on 18 May 1952 Israel officially informed the UNRWA of its agreement to take upon itself responsibility for the internal refugees. Israel did not ask the agency to compensate it in any manner for this move.[152]

In a meeting between Israeli representatives and Blandford at the end of the month, Blandford demanded that the transfer be carried out by 1 July 1952, the end of the agency's budget year. The Israelis argued that they could not commit by this date, but promised that the transfer would be carried out no later than 1 September.[153]

At the outset of June, the first consultation on care for the internal refugees was held by the Ministry of Foreign Affairs. Participating in the gathering were authorized representative of the Ministries of Labor and Agriculture, the state custodian for absentees' property, the advisor on Arab affairs, and a representative of the Jewish National Fund. At the meeting, it was relayed that the number of internal Arab refugees in the country stood at only 17,000 persons. Many thousands ceased to be internal refugees because they returned, little by little, to the places where they had lived previously (mostly to Haifa and Acre). Participants in the discussion decided that, within a month, the relevant ministries would prepare a survey of the socioeconomic status of the internal Arab refugees.[154]

Despite the decision, when the second meeting was convened at the outset of July, no survey had yet been prepared, and therefore it was decided to establish an interministerial committee comprised of representatives from the Ministries of Agriculture, Labor, and Welfare that would prepare the survey and propose a budget to solve the internal refugee problem. During this meeting, procedures were set that were supposed to guide the authorities in their treatment of the internal refugees: (a) the government would take care of welfare and employment for the refugees until their final rehabilitation; (b) care of the refugees would be divided among the ministries, and no special institution would be established for this purpose; (c) the relevant ministries would operate with full cooperation and coordination among them; (d) there would be no official recognition of refugee organizations, and the establishment of such should be prevented.[155]

A short time after the interministerial committee was established, it found that, due to Israel's economic straits, it was impossible to obtain the monetary

Three secondary aspects of the refugee problem 263

budget necessary to prepare the survey, not to mention monies to resolve the internal refugees problem.[156] The absence of financial means led Israel to approach the UNRWA in an unofficial manner to request that it continue to assist internal refugees for two more months, until 1 November 1952.[157] The agency agreed to give aid for the month of September only.[158] During the 31 August cabinet meeting, Foreign Minister Sharett said that Israel must be cautious and take steps to ensure that the support system for internal refugees wouldn't collapse at such a sensitive moment – during the 7th General Assembly. He clarified that there was a need for a budget earmarked to care for this population. The government decided, in keeping with his proposal, that a ministerial committee be established that would convene within days and decide on immediate steps to solve the Arab refugee problem in the country.[159] On 4 September the committee met, with the Ministers of Foreign Affairs, Finance, Labor, and Welfare. The meeting closed after the following decisions were passed: (a) the Ministry of Finance would budget a sum of 29,000 Israeli pounds for the month of October, to cover welfare needs of the refugees. During this time window, needs and abilities for the coming months would be investigated; (b) the Ministry of Finance would examine employment programs for the refugee population; (c) the Ministry of Foreign Affairs would coordinate among the ministries.[160] A week later, the Minister of Finance budgeted 50,000 Israeli pounds to the Ministry of Foreign Affairs to employ refugees (through the Ministry of Labor).[161]

To execute these decisions, on 22 September, Comay proposed that a new committee, the Former Arab Refugee Rehabilitation Committee, be established, whose tasks would be "to advise on rehabilitation matters, to help in implementing programs and to propose suitable proposals to the government." He also recommended the appointment of Alexander Dotan, an official in the Ministry of Foreign Affairs International Institutions Division, as coordinator and chair of the committee. On the committee would be representatives from the Ministries of Labor and Welfare, a representative of the military government, as well as the government's advisor on Arab affairs, Yehoshua Palmon.[162] Comay's proposals were accepted, and at the outset of October 1952, the committee began to operate.[163]

Dotan opened his work as coordinator and chair of the Former Arab Refugee Rehabilitation Committee with a number of tours amongst concentrations of internal refugees and talks with them, as well as meetings with members of the military government, functionaries in the Custodian's Office, and representatives of the Ministries of Welfare and Labor that operated among the refugees. His impressions were written up in a special report. One of his primary conclusions was that the economic situation of the refugees "doesn't need to worry the government in particular"; most had found a livelihood in temporary works, a small number made a living from smuggling and selling black-market goods, and a number had leased small plots of land from which they made a living. In Dotan's estimation, the main problem that bothered the internal refugees was the problem of land. Dotan

264   *Three secondary aspects of the refugee problem*

said, "From his point of view and from his current haven, [the refugee] follows what is happening to his land, [to which he] hopes and wishes to return."[164]

Days after the report was written, Dotan completed another report, this one dealing with the allocation of lands to the Israeli Arab minority, including the internal refugees. In his opinion, in deciding this issue, security needed to be taken into account, and therefore the state should adopt three guiding principles: "(a) not to expand, rather to curtail as much as possible, the land settled by Arabs. (b) not to resurrect Arab villages that had [been] destroyed during the 1948 war. (c) not to create new Arab villages." According to Dotan, the state needed to rehabilitate the majority of the internal refugees in the places where they were currently situated, "on the abandoned lands found in [existing Arab] villages."[165]

This approach, presented by the chair of the Refugee Rehabilitation Committee, was characteristic of Israel's policy towards its Arab refugees. Already in mid 1949, several reports and memorandums appeared that rejected the return of most of the internal refugees to their former settlements, on security and settlement grounds.[166]

As a result, most of the refugees were absorbed in existing Arab settlements, and the lands that they were offered were for the most part lands abandoned by other refugees who had left the country in the course of the war. Over the years, the military government's machinery took on the role, among other things, of implementing Israel's land policy towards the internal refugees.[167]

Although Dotan did not see much room for concern over the economic situation of the refugees Israeli authorities decided to take action with a comprehensive employment program that included public works and agricultural projects. Until mid December 1952, 47 percent of the internal refugees were engaged in full-time work, 30 percent in part-time work, and 23 percent remained welfare recipients.[168]

The primary source of distress for the internal refugees, as Dotan had rightly noted, stemmed from their inability to receive their lands back. The authorities sought to ease their hardships in two ways: (a) the refugees were given priority status in leasing alternative plots; (b) assets whose return to their former owners (i.e. the internal refugees) did not jeopardize the security and settlement interest of the state were released. The assets released were urban assets, moveable assets, and blocked bank accounts.[169]

On 10 March 1953 another step was taken in this direction: the Knesset passed the Land Acquisition Law (Validation of Acts and Compensations), 5713-1953. The law had two objectives: first, to create a legal basis for the acquisition of lands, whether they had belonged to internal refugees or whether they belonged to regular citizens; second, to grant the right for compensation to the original owners of the lands. The body responsible for such transactions was the Development Authority. In most cases compensation was given in cash, but if the land was used for agriculture and was the primary source of income for its owners, and the owners had no other land upon which to make a living, the Development Authority was obliged to offer alternative land. The rate of compensation was set between the Development Authority and the owners. If no agreement could be reached between the parties, the district court had authority to set the sum, at the request of one of the parties.[170] Passage of the Land Acquisition Law led to protests in the Arab states and among Palestinian Arabs. They charged that Israel sought to take over Palestinian assets and use the money they yielded to finance settlement of Jewish immigrants. Israel replied that the law didn't jeopardize in any way its commitment to pay compensation for abandoned Arab property.[171]

By the close of the 1950s, many internal refugees refrained from submitting claims for compensation for their lands (in keeping with the Land Acquisition Law). There were several reasons for this: (a) some internal refugees did not want to occupy alternative lands that belonged to other Arab refugees who one day might return to the country; (b) the level of compensation went against the grain of a portion of the claimants; (c) the large land owners, who didn't make their living from agriculture prior to the establishment of the State of Israel, took a dim view of the arrangement where compensation would be paid in money. They preferred to wait in the hope that, in the future, a way would be found to compensate them with land; (d) submission of claims for compensation and establishment of title over lands was arduous and often encountered difficulties. This state of affairs discouraged some of those entitled to compensation, and they therefore refrained from embarking on the process of filing claims.[172]

Notes

1 ISA, MFA 2451/19, Absentees with Deposits in Israel, by Size of Deposit in Palestine Lirot, and by Place of Deposit (30 September 1952); ISA, MFA 2451/19, The Blocked Deposits, 22 October 1952; ISA, MFA 2451/19, Amount of Absentees' Bank Deposits, undated.
2 DEPI, Vol. 2, Document 485, Memorandum by the Conciliation Commission, 11 April 1949.
3 DEPI, Vol. 4, Document 10, W. Eytan to M. Ethridge, 6 May 1949.
4 DEPI, Vol. 4, Editorial Note, p. 60.
5 ISA, MFA 2447/8, Status of the Question of Unfreezing of Arab Assets, 2 December 1949.
6 UNPCC, A/1367/Rev. 1, p. 16.
7 UNPCC, A/1367/Rev. 1, p. 16; Don Peretz, *Israel and the Palestine Arabs*, Washington, DC: The Middle East Institute, 1958, p. 224.
8 DEPI, Vol. 5, Document 52, G. Rafael to W. Eytan, 28 January 1950.
9 ISA, MFA 2442/1, Interim Report on the Question of the Frozen Accounts, 3 April 1950; UNPCC, A/1367/Rev. 1, pp. 16–17.
10 UNPCC, A/1793, pp. 3–4.
11 ISA, Government Meeting, 12 April 1950, pp. 8–9; ISA, MFA 2550/16, Summary of Conversation with Mr. de Boisanger on 18 February 1951; ISA, MFA 2441/4, G. Rafael to the Director-General of the Ministry of Foreign Affairs, 13 March 1951.

266 *Three secondary aspects of the refugee problem*

12 ISA, MFA 2475/1, Mr. George McGhee's Visit to Israel on the 27th and 28th of March 1951.
13 Peretz, *Israel and the Palestine Arabs*, p. 225.
14 UNPCC, A/1985, p. 22.
15 DEPI, Vol. 6, Document 488, Fischer's Statement before the Palestine Conciliation Commission (Paris, 14 November 1951).
16 DEPI, Vol. 7, Document 1, Memorandum by the Minister of Foreign Affairs, 2 January 1952.
17 DEPI, Vol. 7, Document 9, A. Lourie to M. Sharett, 9 January 1952.
18 ISA, MFA 2345/1, M. Sharett to A. Eban, 13 January 1952.
19 UNPCC, A/2121, p. 4.
20 UNPCC, A/2216, p. 5.
21 ISA, MFA 2451/19, A. Eban to the United States Division in the Ministry of Foreign Affairs, 5 May 1952.
22 ISA, MFA 2451/19, A. Eban to the United States Division in the Ministry of Foreign Affairs, 5 May 1952; DEPI, Vol. 7, Document 142, A. Eban to M. Sharett, 8 May 1952.
23 ISA, Government Meeting, 11 May 1952, pp. 31–5.
24 ISA, MFA 2451/19, M. Sharett to A. Eban, 12 May 1952.
25 ISA, MFA 360/18, Frozen Accounts, 20 May 1952.
26 ISA, MFA 2451/19, On the Release of Arabs' Blocked Accounts in Israel, 30 June 1952.
27 UNPCC, A/2216, pp. 5, 7.
28 ISA, MFA 1965/5, Release of 1,000,000 LS. to Arab Refugees: Summary of Discussions, 27 November 1952.
29 ISA, MFA 3061/8, Release of Blocked Accounts of Arab Refugees, 8 December 1952.
30 ISA, MFA 3061/8, Opposition in Jordan to the Acceptance of the Released Deposits, 30 March 1953; ISA, MFA 116/10, G. Rafael to M. Kidron, 2 April 1953; ISA, MFA 2451/9, The Ministry of Foreign Affairs to the Israel Missions in Washington, London, Paris and Rome, 8 April 1953; ISA, MFA 1965/6, The Opposition to the Acceptance of the Released Deposits is Increasing, 8 April 1953; ISA, MFA 1965/6, The United Nations Division in the Ministry of Foreign Affairs to the Heads of the Divisions in the Ministry, 10 April 1953; Robert L. Jarman (ed.), *Political Diaries of the Arab World: Palestine and Jordan, 1948–1965*, vol. 10, Slough: Archive Editions, 2001, p. 597.
31 ISA, MFA 1965/6, S. Arad to S. Bendor, 16 April 1953.
32 UNPCC, A/2629, p. 2.
33 BGA, Correspondences, Weekly Review No. 58 – Released of Blocked Accounts, 14 April 1953.
34 ISA, MFA 3061/8, Statement of the PCC Concerning the Release of the Arab Refugees Accounts Blocked in Israel, 12 April 1953.
35 UNPCC, A/2629, p. 2.
36 ISA, MFA 3061/8, Press Release on Blocked Accounts of Arab Refugees, 18 June 1953.
37 UNPCC, A/2629, pp. 2–3.
38 ISA, MFA 2474/11, The Overall Release of the Arab Refugees' Deposits, 29 November 1954.
39 ISA, MFA 2451/19, G. Rafael to the United Nations Division in the Ministry of Foreign Affairs, 2 February 1953.
40 ISA, MFA 2451/19, United Nations Division in the Ministry of Foreign Affairs to the Israel Mission in New York, 5 February 1953.
41 ISA, MFA 2451/19, G. Rafael to the United Nations Division in the Ministry of Foreign Affairs, 10 February 1953.

Three secondary aspects of the refugee problem 267

42 See, for example: ISA, MFA 1965/6, Daily Review: Israel-Arab Countries, 19 November 1953; ISA, MFA 2474/11, Subject: New Lawsuit against Barclays for 40,000 Dinars, 19 January 1954; ISA, MFA 2474/11, Subject: Lawsuit against Ottoman Bank for 1,200 Dinars, 20 January 1954.

43 ISA, MFA 3061/8, Aide Memoire, 31 December 1953.

44 ISA, MFA 3743/12, Letter to British Embassy in Tel Aviv, 12 January 1954.

45 Moshe Sharett, *Personal Diary*, vol. 2, Tel Aviv: Am Oved, 1978, p. 331 (Hebrew).

46 Sharett, *Personal Diary*, vol. 2, p. 332.

47 ISA, MFA 2401/22II, G. Rafael to M. Amir, 4 February 1954.

48 ISA, MFA 3743/12, G. Rafael to M. Kidron, 10 August 1954.

49 ISA, MFA 2451/20, Memorandum of Agreement between the Government of Israel and Barclays Bank, 26 September 1954.

50 ISA, MFA 3065/11, Announcement by the Government of Israel, 16 November 1954.

51 UNPCC, A/3199, p. 4.

52 ISA, MFA 2491/6, A. Gordon to P. Eliav, undated; ISA, MFA 1965/8, Press Extracts – Al-Difa, 1 June 1956.

53 ISA, MFA 2451/19, On the Release of Arabs' Blocked Accounts in Israel, 30 June 1952.

54 ISA, MFA 1965/7, M. Meir to G. Rafael, 17 December 1954; ISA, MFA 2475/3II, George Allen's Visit, 20 December 1954.

55 Jarman, *Political Diaries*, p. 745.

56 ISA, MFA 174/2, M. Sharett to W. Eytan, 15 March 1949.

57 DEPI, Vol. 2, Document 448, W. Eytan to M. Sharett, 18 March 1949.

58 DEPI, Vol. 2, Document 477, M. Sharett to W. Eytan, 5 April 1949.

59 DEPI, Vol. 2, Document 494, M. Comay to M. Sharett, 15 April 1949.

60 DEPI, Vol. 2, Document 479, Meeting of the Conciliation Commission with the Prime Minister and Ministry for Foreign Affairs Staff (Tel Aviv, 7 April 1949).

61 FRUS, 1949, VI, pp. 925–7, The Consul at Jerusalem to the Secretary of State, 20 April 1949; ISA, Government Meeting, 21 April 1949, pp. 2–3.

62 The military government was a military-operated machinery established in the closing months of 1948 to address the problems of the Palestinian Arab minority in Israel. On the military government mechanism, see: Yossi Amitay, "The Arab Minority in Israel: The Military Government's Years, 1948–1966," in Anita Shapira (ed.), *Independence: The First Fifty Years*, Jerusalem: The Zalman Shazar Center, 1998 (Hebrew); Dina Greitzer, "Ben-Gurion, Mapai and the Attitude towards the Arab Minority in Israel, 1948–1956," PhD thesis, The Hebrew University, 1995, pp. 82–108 (Hebrew); Sarah Ozacky-Lazar, "The Crystallization of Mutual Relations between Jews and Arabs in the State of Israel: The First Decade, 1948–1958," PhD thesis, University of Haifa, 1996, pp. 70–79 (Hebrew).

63 ISA, GL 17014/3, Family Reunification and Entry and Residency Permits for Refugees and Infiltrators, undated.

64 ILPA, 48/1/4-2, Deputy Military Governor, Western Galilee, Avraham Yaeli to Y. Duvdevani, Ministry of Defence, 21 November 1948.

65 ILPA, 2-11-1949-1, Parliamentary Party Meeting, 28 July 1949; ILPA, 2-11-1949-2, Parliamentary Party Meeting, 1 August 1949.

66 Ian Lustick, *Arabs in the Jewish State: Israel's Control of a National Minority*, Austin, TX: University of Texas Press, 1980, p. 204.

67 DEPI, Vol. 4, Document 19, E. Elath to the Ministry of Foreign Affairs, 11 May 1949.

68 DEPI, Vol. 4, Document 42, J. G. McDonald to D. Ben-Gurion, 29 May 1949.

69 DEPI, Vol. 4, Editorial Note, p. 60.

70 DEPI, Vol. 4, Document 64, M. Sharett to J. G. McDonald, 8 June 1949.

268 Three secondary aspects of the refugee problem

71 ISA, Government Meeting, 14 June 1949, pp. 59–60.
72 *Knesset Minutes*, vol. 1, 15 June 1949, p. 722.
73 DEPI, Vol. 4, Document 92, A. Eban to M. Sharett, 22 June 1949.
74 DEPI, Vol. 4, Document 103, A. Eban to W. Eytan, 24 June 1949.
75 *Davar*, 10 July 1949.
76 *Ha-Boker*, 11 July 1949.
77 *Ha-Tzofe*, 10 July 1949.
78 *Ha'aretz*, 11 July 1949.
79 *Herut*, 7 July 1949.
80 DEPI, Vol. 4, Document 108, W. Eytan to P. de Azcarate, 27 June 1949.
81 ISA, MFA 2451/17, Information to Israel Missions Abroad, 4 July 1949.
82 ISA, MFA 2445/4A, Subject: Entry Permits for Arab Refugees – Family Reunification, 26 July 1949; DEPI, Vol. 4, Document 126, G. Avner to P. de Azcarate, 8 July 1949.
83 Peretz, *Israel and the Palestine Arabs*, p. 52.
84 Rony E. Gabbay, *A Political Study of the Arab-Jewish Conflict – The Arab Refugee Problem (A Case Study)*, Geneve: Librairie E. Droz, 1959, p. 311.
85 ISA, GL 17014/3, Family Reunification and Entry and Residency Permits for Refugees and Infiltrators, undated.
86 DEPI, Vol. 4, Document 115, U. Heyd to E. Herlitz, 1 July 1949.
87 DEPI, Vol. 4, Editorial Note, p. 206.
88 DEPI, Vol. 4, Document 110, Meeting: R. M. Kidron – J. Beith (London, 28 June 1949).
89 FRUS, 1949, VI, p. 1206, The Ambassador in Israel to the Secretary of State, 6 July 1949.
90 ISA, GL 17014/3, Family Reunification and Entry and Residency Permits for Refugees and Infiltrators, undated.
91 ISA, MFA 2444/19A, Bureau of the Minister of Foreign Affairs to Gershon Avner, 26 July 1949.
92 UNPCC, A/1367/Rev. 1, p. 16; Peretz, *Israel and the Palestine Arabs*, p. 53.
93 Henry Rosenfeld, *They Were Peasants: Social Anthropological Studies on the Arab Village in Israel*, Tel Aviv: Hakibbutz Hameuhad, 1964, pp. 14–15, 21–2 (Hebrew).
94 Rosenfeld, *They Were Peasants*, p. 144
95 DEPI, Vol. 4, Document 146, M. Sharett: Guidelines for Israel Missions Abroad, 25 July 1949.
96 DEPI, Vol. 4, Document 154, E. Sasson to M. Sharett, 27 July 1949, Note 3; ISA, MFA 2451/17, Sharett to Sasson, 29 July 1949.
97 ISA, MFA 2447/15, Yohanan Biham to W. Eytan, undated.
98 ISA, MFA 2445/4A, Subject: Return of the Arab Families, 22 November 1949.
99 Peretz, *Israel and the Palestine Arabs*, p. 52.
100 ISA, GL 17014/3, Family Reunification and Entry and Residency Permits for Refugees and Infiltrators, undated.
101 ISA, GL 17103/53, Yehiel Argov to the Ministry of Immigration, 25 December 1949.
102 UNPCC, A/1255, p. 15.
103 ISA, MFA 2566/15, Yehiel Argov to the Ministry of Foreign Affairs, 18 January 1952.
104 ISA, MFA 2566/15, Yehiel Argov to the Ministry of Foreign Affairs, 18 January 1952.
105 ISA, GL 17014/3, Y. Palmon to Y. Sapir, 30 July 1952.
106 Peretz, *Israel and the Palestine Arabs*, p. 54.
107 ISA, GL 17014/3, Family Reunification (Review by the Bureau of the Adviser on Arab Affairs, 16 October 1956).

Three secondary aspects of the refugee problem   269

108 ISA, GL 17014/3, Family Reunification and Entry and Residency Permits for Refugees and Infiltrators, undated.
109 ISA, Government Meeting, 24 February 1952, pp. 48–9.
110 See in this context: ISA, GL 17103/53, R. Levi to A. Biran, 22 June 1952; ISA, GL 17108/39, A. Biran to the Director-General of the Ministry of Foreign Affairs, 27 July 1952; ISA, GL 17108/39, Y. Palmon to the Director-General of the Ministry of Foreign Affairs, 5 August 1952; ISA, GL 17103/53, Subject: Family Reunification – Jordan Policy, 13 August 1952.
111 See, for example: *Knesset Minutes*, vol. 10, 8 October 1951, pp. 234, 264; *Knesset Minutes*, vol. 10, 5 November 1951, p. 315; *Knesset Minutes*, vol. 10, 6 November 1951, pp. 335–6; *Knesset Minutes*, vol. 11, 13 February 1952, p. 1303; *Knesset Minutes*, vol. 12, 9 June 1952, p. 2235; *Knesset Minutes*, vol. 12, 7 July 1952, p. 2533; *Knesset Minutes*, vol. 13, 23 December 1952, p. 310; *Knesset Minutes*, vol. 13, 27 January 1953, p. 573; *Knesset Minutes*, vol. 14, 25 May 1953, p. 1367.
112 ISA, GL 17014/3, Family Reunification (Review by the Bureau of the Adviser on Arab Affairs, 16 October 1956).
113 ISA, GL 17014/3, Subject: Family Reunification for Members of Minority Groups from Syria and Egypt, 20 November 1952.
114 ISA, GL 17014/3, Family Reunification and Entry and Residency Permits for Refugees and Infiltrators, undated.
115 ISA, GL 17014/3, The Division for Minorities in the Ministry of the Interior to the Adviser on Arab Affairs at the Prime Minister's Office, 27 January 1956; ISA, GL 17014/3, Family Reunification and Entry and Residency Permits for Refugees and Infiltrators, undated.
116 ISA, MFA 1989/1, UNRWA Policy in the State of Israel, 13 November 1951.
117 Michal Oren-Nordheim, "The Crystallization of Settlement Land Policy in the State of Israel from Its Establishment and during the First Years of the Israel Lands Administration (1948–1965)," PhD thesis, The Hebrew University, 1999, p. 99 (Hebrew).
118 ISA, 5592/46691 G, The Arab "Present Absentees", "Refugees" and "Evacuees", undated.
119 BGA, Ben-Gurion's Bureau – As Prime Minister, Container 139 (Policy Concerning Israeli Arabs, 1950–1956), Problems of the Arab Minority in Israel, 26 July 1950.
120 Hillel Cohen, *The Present Absentees: The Palestinian Refugees in Israel since 1948*, Jerusalem: The Institute for Israeli Arab Studies, 2000, p. 25 (Hebrew); Majid al-Haj, "The Arab Internal Refugees in Israel: The Emergence of a Minority within the Minority," *Immigrants and Minorities* 7(2), July 1988, p. 157.
121 Cohen, *The Present Absentees*, p. 24.
122 Haj, "The Arab Internal Refugees in Israel," p. 151.
123 Because they were so numerous, it is difficult to establish an exact figure for the very many refugees who moved to Nazareth and its vicinity. In April of 1949, Yosef Weitz reported to the Ministers' Committee on Refugee Affairs that 5,222 refugees were living in Nazareth and an additional 7,334 refugees lived in nearby villages. One quarter of them, he claimed, had come from Haifa. Charles S. Kamen, "After the Catastrophe II: The Arabs in Israel, 1948–1951," *Middle Eastern Studies* 24(1), 1988, p. 78. See also in this regard Mustafa Abbasi, "'City in Distress': Nazareth and the Problem of Internal Arab Refugees, 1948–1949," *Cathedra* 146, December 2012, pp. 122–6 (Hebrew).
124 Cohen, *The Present Absentees*, p. 28.
125 Ronit Barzily and Mustafa Kabha, *Refugees in Their Homeland: Internal Refugees in the State of Israel, 1948–1996*, Givat Haviva: The Institute for Peace Research, 1996, pp. 9–10 (Hebrew).
126 ISA, GL 17108/31, Subject: Termination of UNRWA Activities – List of Settlements, 10 June 1952.

270   *Three secondary aspects of the refugee problem*

127 Cohen, *The Present Absentees*, p. 26.

128 Cohen, *The Present Absentees*, p. 28.

129 Cohen, *The Present Absentees*, p. 41.

130 Cohen, *The Present Absentees*, pp. 41–52; Jacques Kano, *The Problem of Land between Jews and Arabs (1917–1990)*, Tel Aviv: Sifriat Poalim, 1992, pp. 81–2 (Hebrew).

131 ISA, GL 17108/20, Bureau of the Minister of Foreign Affairs to Mr. Y. Weitz, Mr. E. Danin, Mr. Z. Liff, Mr. Y. Palmon and Lieutenant Colonel A. Mor, 11 September 1949.

132 The following two files contain considerable material concerning the activity of the Refugee Rehabilitation Authority: ISA, GL 13924/6; and ISA, GL 17108/28.

133 ISA, MFA 1989/1, Financial Report for the Activity of the Arab Refugee Rehabilitation Authority, dated 1 August 1951; Cohen, *The Present Absentees*, pp. 62–4.

134 See, in this context: ISA, GL 17108/20, The Adviser on Arab Affairs to the Prime Minister's Secretary, 23 June 1950; ISA, GL 17108/28, Minutes of a Meeting of the Refugee Rehabilitation Authority, dated 2 August 1950; ISA, GL 17108/20, Subject: Arab Refugee Rehabilitation Authority in Israel, 17 June 1951.

135 See, in this context: ISA, GL 17108/20, A. Hanoki to the Members of the Authority, 24 April 1950; ISA, GL 17108/20, Subject: Arab Refugee Rehabilitation Authority in Israel, 17 June 1951.

136 See, in this context: ISA, GL 17099/31, Subject: Returning Refugees to their Former Places of Residence, 14 June 1949; ISA, GL 17108/20, A. Hanoki to the Members of the Authority, 24 April 1950; *Knesset Minutes*, vol. 8, 7 March 1951, pp. 1293–4.

137 Cohen, *The Present Absentees*, pp. 53–4.

138 ISA, MFA 2015/1, Subject: UNRWA Assistance to Refugees in Israel, 25 October 1950.

139 Alexander Bligh, "From U.N.R.W.A. to Israel: The 1952 Transfer of Responsibilities for Refugees in Israel," *Refuge* 14(6), November 1994, p. 7; Alexander Bligh, "Israel and the Refugee Problem: From Exodus to Resettlement, 1948–1952," *Middle Eastern Studies* 34(1), 1998, pp. 135–6; Charles S. Kamen, "After the Catastrophe I: The Arabs in Israel, 1948–1951," *Middle Eastern Studies* 23(4), 1987, p. 466.

140 ISA, MFA 1989/1, Record of a Meeting with UNRWA Representative on 8 December 1950.

141 ISA, MFA 1989/1, UNRWA Policy in the State of Israel, 13 November 1951.

142 ISA, MFA 339/7, United States Division in the Ministry of Foreign Affairs to the Israel Missions in the United States, 9 September 1951.

143 In the following years, Israel worked laboriously to utilize this gesture for propaganda purposes. It served as the basis for Israel's criticism of the Arab countries with respect to their inability and unwillingness to absorb the Arab refugees within their territory, in the same manner that Israel had absorbed 28,000 Palestinian refugees who were situated within its territory. Abba Eban, *Voice of Israel*, New York: Horizon Press, 1957, pp. 225–6.

144 ISA, MFA 2477/2A, United Nations Division in the Ministry of Foreign Affairs to the Embassy in Washington, 20 March 1952.

145 Bulent Gokay (ed.), *British Documents on Foreign Affairs: Near and Middle East, 1951*, vol. 2, London: Lexis Nexis, 2005, pp. 350–1.

146 ISA, 7562/12 A, Foreign Affairs and Defense Committee Meeting, 31 December 1951, p. 12.

147 Cohen, *The Present Absentees*, p. 77.

148 ISA, MFA 1989/1, G. Meron to the Director-General of the Ministry of Foreign Affairs, 16 December 1951.

149 ISA, Government Meeting, 16 December 1951, p. 12.

Three secondary aspects of the refugee problem 271

150 ISA, MFA 2491/5, The Embassy in Washington to the United Nations Division in the Ministry of Foreign Affairs, 18 March 1952.
151 ISA, MFA 2406/17A, M. Comay to M. Sharett, 17 April 1952.
152 ISA, MFA 3062/4, The Treatment of the Former Arab Refugees in Israel during the Period 4 September 1952–15 December 1952, 31 December 1952.
153 ISA, MFA 2406/17A, M. Comay to Various Government Ministries, 1 June 1952.
154 ISA, MFA 1989/2, Termination of UNRWA Activities in Israel, 17 June 1952.
155 ISA, MFA 3062/4, The Treatment of the Former Arab Refugees in Israel during the Period 4 September 1952–15 December 1952, 31 December 1952.
156 ISA, MFA 1989/2, A. Dotan to M. Comay, undated.
157 ISA, MFA 1989/2, Record of a Conversation with Mr. Hoover, UNRWA Representative in Israel, 5 August 1952.
158 ISA, MFA 2406/17A, Director of the United Nations Division in the Ministry of Foreign Affairs to M. Sharett, 27 August 1952.
159 ISA, Government Meeting, 31 August 1952, p. 4.
160 ISA, MFA 1989/2, Record of a Meeting of the Ministers' Committee on Arab Refugees in Israel, 8 September 1952.
161 ISA, 5592/4670 G, Subject: Employment and Relief for Arab Refugees in Israel, undated.
162 ISA, MFA 2406/17A, M. Comay to M. Sharett, 22 September 1952.
163 ISA, 5592/4670 G, Subject: Employment and Relief for Arab Refugees in Israel, undated.
164 ISA, MFA 2406/17A, Condition of the Arab Refugees in Israel and Their Problems, 9 November 1952.
165 ISA, MFA 2406/17A, Final Solution for the Problem of the Refugees in Israel and a New Policy toward the Arab Minority, 12 November 1952.
166 ISA, MFA 2401/19A, Report of the Committee for Inquiry the Problems of the Military Government and Its Future, 3 May 1949; ISA, GL 17099/31, Subject: Returning Refugees to Their Former Places of Residence, 14 June 1949; Cohen, *The Present Absentees*, pp. 49–51.
167 Hillel Cohen has shown in his book that Israel also used collaborators from within the Israeli Arab population in order to prevent the return of internal refugees to their land. See Hillel Cohen, *Good Arabs: The Israeli Security Agencies and the Israeli Arabs, 1948–1967*, Berkeley, CA: University of California Press, 2010, pp. 99–110.
168 ISA, MFA 3062/4, The Treatment of the Former Arab Refugees in Israel during the Period 4 September 1952–15 December 1952, 31 December 1952.
169 ISA, MFA 2474/11, United States Division in the Ministry of Foreign Affairs to the Embassy in Washington, 28 December 1953.
170 Aharon Liskovsky, "'Resident Absentees' in Israel," *The New East* 10(3), 1960, pp. 190–1 (Hebrew).
171 UNPCC, A/2629, pp. 3–4; Maha Nassar, "Palestinian Citizens of Israel and the Discourse on the Right of Return, 1948–1959," *Journal of Palestine Studies* 40(4), 2011, p. 52.
172 Liskovsky, "'Resident Absentees'," pp. 191–2.

Conclusion

One of the key results of the 1948 Arab-Israeli war was the creation of a refugee problem: 600,000 to 760,000 Arabs who had lived in territories that had become part of the State of Israel became refugees in neighboring Arab states and in the Arab sectors of Mandate Palestine. The objective of this book was to examine the shaping and crystallization of Israel's policy towards this problem in all its facets: repatriation and resettlement, compensation for abandoned property, blocked bank accounts, family reunification, and internal refugees.

A number of conclusions can be drawn from this research. Already during the evolution of the refugee problem, the Israeli leadership vehemently rejected the repatriation solution and stood firm behind this position throughout the period studied – a position that enjoyed sweeping support among the Jewish public. Israel was able to adopt this approach vis-à-vis the international community and stick with it due to the fact that all the primary actors (except Lebanon) that were involved in the issue – the United Nations, the two western powers (the United States and Britain), and neighboring Arab states where the refugees were (Jordan, Egypt, and Syria) – adopted (each for its own reasons and vested interests) a position that, in essence, sidelined the repatriation solution. Nevertheless, Israel could not be entirely exempted from paying a price, and the coinage with which it was required to pay for removal of the repatriation principle from the political agenda was economic in nature – payment of compensation for abandoned Arab property. Parallel to this but of less importance was the requirement that Israel solve several secondary aspects of the refugee problem, such as blocked bank accounts, family reunification, and internal refugees. It is plain as day that for Israel, this was a small and almost inconsequential sacrifice compared to the formidable burden from an economic, social, political, and security standpoint that would have fallen on its shoulders had the Jewish state been required to repatriate within its territory hundreds of thousands of Palestinian refugees. It is, therefore, not surprising that Israel expressed its willingness, even with conditions, to pay in economic coinage, parallel to the other steps taken to solve the three secondary issues.

Rejecting repatriation

Israel's fundamental stance regarding the Palestinian refugee question in general, and the repatriation issue in particular, was defined, in effect, in the cabinet meeting of 16 June 1948. Prime Minister Ben-Gurion and Foreign Minister Sharett asserted adamantly, garnering the support of most of the cabinet behind them, that under no condition and in no case should the repatriation solution be accepted. At the same time, the two leaders made efforts to blur this position as much as possible, in order to avoid at this time, in the midst of an existential war, both a coalition crisis with Mapam – the most important political movement in the country after Mapai – and a political confrontation with the United States – the strongest power in the world, which at the time supported mass repatriation of refugees. At the outset of 1949, with the establishment of a new government without Mapam, and after the danger of a confrontation with Washington was less troubling due to the end of the war, the leadership in Tel Aviv allowed itself to express more freely its opposition to the repatriation solution.

In justifying this approach, Israel employed the following reasons. First, moral responsibility for resolving the refugee problem lay on the Arab states, which had brutally abrogated an official resolution of the United Nations (Resolution 181) and embarked on a war that gave birth to the refugee problem. This problem developed and ballooned to a tremendous scale due to a series of actions taken by the Arab side in the course of the war. Second, settlement of the refugees in Israel could be expected to encounter difficulties on every hand: masses of returnees would constitute a grave security risk to the Jewish state, whose birth they sought to prevent by force, and whose very existence they repudiated; their presence would create perpetual political and social friction with the Jewish sector; their economic rehabilitation under prevailing circumstances was impossible, for a number of reasons. The country had been hard hit economically by the prolonged and destructive war; enormous resources had been earmarked for mass absorption of Holocaust survivors from Europe and Jews from Muslim countries; the refugees' homes were in ruin or had been occupied by homeless Jewish immigrants and demobilized soldiers; and the pre-state economic infrastructure of the Arab sector of Mandate Palestine had been almost entirely erased. Third, resettlement of the refugees in the Arab states was the only feasible option, and it was preferable from all perspectives compared to their return to Israel. They would not constitute a risk to the national security of the Arab states; their assimilation among the local population was ensured since there were no religious, linguistic, or cultural barriers between the two communities; from an economic standpoint it would be easier for countries such as Iraq, Syria, and Jordan to absorb hundreds of thousands of new citizens since they had sparse populations and immense territories in need of manpower to assist development of their agricultural and industry, based on the water resources at their disposal (the Tigris, the Euphrates, and the Jordan rivers).

274 Conclusion

Israel did not suffice with declarations, and its policy position rejecting repatriation was accompanied by a series of legal and physical steps designed to block any possibility of repatriating refugees. As for the legal perspective, from the summer of 1948, ordinances were issued and laws passed that transferred ownership of abandoned Arab property to the state, which was empowered to utilize it as it saw fit. On the physical plane, during the war (and in the aftermath on a smaller scale) buildings in Palestinian villages and Arab urban neighborhoods in mixed cities were razed, at times entire settlements. Both the moveable and unmovable property of the refugees left behind was seized and diverted towards the absorption of hundreds of thousands of Jews, who came to Israel in the first years after its establishment.

Israel's position vis-à-vis resolution of the refugee problem did not remain "orphaned" or spurned in the international arena. Just the opposite, it quickly found influential supporters. The first was Great Britain. Within weeks of the Israeli leadership's rejection of the repatriation principle, London itself adopted this stance and stuck with this position throughout the entire period under study, convinced that repatriation was unfeasible from both economic and political standpoints and the Palestinian refugee problem should be resolved through resettlement in the Arab states.

When the leading western power – the United States – set out to establish its position on the issue, it took into account Tel Aviv's resolute and consistent approach opposing the repatriation principle and most probably didn't ignore London's negative attitude towards repatriation. The Americans were also cognizant of the fact (which Israel underscored) that, from a purely fiscal standpoint, successful absorption of refugees could take place primarily in the territory of Arab states such as Iraq, Syria, and Trans-Jordan. Due to this, it is not surprising that Washington decided to support basing resolution of the refugee problem on the resettlement principle.

This posture by the Americans was clearly reflected in the weeks leading up to the Lausanne Conference (27 April – 15 September 1949) and particularly in the course of the gathering, when the Americans demanded that Israel agree to absorb between 200,000 and 250,000 refugees. While the scope was quite large, relatively speaking, it was only about a quarter of the total refugee population. In other words, according to the Americans, almost 75 percent of the refugees were supposed to be resettled in the Arab states.

From Israel's perspective, however, this figure constituted a far-reaching and perilous implementation of the repatriation principle. On the eve of the Lausanne Conference (and, in essence, since the summer of 1948), Tel Aviv declared that it was willing to consider the return of a very limited number of refugees, only within the framework of a comprehensive and lasting peace between the Jewish state and its Arab neighbors, a condition that under prevailing political realities appeared unfeasible. Washington, however, was unwilling to retreat from the figure it had cited; in American eyes, the demand to repatriate only a quarter of the refugees expressed its readiness to embrace the essence of the Israeli position.

In the end, long months of American (and UN) pressure led to an Israeli consent to absorb 100,000 refugees – in practice (after taking into account the 30,000 who had already returned), 70,000 refugees, but only in the framework of a comprehensive peace settlement. The number suggested constituted only about 10 percent of the Palestinian refugee population. Thus, despite unrelenting pressure from the most powerful nation on earth, the fledgling state of Israel, as weak and tiny as it was, did not cave in under pressure to change its fundamental position regarding the repatriation issue.

The resounding collapse of the political track at Lausanne led Washington to adopt a new policy: attempts should be made to resolve the Middle East conflict, and the refugee problem at its core, through economic means. The shift of emphasis from a political approach to an economic one was clearly beneficial to the parties who favored resettlement; after all, from an economic standpoint, the rehabilitation of refugees in the Arab states was a lot more feasible than their rehabilitation in the Jewish state. In this context, Washington took another step forward, a very important one, towards the Israeli position: it did not suffice with formulating a declaratory guideline that would give preference to rehabilitating the majority of refugees in the Arab states; rather, it sought to take concrete economic steps to implement its declared position in practice. No less important, commencement of work on the rehabilitation of refugees in Arab territory would create dynamics for resettlement that would render repatriation irrelevant.

The willingness of the United States in the fall of 1949 to anchor the resettlement concept in practice stemmed from the very same factors that prompted Washington in the spring of that year to adopt an approach that based resolution of the refugee problem on this concept. One can assume that the Americans were particularly influenced by Israel's unprecedentedly clear and resolute stand at the Lausanne Conference in the face of fierce pressure to repatriate a large number of refugees.

There was, however, another important factor that spurred the United States (as well as Britain) to set itself steadfastly in the resettlement realm: the attitude of the Arab states towards the refugee problem. Publicly, the Arab states expressed a position diametrically opposed to the Israeli one: a demand that every single refugee be granted the option to realize the principle of repatriation or receive compensation for its property. Yet in diplomatic contacts between their envoys and representatives of the western powers, United Nations officials, and Israeli envoys, their position was very different.

Abdullah's Jordan – where the majority of the refugee population (approximately 55 percent) was situated – labored vigorously, fueled by the vision of a "Greater Syria," to assimilate the West Bank with all its inhabitants – refugees and non-refugees – within the Hashemite Kingdom, as well as tens of thousands of refugees who had crossed the Jordan River eastward into Trans-Jordan. From Amman's perspective, the ultimate and only solution to the refugee problem was founded on the resettlement principle.

Damascus, for its part, during different junctures of the period under study, expressed readiness to absorb between a quarter of a million and half a

276   *Conclusion*

million Palestinian refugees (at the time, there were only 85,000 refugees in Syria). The Syrian rulers hoped that their conciliatory offers on the refugee issue would buy understanding in Washington, and the Americans would be willing to shower their country with economic, military, and political "goodies" in return.

Egypt, the largest and most important Arab state, pushed the question of the Palestinian refugees' fate to the bottom of its political priorities. In interactions that its envoys carried out with representatives of Israel, the western powers, the United Nations, and private parties during the period under study, it was clarified that the primary Egyptian condition (in fact the only one) for any political settlement of the "Palestine Question" hinged on Israel relinquishing the Negev (which constituted about 50 percent of Israeli territory), in order to create territorial contiguity between Egypt and the Arab world to the east. Only after they took care to underscore the border question did the Egyptians go about paying lip service to the Palestinian refugee problem. In their opinion, the chances of realizing the repatriation principle were slim, but nevertheless on a number of occasions they suggested that some of the refugees be settled in territories that Israel would relinquish.

This attitude of the Arab states towards the refugee problem was already revealed during the Lausanne Conference and continued in full force during the years that followed. By virtue of their own approach, the Arabs themselves liberated the United States, as well as Britain and the United Nations, from the necessity to confront and clash with Israel on realization of the repatriation principle. In other words, the Arabs eased Israel's ability to hold firm in its stance that categorically rejected repatriation.

The decisive step that the United States took in the direction of the resettlement principle, as expressed in the American decision to resolve the refugee problem through an "economic approach," fueled and bolstered the Israeli position that rejected the repatriation principle. Thus, if until the end of 1949 Israel had declared that it was willing to discuss the return of a very limited number of refugees "in the framework of a peace settlement" – several tens of thousands, according to "the 100,000 Proposal" – from this point forward, the rehabilitation of the Palestinian refugees (according to Israel) must be carried out *exclusively* in the Arab states. Israel for its part was prepared to allow a token number of refugees – only several thousand – to return to its territory (in the framework of family reunification and humanitarian cases).

Compensation in exchange for resettlement

Up until the summer of 1950, the issue of compensation for the refugees' abandoned property hardly appeared on the agenda of Israel, the United Nations, the west, or the Arabs. The parties focused on the settlement elements of the refugee problem: resettlement or repatriation. Under such conditions, Israel could allow itself not to delve deeply into the compensation issue. In the 16 June 1948 cabinet meeting, Sharett drew the Israeli position on the issue in general terms, and in coming months, this position crystallized into declared policy. The Israeli position was based on a number of principles: (a) Israel was prepared to discuss compensation and bring about its resolution, but only in the framework of a comprehensive peace settlement in which all aspects of the conflict would be resolved; (b) payment would be for cultivated land only; (c) Israel preferred to give full monetary payment of compensation to one central fund that would engage in resettlement of the refugees; (d) compensation to Palestinian refugees was irrevocably tied to compensation Israel deserved from its Arab neighbors for war damages.

The compensation issue took center stage following the decision of the Conciliation Commission in the latter half of 1950 to focus on this matter. The commission, with backing from Washington and London, proposed to Israel a kind of "exchange transaction": Israel would declare its willingness to discuss the compensation question and pay the money outside the framework of a peace settlement and, in exchange, support for resettlement as the vehicle to a solution (a position held by the powers, the United Nations, and Arab states such as Jordan and Syria) would be maintained and even acted on in practice (through the UNRWA, which had just been established). From the perspective of the Conciliation Commission and the western powers, Israel could not hold the stick at both ends: enjoy sidelining the repatriation principle and also dodge payment of compensation. They feared that the Arab states would be unwilling to make progress on the resettlement programs that the UNRWA had just prepared if the Arabs became convinced that Israel was getting away scot-free, so to speak – without paying a price for resolution of the problem.

Sharett was in favor of giving a positive reply to the proposal offered by the Conciliation Commission (and the western powers). Ben-Gurion took issue with this. The compensation question turned out to be the primary bone of contention between the two Israeli leaders in regard to the Palestinian refugee problem: at various political junctures in the course of the period under study, Sharett felt Israel must exhibit more flexibility regarding compensation, while Ben-Gurion presented an unbending position that sought to curtail as much as possible any Israeli willingness to raise a financial contribution.

In the fall of 1950, however, after a lengthy and exhausting pressure campaign that Sharett put on the government (primarily on the prime minister), Ben-Gurion and his supporters in the cabinet changed their minds. They were convinced that the western powers, the Arab states, and the United Nations bodies involved in the Middle East conflict (the Conciliation Commission and the UNRWA) would not agree to exempt Israel from doing its part both on repatriation and payment of compensation alike. They understood that by insisting on an unbending position on the compensation question, they were liable to jeopardize the enormous achievement of sidelining the repatriation principle by all these international parties.

Consequently, in October 1950, the Israeli cabinet decided to express its readiness to embark on resolution of the compensation issue, separate from

278   *Conclusion*

all other aspects of the conflict (that is, outside the framework of a comprehensive peace settlement). In contrast with the vague non-binding pronouncements by Israeli spokespersons in the past, the decision stated clearly and unequivocally that compensation monies would serve for the resettlement of refugees. In addition, the cabinet waived its previous demand that coupled the compensation issue for Palestinian refugees with compensation demanded from the Arab states for war damages.

Within a year, the Israeli government decided (in September 1951) to make a declaratory amendment to its compensation policy. The background to this step was the Conciliation Commission's initiative to convene another Middle East peace conference – the Paris Conference – in the fall of 1951.

According to this amendment, in exchange for an agreement between Israel and the United Nations that would bring about settlement of the compensation issue (separate from all other aspects of the conflict), the United Nations would assert officially and openly that, with this, Israel completed its responsibilities for solving the Palestinian refugee problem, first and foremost in regard to the repatriation issue. This amendment was designed to entrench – from a political-legal standpoint and in an official, public, and unequivocal manner – the "exchange transaction" that the Conciliation Commission (and the western powers) had placed before Israel in the latter half of 1950. Israel was not willing to suffice with assurances given in closed talks (even if genuine) that payment of compensation would take the repatriation principle off the agenda. Israel wanted an official, public seal on this matter from the most important international institution – the United Nations. Such an open commitment, Jerusalem believed, would provide Israel with an "insurance policy" should the part of the "exchange transaction" dealing with resettlement not be realized. Such a possibility was indeed likely, for a number of reasons:

1   It was possible that the money budgeted for resettlement would not be sufficient, and as a result refugees (even many) would remain who would not be rehabilitated in the Arab states. Such a possibility was a distinct reality in light of the chronic deficit under which the UNRWA (which was responsible for the resettlement projects) operated, and the fact that Israel wanted to pay as small a sum as possible due to its own stretched finances. Moreover, even if a large-enough sum could be gathered to resettle the refugees, it was entirely possible that there would be some refugees who would not want to be rehabilitated in the Arab states and would stand adamantly on their "Right of Return" to Israel.
2   The rulers of Jordan and Syria, in whose countries most of the refugees were supposed to settle and who had expressed their consent on this matter, were liable, for different reasons, to change their minds. Moreover, considering the instability of regimes in the Arab world, today's leaders who had taken a positive view towards resettlement of refugees could tomorrow be replaced by rulers who would take the opposite position.

3 The western powers could, for their own reasons, change their position on the solution to the refugee problem. This was particularly true of the United States – the most important player in the region (certainly from Israel's point of view). After all, only two years had elapsed since Washington had given its blessing – by declaration and in practice – to a solution based on resettlement – too short a time frame to know for sure whether Washington had chosen this path for good.

When the Paris Conference convened, it became clearly evident that no pressure was applied on the repatriation issue; nevertheless, the Israeli government anchored the amendment to its compensation policy. By doing so, it sought to assert that the nitty-gritty of the "exchange transaction" – compensation in exchange for resettlement – was sacred (that is, it was "set in stone") in Israel's view.

In the amended compensation policy that Israel presented in September 1951, there was a section in which Israel warned that its "ability to pay" had been diminished by the economic war that the Arabs were conducting against the Jewish state. This declaration referred to the anti-Israel maritime blockade imposed by Egypt in the Suez Canal and the Arab world's economic boycott of Israel. A year later, in October 1952, the warning was turned into a condition. Under Ben-Gurion's lead, Israel announced that while it was still willing to enter negotiations with the United Nations on the compensation question, separate from a comprehensive peace agreement, the sum that would be set for payment would be forthcoming only *after* the Arab states totally ceased their economic war on Israel.

By linking this issue to the compensation issue, Israel sought to achieve two objectives: first, to remove a destructive tool that was very detrimental to its economy; second, to signal to the Arabs, the western powers, and the United Nations that Israel was displeased and worried about the direction Arab-Israel relations were going – entrenchment and even amplification of the conflict. Economic warfare was the most tangible and most extreme expression of the deterioration in relations taking place (not counting *feda'iyin*-based terrorism that Egypt sponsored for a short time). The Arabs, however, didn't want to relinquish their economic warfare and even expanded it, and Israel, in response, pointedly refrained from resolving the compensation issue.

Sharett had doubts concerning the inflexible line that Ben-Gurion led in the fall of 1952, but nevertheless adopted it in full. He was aware that Ben-Gurion's "ungenerous" approach regarding gestures towards the Arabs, taken due to escalating conflict between Israel and the Arabs, had been well received among the public at large and the country's political community. There was another reason, too. Sharett no longer needed to be apprehensive, as he had been in the fall of 1950 and a year later on the eve of the Paris Conference, that Washington would raise the "demon" from the depths – resurrect the repatriation concept in response to an Israeli refusal to make progress on the compensation issue. It became clear that the Eisenhower administration,

280   *Conclusion*

which took office in January 1953, was distinctively pro-Israel as far as the Palestinian refugee issue was concerned, even more than its predecessor, the Truman administration. In two speeches delivered by Secretary of State Dulles in June 1953 and August 1955, for the first time in the history of the Arab-Israeli conflict, the United States granted official and public validity to its policy that was based on resolving the refugee problem on the principle of resettlement. The second speech indicated that, in essence, it was possible to base a solution *only* on this principle. And indeed, the 1955 Anglo-American "Alpha" Plan stipulated that the Arab states would rehabilitate no less than 92 percent of the refugees in their own territory. The remaining 8 percent – 75,000 refugees only – was to return (over a 5-year period) to Israel, and the planners even surmised that in practice no more than 50,000 would opt to do so. Thus, once the shadow of repatriation was almost totally removed, the leadership in Israel could harden its position on the compensation issue, without fear.

Minor gestures

Israel's actual contribution to resolving the Palestinian refugee problem was expressed in three secondary facets of the problem: blocked bank accounts, family reunification, and internal refugees. The resolution, in part or in full, of these problems was designed, first and foremost, to please Washington, which had firmly demanded some sort of Israeli gesture regarding the refugee question, particularly following the sidelining of the repatriation principle. The Americans hoped that an Israeli gesture would prompt the Arabs to implement the resettlement principle all the more forcefully. But this hope had no foundation. The considerations of each of the Arab states regarding resolution of the refugee problem were not tied in any way to these symbolic Israeli gestures.

Among the three issues at stake, the issue of the blocked bank accounts was the only one that approached almost full resolution. In the course of the time frame during which the campaign to unfreeze the accounts took place (in two stages, between March 1953 and August 1956), approximately 2.8 million British pounds were freed from bank accounts, securities, and contents of safety-deposit boxes – approximately 90 percent of all the refugee assets frozen by Israel. This campaign affected 20,000 to 30,000 refugees. In the framework of family reunification, the return of approximately 5,200 refugees was approved between late 1949 and the outset of 1956. In the end, only some 4,300 persons opted to utilize their permits. The problem of internal refugees affected the fate of almost 28,000 persons. Most received housing and employment solutions from the authorities, but their core demand – to return to their previous places of residence – remained, for the most part, unanswered due to security concerns and political considerations.

Resolution of the three secondary issues didn't advance overall resolution of the refugee problem by even the smallest measure, since the number of refugees affected by them was small – in essence, a drop in the bucket. These gestures were the only concrete payments raised by Israel to resolve the Palestinian refugee problem during the period under study (and in essence henceforth).[1] "Payment" in the coinage of repatriation was dropped from the agenda with the direct or indirect support of the western powers, the United Nations, and the Arab states, while "payment" in the form of compensation remains open for discussion.

Note

1 The "family reunification" procedure continued to exist, in various incarnations, for many years after the period discussed here.

Bibliography

Primary sources

Archives

Israel State Archives (ISA), Jerusalem, Israel

> Government Meetings
> Government's Resolutions
> Foreign Affairs and Defense Committee Meetings
> Prime Minister's Office
> Ministry of Foreign Affairs (MFA)
> Bureau of the Adviser on Arab Affairs (GL)

Ben-Gurion Archives (BGA), Sede Boker, Israel

> Ben-Gurion Diary (BGD)
> Ben-Gurion's Bureau – As Prime Minister
> Minutes of Meetings
> Correspondences

Israel Defence Forces and Defence Establishment Archives (IDFA), Tel Aviv, Israel
Israel Labor Party Archives (ILPA), Beit Berl, Israel

> Political Committee Meetings
> Central Committee Meetings
> Council Meetings
> Parliamentary Party Meetings

Ha-Shomer Ha-Tzair Archives (HHA), Givat Haviva, Israel
Yad Tabenkin Archives (YTA), Ramat Efal, Israel
United Kingdom National Archives (UKNA), London, United Kingdom
> Foreign Office Files (FO)

Published documents

State of Israel – Israel State Archives and World Zionist Organization – Central Zionist Archives, *Political and Diplomatic Documents, December 1947–May 1948* (PDD), Jerusalem: The Government Printer, 1979.

Bibliography 283

State of Israel – Israel State Archives, *Documents on the Foreign Policy of Israel* (DEPI), Jerusalem: The Government Printer
Vol. 1 (14 May–30 September 1948), 1981.
Vol. 2 (October 1948–April 1949), 1984.
Vol. 3 (Armistice Negotiations with the Arab States, December 1948–July 1949), 1983.
Vol. 4 (May–December 1949), 1986.
Vol. 5 (1950), 1988.
Vol. 6 (1951), 1991.
Vol. 7 (1952), 1992.
Vol. 8 (1953), 1995.
Vol. 9 (1954), 2004.
Vol. 11 (January–October 1956), 2008.

United States – Department of State, *Foreign Relations of the United States* (FRUS), Washington, DC: United States Government Printing Office.

Vol. V (The Near East, South Asia and Africa, 1948), 1976.
Vol. VI (The Near East, South Asia and Africa, 1949), 1977.
Vol. V (The Near East, South Asia and Africa, 1950), 1978.
Vol. V (The Near East and Africa, 1951), 1982.
Vol. IX: Part I and II (The Near and Middle East, 1952–1954), 1986.
Vol. XIV (Arab-Israeli Dispute, 1955–1957: 1955), 1989.
Vol. XV (Arab-Israeli Dispute, 1955–1957: 1 January–26 July, 1956), 1989.

United Nations, *United Nations Economic Survey Mission for the Middle East* (UNESM). First interim report of the U.N. Economic Survey Mission for the Middle East, Document A/1106 of 17 November 1949.
United Nations, *United Nations Conciliation Commission for Palestine* (UNPCC). General Assembly, Official Records

Sixth Progress Report for the period 9 December 1949 to 8 May 1950. Document A/1255 (29 May 1950).
Seventh Progress Report for the period 8 May to 12 July 1950. Document A/1288 (17 July 1950).
Eighth Progress Report for the period 11 December 1949 to 23 October 1950. Document A/1367/Rev.1 (2 October 1950).
Ninth Progress Report for the period 25 January to 10 March 1951. Document A/1793 (10 March 1951).
Tenth Progress Report for the period 23 January to 19 November 1951. Document A/1985 (19 November 1951).
Eleventh Progress Report for the period 19 November 1951 to 30 April 1952. Document A/2121 (2 May 1952).
Twelfth Progress Report for the period 1 May to 24 November 1952. Document A/2216 (8 October 1952).
Thirteenth Progress Report for the period 28 November 1952 to 31 December 1953. Document A/2629 (4 January 1954).
Fourteenth Progress Report for the period 31 December 1953 to 31 December 1954. Document A/2897 (3 March 1955).
Fifteenth Progress Report for the period 1 January 1955 to 30 September 1956. Document A/3199 (4 October 1956).

284 *Bibliography*

United Nations, *United Nations Relief and Works Agency for Palestine Refugees in the Near East* (UNRWA). General Assembly, Official Records
Fifth Session, Supplement No. 19 (A/1451/Rev. 1), Interim report of the director.
Sixth Session, Supplement No. 16 (A/1905), Annual report of the director covering the period 1 May 1950 to 30 June 1951.
Seventh Session, Supplement No. 13 (A/2171), Annual report of the director covering the period 1 July 1951 to 30 June 1952.
Eighth Session, Supplement No. 12 (A/2470), Annual report of the director covering the period 1 July 1952 to 30 June 1953.
Ninth Session, Supplement No. 17 (A/2717), Annual report of the director covering the period 1 July 1953 to 30 June 1954.
Tenth Session, Supplement No. 15 (A/2978), Annual report of the director covering the period 1 July 1954 to 30 June 1955.
Eleventh Session, Supplement No. 14 (A/3212), Annual report of the director covering the period 1 July 1955 to 30 June 1956.
Twelfth Session, Supplement No. 14 (A/3686), Annual report of the director covering the Period 1 July 1956 to 30 June 1957.

Gokay, Bulent (ed.), *British Documents on Foreign Affairs: Near and Middle East, 1951*, vol. 2, London: Lexis Nexis, 2005.
Hurewitz, J.C. (ed.), *Diplomacy in the Near and Middle East: A Documentary Record, 1914–1956*, New York: Octagon Books, 1972.
Jarman, Robert L. (ed.), *Political Diaries of the Arab World: Palestine and Jordan, 1948–1965*, vol. 10, Slough: Archive Editions, 2001.
Medzini, Meron (ed.), *Israel's Foreign Relations: Selected Documents, 1947–1974*, Jerusalem: Ministry for Foreign Affairs, 1976.
Rosenthal, Yemima (ed.), *Moshe Sharett – The Second Prime Minister: Selected Documents (1894–1965)*, Jerusalem: Israel State Archives, 2007 (Hebrew).
Sharett, Yaakov and Rina Sharett (eds), Speaking Out: Israel's Foreign Minister's Speeches, May-December 1948, Tel Aviv: Moshe Sharett Heritage Society, 2013 (Hebrew).
Tomeh, George J. (ed.), *United Nations Resolutions on Palestine and the Arab-Israeli Conflict, 1947–1974*, vol. 1, Washington, DC: Institute for Palestine Studies, 1975.

Published minutes

Knesset Minutes (Israel Parliament), vols 1, 2, 8, 10, 11, 12, 13, 14, 19.

Official publications

United States Congress – Committee of Foreign Affairs, *The Arab Refugees and Other Problems in the Near East*, Washington, DC: U.S. Government, 1954.
Sicron, Moshe, *Immigration to Israel, 1948–1953*, Jerusalem: The Falk Institute for Economic Research in Israel and the Central Bureau of Statistics, 1957.
Chief Education Officer (Information Branch), *The War of Independence*, Jerusalem: Israel Information Center, 1980 (Hebrew).

Newspapers

Israel: *Davar, Al Ha-Mishmar, Herut, Ha-Modia, Kol Ha-Am, Ha-Boker, Ha-Tzofe, Lamerhav, Shaarim, Zmanim, Ha'aretz, Ma'ariv, Yedioth Ahronoth, The Jerusalem Post*
United States: *The Washington Post, The New York Times, USA Today.*

Bibliography 285

Memoirs

Azcarate, Pablo, *Mission in Palestine, 1948–1952*, Washington, DC: The Middle East Institute, 1966.

Beilin, Yossi, *Manual for a Wounded Dove*, Tel Aviv: Yedioth Ahronoth, 2001 (Hebrew).

Ben-Ami, Shlomo, *Scars of War, Wounds of Peace: The Israeli-Arab Tragedy*, Oxford: Oxford University Press, 2007.

Ben-Gurion, David, *Negotiations with Nasser*, Jerusalem: Israel Information Center, 1970.

——, *War Diary*, Tel Aviv: Ministry of Defence, 1982 (Hebrew).

Bernadotte, Folke, *To Jerusalem*, trans. Joan Bulman, London: Hodder and Stoughton, 1951.

Clinton, Bill, *My Life*, New York: Alfred A. Knopf, 2004.

Danin, Ezra, *Unconditional Zionist*, Jerusalem: Kidom, 1987 (Hebrew).

Dayan, Moshe, *Story of My Life*, Jerusalem: Steimatzky's Agency, 1976.

Eban, Abba, *An Autobiography*, New York: Random House, 1977.

——, *Personal Witness: Israel through My Eyes*, New York: G.P. Putnam's Sons, 1992.

Elath, Eliahu, *Through the Mist of Time: Reminiscences*, Jerusalem: Yad Izhak Ben-Zvi, 1989 (Hebrew).

Glubb, John Bagot, *A Soldier with the Arabs*, London: Hodder and Stoughton, 1957.

Indyk, Martin, *Innocent Abroad: An Intimate Account of American Peace Diplomacy in the Middle East*, New York: Simon and Schuster, 2009.

Jackson, Elmore, *Middle East Mission*, New York: Norton and Company, 1983.

Kirkbride, Alec, *From the Wings: Amman Memoirs, 1947–1951*, London: Frank Cass, 1976.

Kollek, Teddy, *For Jerusalem*, Jerusalem: Steimatzky's Agency, 1978.

Macmillan, Harold, *Tides of Fortune, 1945–1955*, London: Macmillan, 1969.

McDonald, James G., *My Mission in Israel, 1948–1951*, New York: Simon and Schuster, 1951.

McGhee, George, *Envoy to the Middle World: Adventures in Diplomacy*, New York: Harper and Row, 1983.

Rafael, Gideon, *Destination Peace: Three Decades of Israeli Foreign Policy – A Personal Memoir*, London: Weidenfeld and Nicolson, 1981.

Ross, Dennis, *The Missing Peace: The Inside Story of the Fight for Middle East Peace*, New York: Farrar, Straus and Giroux, 2004.

Sasson, Moshe, *Talking Peace*, Or Yehuda: Ma'ariv, 2004 (Hebrew).

Sharett, Moshe, *Personal Diary*, vols 1–5, Tel Aviv: Am Oved, 1978 (Hebrew).

Sher, Gilead, *The Israeli-Palestinian Peace Negotiations, 1999–2001: Within Reach*, London, Routledge, 2006.

Shuckburgh, Evelyn, *Descent to Suez: Diaries, 1951–1956*, London: Weidenfeld and Nicolson, 1986.

Weitz, Joseph, *My Diary and Letters to the Children*, vols 3 and 4, Ramat Gan: Massada, 1965 (Hebrew).

Secondary sources

Books, articles, dissertations

Abbasi, Mustafa, "'City in Distress': Nazareth and the Problem of Internal Arab Refugees, 1948–1949," *Cathedra* 146, December 2012, pp. 117–43 (Hebrew).

286 Bibliography

Abd el-Wahab Sayed-Ahmed, Muhammad, *Nasser and American Foreign Policy, 1952–1956*, London: Laam, 1989.

Abu Massara, Muhammad, "The Refugees Issue in Israeli Policy in 1948–49," *International Problems, Society and Politics* 28 (53/3–4), 1989, pp. 36–57 (Hebrew).

Abu Nowar, Maan, *Jordanian-Israeli War, 1948–1951: A History of the Hashemite Kingdom of Jordan*, Ithaca, NY: Reading, 2002.

Alexander, D., "U.N. Aid to Palestine Refugees," *The New East* 5(1), 1953, pp. 1–13 (Hebrew).

Alteras, Isaac, *Eisenhower and Israel: U.S.- Israeli Relations, 1953–1960*, Gainesville, FL: University Press of Florida, 1993.

Alterman, Jon, "American Aid to Egypt in the 1950s: From Hope to Hostility," *The Middle East Journal* 52(1), 1998, pp. 51–70.

Amitay, Yossi, *The United Workers' Party (Mapam), 1948–1954: Attitude on Palestinian-Arab Issues*, Tel Aviv: Tcherikover, 1988 (Hebrew).

——, "The Arab Minority in Israel: The Military Government's Years, 1948–1966," in Anita Shapira (ed.), *Independence: The First Fifty Years*, Jerusalem: The Zalman Shazar Center, 1998, pp. 129–49 (Hebrew).

Aridan, Natan, *Britain, Israel and Anglo-Jewry, 1949–1957*, London and New York: Routledge, 2004.

Aronson, Geoffrey, *From Sideshow to Center Stage: U.S. Policy toward Egypt, 1946–1956*, Boulder, CO: Lynne Rienner Publishers, 1986.

Ashton, Nigel John, *Eisenhower, Macmillan and the Problem of Nasser: Anglo-American Relations and Arab Nationalism, 1955–1959*, London: Macmillan, 1996.

Asia, Ilan, *The Core of the Conflict: The Struggle for the Negev, 1947–1956*, Jerusalem: Yad Izhak Ben-Zvi, 1994 (Hebrew).

Avidan, Meir, *Main Aspects of Israel-United States Relations during the 1950's*, Jerusalem: The Hebrew University, 1982 (Hebrew).

Baily, Clinton, *The Participation of the Palestinians in the Politics of Jordan*, Ann Arbor, MI: University Microfilms, 1972.

Bambaji-Sasportas, Haya, "Whose Voice Is heard/Whose Voice Is Silenced: The Construction of 'The Palestinian Refugees Problem' Discourse in the Israeli Establishment, 1948–1952," MA thesis, Ben-Gurion University, 2000 (Hebrew).

Barkai, Haim, *The Beginnings of the Israeli Economy*, Jerusalem: Bialik Institute, 1990 (Hebrew).

Bar-On, Mordechai, *The Gates of Gaza: Israel's Road to Suez and Back, 1955–1957*, New York: St. Martin's Press, 1994.

——, "Status Quo Before – or After? Commentary Notes on Israel's Defense Policy 1949–1958," *Iyunim Bitkumat Israel* 5, 1995, pp. 65–112 (Hebrew).

——, *Of All the Kingdoms: Israel's Relations with the United Kingdom during the First Decade after the End of the British Mandate in Palestine, 1948–1959*, Jerusalem: Yad Izhak Ben-Zvi, 2006 (Hebrew).

Bar Siman Tov, Yaacov, "Ben-Gurion and Sharett: Conflict Management and Great-Power Constraints in Israeli Foreign Policy," *Middle Eastern Studies* 24(3), 1988, pp. 330–57.

Barzily, Ronit and Mustafa Kabha, *Refugees in their Homeland: Internal Refugees in the State of Israel, 1948–1996*, Givat Haviva: The Institute for Peace Research, 1996 (Hebrew).

Bar-Zohar, Michael, *Ben-Gurion: A Political Biography*, Tel Aviv: Am Oved, 1977 (Hebrew).

Bibliography 287

Beker, Avi, *The United Nations and Israel: From Recognition to Reprehension*, Lexington, MA: Lexington Books, 1988.

Ben-Dor, Gabriel (ed.), *The Palestinians and the Middle East Conflict*, Ramat Gan: Turtledore Pub., 1978.

Ben-Dror, Elad, *The Mediator: Ralph Bunche and the Arab-Israeli Conflict, 1947–1949*, Sede Boqer: The Ben-Gurion Research Institute, 2012 (Hebrew).

Ben-Horin, Daniel, "The Crystallization of Two Orientations to the Arab-Israel Conflict: David Ben-Gurion and Moshe Sharett," PhD thesis, University of Haifa, 1991 (Hebrew).

Benziman, Uzi and Atallah Mansour, *Subtenants: Israeli Arabs – Their Status and the Policy toward Them*, Jerusalem: Keter, 1992 (Hebrew).

Ben-Zvi, Abraham, *Decade of Transition: Eisenhower, Kennedy and the Origins of the American-Israeli Alliance*, New York: Columbia University Press, 1998.

Bialer, Uri, "Ben-Gurion and Sharett – Two Perceptions of the Arab-Israeli Conflict," in Benyamin Neuberger (ed.), *Diplomacy and Confrontation: Selected Issues in Israeli Foreign Relations, 1948–1978*, Tel Aviv: The Open University, 1984, pp. 189–206 (Hebrew).

——, *Between East and West: Israel's Foreign Policy Orientation, 1948–1956*, Cambridge: Cambridge University Press, 1990.

Bishku, Michael B., "The Other Side of the Arab-Israeli Conflict: Great Britain and the Issue of Iraqi Jewry Prior to 'Operation Ezra and Nehemia'," *Studies in Zionism* 12(1), 1991, pp. 29–41.

Bligh, Alexander, "From U.N.R.W.A. to Israel: The 1952 Transfer of Responsibilities for Refugees in Israel," *Refuge* 14(6), November 1994, pp. 1–7.

——, "Israel and the Refugee Problem: From Exodus to Resettlement, 1948–1952," *Middle Eastern Studies* 34(1), 1998, pp. 123–48.

Bodansky, Yossef, *The High Cost of Peace: How Washington's Middle East Policy Left America Vulnerable to Terrorism*, Roseville, CA: Prima Publishing, 2002.

Botsai, Sarah Lillian, *The United States and the Palestine Refugees*, Ann Arbor, MI: University Microfilms, 1972.

Brand, Laurie, "Building the Bridge of Return: Palestinian Corporate Mobilization in Egypt, Kuwayt and Jordan," PhD thesis, Columbia University, 1985.

——, "Palestinians in Syria: The Politics of Integration," *The Middle East Journal* 42 (4), 1988, pp. 621–38.

Brecher, Michael, *Decisions in Israel's Foreign Policy*, London: Oxford University Press, 1974.

Buehrig, Edward H., *The U.N. and the Palestinian Refugees*, Bloomington, IN: Indiana University Press, 1971.

Campbell, John C., *Defense of the Middle East: Problems of American Policy*, New York: Harper and Brothers, 1960.

Caplan, Neil, *The Lausanne Conference, 1949*, Tel Aviv: Tel Aviv University Press, 1993.

——, *Futile Diplomacy: The United Nations, the Great Powers and Middle East Peacemaking, 1948–1954*, Portland, OR: Frank Cass, 1997.

——, *Futile Diplomacy: Operation Alpha and the Failure of Anglo-American Coercive Diplomacy in the Arab-Israeli Conflict, 1954–1956*, London: Frank Cass, 1997.

Carmy, Shulamit and Henri Rosenfeld, "The Time When the Majority of the Israeli 'Cabinet' Decided 'Not to Block the Possibility of Return of the Palestinian Refugees', and How and Why This Policy Was Defeated ?," *Medina Vechevra* 2(3), 2002, pp. 371–99 (Hebrew).

288   Bibliography

Chill, Dan S., *The Arab Boycott of Israel: Economic Aggression and World Reaction*, New York: Praeger, 1976.

Cohen, Aharon, *Israel and the Arab World*, New York: Funk and Wagnalls, 1970.

Cohen, Hillel, *The Present Absentees: The Palestinian Refugees in Israel since 1948*, Jerusalem: The Institute for Israeli Arab Studies, 2000 (Hebrew).

——, *Good Arabs: The Israeli Security Agencies and the Israeli Arabs, 1948–1967*, Berkeley, CA: University of California Press, 2010.

Cohen, Orna, "The Arabs of Majdal (Ashqelon): Changes of Their Situation between the War of 1948 and Their Evacuation from the State of Israel," MA thesis, The Hebrew University, 1999 (Hebrew).

Daneels, Isabelle, *Palestinian Refugees and the Peace Process: An Analysis of Public Opinion Surveys in the West Bank and the Gaza Strip*, Jerusalem: Jerusalem Media and Communication Centre, 2001.

Dekmejian, R. Hrair, *Egypt under Nasir: A Study in Political Dynamics*, Albany, NY: State University of New York Press, 1971.

Dessouki, Ali E. Hillal, "Nasser and the Struggle for Independence," in Roger Louis and Roger Owen (eds), *Suez 1956: The Crisis and Its Consequences,* Oxford: Clarendon Press, 1991, pp. 29–47.

Donohue, James T., "Before Suez: John Foster Dulles and the Arab-Israeli Conflict, 1940–1954," PhD thesis, University Microfilms, 1989.

Douglas-Home, Charles, *The Arabs and Israel: A Background Book*, London: The Bodley Head Ltd., 1968.

Doyle, Chris, *Camp David II – A Synopsis: What Was Discussed at the Camp David Summit, July 2000*, London: Council for the Advancement of Arab-British Understanding, 2000.

Druks, Herbert, *The Uncertain Friendship: The U.S. and Israel from Roosevelt to Kennedy*, Westport, CT: Greenwood Press, 2001.

Eban, Abba, *Voice of Israel*, New York: Horizon Press, 1957.

Efrat, Moshe, "The Palestinian Refugees: Social and Economic Survey 1949–1974," MA thesis, Tel Aviv University, 1976 (Hebrew).

——, "The Palestinian Refugees: The Socio-Economic Integration in their Host Countries," *Orient* 42(1), 2001, pp. 45–71.

Elizur, Yuval, *Economic Warfare: The Hundred-Year Economic Confrontation between Jews and Arabs*, Tel Aviv: Kinneret, 1997 (Hebrew).

Epstein, Alec D. and Michael Uritsky, "What Happened and What Did Not Happen: The Yishuv, the End of the Mandate, and the Emergence of the Refugee Problem," *Gesher* 149, 2004, pp. 57–79 (Hebrew).

Erlich, Reuven, *The Lebanon Tangle: The Policy of the Zionist Movement and the State of Israel towards Lebanon, 1918–1958*, Tel Aviv: Ma'arachot, 2000 (Hebrew).

Eshed, Haggai, *One Man "Mossad": Reuven Shiloah – Father of Israeli Intelligence*, Tel Aviv: Edanim, 1988 (Hebrew).

Evron, Yair, "Foreign and Defence Policy: Structural and Personal Aspects, 1949–1956," *Zionism* 14, 1989, pp. 219–31 (Hebrew).

Eytan, Walter, *The First Ten Years: A Diplomatic History of Israel*, London: Weidenfeld and Nicolson, 1958.

Feiler, Gil, *From Boycott to Economic Cooperation: The Political Economy of the Arab Boycott of Israel*, London: Frank Cass, 1998.

Fischbach, Michael R., "The United Nations and Palestinian Refugee Property Compensation," *Journal of Palestine Studies* 31(2), 2002, pp. 34–50.

Bibliography 289

——, *Records of Dispossession: Palestinian Refugee Property and the Arab-Israeli Conflict*, New York: Columbia University Press, 2003.

Flapan, Simha, *The Birth of Israel – Myths and Realities*, London: Croom Helm, 1987.

Forsythe, David P., "UNRWA, the Palestine Refugees and World Politics: 1949–1969," *International Organization* 25(1), 1971, pp. 26–46.

——, *United Nations Peacemaking – The Conciliation Commission for Palestine*, Baltimore, MD: The Johns Hopkins University Press, 1972.

Freiberger, Steven Z., *Dawn over Suez: The Rise of American Power in the Middle East, 1953–1957*, Chicago: Ivan R. Dee, 1992.

Fried, Shelly, "Precious Land – Israel's Policy on Compensation for Abandoned Palestinian Property, 1947–1951: From the UN Partition Resolution to the Paris Conference," MA thesis, Tel Aviv University, 1998 (Hebrew).

——, "'They Are Not Coming Back' – The Crystallization of Israeli Foreign Policy toward Possible Solutions of the Palestinian Refugee Problem, 1947–1956: From the UN Partition Resolution to the Suez Campaign," PhD thesis, Tel Aviv University, 2003 (Hebrew).

Gabbay, Rony E., *A Political Study of the Arab-Jewish Conflict – The Arab Refugee Problem (A Case Study)*, Geneve: Librairie E. Droz, 1959.

Gama, Abid Husni, *The United Nations and the Palestinian Refugees: An Analysis of the United Nations Relief and Works Agency for the Palestine Refugees in the Near East, 1 May 1950–30 June 1971*, Ann Arbor, MI: University Microfilms, 1972.

Gat, Moshe, *The Jewish Exodus from Iraq, 1948–1951*, London: Frank Cass, 1997.

Gazit, Mordechai, "American and British Diplomacy and the Bernadotte Mission," *The Historical Journal* 29(3), 1986, pp. 677–96.

——, "Ben-Gurion's Proposal to Include the Gaza Strip in Israel, 1949," *Zionism* 12, 1987, pp. 315–32 (Hebrew).

——, "The Israel-Jordan Peace Negotiations (1949–1951): King Abdallah's Lonely Effort," *Journal of Contemporary History* 23(3), July 1988, pp. 409–24.

Gelber, Yoav, *Jewish-Transjordanian Relations, 1921–1948*, London: Frank Cass, 1997.

——, *Palestine 1948: War, Escape and the Emergence of the Palestinian Refugee Problem*, Brighton: Sussex Academic Press, 2001.

Gerges, Fawas A., *The Superpowers and the Middle East Regional and International Politics, 1955–1967*, Boulder, CO: Westview Press, 1994.

Gerner, Deborah J., "Missed Opportunities and Roads Not Taken: The Eisenhower Administration and the Palestinians," *Arab Studies Quarterly* 12(1–2), 1990, pp. 67–100.

Ginat, Rami, *The Soviet Union and Egypt, 1945–1955*, London: Frank Cass, 1993.

Golan, Arnon, *Wartime Spatial Changes: Former Arab Territories within the State of Israel, 1948–1950*, Sede Boqer: The Ben-Gurion Research Institute, 2001 (Hebrew).

Golan, Shimon, *Hot Border, Cold War: The Formulation of Israel's Security Policy, 1949–1953*, Tel Aviv: Ma'arachot, 2000 (Hebrew).

Golan, Shimon and Shaul Shay, "The Challenges of Infiltration and the Response to Them, 1949–1956," in Haggai Golan and Shaul Shay (eds), *When the Engines Roared: 50th Anniversary to the Sinai War*, Tel Aviv: Ma'arachot, 2006, pp. 175–201 (Hebrew).

Golani, Motti, *Israel in Search of a War: The Sinai Campaign, 1955–1956*, Brighton: Sussex Academic Press, 1998.

Goldstein, Yossi, "The Great Aliyah and the Palestinian Villages: The Settlement Dynamics, 1948–1951," *Social Issues in Israel* 12, 2011, pp. 32–62 (Hebrew).

Goren, Tamir, *The Fall of Arab Haifa in 1948*, Sede Boqer: The Ben-Gurion Research Institute, 2006 (Hebrew).

290   Bibliography

Goria, Wade R., *Sovereignty and Leadership in Lebanon, 1943–1976*, London: Ithaca Press, 1985.

Greitzer, Dina, "Ben-Gurion, Mapai and the Attitude towards the Arab Minority in Israel, 1948–1956," PhD thesis, The Hebrew University, 1995 (Hebrew).

Haddad, Simon, *The Palestinian Impasse in Lebanon: The Politics of Refugee Integration*, Brighton and Portland: Sussex Academic Press, 2003.

Hahn, Peter L., *The United States, Great Britain and Egypt, 1945–1956: Strategy and Diplomacy in the Early Cold War*, Chapel Hill, NC: The University of North Carolina Press, 1991.

Haj, Majid al, "The Arab Internal Refugees in Israel: The Emergence of a Minority within the Minority," *Immigrants and Minorities* 7(2), July 1988, pp. 149–65.

Hanieh, Akram, "The Camp David Papers," *Journal of Palestine Studies* 30(2), 2001, pp. 75–97.

Haron, Miriam Joyce, *Palestine and the Anglo-American Connection, 1945–1950*, New York: Peter Lang, 1986.

Heikal, Mohamed Hassanein, *The Cairo Documents: The Inside Story of Nasser and His Relationship with World Leaders, Rebels and Statesmen*, Garden City, NY: Doubleday and Company, 1973.

Holland, Matthew F., *America and Egypt: From Roosevelt to Eisenhower*, London: Praeger, 1996.

Howley, Dennis C., *The United Nations and the Palestinians*, Hicksville, NY: Exposition Press, 1975.

Ilan, Amitzur, *Bernadotte in Palestine 1948: A Study in Contemporary Humanitarian Knight-Errantry*, Basingstoke: Macmillan, 1989.

Jelinek, Yeshayahu A., *Deutschland und Israel, 1945–1965: Ein Neurotisches Verhaltnis*, Munchen: R Oldenbourg Verlag, 2004.

Joffe, Alexander H. and Asaf Romirowsky, "A Tale of Two Galloways: Notes on the Early History of UNRWA and Zionist Historiography," *Middle Eastern Studies* 46(5), 2010, pp. 655–75.

Junod, Dominique D., *The Imperiled Red Cross and the Palestine–Eretz-Yisrael Conflict 1945–1952*, London: Kegan Paul International, 1996.

Kafkafi, Eyal, "Ben-Gurion, Sharett ant the Johnston Plan," *Studies in Zionism* 13(2), 1992, pp. 165–86.

Kamen, Charles S., "After the Catastrophe I: The Arabs in Israel, 1948–1951," *Middle Eastern Studies* 23(4), 1987, pp. 453–96.

——, "After the Catastrophe II: The Arabs in Israel, 1948–1951," *Middle Eastern Studies* 24(1), 1988, pp. 68–110.

Kano, Jacques, *The Problem of Land between Jews and Arabs (1917–1990)*, Tel Aviv: Sifriat Poalim, 1992 (Hebrew).

Kaplan, Deborah, *The Arab Refugees: An Abnormal Problem*, Jerusalem: Rubin Mass, 1959.

Kark, Ruth, "Planning, Housing, and Land Policy 1948–1952: The Formation of Concepts and Governmental Frameworks," in Ilan S. Troen and Noah Lucas (eds), *Israel First Decade of Independence*, Albany, NY: State University of New York Press, 1995, pp. 461–95.

Karsh, Efraim, "Falsification Out of Awareness? Falsification Out of Blindness? – Benny Morris on the 'Transfer' Issue," *Alpayim* 13, 1996, pp. 212–32 (Hebrew).

——, *Fabricating Israeli History: The "New Historians"*, London: Frank Cass, 1997.

Bibliography 291

Katz, Yossi, "Yoseph Weitz and the Transfer of Arab Population," *Iyunim Bitkumat Israel* 8, 1998, pp. 347–54 (Hebrew).

Kedar, Alexander, "Israeli Law and the Redemption of Arab Land, 1948–1969," SJD thesis, Harvard University, 1996.

Kertin, Amnon, "The Program for Rehabilitating Palestinian Refugees in the Eastern Ghor in the Kingdom of Jordan," *Studies in the Geography of Israel* 13, 1992, pp. 49–62 (Hebrew).

——, "A Geographical Study of the Impact of Hostile Relations between Neighboring Countries on the Characteristics of Settlement in their Common Frontier Zones: The Case of Israel's Frontier Zones," PhD thesis, Tel Aviv University, 1995 (Hebrew).

Khouri, Fred J., "United Nations Peace Efforts," in Malcolm H. Ker (ed.), *The Elusive Peace in the Middle East,* Albany, NY: State University of New York Press, 1975, pp. 19–102.

Kimmerling, Baruch, *Zionism and Territory: The Socio-Territorial Dimensions of Zionist Politics,* Berkeley, CA: University of California Press, 1983.

Kimmerling, Baruch and Joel S. Migdal, *Palestinians: The Making of a People,* New York: The Free Press, 1993.

Kolinsky, M., "The Efforts of the Truman Administration to Resolve the Arab–Israeli Conflict," *Middle Eastern Studies* 20(1), 1984, pp. 81–94.

Kushner, Arlene, "The UN's Palestinian Refugee Problem," *Azure* 22, 2005, pp. 57–77.

Lahav, Mordechai, *50 Years of the Palestinian Refugees, 1948–1999,* Haifa: self-published, 2000 (Hebrew).

Leibovich, Ariel, "The Palestinian Refugee Issue in Israeli Foreign Policy 1948–1967," PhD thesis, University of Haifa, 2012 (Hebrew).

Lesch, David W., *Syria and the United States: Eisenhower's Cold War in the Middle East,* Boulder, CO: Westview Press, 1992.

Levey, Zach, *Israel and the Western Powers, 1952–1960,* Chapel Hill, NC: The University of North Carolina Press, 1997.

Levin, Itamar, *Locked Doors: The Seizure of Jewish Property in Arab Countries,* London: Praeger, 2001.

Lewis, Frank D., "Agricultural Property and the 1948 Palestinian Refugees: Assessing the Loss," *Explorations in Economic History* 33(2), 1996, pp. 169–94.

Liskovsky, Aharon, "'Resident Absentees' in Israel," *The New East* 10(3), 1960, pp. 186–92 (Hebrew).

Little, Douglas, "Cold War and Covert Action: The United States and Syria, 1945–1958," *The Middle East Journal* 44(1), 1990, pp. 51–76.

——, *American Orientalism: The United States and the Middle East since 1945,* Chapel Hill, NC: The University of North Carolina Press, 2002.

Lorech, Natanel, *The History of the War of Independence,* Tel Aviv: Massada, 1958 (Hebrew).

Lowi, Miriam R., *Water and Power: The Politics of a Scarce Resource in the Jordan River Basin,* Cambridge: Cambridge University Press, 1993.

Lucas, Scott, *Divided We Stand: Britain, the U.S. and the Suez Crisis,* London: Sceptre, 1991.

Lucas, Scott and Ray Takeyh, "Alliance and Balance: The Anglo-American Relationship and Egyptian Nationalism, 1950–1957," *Diplomacy and Statecraft* 7(3), 1996, pp. 631–51.

Lustick, Ian, *Arabs in the Jewish State: Israel's Control of a National Minority,* Austin, TX: University of Texas Press, 1980.

292 Bibliography

Maddy-Weitzman, Bruce and Shimon Shamir (eds), *The Camp David Summit: What Went Wrong?*, Brighton and Portland: Sussex Academic Press, 2005.

Malley, Robert and Hussein Agha, "Camp David: The Tragedy of Errors," *New York Review of Books*, 9 August 2001.

Ma'oz, Moshe, *Syria and Israel: From War to Peacemaking*, Oxford: Clarendon Press, 1995.

Mazar, Ofer, *In the Shadow of the Sphinx: Gamal Abdel Nasser and the Making of the Special U.S.-Israel Relations*, Tel Aviv: Ministry of Defence, 2002 (Hebrew).

Meir-Glitzenstein, Esther, "The Palestinian Dispute and Jewish-Muslim Relations in Iraq in the 1940s," *Pe'amim* 62, 1995, pp. 111–32 (Hebrew).

——, "The Riddle of the Mass Aliya From Iraq – Causes, Context and Results," *Pe'amim* 71, 1997, pp. 25–55 (Hebrew).

Meron, Jacob, "The Expulsion of the Jews from the Arab States and the Position of the Palestinians toward It," *State, Government and International Relations* 36, 1992, pp. 27–56 (Hebrew).

Mishal, Shaul, "The Conflict between the West and East Banks under Jordanian Rule and Its Impact on the Governmental and Administrative Patterns in the West Bank (1949–1967)," PhD thesis, The Hebrew University, 1974 (Hebrew).

Morris, Benny, *The Birth of the Palestinian Refugee Problem, 1947–1949*, Tel Aviv: Am Oved, 1991 (Hebrew).

——, *Israel's Border Wars, 1949–1956: Arab Infiltration, Israeli Retaliation and the Countdown to the Suez War*, Tel Aviv: Am Oved, 1996 (Hebrew).

——, *Correcting a Mistake: Jews and Arabs in Palestine, 1936–1956*, Tel Aviv: Am Oved, 2000 (Hebrew).

——, "The Historiography of Deir Yassin," *The Journal of Israeli History* 24(1), 2005, pp. 79–108.

Naff, Thomas and Ruth C. Matson, *Water in the Middle East: Conflict or Cooperation?*, Boulder, CO: Westview Press, 1984.

Nassar, Maha, "Palestinian Citizens of Israel and the Discourse on the Right of Return, 1948–1959," *Journal of Palestine Studies* 40(4), 2011, pp. 45–60.

Nets-Zehngut, Rafi, "Origins of the Palestinian Refugee Problem: Changes in the Historical Memory of Israelis/Jews, 1949–2004," *Journal of Peace Research* 48(2), 2011, pp. 235–49.

Neuberger, Benyamin, *Political Parties in Israel*, Tel Aviv: The Open University, 1997 (Hebrew).

Nevo, Joseph, *King Abdallah and Palestine: A Territorial Ambition*, Oxford: Macmillan, 1996.

Nimrod, Yoram, *Anger Waters: The Controversy over the Jordan River*, Givat Haviva: Center for Arabic and Afro-Asian Studies, 1966 (Hebrew).

——, *War or Peace? Formation of Patterns in Israel-Arab Relations, 1947–1950*, Givat Haviva: The Institute for Peace Research, 2000 (Hebrew).

Ninburg-Levy, Ruth, "The Arab Position at Lausanne Conference, 1949," MA thesis, University of Haifa, 1987 (Hebrew).

Oren, Michael B., *Origins of the Second Arab-Israel War: Egypt, Israel and the Great Powers, 1952–1956*, London: Frank Cass, 1992.

Oren-Nordheim, Michal, "The Crystallization of Settlement Land Policy in the State of Israel from Its Establishment and during the First Years of the Israel Lands Administration (1948 –1965)," PhD thesis, The Hebrew University, 1999 (Hebrew).

Orren, Elhannan, "From the Transfer Proposal of 1937–1938 to the 'Transfer De Facto' of 1947–1948," *Iyunim Bitkumat Israel* 7, 1997, pp. 75–85 (Hebrew).

Bibliography 293

Ozacky-Lazar, Sarah, "The Crystallization of Mutual Relations between Jews and Arabs in the State of Israel: The First Decade, 1948–1958," PhD thesis, University of Haifa, 1996 (Hebrew).

Pappe, Ilan, *Britain and the Arab-Israeli Conflict 1948–1951*, New York: St. Martin's Press, 1988.

——, *The Making of the Arab-Israeli Conflict 1947–1951*, New York: St Martin's Press, 1992.

Patinkin, Don, *The Israel Economy: The First Decade*, Jerusalem: The Falk Institute for Economic Research in Israel, 1967.

Paz, Shaul, "Between Ideology and Pragmatism: Mapam's Perceptions and Positions with Regard to Israel's Foreign and Defence Policy in the Years 1948–1954," PhD thesis, The Hebrew University, 1993 (Hebrew).

Pelcovits, Nathan A., *The Long Armistice – UN Peacekeeping and the Arab-Israeli Conflict, 1948–1960*, Boulder, CO: Westview Press, 1993.

Peretz, Don, *Israel and the Palestine Arabs*, Washington, DC: The Middle East Institute, 1958.

——, *The Palestine Arab Refugee Problem*, New York: Rand Corporation, 1969.

Perla, Shlomo, "Israel and the Palestine Conciliation Commission," *Middle Eastern Studies* 26(1), 1990, pp. 113–19.

Persson, Sune, *Meditation and Assassination: Count Bernadotte's Mission in Palestine, 1948*, London: Ithaca Press, 1979.

Pinner, Walter, *How Many Arab Refugees? A Critical Study of UNRWA's Statistics and Reports*, London: Macgibbon and Kee, 1959.

Plascov, Avi, *The Palestinian Refugees in Jordan, 1948–1957*, London: Frank Cass, 1981.

Prittie, Terence and Bernard Dineen, *The Double Exodus – A Study of Arab and Jewish Refugees in the Middle East*, London: The Goodhart Press, 1970.

Rabinovich, Itamar, "Egypt and the Palestine Question before and after the July Revolution," *Zmanim* 32, 1989, pp. 78–88 (Hebrew).

——, *The Road Not Taken: Early Arab-Israeli Negotiations*, New York: Oxford University Press, 1991.

——, *The Lingering Conflict: Israel, the Arabs and the Middle East 1948–2011*, Washington, DC: Brookings Institution Press, 2011.

Radai, Itamar, "Jaffa, 1948: The Fall of a City," *The Journal of Israeli History* 30(1), 2011, pp. 23–43.

Richardson, Channing B., "The United Nations and Arab Refugee Relief, 1948–1950: A Case Study in International Organization and Administration," PhD thesis, University Microfilms, 1951.

Rosenfeld, Henry, *They Were Peasants: Social Anthropological Studies on the Arab Village in Israel*, Tel Aviv: Hakibbutz Hameuhad, 1964 (Hebrew).

Rosenthal, Yemima, "David Ben-Gurion and Moshe Sharett Facing Decisions on Israeli Foreign Policy, 1949," *Monthly Review* 25(11), 1988, pp. 15–22 (Hebrew).

——, "Shaping Israeli Policy for the Palestine Conciliation Conference," *Zionism* 13, 1988, pp. 53–69 (Hebrew).

——, "Israel's Foreign Policy: Between Security and Diplomacy," in Hanna Yablonka and Zvi Zameret (eds), *The First Decade: 1948–1958*, Jerusalem: Yad Izhak Ben-Zvi, 1997, pp. 169–96 (Hebrew).

Rubin, Barry, *The Arab States and the Palestine Conflict*, Syracuse, NY: Syracuse University Press, 1981.

294   Bibliography

Sachar, Howard M., *Egypt and Israel*, New York: Richard Marek Publishers, 1981.

Saliba, Samir N., *The Jordan River Dispute*, The Hague: Martinus Nijhoff, 1968.

Sandberg, Haim, *The Lands of Israel: Zionism and Post-Zionism*, Jerusalem: self-published, 2007 (Hebrew).

Sarna, Aaron J., *Boycott and Blacklist: A History of Arab Economic Warfare against Israel*, Totowa, NJ: Rowman and Littlefield, 1986.

Saunders, Bonnie F., *The United States and Arab Nationalism: The Syrian Case, 1953–1960*, London: Praeger, 1996.

Schechtman, Joseph B., *The Arab Refugee Problem*, New York: Philosophical Library, 1952.

Schiff, Benjamin N., *Refugees unto the Third Generation: U.N. Aid to Palestinians*, Syracuse, NY: Syracuse University Press, 1995.

Schueftan, Dan, *A Jordanian Option: The Yishuv and the State of Israel vis-à-vis the Hashemite Regime and the Palestinian National Movement*, Tel Aviv: Yad Tabenkin, Hakibbutz Hameuhad, 1986 (Hebrew).

Segev, Tom, *1949: The First Israelis*, New York: The Free Press, 1986.

Sela, Avraham, "The Palestinian Arabs in the 1948 War," in Moshe Maoz and Benjamin Z. Kedar (eds), *The Palestinian National Movement: From Confrontation to Reconciliation?*, Tel Aviv: Ministry of Defence, 1996, pp. 115–203 (Hebrew).

Shalev, Aryeh, *The Israel-Syria Armistice Regime, 1949–1955*, Boulder, CO: Westview Press, 1993.

Shalom, Zaki, "From the PRO," *Iyunim Bitkumat Israel* 3, 1993, pp. 582–87 (Hebrew).

——, *Policy in the Shadow of Controversy: The Routine Security Policy of Israel, 1949–1956*, Tel Aviv: Ma'arachot, 1996 (Hebrew).

——, "Positions of Israeli Leaders Regarding the Territorial Status Quo – A New Perspective," *Iyunim Bitkumat Israel* 8, 1998, pp. 110–50 (Hebrew).

——, "Gideon Raphael's Summary and Lesson from the Negotiations with Egypt, 1949–1955," *Iyunim Bitkumat Israel* 10, 2000, pp. 753–83 (Hebrew).

——, *David Ben-Gurion, the State of Israel and the Arab World, 1949–1956*, Brighton: Sussex Academic Press, 2002.

Shamir, Shimon, "The Collapse of Project Alpha," in Roger Louis and Roger Owen (eds), *Suez 1956: The Crisis and Its Consequences*, Oxford: Clarendon Press, 1991, pp. 73–100.

Sheffer, Gabriel, *Resolution vs. Management of the Middle East Conflict: A Reexamination of the Confrontation between Moshe Sharett and David Ben-Gurion*, Jerusalem: Magnes Press, 1980.

——, *Moshe Sharett: Biography of a Political Moderate*, Oxford: Clarendon Press, 1996.

Shemesh, Moshe, "The Kadesh Operation and the Suez Campaign: The Middle Eastern Political Background, 1949–1956," *Iyunim Bitkumat Israel* 4, 1994, pp. 66–97 (Hebrew).

Shenhav, Yehuda, "Bringing Iraqi Jews to Israel," *Theory and Criticism* 12–13, 1999, pp. 67–77 (Hebrew).

Shiffer, Varda, "The 1949 Israeli Offer to Repatriate 100,000 Palestinian Refugees," *Middle East Focus* 9, 1986, pp. 13–18.

Shimoni, Yaacov and Evyatar Levine, *Political Dictionary of the Middle East in the Twentieth Century*, London: Weidenfeld and Nicolson, 1972.

Bibliography 295

Shlaim, Avi, "Conflicting Approaches to Israeli Relations with the Arabs: Ben-Gurion and Sharett 1953–1956," *The Middle East Journal* 37(2), 1983, pp. 180–201.

——, "Husni Za'im and the Plan to Resettle Palestinian Refugees in Syria," *Journal of Palestine Studies* 15(4), 1986, pp. 68–80.

——, *Collusion across the Jordan – King Abdullah, the Zionist Movement and the Partition of Palestine*, Oxford: Clarendon Press, 1988.

Sinaisky, S., "USSR-Egypt Military Cooperation Revisited," *International Affairs: A Russian Journal of World Politics, Diplomacy and International Relations* 59(2), 2013, pp. 150–61.

Slutsky, Yehuda, *History of the Hagana (Vol. 3: From Resistance to War)*, Tel Aviv: Am Oved, 1972 (Hebrew).

Smith, Charles D., *Palestine and the Arab-Israeli Conflict*, New York: St. Marin's Press, 1988.

Tal, David, "Israel's Retaliation Attacks: From Tactical to a Strategic Tool," in Motti Golani (ed.), *Black Arrow: Gaza Raid and Israeli Policy of Retaliation during the Fifties*, Tel Aviv: Ma'arachot, 1994, pp. 65–91 (Hebrew).

——, *Israel's Day-to-Day Security Conception: Its Origin and Development, 1949–1956*, Sede Boqer: The Ben-Gurion Research Institute, 1998 (Hebrew).

——, *War in Palestine, 1948: Strategy and Diplomacy*, London: Routledge, 2004.

Talmy, Ephraim, *Who's and Who's: The Lexicon of the War of Independence*, Tel Aviv: Davar, 1965 (Hebrew).

Tessler, Mark, *A History of the Israeli-Palestinian Conflict*, Bloomington, IN: Indiana University Press, 2009.

Teveth, Shabtai, "The Palestinian Refugee Problem and Its Origins (Review Article)," *Middle Eastern Studies* 26(2), 1990, pp. 214–50.

——, "Integrity and Rewriting Documents," *Alpayim* 13, 1996, pp. 233–56 (Hebrew).

Tiller, Stian Johansen and Hilde Henriksen Waage, "Powerful State, Powerless Mediator: The United States and the Peace Efforts of the Palestine Conciliation Commission, 1949–51," *The International History Review* 33(3), 2011, pp. 501–25.

Touval, Saadia, *The Peace Brokers: Mediators in the Arab-Israeli Conflict, 1949–1979*, Princeton, NJ: Princeton University Press, 1982.

Tovy, Jacob, "Israeli Policy in the Gaza Strip and the Palestinian Refugees, November 1956– March 1957," *Jama'a* 7, 2001, pp. 9–54 (Hebrew).

——, "Negotiating the Palestinian Refugees," *Middle East Quarterly* 10(2), 2003, pp. 39–50.

——, "David Ben-Gurion, Moshe Sharett and the Status of the Gaza Strip, 1948–1956," *Iyunim Bitkumat Israel* 13, 2003, pp. 139–63 (Hebrew).

Vander Clute, Norman, *Legal Aspects of the Arab Boycott*, New York: Practising Law Institute, 1977.

Viorst, Milton, *UNRWA and Peace in the Middle East*, Washington, DC: The Middle East Institute, 1989.

Wishart, David M., "The Breakdown of the Johnston Negotiations over the Jordan Waters," *Middle Eastern Studies* 26(4), 1990, pp. 536–47.

Wolf, Aaron T., *Hydropolitics along the Jordan River: Scarce Water and Its Impact on the Arab-Israeli Conflict*, Tokyo: United Nations University Press, 1995.

Ya'ari, Ehud, *Egypt and the Fedayeen, 1953–1960*, Givat Haviva: Center for Arabic and Afro-Asian Studies, 1975 (Hebrew).

Yitzhak, Ronen, "The Assassination of King Abdallah: The First Political Assassination in Jordan: Did it Truly Threaten the Hashemite Kingdom of Jordan?," *Diplomacy and Statecraft* 21(1), 2010, pp. 68–86.

296 Bibliography

Youngs, Tim, *The Middle East Crisis: Camp David, the "Al-Aqsa Intifada" and the Prospects for the Peace Process*, London: UK House of Commons Library, 2001.

Zeitune, Shaul, *Deterrence and Peace: Israel's Attempts to Arrive at a Settlement*, Tel Aviv: Tcherikover, 2000 (Hebrew).

Zimhoni, Dafna, "The Government of Iraq and the Mass Aliya of Jews to Israel," *Pe'amim* 39, 1989, pp. 64–103 (Hebrew).

Internet websites (valid to December 2008)

http://spirit.tau.ac.il/socant/peace/peaceindex/2000/data/july2000d.doc
http://www.jmcc.org/publicpoll/results/1999/no.34.htm
http://www.jmcc.org/publicpoll/results/2000/no.37.htm
http://www.nad-plo.org
http://mondediplo.com/2001/09/01middleeastleader?var_research-camp+david

Index

Please note that page numbers relating to Notes will have the letter 'n' following the page number.

1929 Disturbances 160

Abandoned Areas Ordinance (5708–1948), 28–9
Abandoned property *see* Jewish property, abandoned; Palestinian property, abandoned
Abdullah I bin al-Hussein, King of Jordan, 23, 87–9, 93–5, 97, 99–102, 106n, 174, 202; assassination (July, 1951), 102, 139, 155; blocked bank accounts, 102; compensation, 92, 94–5, 102; political settlement with Israel, 89–95, 97, 100–2; repatriation and resettlement, 89–92, 94–6, 99, 101–2, 103n, 120, 275
"Absentee" concept, defined, 30
Absentees' Property Law (5710–1950), 29–30, 93
Acheson, Dean, 40–1, 43, 45–6, 66n, 119; economic approach, 72–4; Lausanne Conference, 54, 60–1, 64; Paris Conference, 137–8, 149, 151; UNRWA, 82
Acre, 4, 259, 262
Afghanistan, 171
Afro-Asian conference of unaligned nations, Bandung (1955), 224
Agudat Israel (party), 148
Ahduth Ha-Avodah – Po'alei Zion (party), 15, 228
Alexandria, 55, 219
al-Defaa (newspaper), 184

Al Ha-Mishmar (newspaper), 15–16, 63, 148, 209
Al-Habbaniyah Lake valley, Iraq, 39
Allen, George, 229, 232
Alpha Plan (1955), 222–6, 230–6, 237n, 238n, 280; failure, 235–6; Israeli press attitudes, 228–9
American Council for Foreign Relations, 226, 238n
American Jewish community, assistance to Israel, 124
American Red Cross, 72
Amman, 95, 162
Andersen, Holger, 136–7
Anderson, Robert, 233–5, 241n
Anglo-Egyptian agreement (1954), 225
Aqaba, 55
Arab Higher Committee, 1, 5
Arab League 1, 17, 28, 38–9, 93, 189–90, 209, 219, 223; blacklist 160; council 101, 160; economic boycott 160, 202; political committee 23
Arab Legion 87–9, 223
Arab Liberation Army 1–2, 4, 9n
Arab minority in Israel, 6, 18, 20, 42–3, 48–9, 63, 186, 197n, 212, 267n; *see also* family reunification; internal refugees
Arab property, abandoned *see* Palestinian property, abandoned
Arab Revolt (1936–1939) 160
Arab-Israeli War (1948) xiii, xiv, 1–8, 9n, 10n, 11n, 13–17, 21–2, 26, 28, 38–9, 77, 87, 92, 152–4, 161–2, 181,

298 *Index*

203, 232, 258–9, 264, 272–4;
see also war damages (1948)
Arab-Israeli War (1967) xiii
Aranne, Zalman 134n
Aras, Tevfic Rustu 116
Argentina 185, 197n
armistice (agreements/negotiations) 36,
39, 49, 52, 65, 68n, 93–4, 100, 138–9,
145, 155, 161, 176, 181, 206, 222, 231,
237n, 258; *see also* Mixed Armistice
Commissions
Ashkelon *see* Majdal
Authority for the Development of the
Country (the Development Authority)
31, 264–5; *see also* Development
Authority Law (Transfer of
Properties) 5710–1950
Avner, Gershon 46
Azazme tribe 182
de-Azcarate, Pablo 120, 131, 140, 252
Azzam, Abd al-Rahman 17

Baghdad 1, 162–3
Baghdad Pact (1955) 224–5, 231
Bambaji-Sasportas, Haya 33n
Bandung Conference *see* Afro-Asian
Conference of unaligned nations,
Bandung (1955)
Bank accounts, blocked xiv, 79, 100,
102, 137–8, 144–5, 147–8, 150, 155
166, 194n, 200, 220, 232, 242–50, 261,
264, 272, 280; value 28, 242
Barclays Bank 242, 245–9
Barco, James 146, 151, 154, 247
Bar-Siman Tov, Yaacov 241n
Bat Galim (vessel) 219
Bedell Smith, Walter 205, 210
Bedouin population 6–7, 59, 181, 251;
see also Azazme tribe
Beersheva 6, 54, 56, 221
Begin, Menachem 209
Beirut 1, 17, 39, 77 81, 90, 99, 207, 256
Beit Guvrin 55
Beit Shaan 14–15, 89
Ben-Gurion, David 5, 29, 182, 196n,
197n, 211, 217n, 231, 235, 251;
blocked bank accounts 147, 245;
compensation 47, 57, 98, 115–16, 147,
150–1, 201–2, 204, 207–8, 211, 214,
231–2, 235, 250, 277, 279; Egypt 48,
52, 234–5; family reunification 57–8,
235, 250–1; Gaza Plan 47– 9, 51–2,
56; internal refugees 259, 261; Iraq
147; Jordan 48, 52, 93, 95; Lausanne

Conference 39, 46–7, 250; "the
100,000 Proposal" 59–61; Paris
Conference 141, 146–8, 150–2;
repatriation and resettlement 13–16,
19–22, 37–8, 40, 57, 95, 130, 176,
207–8, 234, 251, 273, 277; Syria 176
Bentov, Mordechai 21
Bergus, Donald 183
Bernadotte, Folke 14, 17–18, 32n;
assassination 22–3; Report
(September 1948) 22–5
Berncastle, John 136, 200, 214
Berry, Burton 121
Bevin, Ernest 55; repatriation and
resettlement 45–6, 75–6
Biran, Avraham 95, 97, 117–18, 131, 173
Blandford, John 120–1, 141–2, 205,
261–2; *see also* Three-year plan
(Blandford Plan)
BMEO (British Middle East Office) 45
borders (core problem between Israel
and the Arabs) 20, 23, 25, 36, 39, 47,
51, 53, 56, 74–5, 107, 138, 140, 143–4,
146, 148, 155, 181, 208, 210, 221–2,
225–8, 230–2, 237n, 244, 251; Egypt
51–5, 178–9, 206, 220, 222, 225, 227,
232–5, 239n, 276; Jordan 48, 52–3, 55,
90–2, 94–5, 100, 102, 206, 222, 232;
Palestinians xiii; Syria 176; *see also*
Negev; partition of Palestine (plan –
1947/borders)
Brazil 187
British Mandate, Palestine 1, 4–5, 27,
38, 160–1, 200, 209
Bunche, Ralph 24
Burdett, William 42–3, 72
Byroade, Henry 203–4, 207, 210, 224–5

Cairo 1, 23, 101, 219, 224, 233–5
Camp David xv
Caplan, Neil 65
Carmy, Shulamit 34n
Carver, Leslie 207
Central Council on Arab Affairs 197n
Chambers of Commerce, Arab states
160
Church World Service Committee 72
CIA (Central Intelligence Agency) 233
Cidor, Hanan 214
Clapp, Gordon 77–80, 82, 103n
Cohen, Aharon 12n
Cohen, Hillel 271n
Cohen, Leo 45
Cold War 41, 123

Columbia 171
Comay, Michael 17, 184, 213, 221, 237n, 261–3
Communism 41, 121, 162
Compensation (for Palestinian refugees) xiii, xiv, 14, 17 –18, 22, 24, 27, 37, 42, 45, 47, 57, 77–78, 92–102, 110–31, 134n, 136–9, 143–55, 162, 165–6, 171–3, 176, 179, 186–7, 191n, 200–4, 206–8, 210–15, 215n, 220–32, 235, 237n, 242, 244, 250, 264–5, 272, 275 –81; Jewish refugees (from the 1948 war) 223, 231–2; wealthy (Palestinian) refugees 95–9, 102, 139, 212; *see also* economic warfare; Jewish property, abandoned (in Iraq); Palestinian property, abandoned; reparations agreement (Israel–West Germany, 1952); war damages (1948)
Conciliation Commission *see* United Nations Conciliation Commission for Palestine (UNPCC)
Cyprus 246
Czechoslovakia 230

Damascus 1, 18, 160, 220
Danin, Ezra 19, 143, 185, 259
Davar (newspaper) 148, 209, 228, 252
Davis, Monnett 165, 210
Dayan, Moshe 89, 92–5, 180
de-Azcarate, Pablo 120, 131, 140, 252
de Boisanger, Claude 37, 40, 101, 117–18, 140
de Shalit, Meir 182–3
Democratic Party, US 204
Denaturalization Law (Iraqi Jews, March 1950) 164
Development Authority Law (Transfer of Properties) 5710–1950, 31
Dir Yassin massacre 5
Divon, Shmuel 141
Dodge, Bayard 40
Dotan, Alexander 187, 263–4
Douglas-Home, Charles 10n, 11n
Dulles, John Foster 188, 203, 205–10, 219, 225–35, 239n; compensation 226–7, 229; repatriation and resettlement 206–10, 226–30, 233–4, 238n, 280
Dulles speech (June 1953) 207; Israeli press attitudes 208–9
Dulles speech (August 1955) 226; Israeli press attitudes 228–9

Eban, Abba 45, 49, 53, 55, 57–8, 60, 64–5, 96–7, 113–14, 116, 121, 127, 150–1, 172, 203, 205, 210–11, 213, 221, 225, 229, 231–2, 239n, 244–5, 252
economic boycott 153–4, 160–2, 202–4, 207, 213–15, 221, 223, 227, 229, 237n, 279
"economic refugees" 94, 181, 206, 222
economic warfare *see* economic boycott; maritime blockade, Egyptian
Eden, Anthony 157n, 224, 231, 236n, 261
Egypt 4, 25, 30, 36, 44, 49, 52–3, 77, 85n, 95, 107, 109, 136, 139, 144, 155, 160, 163, 172, 178, 182, 194n, 206, 219, 224–5, 230–1, 233–5, 237n, 238n, 239n, 276, 279; Alpha Plan 222–7, 230, 237n; blocked bank accounts 194n, 246–7; compensation 179, 225, 234; Egyptian-Czech arms deal (September 1955) 225, 230–1, 235; family reunification 194n, 234, 252, 256–7; Gamma Plan 233–5; Gaza Plan 48–9, 51–6; Gaza Strip 44, 48–9, 51–2, 54–6, 80, 178–9, 181–2, 220, 224; Negev 51–6, 138, 178–9, 206, 220–2, 225, 227, 232–5, 239n, 276; political settlement with Israel 51–3, 55–6, 101, 178–9, 202, 224, 226, 230–1, 233–5, 237n, 239n, 276; repatriation and resettlement 52, 99, 142, 174, 179–80, 182–4, 194n, 223, 225, 234, 272, 276; *see also* Jewish property, abandoned (in Egypt); maritime blockade, Egyptian
Eilat 52, 55, 161, 222
Eisenhower, Dwight 188, 203, 205, 207, 226–7, 233; Eisenhower Administration, 189, 203–6, 210, 226, 279–80
El-Arish, Egypt 179–80, 183
Elath, Eliahu 61, 64, 97, 157n, 193n, 267n, 225–6,
Eliash, Mordecai 55
Eliav, Pinhas 183–4
Elizur, Michael 184
Emergency Regulations Relating to Absentees' Property (5709–1948) 29, 42, 66n, 242
Eretz Yisrael (Mandate Palestine in Jewish terminology) 1
Erim, Beck 136

300   *Index*

Eshkol, Levi 213, 248–9
Ethridge, Mark 39–41, 47–9, 52, 64, 72, 90, 250
Evans, Trefor 130
Eytan, Walter 46–50, 52, 57, 60, 64, 72, 90–1, 95–6, 121, 127–8, 146–7, 149–50, 173, 184, 186, 203, 231, 250–2

family reunification xiii, xiv, 57–9, 62, 79, 194n, 221, 232, 234–5, 250–8, 261, 272, 276, 280–1, 281n; Israeli press attitudes 252
Faruq, King 178
Fawzi, Mahmud 225
feda'iyin 224, 279
Fischbach, Michael R. 134–5n
Fischer, Maurice 141, 145–6, 148–50, 154
Fisher, Hamilton 95, 102
Former Arab Refugee Rehabilitation Committee 263
France 36, 56, 72, 76–7, 81, 87, 128, 157n, 158n, 171–2, 222
Free Officers Revolution (Egypt) 178
Fried, Shelly 32n, 134n
Furlonge, Geoffrey 120, 126

Galilee region 6, 53, 208, 210, 259
Galilee, Sea of 176, 188–9
Gamma Plan (1956) 233–6
Gaon, Haim 257
Gardiner, Arthur 182–3, 205, 220
Gaza Plan (1949) 47–58, 61, 64, 70n; Israeli press attitudes 50–1
Gaza Raid (February 1955) 224, 238n
Gaza Strip 6, 8, 42, 44, 48–52, 54–5, 63, 102, 146, 177–8, 182, 220, 223, 253, 256; infiltration 180–2, 219, 224; rehabilitation (resettlement) projects 80, 100, 179; *see also* Gaza Plan; Gaza Raid; Palestinian state
Gelber, Yoav 10n
General Refugee Congress for Palestine 69n
General Zionists Party 50, 63
Geneva 40, 81, 107
Geneva talks (1950) 107–9, 111, 139, 142, 156, 202
Germany *see* reparations agreement (Israel–West Germany, 1952)
Ginossar, Shlomo 112–13
Glubb, John Bagot 45, 103n
Goldmann, Nahum 32n

Good Offices Committee 171
Government House (Jerusalem), Conciliation Commission headquarters at 36, 136
Great Arab Revolt (1936–39) 160
"Greater Israel" 50
"Greater Syria" 87, 275
Gush Halav area 197n

Ha'Aretz (newspaper) 63, 149, 209, 228–9, 252
Ha-Boker (newspaper) 50, 63, 148, 209, 252
Haganah (military arm of organized Jewish community of Mandate Palestine) 3–4, 10n, 11n, 13, 26, 28
Haifa 3–4, 10n, 13–14, 89, 253, 259, 262, 269n; Port 55, 138, 146, 155, 232
Haikal, Yusuf 92
Ha-Modia (newspaper) 148, 209, 228
Harari, Izhar 50
Hare, Raymond 57
Harkabi, Yehoshafat 95
Hashemite Kingdom of Jordan *see* Jordan, Kingdom of
Ha-Shomer Ha-Tzair (party) 12n, 15–16
Ha-Tzofe (newspaper) 63, 148, 209, 228, 252
Hebron 4, 90
Heikal, Mohamed Hassanein 234–5
Herlitz, Esther 254
Herut (newspaper) 50, 63, 209, 228, 252
Herut (party) 50, 63, 209, 252
Herzog, Yaacov 221
Heyd, Uriel 58, 254
Hickerson, John 151, 245
Hilldring, John 60–1
Holocaust survivors 273
Hoover, Herbert 221
Horowitz Committee 210–13
Horowitz, David 19, 78–9, 210
House of Representatives, Foreign Relations Committee 205–6, 220
Huber, Max-Henry 187
al-Huda, Tawfiq Abu 89–90
Hula Valley, clash between Syria and Israel over draining of (1951) 139, 156
Hussein bin Talal, King of Jordan 174
al-Husseini, Haj Amin 1

IDF (Israeli Defense Forces) 6–7, 13, 26, 41, 112, 180, 182, 194n, 219, 238n, 258

Index 301

infiltration (of refugees into Israel) 25, 59, 180–2, 184, 194n, 202, 219, 224, 258; *see also* retaliatory actions
internal refugees xiv, 8, 30, 79, 258–65, 269n, 270n, 272, 280–1
International Red Cross 17, 251
Iraq 25, 30, 44, 77, 87, 160, 162, 168n, 206, 224–5, 243–4; blocked bank accounts 147–8, 155, 243–6; compensation 162, 165–6, 229; exchange of populations 163–4; expulsion of Iraqi Jews 162; repatriation and resettlement 18–20, 37, 39, 44–5, 47, 66n, 76, 78, 83, 84n, 99, 101, 112, 163, 177, 183, 185, 221, 223, 233, 273–4; *see also* Baghdad Pact (1955); Denaturalization Law (Iraqi Jews, March 1950); Jewish property, abandoned (in Iraq); Property Freeze Law (Iraqi Jews, March 1951)
Iran 224, 233
Israeli Communist Party *see* Maki (party)
Israeli Defense Forces *see* IDF (Israeli Defense Forces)
Israeli Electric Company 249

Jackson, Elmore 193n
Jaffa 3–4, 10n, 11n, 13–14, 48, 53, 182, 253
Jerusalem 1, 3–4, 22, 28, 36, 97, 100, 109, 114, 136–7, 171, 214, 233, 246, 253; as a political issue xiii, xiv, 20, 23, 36, 39, 90, 92–3, 96, 107, 209, 222, 228
Jerusalem Post, The (newspaper) 149, 209, 229
Jessup, Philip 17
Jewish Agency 13, 204
Jewish emigration (to Israel) 27
Jewish National Fund 31, 35n, 262
Jewish property, abandoned xiii, 17, 27, 154, 223, 228, 230, 248; in Egypt 169n; in Iraq 34n, 153–4, 163–7, 203, 229–30, 243–5; in Jordan, 223; in Lebanon, 169n; in Libya, 186; in Syria, 169n
Jezirah region 39
Johnston, Eric/Johnston Plan 188–90, 232
Jordan, Kingdom of 4, 6–8, 23, 30, 34n, 36, 44, 50, 53–5, 67n, 68n, 77, 85n, 87–8, 99–101, 102n, 103n, 106n, 107,

109, 112, 136, 138, 144, 155–6, 160, 162, 177, 180–2, 187–190, 206, 220–3, 230, 232, 256, 275; Alpha Plan 222–3; blocked bank accounts 100, 102, 246–8, 250; compensation 37, 92–8, 100–2, 112, 220; family reunification 252, 256–8; Gaza strip 48, 51–2, 55–6, 102; Jerusalem 90, 92–3, 96; political settlement with Israel 89–98, 100–1, 105n, 138, 155–6, 202; repatriation and resettlement 19–20, 37, 39, 44, 46–7, 66n, 75, 78, 80, 83, 84n, 88–96, 98–102, 103n, 110, 112, 119–20, 123, 174–5, 180, 182–4, 188 –90, 191n, 206–7, 220, 223, 232, 272–5, 277–8; West Bank 6, 48, 54, 87–8, 90–2, 95, 100–1, 183, 275; *see also* "economic refugees"; "Greater Syria"; Jewish property, abandoned (in Jordan)
Jordan River/Valley 39, 75, 89, 174, 177, 180, 183, 188–9, 207, 223, 232, 273

Kaplan, Eliezer 19, 29, 77, 110–11, 125, 261
al-Karmi, Abd al-Ghani 98
Keeley, James 176
Kennedy, Howard 34n, 81, 112, 119
al-Khalil, Ahmad 96
Khouri, Fred J. 25
kibbutzim 16
Kidron, Mordecai 97, 105n, 186, 254
Kimmerling, Baruch 30
Kirkbride, Alec 75, 156, 162
Knesset (Israeli Parliament) 16, 26, 30, 32n, 57, 62, 93, 98, 134n, 152–3, 165, 190n, 202–3, 217n, 230–1, 233, 251, 257, 264 ; Foreign Affairs and Defense Committee 47, 50, 62, 94, 113, 127, 129, 133n, 180, 189
Knight, Sir Henry 83, 99, 103n, 112, 142
Knox Helm, Alexander 126, 165
Kol Ha-Am (newspaper) 63, 228
Kollek, Teddy 121, 185
Korean War 120–1, 123

Labor movement, Israeli 123, 209
Lake Success 77
Lamerhav (newspaper) 228
Land Acquisition Law (Validation of Acts and Compensation) 5713–1953, 264–5

302 *Index*

Lausanne Conference (1949) xvi, 39,
  46–7, 56–8, 64, 73–6, 78–9, 90–1, 107,
  109, 139–40, 142, 156, 163, 202, 243,
  250–2, 254–5, 274–6; failure 64–5;
  see also Gaza Plan (1949); "the
  100,000 Proposal" (1949)
Lawson, Edward 229
Lebanon 4, 6, 8, 25, 30, 36, 56, 77, 87,
  107, 136, 144, 160, 175, 177, 188–90,
  206–7, 256; blocked bank accounts
  246–7; compensation 207; family
  reunification 251–2, 255–8;
  repatriation and resettlement xiii, 80,
  100, 142, 174–5, 207, 223, 272; *see
  also* Jewish property, abandoned
  (in Lebanon)
Levin, Itamar 168n
Lewis, Frank D. 28
Libya 185–7, 196n
Lie, Trygve 17, 49, 157n
Liff Committee 111–14, 210
Liff, Zalman 19, 29–30, 46, 111–12,
  196n, 259
Litani River 189
Lod 6, 89, 182; airport 1
London 75, 101, 219, 221–2, 231
Lourie, Arthur 60–1, 121
Lovett, Robert 42

Ma'ariv (newspaper) 51, 63, 149,
  209, 229
Mack, Sir Henry 76
Main, Charles/Main Plan 188–9
Majdal 6, 52, 182
Majd al-Kurum 259
Maki (party) 62–3, 70n
Mandate Palestine *see* British Mandate,
  Palestine
Mandatory Regulations of Commerce
  with the Enemy (1939) 29
Mandelbaum Gate, Jerusalem 253,
  256
Mapai (party) 13, 16, 32n, 62, 148, 189,
  196n, 213, 233, 273
Mapam (party) 15–17, 21–2, 32n, 37,
  50, 62–3, 148, 158n, 273
Marchal, Leon 140, 151, 157n
Mardam, Jamil 18, 33n
Maritime blockade, Egyptian 153,
  161–2, 202–4, 211, 213–14, 221,
  223, 227, 229, 279
Marshall, George 13, 34n
Marshall Plan 74
Maymon, Yehuda Leib 115–16

McDonald, James G. 12n, 18, 20, 43,
  51, 60
McDonald, John 42
McGhee, George 41–2, 44, 61, 64, 66n,
  72–3, 90, 92, 123, 150
Mediterranean Sea 51, 89, 92, 95
Meir, Golda 13, 125, 147, 213
Mikunis, Shmuel 62
Military Government (Israel) 182,
  250–1, 253–4, 263–4, 267n
Mixed Armistice Commissions 139, 161,
  182, 252–3, 257; *see also* armistice
  (agreements/negotiations)
Morris, Benny 9, 11n,
Morton, Desmond 103n
Mount Scopus 93
al-Mufti, Sa'id 94, 100
al-Mulqi, Fawzi, 92–4, 206
Mustafa, Abd al-Mun'im 51–2, 54, 56

Nabi Rubin 6
Nablus 3–4
Najar, Emile 141
al-Nashashibi, Azmi 97
al-Nasser, Gamal Abd 224, 230–1,
  233–5; Alpha Plan 224–5, 230–1;
  compensation 234; Gamma Plan
  233–5, 241n; political settlement with
  Israel 224–5, 230–1, 234–5;
  repatriation and resettlement 234
Nazareth 3, 256, 259, 269n
Near East Foundation 72
Negev 6, 23, 48–9, 51–6, 59, 89, 161,
  176, 178–9, 181, 190, 210, 221–2,
  226–8, 232–4, 239n, 251, 276
New York 41, 53, 107, 146, 171, 178,
  200, 214, 221
New York Herald Tribune (newspaper)
  16
nonalignment policy (Israel) 123

Operation Yochanan 197n
Ottoman Bank 242, 245–9

Pakistan 127, 224
Palestine Post, The (newspaper) 51
Palestinian property, abandoned, scope
  and value 27–8
Palestinian refugees, their number 7–9
Palestinian state xiii, xiv, 54
Palmer, Ely 114, 116, 118–19, 137–42,
  144–6, 148–51, 154, 156n, 165, 200,
  244
Palmon, Yehoshua 143, 186, 256, 263

Paris 22–3, 137, 140, 146, 170, 178
Paris Conference (1951) 136–45, 152–3, 157n, 158n, 170, 202, 215n, 244, 278–9; failure, 155–6; five proposals 145–52, 154–5, 173, 244; Israeli press attitudes 148–9; non aggression declaration, 138, 144–52, 154
partition of Palestine (plan – 1947/ borders) 4, 25, 34n, 41, 45, 51, 53, 148, 208, 231; *see also* United Nations Resolutions (Resolution 181)
Pasha, Khashaba 54–5
Peel commission (1936–1937) 11n
Plan D (Haganah plan of action, 1948) 3–4
Porter, Paul A. 64, 73
"present absentees" *see* internal refugees
Progressive Party 50, 228
Property Freeze Law (Iraqi Jews, March 1951) 164–6, 243

Qybia 182

Rafael, Gideon 69n, 96, 121, 173, 194n, 220, 247, 249
Ramle 6, 53, 89, 182, 253
"refugee march" 182
Refugee Rehabilitation Authority 260
Refugees Office 27–8, 114, 128–9, 131, 136–7, 145, 152, 173, 200, 213
al-Reine 259
Reintegration Fund 122–8, 130, 165, 170
reparations agreement (Israel–West Germany, 1952) 201, 212, 215n
repatriation xiii, xiv, 13–26, 31n, 37–47, 57–64, 66n, 70n, 74–5, 77–9, 82–3, 89–90, 92–6, 101–2, 107–10, 112–16, 118–23, 128–31, 135n, 136–40, 142–5, 148–9, 151–5, 157n, 166, 171–4, 178–9, 190n, 204, 206–10, 212, 216n, 220 –3, 225–9, 231–4, 237n, 239n, 242, 244, 250–2, 254, 257, 261, 272–81
Republican Party, US 203–4
resettlement xiv, 13–14, 18–20, 22–4, 31n, 37–47, 61, 63, 66n, 74–83, 84n, 88–91, 94, 96, 98–102, 103n, 109–14, 117–23, 125–6, 128, 130–1, 133n, 141–2, 144, 148, 158n, 163, 173–90, 191n, 194n, 196n, 205–10, 212, 220–3, 226–30, 232–4, 239n, 242, 261, 270n, 272–80
retaliatory actions 182, 224
Retroactive Transfer Committee 19–20, 33n, 37

Rhodes agreements *see* armistice (agreements/negotiations)
al-Rifa'i, Samir 92–5, 99–101, 162
"Right of Return" xiv, 24–5, 278
Riley, William 173, 176
Rishon Le-Zion 6
Robinson, Yaacov 23
Rockwell, Stuart W. 54
Rosen, Pinhas 29
Rosenfeld, Henri 34n
Rosenne, Shabtai 176, 184
Rosenthal, Yemima 65, 70n
Rosh Haniqra 253, 255
Ross, John 121
Rubin, Barry 194n
Rusk, Dean 41
Russell, Francis 220, 232

Safed 4, 100
al-Sa'id, Nuri 101, 162–3, 165
Sapir, Yosef 50
Sasson, Eliahu 16, 22, 46, 51–3, 64, 91–2, 183–4, 186, 255
Sasson, Moshe 98, 186
Saudi Arabia 25, 30, 101, 160, 206
Schuman, Robert 23
Second World War 87, 160
Selo, Fawzi 176–8
Servoise, Rene 136
Shaarim (newspaper) 228
Sham'un, Camille 207
Shapira, Moshe 21, 118
Sharett, Moshe 13, 19, 29, 32n, 33, 37–8, 53–4, 57, 73, 76–7, 112–19, 123–5, 128–30, 134n, 140–1, 144, 146, 173, 182, 186, 189, 196n, 197n, 204, 210–12, 217n, 221, 226–8, 231–3, 244–5, 250; blocked bank accounts 232, 244–5, 248–9; compensation 14, 17, 47, 78, 98, 110–11, 114–20, 124–5, 129, 133n, 143–4, 147, 150, 152–4, 163, 165, 191n, 201–2, 204, 207, 210–14, 215n, 227, 229–30, 232, 234, 250, 276–7, 279; Egypt 153, 213, 234–5; family reunification 58–9, 62, 232, 234, 250–1, 254–5, 258; Gaza Plan 48–9, 51–2, 55–6, 58; internal refugees 259–61, 263; Iraq 18, 37, 153–4, 163, 165, 229, 245; Jordan 37, 55–6, 89–91, 93–4, 120, 232; Lausanne Conference 46, 140; Lebanon 56; "the 100,000 Proposal" 58–64, 78–9, 209, 254; Paris Conference 140–6, 150–2, 154;

304   *Index*

repatriation and resettlement 13–14, 16–18, 20–23, 26, 32n, 37–8, 40–1, 46–7, 57, 59, 73, 78, 90–1, 94–5, 113–20, 123–5, 129–30, 133n, 143, 145, 151–3, 163, 173, 185–6, 189, 190n, 196n, 201, 204, 207–8, 210, 221, 226–7, 229, 232–4, 244, 250, 273, 279; Syria, 18, 33n, 37, 56, 120, 176
Sharon region 3–4, 48, 53
Sheringham, John 45
Shiloah, Reuven 19, 46, 60, 63–4, 73, 92–5, 100, 113–14, 117, 121, 146, 221, 227, 229, 232
Shimoni, Yaacov 19, 22
al-Shishakli, Adib 176, 178, 206, 256; political settlement with Israel 176; repatriation and resettlement 177, 206–7
Shitreet, Behor 10n, 19, 29, 259
Shlaim, Avi 64–5
Shuckburgh, Evelyn 219–22, 225–6, 236n
Shuneh 89
Sinai Campaign (1956) 161, 180
Sinai Peninsula 7, 179, 181, 183, 194n, 223, 233, 251
Six-Day War *see* Arab-Israeli War (1967)
Smith, R. 249
Somalia 186
Stabler, Wells 90
state custodian for absentees' property 27–31, 136, 187, 246, 249, 262–3
Sudan 178, 187, 196n
Suez Canal 55, 139, 161, 178–9, 206, 213, 219, 223, 225, 237n, 279
Suez (city) 55
Syria 4, 8, 25, 30, 33n, 56, 77, 85n, 87, 107, 109, 136, 142, 144, 160, 175–6, 178, 188, 190, 206, 220, 252, 256; blocked bank accounts 243–4, 246–7; compensation 176; family reunification 256–7; political settlement with Israel 101, 138, 176, 179; repatriation and resettlement 18–19, 37, 39, 44–7, 66n, 76, 78, 80, 83, 91, 99–100, 110, 112, 119–20, 174–8, 180, 183, 185, 206–7, 221, 223, 272–8; *see also* "Greater Syria"; Hula Valley, clash between Syria and Israel over draining of (1951); Jewish property, abandoned (in Syria)

Taba xv
al-Taji, Muhammad 97, 105n

Talal bin Abdullah, King of Jordan 174
Tamra 259
Tel-Aviv 4, 6, 13, 37, 130, 229, 235, 254–5
Tennessee Valley Authority 187–8
"the 100,000 Proposal" (1949) 58–64, 70n, 78–9, 209, 223, 254, 275–6; Israeli press attitudes 62–3
Third Reich 142
Three-year plan (Blandford Plan) 158n, 170–5, 177, 180, 186, 261
Tiberias 4, 47, 89
Trans-Jordan *see* Jordan, Kingdom of
"Triangle", the (concentration of Arab-Palestinian settlements) 50, 56, 68n, 94, 102, 258–9
Troutbeck, John 45
Truman, Harry 41, 47, 57, 60–1, 92, 204, 251; Truman Administration, 74, 203–6, 216n, 223, 280
Tuqan, Ahmad 96, 156
Tuqan, Jamal 94
Turkey 36, 72, 77, 81, 127–8, 171–2, 224–5

United Kingdom 2, 8, 24, 34n, 42, 44–5, 55, 72, 75–7, 81, 83, 87, 117, 121, 127–8, 136, 139, 142, 156n, 157n, 158n, 162–3, 165–6, 171–2, 178, 197n, 206, 219, 224–5, 236n, 237n, 279; Alpha Plan 219–20, 222–7, 230–1, 233, 236, 237n, 238n, 280; blocked bank accounts 248, 250; compensation 45, 111–13, 117, 119–20, 124, 126–7, 162, 166, 201, 221–3, 277; family reunification 221, 254; Gaza Plan 54–5; internal refugees 261; Negev 54–5, 221–2, 239n; repatriation and resettlement 44–6, 75–6, 81–3, 90, 98 –101, 103n, 111–13, 119–20, 123, 130, 142, 163, 177, 179–80, 185, 196n, 221–3, 226, 237n, 261, 272, 274, 276–7; *see also* British Mandate, Palestine
United Nations 4, 6, 25, 34n, 40, 45, 58, 60, 64, 72–3, 81, 89, 91–2, 101, 110, 112–13, 117, 119, 121, 123, 125, 138, 140–5, 150, 152–5, 165, 171, 174–5, 177, 180, 183, 186–7, 200, 202–3, 206–7, 237n, 242, 244–6, 250, 254, 261, 272, 275–9, 281
United Nations Ad Hoc Political Committee 23, 80, 123, 127–8, 170–3, 203, 213, 220–1

United Nations Conciliation Commission for Palestine (UNPCC) 22, 24, 27–8, 36–40, 66n, 72–3, 95, 107, 114–16, 119, 122, 124, 128–9, 131, 136–41, 156n, 158n, 162, 170–4, 200–2, 213–14; blocked bank accounts 137, 144–5, 148, 150, 155, 200, 242–8; compensation 24, 47, 101, 110–12, 114 –20, 122, 124, 126, 134n, 136–9, 143–5, 148, 150–4, 165, 173, 200–2, 213–14, 230, 244, 277–8; establishment of the Economic Survey Mission 73–7; establishment of the Refugee Office 27, 119, 128–9, 131, 136–7, 173; family reunification 250–2, 255; Gaza Plan 47, 49, 52; Geneva talks 107–9, 111, 202; Lausanne conference 39, 46–7, 49, 52, 56–7, 63–5, 74–6, 107, 202, 250; "the 100,000 Proposal" 63–4; Paris conference 137–56, 157n, 170, 173, 202, 244, 278; repatriation and resettlement 24, 37–8, 40, 43, 74–6, 90, 101, 109–10, 114–15, 117–20, 122–4, 130–1, 134n, 137–8, 140, 143–5, 148–9, 151, 157n, 172–4, 230, 250, 277–8; see also Refugees Office; United Nations Economic Survey Mission for the Middle East

United Nations Economic Survey Mission for the Middle East (UNESM) 8, 77–82, 91, 103n, 110, 122, 163

United Nations General Assembly, Second 1; Third 20, 23–5, 36; Fourth 79–80, 117; Fifth 80, 95–6, 100, 112–14, 116–20, 123, 127–31, 136; Sixth 139, 141, 146, 149, 154–5, 170–4, 177, 182, 244, 261; Seventh 201–2, 262–3; Eighth 211; Ninth 249; Eleventh 214

United Nations High Commissioner for Refugees 81

United Nations Relief and Works Agency for Palestine Refugees in the Near East (UNRWA) 7–8, 54, 80–1, 83, 87, 89, 99, 113, 122, 127, 170, 172, 187–8, 207, 220, 261–2, 278; advisory commission 81–2, 99, 103n, 112, 119–20, 122, 131, 141–2, 183; blocked bank accounts 245–7; compensation 110, 112, 119, 126, 277; internal refugees 260–3; Paris Conference 141–2, 158n; repatriation and

resettlement 81–3, 99–101, 110–12, 119–20, 122–3, 130–1, 141–2, 172, 174–5, 177–9, 182–8, 191n, 205, 207, 223, 277–8; see also Reintegration Fund; Three-year plan (Blandford Plan)

United Nations Relief for Palestinian Refugees (UNRPR) 24, 34n, 72, 80

United nations Resolutions; Resolution 181 1, 27, 51, 91, 108, 273; Resolution 194(3) 24–6, 36, 42, 57, 66n, 77, 85n, 107–9, 115, 119, 123, 127–9, 136, 141, 172–3; Resolution 302(4) 80–2; Resolution 393(5) 127, 130–1; Resolution 394(5) 128–9, 131, 136–7; Resolution 512(6) 172–3, 190n, 200; Resolution 513(6) 173

United Nations Secretary General 7, 17, 36, 40, 49, 81

United Nations Security Council 3, 36

United Religious Front 21

United States 2–3, 8, 12n, 20, 24, 36–7, 40–1, 44–5, 58, 77, 81, 116 –17, 120–1, 123, 127–8, 137–9, 156n, 157n, 163–6, 171–2, 176–8, 188, 190, 202–10, 219–22, 225–33, 236, 236n, 237n, 239n, 244–5, 250–1, 261, 279–80; aid to the Palestinian refugees 14, 57–9, 72; Alpha Plan 219–20, 222–7, 230, 232–3, 236, 237n, 238n, 280; blocked bank accounts 137–8, 200, 232, 244–5, 247, 261, 280; compensation 42, 45, 57, 92, 113, 116–17, 119–22, 124–6, 135n, 137–9, 150, 166, 200–4, 206–7, 210–11, 213, 215n, 220–4, 226–30, 232, 234–5, 277, 279; economic approach 72–5, 82, 91, 275–6; family reunification 57, 232, 234–5, 250–2, 254, 280; Gamma Plan 233–6; Gaza Plan 49, 51–8, 61, 64; internal refugees 261–2, 280; Israel's economic dependence on 123–4; Lausanne Conference 56–7, 75, 139; "the 100,000 Proposal" 58–64, 70n, 79; Paris Conference 138–9, 142–3, 147, 149–51, 156, 157n, 158n; repatriation and resettlement 17, 20, 22, 40–6, 57–9, 66n, 67n, 72, 76, 79, 82–3, 84n, 90–1, 95, 98–9, 113, 119–23, 125, 130–1, 135n, 137–9, 153, 163, 176–7, 182–3, 188–9, 204–10, 216n, 220–3, 225–30, 232–4, 239n, 244, 250–1, 261, 272–7, 279–80

306 *Index*

USSR (Soviet Union) 41, 121, 123, 139, 219, 226, 230, 233, 239n

Wadi Ara 259
Wailing Wall 93
war damages (1948) 47, 78, 110, 113, 115, 117, 119, 125–6, 145, 147, 154–5, 223, 228, 277–8
Washington 222
Webb, James 41, 130–1
Weitz, Yosef 19, 143, 197n, 259, 269n
Weizmann, Chaim 12n, 20, 47
West Bank xiii, xiv, 6, 42, 48, 54, 63, 87–8, 90–2, 94–5, 100–1, 180–3, 206, 222, 275
World Jewish Congress 32n
Wright, Michael 45–6, 75–6

Ya'ari, Meir 15
Yahudiya 6
Yalcin, Huseyin 39
Yarmuk (River/Valley) 174, 187–8, 206
Yedioth Ahronoth (newspaper) 50, 63, 149, 229
Yemen 25, 30, 160
Yibna 6
Yosef, Dov 37–8, 40, 59

Za'im, Husni 175–6
Zeitune, Shaul 65
Zionism 25, 162, 168n
Zisling, Aharon 15, 21, 29
Zmanim (newspaper) 228